"Absolutely indispensable. A concise and helpful work that saves time and money with its practical, hands-on approach."

— Randy Holland, Producer/Director,
The Fire This Time (Sundance Channel, PBS)

"This book answered questions I didn't even know I had. A great resource."

— Amy Poncher, first-time documentary filmmaker

"This book is considered to be the industry standard and is the best guide to budgeting that there is."

— *Reelscene* Magazine

"Deke Simon has accomplished the impossible — explaining budgeting and planning in a clear, non-threatening way. Improve how you envision, plan, and pay for your next project, and decrease your stress."

— Larry Jordan, Author, Final Cut Studio expert,
host of *Digital Production Buzz*

"I wish I'd had this book when I started making movies; it would have saved me from years of plodding."

— Norman Berns, Producer and Founder of
www.Reelgrok.com

"My students consider *Film and Video Budgets* the bible of filmmaking."

— Pamela Elder, Professor, Meadows School of the
Arts, Southern Methodist University

"Film students get an easy-to-read, thorough grounding in budgets. Tremendously helpful."

— Glenn Gebhard, Professor, Loyola Marymount
University, School of Film & Television

"The first item in your budget should be this book!"

— Don Schroeder, Ph.D., Emmy-winning Producer
and Instructor, Loyola Marymount School of
Film and Television

"Easy to read and understand. You'll find answers in this book."

— Dana Gasparine, Film & TV student, Loyola
Marymount University

"I am not naturally good with numbers, but this book helped me create a solid budget for my first film, all by myself!"

— Courtney Hardebeck, film student, Loyola
Marymount University

DEKE SIMON

FILM
+VIDEO
BUDGETS

5TH EDITION

Published by Michael Wiese Productions
12400 Ventura Blvd. # 1111
Studio City, CA 91604
tel. 818.379.8799
fax 818.986.3408
mw@mwp.com
www.mwp.com

Cover design: MWP
Interior book design: Gina Mansfield Design
Editor: Paul Norlen

Printed by McNaughton & Gunn, Inc., Saline, Michigan
Manufactured in the United States of America

Library of Congress Cataloging-in-Publication Data

Simon, Deke, 1945-
 Film & video budgets / Deke Simon. -- 5th updated ed.
     p. cm.
 Includes index.
 ISBN 978-1-932907-73-5
1. Motion picture industry--United States--Finance. 2. Video recordings
industry--United States--Finance. I. Title. II. Title: Film and video budgets.
PN1993.5.U6W4915 2010
384'.83'0973--dc22

                                     2009054400

For my wonderful wife Esther,
and our two great daughters, Sarah and Lena Simon.
Without you I would be a poorer man indeed.

Deke Simon

TABLE OF CONTENTS

ACKNOWLEDGMENTS

Many professionals contributed time and advice to make the information in *Film and Video Budgets* as accurate as possible. To them, we say, "Thank you! We owe you one."

- Michael W. Barnard, filmmaker, Lightning Bolt Pix, Santa Monica, CA
- Morgan Barnard, filmmaker, Lightning Bolt Pix, Santa Monica, CA
- Craig Barnes, CCI Digital, Inc., Burbank, CA
- Laurie Beale at Gary Krouse Insurance Services, Inc., Chatsworth, CA
- Ed Bishop at Odd Sprocket, Hollywood, CA
- Mark Bosko, author of *The Complete Independent Movie Marketing Handbook*
- Entertainment Partners payroll service, Burbank, CA
- Breakdown Services Ltd., Los Angeles, CA — for information about casting
- Tony Casala, Casala Ltd., Beverly Hills, CA — Teachers/welfare workers
- Michael Cioni, post-production wizard, www.lightirondigital.com
- Ron Clark, Art/FX, Inc. Burbank, CA Graphic Design
- Eric Cohen, FotoKem, Burbank, CA
- Bob Dunn of Animal Services of Sylmar, CA
- Thom Ehle, Dolby Laboratories, Burbank, CA
- Lin Ephraim of Percenterprises Completion Bonds, Inc. Los Angeles, CA
- Katie Fellion, post-production producer
- Tom Fineman, attorney, Myman, Abell, Fineman, Greenspan & Rowan, Brentwood, CA
- Alex Garcia, Nice, France, music video website *www.mvdbase.com*

▸ Fred Ginsburg of Equipment Emporium Inc., Mission Hills, CA and *www.Equipmentemporium.com* for audio advice

▸ Georgette Green, accountant, Santa Monica, CA

▸ Doug Greenfield at Dolby Labs *www.Dolby.com*

▸ Barbara Gregson at Miller-Gregson Productions, Toluca Lake, CA — Clearances for feature film clips, stock shots, and archive footage

▸ David Grober, Motion Picture Marine, Marina del Rey, CA — Underwater and topside photography and production

▸ Dorain Grusman, Los Angeles, CA, choreographer

▸ Jim Hardy at HTV/illuminate, Hollywood, CA

▸ David Hays at EFILM, Hollywood, CA

▸ Stephen D. Hubbert, Instructional Support Technician, California State University Long Beach, Long Beach, CA

▸ Charles Kelly, Sound Mixer, Los Angeles, CA

▸ Robert Lakstigala, Designer/Producer and Dragon, Director of Digital Effects, Title House, Hollywood, CA

▸ Howard Lavick, Department of Communications Arts, Loyola Marymount University, Westchester, CA

▸ Greg Le Duc, Le Duc Productions, Santa Monica, CA

▸ Mark Leemkuil, filmmaker, Vancouver and Toronto

▸ Elizabeth "Tig" McKenzie of Point 360, Burbank, CA

▸ Larry Michalski, FotoKem, Burbank, CA

▸ Matt Miller and Anita LeGalt of AICP

▸ Mike Minkow, Cinema Research Corp., Los Angeles, CA

▸ Brick Price of WonderWorks, Canoga Park, CA — Miniatures

▸ Mark Rains, Production Executive, Van Nuys, CA

▸ David Robertson, music video producer

▸ Sean Romano, VP Operations, Deluxe, Hollywood, CA

▸ Judy Sand at Halmote Music Payroll, Los Angeles, CA

▸ Gabrielle Schary, Casting Director, Venice, CA

▸ Nancy Severinsen, Film and TV Music Supervisor

▸ Stefan Sonnenfeld, Company 3, Santa Monica, CA

▸ Title House, Hollywood, CA — Titles and opticals

▸ Bryan Thompson, Venice, CA

▸ Dylan Weiss and the good folks at Cry Havoc Productions, Lake Elsinore, CA

- Juerg Walthers, Director of Photography, Los Angeles, CA
- Shalini Waran, Producer, Los Angeles, CA
- Tam Warner, Van Nuys, CA, Choreographer
- Dave Weathers, Supervising Sound Editor, and Brian Murray, Sound Engineer
- West Coast Helicopters, Van Nuys, CA, Aerial Photography
- Arthur Williams of AICE
- Beverly Wood of Deluxe, Hollywood, CA
- Woody Woodhall of Allied Post Audio, Santa Monica, CA
- David Yang at Dolby Labs *www.Dolby.com*
- Dick Ziker of Stunts Unlimited, Hollywood, CA

INTRODUCTION

INTRODUCTION TO THE 5TH EDITION

The book you hold in your hands may be one of the most powerful tools you will ever encounter to help you produce your films and videos. Understanding budgets is the key to production. Without a roadmap you'll never come in on time or on budget. This book is that roadmap.

This book was first written in 1984 by Michael Wiese to supplement his first book, *The Independent Film & Videomaker's Guide*, which is devoted to the financing and distribution of films and videos. In 1995, having been friends and producing partners, Michael asked me to join the enterprise for the 2nd edition, and we've been revising editions to keep up with changing technologies every few years.

These editions have sold more than 45,000 copies, probably because it is one of the few places you can find hard information about budgeting for low-budget features, documentaries, music videos, student productions, and other forms of programs. The book is used as a textbook in production management courses throughout the world, and by professionals who are crossing genres into new territory, and want a helping hand.

Since production technologies are ever changing, we have revised the book yet again, with updates to the budgets in digital acquisition and post, revised sections on Digital Intermediates and Tape-to-Film Transfer and Digital Cinema projection, and High Definition and Development and Marketing.

This is not, however, a book about what things cost. The purpose of this book is to get you to seriously think about the production you are budgeting. This book is a friendly and easy-to-use guide, and will give you many ideas about how to approach budgeting, how to look for savings, how to negotiate, and so forth. Sorry, there is no magic formula. **Do not use the prices in this book for your own budgeting**. Our numbers will get you in the ballpark, but in the end you're going to have to research the costs yourself.

The one who actually benefits the most from doing a budget is you, the producer. The process of figuring out what personnel, equipment and services your project needs, and how long you will need each item makes you the expert. And you need to know your project inside out. But besides you, others will want to see a budget, like your boss, your investor, your client, a foundation, a government agency, or a department within your corporation.

The budget is normally Step 3 in a three-step process. Budgets are determined first by examining the script, storyboard, or breakdown in great detail. Then you do a schedule, and finally, a budget. Once the budget is defined, it becomes a blueprint for bringing your ideas into reality. Budgeting can excite you by this fact alone: you are moving closer and closer to making your ideas real.

Film and video projects do not allow for too many mistakes. Reputations are made and lost on the question "Did you come in on budget?" So it's best to prepare an accurate and detailed budget and know what you can and cannot afford.

For many people the idea of writing a budget brings on a cold sweat. But sooner or later, if you pursue the film or video production business, you will be called upon to account for costs, i.e. to prepare a budget. This book may ease your mind and give you confidence.

For 35 years, I have been producing or overseeing the production of hundreds of hours of film or video programming. It has been my responsibility to negotiate rates with agents, crews, actors, narrators, composers, film labs, film and video equipment houses, post-production and special effects houses, and shipping companies. I've produced pay TV segments, documentaries, drama, political television commercials, marketing reels, television spots, promos, shorts, educational films, television programs, infomercials, and all kinds of home videos. Each and every project had a budget.

This book represents a lot of accumulated knowledge and experience. What Michael and I didn't know, we asked the experts. The budget formats in this book use the "standard" methods of production and equipment that most producers use. Study them, because besides being a list of necessary expenses, they also demonstrate a very well thought-out production process.

On some of our own projects we've saved tens and even hundreds of thousands of dollars. On a few occasions we've blown it and made some expensive mistakes. What we will do in this book is share our insights so you can avoid costly errors and even find savings in your budgets.

Study this book. Challenge it. Make it your own. You may discover many items you would have otherwise overlooked, which will be worth the price of the book. Hopefully, these budgets will spark your imagination so that you will find innovative ways to bring more value onto the screen.

When you've completed your budget, your anxiety will most likely be replaced with a calm confidence. You'll know what you can do and what you can't. You'll know how to make your budget go further, and make a real contribution to the production. I sincerely hope that this book increases your ability to successfully produce your films and videos. Now go get 'em.

Best wishes,
Deke Simon
Los Angeles, California
May 2010

HOW TO USE THIS BOOK

Don't read the whole thing! (Feel better already?) However, you will need to understand every line item in your budget, and therefore I recommend that you first read the Line Items section to familiarize yourself with the meanings of the budget items I use in these budgets.

Next, flip directly to the budget that is closest to the project that you are doing. These budgets should get you 80% or more of the way to determining your own budgets.

If your type of production is not listed, then go through the Line Items, selecting those items you'll use in your production. Most producers go over budget because they forget something! That's where the information in this book will help. It is very thorough and should give you the confidence that you are covered.

Another thing. Do not take the numbers that I use as gospel. These numbers only approximate what things cost. You can't just take these numbers and plug them into your own budgets. Instead, research your own production costs. You may find that your line items may be lower. In addition, you must negotiate (more on this later) to get the best budget possible. **Do not copy the rates in these budgets**. Sorry, folks, there are no shortcuts when it comes to budgeting. You may grumble now, but thank me when you finish your production and still have some money left!

Finally, as the owner of this book, you have the privilege of downloading, at NO CHARGE, its budgets from our website at *www.mwp.com*. Adapt them for your own use. Make templates, add or take away line items, and most importantly, input your own numbers.

INSTRUCTIONS ON DOWNLOADING BUDGETS:

- Go to *www.mwp.com*
- Click on "Virtual Film School"
- Scroll down on menu to "Resources"
- Download Excel Spreadsheets
- Save to your desktop
- *Happy Budgeting!*

chapter 1

SETTING UP A PRODUCTION COMPANY

He has half the deed done, who has made a beginning.
— Horace, 65–8 BC

Horace had that right.

Everyone has to begin at the beginning. If you carefully follow the advice in this book these activities will help you get your own production company up and running. Think of that warm satisfaction that will come over you every morning, when you read your company's name on the door as you enter your office. Hey, we did it! We're a real company!

For many, starting your own production company may seem daunting. This chapter will help dissolve that feeling of being overwhelmed. Take things one step at a time and you'll get there. Once it's done, you'll have a foundation to build on, dreams to achieve, and a snazzy new business card to flash around.

INCORPORATION

To incorporate... or not to incorporate? Most lawyers will suggest that you incorporate in order to protect your personal assets from liability.

If you are a United States resident, and plan to have 35 or fewer stockholders (or maybe just one stockholder, you), most accountants will recommend a Sub-S Corporation or the new kid on the block, the Limited Liability Company (LLC). With a Sub-S or LLC, your company owes no Federal income tax on profit. The profit passes through the company directly to stockholders (that includes you!). The company will still pay state income tax, which, if you pay out or reinvest all your profits at year-end, may only be the minimum.

1

How much does it cost to incorporate? It depends on the state, and on the fees of the attorney or accountant in charge. In California, the Secretary of State gets $900, plus $275 for a seal and stock certificates, plus fees. Shop around for an accountant or lawyer and compare fees. If you already have an accountant, maybe he or she will do it for you inexpensively.

If you choose not to incorporate, then it's probably a good idea to name your company and apply for a 'dba' (Doing-Business-As). Your accountant can handle this for you, or you might have a local newspaper that will send you the forms and charge $50 or so for the required announcement in its pages.

FEDERAL ID

Whether you are a dba or incorporated, you still must apply for a Federal ID number, which you need if you plan to pay the people who work on your projects. The ID number exists to help the IRS with its accounting. You can get a File SS4 form from the IRS (*www.federaltaxid. us*) or go through your accountant. Remember, if you are a sole owner, you are not on the payroll. You take your salary from company profit, and yes, you do owe Federal tax on your salary.

Every payment you receive will now be written to the corporation and not to you personally.

BUSINESS LICENSE

Even if you operate your business out of your house, strictly speaking, you should have a city business license if you are a dba or incorporated. It's a city's way of keeping track of commerce, and making a little money — actually a lot of money! In Los Angeles, the minimum fee for motion picture producers whose productions cost less than $50,000 in a given year is $158.89. It goes up from there on a scale. If you are in the maximum production range of $4 million and up, the fee is $13,665.29, but by then you're so rich you don't care. Be sure to check locally for any special allowances for production companies or small businesses — anything for a break. For the first year you usually pay a standard fee, then you pay on the preceding year's gross income. The City Hall Clerk can get you an application form. They will love to help you because this is more money for the city's coffers.

2

BANK ACCOUNT

You cannot open a corporate bank account until you have your articles of incorporation (which you prepare before filing for a corporation), or your Operating Agreement if you're an LLC, and your Federal ID number. The bank will require copies of these documents.

For smaller companies, one business checking account should suffice. Ask if it can be an interest-bearing account, which might help offset fees banks charge for business accounts.

If you have a sizable payroll, you may want to set up a separate payroll account and have a payroll service do the paperwork and actual payments. For small payrolls, most businesses do it themselves.

Be sure to go to the bank, and introduce yourself to the bank manager, president, or vice president. Get to know them. The day will come when you'll want to borrow money, set up an escrow account, or employ other services. All this will come much easier if they feel they know you.

CORPORATE TAXES

Surprise — your new business owes the state! Your accountant prepares the state income tax return and calculates what you owe. Happily, there's no federal corporate income tax if you are a Sub-S Corporation or an LLC.

ACCOUNTING SOFTWARE

We've heard good things about the QuickBooks accounting program (*intuit.com*) for small businesses. In most small companies, people do their own bookkeeping, or hire a bookkeeper who may come in once a week or more. Production accountants sometimes use high-powered software.

ACCOUNTANT

Your accountant can help you incorporate, give business planning advice, project a business budget, supply you with W-2 and I-9 tax payroll forms, and file your corporate and personal tax returns.

Your accountant will become one of your greatest allies. First, he or she will help you set up your business, making sure you don't miss

3

any filing or tax deadlines. This is their business. What may be hard for you is extremely easy for them. They will enjoy their relationship with a film or video producer because in the same way that numbers baffle you, movies baffle them!

ATTORNEY

Your attorney should be an *entertainment* attorney, distinct from the garden variety corporate type. Entertainment attorneys know things the rest of us don't but should — like production contracts, options and rights acquisition, licensing, releases of every stripe, and where to have power lunches.

Your attorney should be someone whom you know and respect. Someone who can get things done in the entertainment community. Even if this costs more (on an hourly basis), you will be way ahead of the game when you want to do something, whether it's closing an investment deal or getting a distribution contract. In addition, as you work with your attorney you will gain a great deal of knowledge yourself that will be of immeasurable benefit over the years.

EMPLOYEES

Even in Hollywood, many incorporated production companies are made up of no more than one or two people. When you are in production you have many people on salary. When you are developing your projects you want to have few employees to keep your overhead costs down.

In the beginning you will probably hire a full-time secretary or assistant to help with the administrative chores, which will be many. As your business grows, others will be brought on. Here's where you want to hire the right people for the job. You want people that supplement — no, complement — your skills. If you are not extremely well organized, then look for this quality in those you hire. If you are well organized, then you may want more creative types for those aspects of your business. Do not hire someone just like you, because your aim is to balance your company.

4

Create a fun atmosphere for people to work in and your productivity will soar. Make sure they are free to make contributions to the projects and credit them appropriately. Giving credit is one of the easiest (and cheapest) things you can do. It's a way of saying thanks that goes a long way.

BECOMING A SIGNATORY TO GUILDS AND UNIONS

You may or may not have to deal with guilds, but in case you do, these are the main guilds (see Appendix for addresses): the Writers Guild of America (WGA), Directors Guild of America (DGA), Screen Actors Guild (SAG), and the American Federation of Radio and Television Artists (AFTRA).

The prevailing wisdom is that by using guild members, you get more experienced actors, writers, and directors, and that's mainly true. On the other hand, it all boils down to who you want to work with. Guild membership doesn't instantly qualify anyone for anything. You have to meet your prospective collaborators and decide for yourself.

Technically, guild members are not supposed to work with a production company that has not signed an agreement with their guild. A writer, actor or director may do it anyway, and sometimes use another name in the credits. Some work non-guild jobs happily, others do it grudgingly. Still others choose not to work with non-signatory companies at all. When guild members choose to work on a non-guild project, make it clear that they do so at their own risk, not the production company's.

One producer we know has three different companies: one signatory to SAG and AFTRA, one signatory to SAG, AFTRA, and the DGA, and one that is not signatory to anything. Why go through that paperwork nightmare? He wants to avoid dealing with residual payments for certain projects, and avoid paying the extra expense of pension and health (P&H) that guilds demand — usually around 10% to 13% of the member's gross salary. (For really high salaries, like a star's, there is a cut-off beyond which the company does not have to pay P&H. Check with each guild for what it is.)

WGA (*Writers Guild of America*) — To become signatory and hire WGA writers, your company must be legally structured, as in a Sub-S corporation (not a dba). Simply call and request the application forms. There is no fee to become signatory. Your company cannot disengage from signatory status until the current WGA agreement expires, and these agreements run for about five-year terms. You can check out the current Minimum Basic Agreement (MBA) on-line, as well as other Agreements and Contracts, e.g. "Low-Budget" and "Standard Theatrical."

AFTRA (*American Federation of Radio and Television Artists*) and **SAG** (*Screen Actors Guild*) — The company must be legally structured (not a dba, although there may be exceptions). There are a number of contracts companies can sign, depending on what type of programming they produce (i.e., free TV, cable, public TV, interactive, etc.). There is no fee, but a new company may have to provide a bond to cover payment of actors. Bonds can be in the form of a certified check, or a letter from a payroll service attesting that money is on account. Check the respective websites for contracts and/or digests of agreements.

DGA (*Directors Guild of America*) — The company could be a dba or incorporated or a partnership. The application requests information about stockholders and ownership. It asks for documentation, like a copy of the fictitious name statement or articles of incorporation. In most cases, the company must have a project lined up in order to become signatory. They want to know what the project is, what DGA member functions you'll be hiring, where the financing comes from, and if you have a distributor. Basically, they want to make sure members will be paid. If the financing looks shaky, they may ask to put the DGA money in escrow. For TV movies and features, they may demand a security agreement that puts a lien on the film in case you go bankrupt. That way they can better collect any residuals. There is no fee to sign up.

IATSE — The crafts people and technicians who work in television and movies are represented by the International Alliance of Theatrical and Stage Employees (IATSE), and a host of other locals, including the Teamsters (the people who drive all the studio trucks and vans). Because it is such a complicated web, it can be extremely frustrating to get signatory information. You may end up gabbing with the secretary at the Plasterers and Cement Finishers local.

6

First of all, if you're a small production company doing low-budget projects, you probably won't want to become signatory to the IATSE. The problem for little guys is that the sometimes restrictive practices and benefits packages make it too expensive. But just in case you need to know, here is some information.

Why become signatory to IATSE? The theory goes that union crews (camera operators, sound mixers, grips, electrics, etc.) are more experienced, hence more efficient. This is usually true — although there are plenty of excellent people who are not union members.

When you hire union crews for scale (some feature productions are over-scale), there's no negotiating; you pay whatever the going rate is for that job, plus the usual payroll taxes. Plus you'll pay union fringes: Health/Retiree Health and Pension, Vacation/Holiday. Check with your local to get all the current rates, rules and regulations.

To become signatory, write a letter expressing interest in becoming signatory. The address for the Los Angeles office is in the Resources section, but there are offices in most major cities. They send back a three-page questionnaire. If you are approved, you're in. For production companies, there's no fee. If you can't find the right office, call a payroll service (a company that handles union and non-union payroll for production companies), since these people seem to know the most about unions.

BON VOYAGE

It may take you a week or two or several months to do all the paperwork required to set up your production company and become signatory to some or all of the unions.

If you are just getting started and want to get your feet wet on a production or two, then you probably won't go through this step. When you do set up your first corporation you'll find that it isn't as intimidating as you thought, and you'll feel empowered because now you are just like the big guys with all the same rights and privileges. Not only that, as president of your own corporation your parents will have something new to brag about around the neighborhood!

What follows are the nuts and bolts of budgeting; a potpourri of ideas that will help you think through and prepare your own production budgets.

If you come in under budget you'll be a hero. If you go over budget, the reputation will come to haunt you. This book is designed to help you become remembered for your remarkable foresight and ability to deliver a project on time and on budget. That's what clients, backers, and employees expect.

By careful planning and researching you can create a very accurate budget before the cameras roll.

chapter 2

PRE-PRODUCTION

I know... why don't we put on a show!!

Ask any production veteran — Pre-Production will make you or break you. This is where you make the plans you live with in Production and Post. It's a grand scheme made up of a dizzying number of details. One production manager we know made big points with the executive producer by handing him a cup of espresso while on location in the middle of nowhere. Of course, that wouldn't have amounted to a hill of coffee beans if the guy had forgotten to order lunch for the crew.

There is a method to Pre-Production, but the method for fiction films is different than for non-fiction. There are whole books written about both, so let's just sketch out the two approaches.

PRE-PRODUCTION FOR FICTION FILMS

Once the script is "locked," meaning the major characters, major locations, stunts, effects, big scenes, and major sets are decided upon, you go through a process called "script breakdown." There is software to help (see *www.writersstore.com*). What we are doing is combing through each scene of the script and highlighting everything in that scene (every character, prop, vehicle, significant wardrobe, set dressing, extra, special effect, etc.) that we will need to shoot it.

That information is carefully entered into a Scheduling program, of which there are several that are very good. I prefer Movie Magic Scheduling. When that process is complete, we create a shooting schedule that makes sense according to a number of factors. The usual ones are:

1. Location

Let's say we have nine scenes to shoot, three each in Canada, the U.S. and Mexico. Obviously, we would not shoot one scene in Canada, hop a plane to the U.S. location, shoot a scene, travel to Mexico and shoot a scene, then return to Canada and so on. We would "shoot out," as they say, all our Canada scenes, then move to the U.S., then finish in Mexico. The same logic applies regionally. If possible, shoot all the scenes in "A" County or City, then move to "B" County or City. Try to order scenes by locations, so you keep your globe-trotting to a minimum.

2. Set

The same logic applies to sets. If we're shooting in a house or on a stage with multiple sets, when possible, try to "shoot out" each set to avoid returning to the same set twice. Why be upstairs in a Bedroom, go to the trouble of dressing it and lighting it, and then return to it two days later to repeat the whole process for another scene unless you absolutely have to?

3. Cast

The rule of thumb is, try to schedule actors so they work consecutive days.

For SAG/AFTRA shoots, in-between days are "Hold" days, and actors get paid. More than ten Hold days and you must do a "Drop/Pick-up," meaning the actor is dropped from his/her contract and picked up again. This can only happen once per film. For non-union actors these rules do not apply but try to work them consecutively anyway. It's more efficient.

4. Day/Night

▶ Be aware of turnaround — the time between camera wrap and the next crew call. A ten-hour turnaround (or rest period) is customary for crew, 12 for SAG/AFTRA actors. Be sure to check local rules.

▶ So don't schedule an EXTERIOR (EXT) NIGHT that goes all night followed by an EXT DAY. There must a break in between.

▶ Try to schedule all EXT NIGHTS together so people are on the same biological clock. Allow a day off before resuming a day schedule.

5. Exterior/Interior

▶ It's generally wise to shoot exteriors early in the schedule. That way, if there's bad weather, cover yourself with the option of shooting interiors (aka "cover sets"). If you wait until the end of the schedule to shoot exteriors, and bad weather hits, you pay your cast, crew and equipment rentals to sit around playing pinochle while you wait for the sun.

▶ Arrange all cover sets/locations with owners in advance. The First Law of Production is "Never Assume Anything."

6. Children

Children under 18 have special rules from both SAG/AFTRA and the state's Dept. of Labor about special permits, working hours, rest breaks, meals and school. You may also need to budget for a Teacher and a Social Worker on set, or maybe more than one depending on the number of children. Also find out the driving distance from the child's home to set. If they are outside certain pre-set limits (in L.A. it's "the 30 Mile Zone"), the child's day may begin earlier than you think.

7. Time of Year/Climate

▶ How much available light do you have this time of year?

▶ What's the prevailing weather in this season?

▶ Always check weather/wind forecasts before and during your shoot.

8. Special Effects/Stunts

Is a Stunt Coordinator on hand for run of show? If not, try to schedule all stunts and special effects (mechanical, aka physical) together. Major stunts/effects will need prep time.

9. Key Scenes

▶ It's usually wise to make the first shoot day light work to allow for crew and talent to get up to speed.

▶ Highly emotional scenes need consideration about when to be scheduled. Discuss with your actors and team.

There are a couple good books about fiction film scheduling: *Film Scheduling* by Ralph Singleton, and *The Hollywood Guide to Film Budgeting and Script Breakdown for Low Budget Features* by Danford Chamness.

Once you have a Schedule, you know a lot more about your production, such as how many shoot days, how many actors and extras, what your props are, your locations and when you'll be using them, major sets and when you'll need them, key picture vehicles, how much prep time for any special effects, and much more. Armed with this knowledge, you can now begin the next phase of Pre-Production, the Budget. You'll find several sample budgets for fiction projects in this book ($5 Million Feature Film, Digital Feature Film, Digital "No-Budget" Feature Film, and the Student Film).

Doing a budget is not the end of the pre-production process. If you were thinking it was, stop reading and take a little nap. You'll need fresh eyes when you see what remains to be done before you shoot:

PRE-PRODUCTION CHECKLIST

Completed Prior to Three Weeks Before Production
▶ Script Revisions ("final" draft script)
▶ Script Research Report
   (send "final" draft to script research co. for clearance)
▶ A.D. Breakdown Pages Complete
▶ Shooting Schedule
▶ Locked Budget
▶ Cost Report on Development Costs
   (or Close Out of Development Costs)
▶ Payroll Service (make deal/prelim schedule)
▶ Crewing Keys and Rest of Crew
▶ Casting — Stars and Support Cast
▶ Crew Deal Memos
▶ Union Negotiations (as needed)
▶ Crew List (names/contact info)
▶ Cast Contracts
▶ Cast List (names/contact info)
▶ Travel Arrangements for Cast/Crew
▶ Studio (sound stage)

▷ Locations Scouting/Surveying
▷ Post House (make selection/discuss workflow/negotiate deal/do tests/prelim schedule)
▷ Digital/Film/Audio Stock (place orders)
▷ Equipment Orders (all departments — prelim orders)
▷ Insurance (prod. ins./general liability/workers comp)
▷ Completion Bond (or Completion Guarantee)
▷ *ISAN* Application*
▷ Other Suppliers (place orders)
▷ Unit Publicity Plan (Online & On Set)
▷ Set Up Office and FTP Site
▷ Catering Choice (make selection/negotiate/prelim schedule)

Two Weeks Before Production

▷ Stunt Contracts
▷ Pre-Calculate Extra Day Costs, Extra OT Costs
▷ Rehearsal Room (book and schedule)
▷ Choose Forms for Call Sheet and Production Report
▷ Catering Deal Memo
▷ Digital/Film/Audio Stock in
▷ Craft Service (place orders)
▷ Battery Stock in
▷ Polaroid Film Stock (or digital still cams)
▷ Expendibles Order
▷ Production and Department Meetings
▷ Location/Tech Surveys

One Week Before Production

▷ Final Production Meeting (all departments)
▷ Final Location/Tech Surveys
▷ First Call Sheet
▷ Camera Test/Equipment Pickup
▷ Crew Deal Memos Done

* *ISAN* (International Standard Audiovisual Number) is a new global identifier for audio-visual projects, a numerical version of your project title. The ISAN number is constant, so it's helpful, for example, for Producers

13

tracking global revenue for their project even if the program was aired with a different title that the Producer didn't know about. The ISAN number is also useful for international distributors and festivals; they scan the visual bar code, and they have consistent descriptive data about the project. ISAN is a required deliverable for Blu-Ray release, and required if you get financing in the UK. The requirement is spreading (see *www. isan.org*).

The above Pre-Production Checklist is just a taste. I have edited it from a more complete list courtesy of Deborah S. Patz and her fine book, *Film Production Management 101* (*www.mwp.com*). (Also see Resources.) If you want to know how to line produce features, check it out. And yes, it's true, production management takes up entire books.

Let's move on to Pre-Production for Non-Fiction.

PRE-PRODUCTION FOR NON-FICTION FILMS

I'm referring to "non-fiction" rather than "documentary" because the "D" word usually conjures up specific images, like penguins, or shaky black-and-white WWII aerial combat, or following a person as he or she recovers, or not, from an addiction. The point is that these are worthy topics, but there are many ways, or genres, in non-fiction through which these and other topics can be expressed. Here's a list of some of them:

1. The personal essay
2. Biography
3. Cinema vérité (filmmaker may intervene)*
4. Diary
5. Direct cinema (filmmaker observes — no intervention)*
6. Educational
7. Experimental
8. Historical
9. How-to/Instructional
10. Nature
11. Persuasive
12. Political
13. Science
14. Training
15. Travel

*For an interesting discussion of the history, aesthetics, and differences between Cinema Vérité and Cinema Direct, see Chapter 14 of the excellent book, *A New History of Documentary Film*, by Jack C. Ells and Betsy A. McLane.

Pick your topic, choose your genre, and depending on your choices, you have completely different pre-production approaches.

Suppose, for example, we decide to make a film about a famous sculptor who works in stone. Let's look at three possible approaches:

▸ Direct Cinema to follow her and see her at life and work.
▸ How-to/Instructional to teach others her technique.
▸ Experimental/Art to immerse the viewer in an experience.

Direct Cinema Pre-Production

In this example, assuming we have all the necessary permissions, we might begin by asking questions like:

▸ Who will see this film? (And what are its likely distribution outlets?)
▸ What is its purpose?

Let's assume we are making a sixty-minute film, aiming for broadcast to a wide audience on cable or TV, like PBS, with DVD sales. Our purpose is to convey the artist's ideas about people and nature and our journey through space and time. (If we were doing this film in real life, we'd spend a lot more time refining these ideas.)

Research

So, assuming that the sculptor has agreed to the project, we might begin by researching the sculptor's history, past work, writings, what others have written about her, her family, photos and films, and finally, visiting the sculptor at her home/studio without cameras. By becoming acquainted, we can be more relaxed around each other. We are building trust. This is an important part of pre-production that may take some time: a few days, a week.

If there are photos or film, who has them? Who owns the rights? We will have to license them. How much will it cost?

Are there family members and colleagues whom we also want to interview or get on film? Certain names might emerge in research, and during the days of being with her without a camera. How does she feel about our talking with these people? Are they open to being in the film? Will they be good on camera and worth the effort of filming them?

As you can see, once we go down the Direct Cinema road, there are many choices that pop up in pre-production. Each one takes time and probably money.

Treatment

Once we have enough research, it's helpful, some argue even critical, to start writing a Treatment or Script. We should have a sense of the story we want to tell about our sculptor. We have an idea of who else we want to bring into the film and roughly what they will contribute. We have a sense of what other materials, photos and films, we will have access to. So we write out a narrative that lays out and juxtaposes all the scenes we believe we can really shoot and is the most compelling story that we can fashion. Will it change as we shoot it? Sure it will. Maybe a lot. And we want to be open to change and serendipity. But with a story in our hip pocket we have a structure with which to begin.

Schedule

With a story in our pocket, we know which family and colleagues we probably want to visit, which photos and films we probably want to license, and how much time we probably want to shoot with our sculptor. With this information, we can now revise our schedule. In this case, our schedule might look like this:

Weeks 1-5
Research:
History of sculptor/past work/photos/films/rights/family/colleagues

Weeks 6-11
Pre-interview family/colleagues (by phone if distant)
Write Treatment
Pencil Crew/Gear for shoot Week 16 and 18
Pencil Editor Week 17 on

Weeks 12-13
On-site visit/location scout (sculptor)
On-site visit/location scout — selected family/colleagues
Releases signed

Schedule shoot dates for Week 16 and 18
Book crew/gear for Week 16 and 18
Book hotel for crew for Week 16 and 18
Book editor for Week 17 on

Weeks 14–15
Research — follow-up from visits re: family/colleagues
Prep permits for Week 16 and 18
Production insurance
Book Family/Colleagues shoots Week 18

Week 16
Shoot sculptor on site

Week 17
Log/capture footage from Week 16

Week 18
Shoot family/colleagues

Week 19
Log/capture footage from Week 18
Transcribe interviews

Week 20
Start edit assembly
Paper cut interviews

Weeks 21–30
Continue edit
Bring in licensed photos/film
Additional shooting as needed

Weeks 30–31
Continue edit
Fine cut to composer for score

Weeks 31–32
Composer for score
Sound design
Audio clean-up/sound editing
Final mix

Week 33
Color correction
Mastering

Budget
Now that we have a Treatment and a Schedule, we have thought through enough items that we can make a Budget. For sample non-fiction budgets in this book, see the Documentary Video Budget, the Industrial Budget, and the Music Video Budget.

So that might be our pre-production method with a Direct Cinema approach to this topic. Let's look at example number two to see how pre-production differs depending on our choice of genre.

How To/Instructional Pre-Production
How might we approach a How-To/Instructional video of our famous sculptor's techniques? First, we might begin by asking the same questions:

▶ Who will see this film? (And what are its likely distribution outlets?)
▶ What is its purpose?

Let's assume we are making a 45-minute DVD that will be sold to college art departments, art schools, sculpture studios, and to artists in general via educational film catalogues and a website under the sculptor's name. The audience is fellow sculptors and students interested in technique. The purpose is to transmit learning, so that viewers will walk away knowing how to achieve practical techniques in stone sculpture.

Research
We might begin this project by asking our sculptor what areas of her techniques she wants to focus on, and get her ideas about how to teach them. This may involve a visit. We may also want to research the marketplace, and ask potential customers what they'd like to learn from this sculptor. Hopefully, there's a "harmonic convergence" here. Next, we might research other art and sculpture instructional DVDs to see what we like and dislike. We may have a particular vision about how best to transmit this information.

Script

Finally, we'll write a script, which lays out all our ideas, and the actual content of what our sculptor will teach, in a sequence of scenes that we can realistically shoot. Then we'll re-write it until it's right. It would be smart to get the script approved by the sculptor, and by whoever is paying for this project.

Schedule

With a script, we now know what materials we need, where we'll be shooting, how many days we'll shoot, what kinds of shots we'll make... which tells us what kind of gear we'll need, and how many crew we'll need and what positions they'll fill. With that information, we're well on or way to revising our Schedule. It might look like this:

Week 1–4

Research other DVDs
Research sculptor's work
Research marketplace
Preliminary ideas for DVD
Meet with sculptor

Weeks 5–8

Write/revise script
Hire and meet with Graphic Designer
Scout locations
Scout production requirements (tools/sculptor assistants/machinery, etc.)
Incorporate all of above into script
Pencil Crew/Gear for shoot Week 11
Pencil Editor Week 12

Week 9

Script approval and re-writes
Book Crew/Gear for shoot Week 11
Book editor Week 12
Production insurance

Week 10

Prep week/locations/materials

Week 11
Shoot

Weeks 12–15
Log/capture footage
Edit
Graphic Designer — refine and lay in graphics

Week 16
Sound design
Audio clean-up/sound editing
Lay in library music
Final mix

Week 17
Color correction
Mastering
Authoring for DVD
Replication

Budget

And now that we've done all this planning and thinking through the Script and the Schedule, we can design a Budget that reflects the crew positions, crew time, gear type and time, locations, hotel if any, editor time and so forth. This is a very different non-fiction project from Direct Cinema, all because we changed our creative approach and our purpose, to suit our goal — we wanted to reach a specific audience with a specific message.

Let's look at our final example to see how pre-production differs depending on our choice of genre.

Experimental/Art Pre-Production

How might we approach an Experimental or Art video that gives viewers an experience that is in tune with the sculptor's own artistic vision? Let's ask the same questions:

▶ Who will see this film? (And what are its likely distribution outlets?)
▶ What is its purpose?

Let's assume we are making a 15-minute DVD that will be seen in festivals, and sold to college art departments, art schools, and to art lovers via educational film catalogues and a website under the sculptor's name. The audience is art lovers, and fellow artists. The purpose is to transmit an experience, through images and sound, of the sculptor's artistic vision about objects in nature undergoing natural change in space and time.

Research

Assuming we have permission from, and an affinity with the sculptor, we'll probably want to spend some time with her just hanging out, if that's possible, talking about how to achieve a happy result with the film. What to shoot, what kind of equipment, what sounds, what music if any, what visual effects if any, are all interesting questions.

Treatment

We may or may not need a treatment. We may want to storyboard certain sequences if they require camera moves or some special equipment. Maybe we'll want to shoot time-lapse of a stone sculpture being assembled in a tidal flat, and then watch as the tide rushes in under a full moon and rising sun to wash the sculpture away (with apologies to famed British sculptor Andy Goldsworthy).

Schedule

Once we have our ideas fleshed out, we can make a schedule. It might look like this:

Weeks 1–2
Research:
Time with the sculptor
Releases signed
Location scouting

Weeks 2–3
Write Treatment/Storyboards
Prep permits for Week 6
Production insurance
Pencil Crew/Gear for shoot Week 6
Pencil Editor Week 7

Weeks 4-5
On-site location scout (sculptor)
Schedule shoot dates for Week 6
Book crew/gear for Week 6
Book hotel for crew for Week 6
Book editor for Week 7

Week 6
Shoot sculptor /other footage on locations

Week 7
Log/capture footage from Week 6

Weeks 8-10
Edit

Weeks 11-12
Fine cut to composer for score

Weeks 12-13
Sound design
Audio clean-up/sound editing
Final mix

Week 14
Color correction
Mastering

Budget

With Storyboards and a Schedule, we can make a Budget. This book does not contain an Art Film budget, but if you ever need to make one, the lessons learned from the other budgets will take you pretty far along the road.

In these three non-fiction examples, we've seen that the creative approach that we take, or the genre that we choose, sends us in a definite direction that in turn determines what we shoot, how and when we shoot it, and how much it costs: script, schedule, and budget.

Line Items Checklist

Pre-Production for fiction or non-fiction is made easier by having a checklist that contains practically every personnel function, every service, and every piece of equipment you might use. For our purposes, that's the budget Line Items section in this book. Use it to help you think through every phase of Pre-Production, Production, and Post. What you don't need from the list, discard.

We find it helpful when doing a budget to actually visualize a shoot, day by day, hour by hour, imagining what everyone is doing at any given time. This kind of detailed thinking also helps to work out the daily schedules and avoid conflicts.

It's important to think about contingencies during this phase. What if the weather turns bad? Do we have an alternate location ready to go? Is there something else we can shoot so we don't waste the day? What if we need something we don't have? Where are the nearest hardware stores, gas stations, restaurants, groceries, rental cars, and so on? If a crew member calls in sick, do we have a list of people we can call? (For more tips and wise thoughts from old-timers, see the Money-Saving Ideas section.)

While the budget Line Items is the ultimate Pre-Production checklist, here are some other goods and services you'll need during this stage.

Legal

If you don't have one, find an entertainment lawyer you can work with. Don't be afraid to call several. You can find them in or around the larger entertainment industry cities like New York and Los Angeles. Explain that you are interviewing prospective lawyers and you'd like to meet and talk about your project. Our experience has been that they are nice people who won't eat you for lunch — they may even take you to lunch. If you're not familiar with things legal, don't be afraid to ask all the questions people are too afraid to ask, like "Are you charging us for this meeting?"

In the meeting, explain the project, and ask about what services your lawyer will perform, and how much it will cost. For budgeting, you'll need to know how much to allot for the entire project. Some lawyers charge by the hour, but many accept a flat fee for a project, or a percentage of the budget. An average TV movie, for example, might have a budget of $2.5 million, of which 1% to 1.5% might go for legal fees. Once you've interviewed a few attorneys, you'll have a good sense of the range of prices for your project.

Your lawyer will probably generate various deal memos, contracts, personal release forms/materials releases/location releases, rights options, and the like. Tons of carefully worded paper will cross your desk and make you cross-eyed. Eventually you'll get used to it. Then it'll actually start to make sense.

One way to save money in the future is to enter these documents into your computer. On your next project, you may need to merely alter some details. Discuss this with your lawyer first, because laws change, and you may waste time generating your own document only to have your lawyer recommend a new one. In any case, you'll still want him or her to review documents before they go out for signature.

Some specialized stationers and bookstores, like Enterprise Printers and Samuel French Books (see Resources section), have sample contract books for sale. These can often get you started, but the safest tack is to have your attorney examine any proposed contract.

Rights Acquisition

Is your project based on a book, article, stage play, screenplay, radio play, or someone's life story? If so, you'll need to get the rights to produce it. If it's published, call the publisher, and ask who owns the copyright. If that doesn't work, try a large copyright search firm like Thomson and Thomson (800) 692-8833, or Universal Media (202) 234-7292. If you're really desperate, try calling the U.S. Copyright Office, Washington, D.C., (202) 707-3000 (*www.copyright.gov*). (A search of registrations, renewals, and recorded transfers of ownership made before 1978 requires a manual search of their files at $150/hour, and you can talk to the research people there for an estimate of how long it will take.) When you've tracked down who actually owns the rights you can negotiate to buy the rights or buy an option. You'll probably want your lawyer to advise you, since rights acquisition can be tricky.

An option gives you the exclusive right to later acquire the rights to a book or some other property. Here's how it works. An option allows you to tie up the property for a specified period of time (usually a year or two). This means no one else can take the project from you. During the option period, you will look for financing, write script drafts, and attract stars. The option agreement usually states that if the term ends with no production agreement, and if the option is not renewed, then the rights revert back to the original owner. If, however, the project goes forward, the option will spell out the terms for actually buying the rights, including how much money and profit participation (if any) the owner will get. Option agreements can be simple or complex, depending on the property and who is involved. We've bought options for a dollar. We argue that our time trying to get the property into production is worth something and refuse to pay for an option. Other times, when it's clear the property has immediate value, you must pay for an option. If it's Liz Taylor's life story, expect to pay, well, a lot.

On the other hand, if the property you want to produce has been published in another form, then you must acquire the rights. Having control of a property is the first element you need to begin to leverage your project into reality. If you don't write a script yourself then you'll have to option or buy the rights to one.

Staff Contracts

If your company has become a signatory to one or more of the guilds, you may want to use standard deal-memo forms for personnel such as writers (WGA), directors, stage managers, associate directors, unit production managers (DGA), and actors, dancers, narrators (SAG and AFTRA).

Call the guilds (see Appendix) and ask for copies of the standard forms appropriate to your project (i.e., feature film, videotape music concert, etc.). Have your lawyer review the forms just in case they need to be customized. If a guild doesn't have forms, it's up to your lawyer to create the contract, which, in most cases, is fairly simple.

The deal memos state that you agree not to pay less than the guild minimum scale. To find out how much that scale is, as well as basic guild rules, you need to refer to the appropriate rate cards and Basic Agreement books, which you get from the guilds. (Also see Resources section for *The Labor Guide*.) We advise getting the books and cards, even though you may wind up calling back several times to confirm the rates, residuals, and other matters for your specific project. It's now a running joke in our office that whoever gets to confirm rates with a certain guild (which shall remain nameless) also gets a free hour of psychotherapy and a group hug. That's because the rates seem to change overnight depending on whom you talk to. We usually go back and forth a few times until it's finally settled. (Also see "Negotiating with Crews" later in this chapter.)

Music Clearance

If copyrighted music is an important part of your project, start the clearance process as soon as the script is "locked," that is, approved. Why start early? Some music may be too expensive, or perhaps the owner won't give permission for its use. Until you know what you can use, and how much it will cost, your budget — and your show — will be incomplete.

When you clear a piece of music, you pay a license fee to the copyright owner in exchange for the right to use that music in your show. The price depends on what medium you use (i.e., feature film, television, DVD, CD-ROM, the Internet, etc.), what territories you'll distribute to (U.S., North American, European, etc.), and what term you want, or can afford (three years, five years, perpetuity).

Many producers use a Music Supervisor, music clearance person or service to track down copyright owners and negotiate prices. If your needs are at all complex, this is the way to go, since it is a specialized business. If clearances are not obtained correctly, and if you're caught, owners can get nasty and throw injunctions at you, forcing you to re-edit or even destroy release prints or copies.

Music clearance services do charge different fees for their work, so call a few to compare. If you're in New York or Los Angeles (or at your public library), check the Business to Business phone directory for either city to get a listing. Clearance people are also listed in such production guides as *L.A. 411*, and the *NYPG* (*New York Production Guide*), available at many bookstores or online.

It is prudent to contact a clearance service or your attorney, even if you believe your music to be in the public domain, or if you intend to claim "fair use." Public domain music must be verified as such, and "fair use," while it may apply to limited use of music in news, criticism or scholarship, may or may not be appropriate for your project. And one last little tip. Somebody started the rumor that producers can use up to eight bars of a song without paying for it. Sorry — no can do.

Fair Use

By the way, the concept of "fair use," whether you intend to use it with music, clips or what your own camera sees, requires your careful study. If you incorporate music or footage under fair use, and later discover that you cannot use it, you may face a host of issues, including: a court battle, cutting out the footage, leaving in the footage but not being able get Errors and Omissions insurance and therefore not being able to get a Distributor. That said, fair use, properly applied, can be your good friend. For a great source of information on the topic, see American University's Center for Social Media (*www.centerforsocialmedia.org/resources/fair_use/*).

Feature Film Clips

If you want to use clips from Hollywood feature films in your project, you may be in for a trip on a long and winding road. With patience and perseverance you will prevail. The cost per clip depends on the rights you or your distributor need. So the first step is to call your distributor and find out. If you don't have one yet, then anticipate what rights you'll need by talking to a few producers of similar projects who have been through the distribution wars.

What rights are there to be had? The big banana is "worldwide" (or as they sometimes say, "throughout the universe"), "in all media, in perpetuity," which means you can use the clip in any territory (or on any planet), in films, television, interactive, and on DVD for all eternity. Ask for these rights first, because you never know, you just might get them. On the other hand, if you really don't need these rights (they will cost more), go for what you do need. Most major studios, for example, won't grant rights in perpetuity — the usual term is three years or so. (This is usually not long enough for DVD distribution, which generally requires seven years.)

Rights are broken down by territory and by media/distribution format. For example you could ask for:

- U.S. & Territories TV rights
- North American TV rights
- World TV rights/World TV
- All Rights (includes free TV/pay TV/cable TV/satellite-delivered TV)/DVD/Airline/Non-Theatrical (educational)/Interactive, New Media, and so forth.

Be clear about what rights and clips you need from the outset; otherwise, the conversation gets confusing very fast. After you know what rights you want and what clips you want, how do you find out who owns the feature film so you can start negotiating?

First, try calling the studio directly. Remember that over the years, many film libraries have been sold, and you need to find the current owner. If you've rented the DVD, check the front or tail credits for the distribution company's logo.

Or, you can try a number of reference books:

The *BIB Books* is a three-volume series from the Broadcast Information Bureau in Philadelphia (800/777-8074 or *www.bibnet.com*). The books are a compilation of all films, TV films, series, specials, etc., appearing on television. Distributor information is provided. The cost is a mere $799 for all three volumes, or for the online version. If you live in Los Angeles, try the poor man's way and see if there's a set of the books at the Academy of Motion Picture Arts and Sciences Library. If you live elsewhere, try charming your way into a local television station that may have a copy.

There is also an international group called Focal (Federation of Commercial Audio Visual Libraries Ltd.) in London (*www.focalint.org*). Email them at *info@focalint.org*. Their publication and website lists many sources for footage around the world.

The U.S. Copyright Office, Washington, DC, (202) 707-3000 will do a search to determine ownership or whether a film is in the public domain. There is an hourly charge. Contact the office for the latest rate.

Finally, you can hire a research and clearance service to locate the owners and negotiate the rights. Services charge by the hour, or anywhere from $1,000 to $2,000 per week, depending on the show, its length, the nature of the clips, etc. Finding a research and clearance person can be an interesting challenge, since they usually aren't listed in the yellow pages. Some of the above clip reference books may have lists. Or ask for a recommendation from a friendly person at a major movie studio's clip licensing department. Warner Brothers, Sony, and Universal are all candidates. Even if you've used a service, have your own attorney review the license agreements from the studios before you sign.

So now you've located the owner and negotiated the rights for the license fee. Are you done? Nope. Many producers forget the next step, and pay dearly when they go over budget.

The use of many clips requires the producer to get permission from, and pay residuals to, "third parties" like actors, writers, and directors. (On many pre-1960 features, you don't need to do this, but ask the studio if there are any outstanding items to clear with third parties, regardless of the year of release. Fred Astaire, for example, had a permission clause put into his contracts as early as the 1940s, and now producers must go through his estate!)

All actors *recognizable in a scene* must give their permission, and be paid at least SAG/AFTRA scale (call the respective guild for clip rates). Stunt people get more money and may even ask for what they originally got for the stunt! You are excused from crowd scenes with extras, but crowd scenes with recognizable credited actors must be cleared. For the writers and directors of the film with your desired clip, call the respective guild for clip rates.

Somehow, producers can get the idea that since they worked so hard and paid so much to license a film clip, the musical score ought to be part of the deal. Sometimes it is, but most of the time it's not. If not, add that to the list for the music clearance (see above).

Michael Wiese, my publisher and co-author on earlier editions of this book, tells this story. "*I executive-produced a feature documentary,* The Beach Boys: An American Band. *The rights clearances filled two books larger than two New York City phone books. For every clip we used, even if it was only a few feet long, we had to get something like nine underlying rights; the master recording license, the sync license, the footage rights, celebrity appearances, background actors, plus guild payments to writers, directors, and musicians (other than the Beach Boys). It was horrendous and consumed an extraordinary amount of time. I believe a paralegal worked on the project for a year and a half just clearing rights. When all was said and done we learned that we had missed a few that almost resulted in major litigation and required an additional $60,000 to make the suit 'go away'. You've got to really make sure the bases are covered when you do programs that use so much of other people's source materials.*"

Archive Film Clips and Stock Footage

Need clips from old movies, newsreels, old cartoons, educational films and the like? Need a stock shot of a 1977 Mustang cruising Hollywood Boulevard?

Studios have a *stock footage department* where standard fees average $50 per foot (on 35mm) with a 10-foot minimum cut ($500). Or go to a *stock footage library*. Some have both stock and archival footage, while some specialize in one or the other.

Here's the way archive footage works by way of an example.

We needed a series of "impact" shots for an athletic shoe commercial — funny shots of old cars, planes, people, and cartoon characters crashing into things or getting creamed in imaginative ways. We searched the web for stock footage companies and found a few that specialized in what we wanted. Most of them operate like this. Enter the keyword search or category search and find demos of clips you like. Register as a customer. Then download a free, watermarked, "low-resolution" version of your clip that you can place in your editing timeline to see how it works. You can save a copy of it to put in your customer bin on the website. If you like the look of the clip, return to the website, pay the nice people by credit card, and download the high-resolution version. You may have to render it in your timeline. Prices are usually for a minimum of a certain number of seconds, like 30, so even if you only need 5 seconds, you still pay for 30. But check their terms; most companies offer "royalty free," meaning you pay a one-time fee for use in your project forever, some companies also offer "editorial use," which is a lower rate for documentary and educational projects. If in doubt, call them and negotiate.

The Budget

A "detailed" budget lists each and every line item. A multimillion-dollar feature budget could run a hundred pages. A student documentary film could run five pages. But both should be as detailed as possible. A "summary" budget, also called a "topsheet," is just that — a summary. It groups the line items into categories so that an investor or client need only look at one short page to see how the money is allocated. The categories of a "summary budget" or "topsheet" might be grouped like this:

01-00 Story Rights
02-00 Script
03-00 Producer's Unit
04-00 Direction
05-00 Cast
06-00 Travel and Living – Producers/Director
07-00 Travel and Living – Cast
08-00 Residuals
09-00 Above-the-Line Fringe
10-00 Production Staff

11-00 Extra Talent
12-00 Sound Stage
13-00 Production Design
14-00 Set Construction
15-00 Set Operations
16-00 Special Effects
17-00 Set Dressing
18-00 Property
19-00 Wardrobe
20-00 Make-Up and Hair
21-00 Electrical
22-00 Camera
23-00 Sound
24-00 Transportation
25-00 Location Expenses
26-00 Picture Vehicles/Animals
27-00 Film and Lab
28-00 Travel and Living-Crew
29-00 Below-the-Line Fringe
30-00 Editorial
31-00 Post-Production Videotape/Film and Lab
32-00 Optical Effects/Visual Effects/Digital Intermediate
33-00 Music
34-00 Post-Production Sound
35-00 Titles and Graphics
36-00 Stock Footage
37-00 Insurance
38-00 General and Administrative Expenses

This sequence of categories is fairly standard, but different producers and studios often create their own versions. Once you have assessed all your categories and line items, feel free to group them in any way you (and your accountant) like. You will be assigning each category code numbers (Chart of Accounts) for tracking purposes, as above, but more on that later.

There are standardized budget formats, like those used by the AICP (Association of Independent Commercial Producers — see Appendix), which are used for commercial bidding. With this format, an ad agency or client can quickly review competitive bids from different producers and compare costs on a line-by-line basis before awarding a contract. Other producers who like the AICP format simply borrow it for their own use.

The budgets in this book are arranged according to the Summary Budget above. It is a format that has been useful for us, but feel free to adapt it to your own needs. Use whatever format works for you. All the budgets in this book are available for free from MWP as Excel documents. (See each budget's title page for download instructions.)

Negotiations

Negotiating is a fundamental skill in producing. Actually, it is just clear communication. If you are good at it, you can reduce your costs 10%, 20%, 30%, or more. Webster's definition of *negotiation* is "to confer, bargain, or discuss with a view of reaching agreement, to succeed in crossing, surmounting, moving through." For our purposes, it is when two or more people settle on the specific terms of the exchange. This could take the form of cash payment, deferred payment, title credits, profit sharing, or any number of other elements. (We believe there should always be some form of an exchange even if you are getting something for free — such as a thank you note or flowers.)

An agreement is only an agreement when both parties agree upon the terms of the exchange. If this is not the case, you are still negotiating. You're going to have to negotiate. There's no way around it. This skill allows you to do "more with less." It gives you the opportunity to clearly define the exchange with the people with whom you'll work.

Too often, wages and prices are not fully discussed. Each person has only a partial understanding of the arrangement. Assumptions are made and it's not until the bill comes and all hell breaks loose that the differences are apparent. Then it's too late. Feelings are hurt. Trust and confidence are broken. Friends are lost. And to top it all off, more money is spent than planned — all because the terms of the agreement were not clear. This just cannot happen if you want to produce films. Life is too short. It's better to learn how to negotiate, come to an honorable agreement, and get on with it.

In America and most Western countries people somehow feel funny about negotiating. They pay the full price rather than face the embarrassment of negotiating. But in the Far East, Southeast Asia, India and Africa, negotiating is considered polite. If you negotiate, you get involved with people, you learn something about each other. It's extremely rude in Java to pay the first price asked. It's expected that one will banter back and forth two or three times before settling on a price. It's part of the accepted social exchange.

(An interesting note: In Indonesia it's not buyer beware but seller beware. If you charge an unfair price you will be ostracized. It's considered very poor manners to charge too high a price.)

In the Western world — where the attitude is there's a sucker born every minute — remarkably, people are still embarrassed to question a price tag or a rate card even when it seems too high. But when they do, more often than not the price will be reduced. You *can* get a discount on a refrigerator at Sears or an Eclair at Camera Mart, but first you've got to ask.

Question every price. Could the price be lower? Assume it can. Don't accept the first quote offered. Write it down. Don't worry, it'll still be there when you come back. In film and tape production, prices are more flexible than you might assume. Freelancers' rates are flexible. So are rates at labs, equipment rental houses, and video editing facilities. You simply have to ask! It's not unusual to receive anywhere from 5% to 50%.

Shop around. Check at least three sources for the same job or piece of equipment — prices can vary tremendously. Once when we needed a special effect, we were quoted three prices: $4,500, $2,000, $600. Through these discussions we studied the effect and found a way to do it for $300. It finally cost 15 times less than the first estimate!

Give yourself time. Do the necessary research to find the best price and the best quality. If you are forced to do something right away (for example, typeset titles on a Sunday), you will spend two or three times the normal price for "rush charges." Furthermore, with added pressure the job may not come out as well as you hoped. Rush shipping is usually an unnecessary waste. The difference between a next-day delivery ($17) and same-day delivery ($150) is significant. Leave enough time to do the job well. Plan ahead and save money.

Collect information. Give yourself time to collect information, and you'll be ahead of the game. Most information is free. If you are too busy, hire a research assistant. The more you learn, the more options you'll discover. You'll find new technical processes, locate facilities, and be less willing to pay the first price quoted. The more "mystical" or complex a job seems to you, the more it will cost. Once understood, these things lose their mystique. With enough time and information, and the willingness to negotiate rates, you'll gain that necessary edge to make the best deal possible and save money. You'll also find better ways of doing the job.

Negotiating with Crews

Take time to talk with the person you want to hire. Describe the shoot, what you want to accomplish, the working conditions, who else will be in the crew and cast. Learning about the project will increase his or her interest in joining you. The person will get an image of what the shoot will be like and all its intangible benefits. Perhaps the shoot includes locations in Taiwan and he's always wanted to go there. Perhaps she'll be working with a favorite actor or personality. Maybe the cause of the film is close to his heart. Or maybe none of the above counts and it's strictly business, but at least you tried.

Michael says, "*I once spent a few weeks in Sydney, Australia, interviewing directors of photography, production managers, and art directors for a feature I'd like to do in Bali. I chose Australia because the strong dollar's exchange rate immediately gave me a 25% edge. But more important, I found out that Australians have worked throughout the South Pacific, so they are accustomed to the weather, working conditions, and accommodations. Many had even worked in Bali before. Each person had his own strengths and weaknesses, but overall of the twenty some people I interviewed I only found two with whom I wouldn't want to work. Now that's the kind of situation you want to be in when looking for department heads and crews.*

"*I was also able to place these people (by asking their colleagues) into A, B, and C categories in regard to their experience and fees. This gave me a financial and experience palette with which to work.*"

What follows may get a little thick. For many readers, this is more information than you will need to know. For others, as your production budgets increase your knowledge of negotiations will necessarily have to increase as well. We decided we'd lay out the details for you so you'd know what you will one day have to face. Hang in there, take it a chunk at a time, and you'll see it's not as intimidating as it seems at first glance.

Flat Rates vs. Hourly Rates

There is great confusion in the industry about hiring a crew member for a flat rate of, say, $300 for a day's work, a "day" being anything the producer says it is. Exploitive producers love this approach because they can work crews until they drop from exhaustion and not pay any overtime. Crew people hate these kinds of flats, for obvious reasons.

The fact is, except for some positions (see Exceptions to the overtime rule below), the labor law says people must be paid at regular, straight time wages for the first 8 hours of work per day, or for the first 40 hours of work per week. For non-union workers the wages are negotiable, for union workers they are set. Any hours worked over those must be paid at 1.5 times the regular rate (time and a half) up to 12 hours in a day. In some states, after 12 hours, the employer must pay double time. Other states do not have such a rule, and the worker continues to be paid at time and a half. Call a payroll service to find out the rules that apply to the state in which you are shooting. (Do an Internet search for "payroll service entertainment," or a similar combination of key words, and your city, and you'll likely find some local payroll services familiar with the arcane rules and regulations of paying cast and crew.)

Exceptions to the overtime rule

Such positions as Production Designer, Director of Photography, Art, Director, Production Accountant, or a Costume Designer are "on call." These people are regarded as "management" of a sort, since they head their departments. This means that in non-union situations, the person can be hired by the week, at a flat rate, with no allowance for overtime. In union cases, there are limits, and overtime pay, that vary by the job and by state.

Here's an example of how the wage structure can work for regular employees:

Key Grip (non-union)

Let's say you offer the Key Grip the hourly rate of $20. This means you'll pay him $20 per hour for 8 hours of work. That's a minimum guarantee. If you let him go after 7 hours, he still gets $160. (A half-hour for lunch is not counted as work time.) Every hour after 8, and up to 12, he gets time and a half, in this case $30. If he works 12 hours (a typical day), he gets $280. Any time after 12 hours may be double time (some states have it, others do not), in this case $40, and the second meal is counted as work time (i.e., do not deduct it). If he works for eleven and three quarter hours, you prorate the hourly wage to the nearest quarter hour. Because he is non–union, he gets no benefits for pension, health, vacation and holiday. You do apply normal employer contributions for Social Security, etc., in the form of an approximately 21% payroll tax.

Key Grip (union)

With the union worker, in this case IATSE, the minimum straight time wage is set. For First Company Grips in Los Angeles, for a certain bracket of production budget, it's $33.53 for the first 8 hours. If you are budgeting for a 12-hour day, that's $268.24 for 8 hours, and $50.30/hour (time and a half) for 4 hours, or $201.20. (After 12 hours, it's double time.) The total for 12 hours is $469.44.

Because he is an IATSE member, he also gets Pension and Health benefits to the tune of $3.8975 for every hour worked ($3.8975 x 12 = $46.77). Plus 7.719%, based on straight time pay for Vacation and Holiday ($46.77 x 8 hours x .07719% = $28.88). The grand total (without payroll tax) is $469.44 + $46.77 + $28.88= $545.09 for 12 hours of work. The payroll tax is figured on the gross wages not including benefits, in this case $469.44.

Let's say you're doing a non–union show, you're fat on script and lean on money. You anticipate going 12-hour days. So calculate your hourly rates for crew by working backward.

For example, you figure the show can afford to pay a Key Grip $300 for a day's work of 12 hours, with no double time. If you break that out, it becomes $21.42 per hour for 8 hours, and $32.13 per hour (time and a half) for 4 hours.

When you call the Key Grip, explain that you're paying $21.42 per hour for 8, and time and a half after that. Now there's no potential for confusion.

Work Hours and Pay Hours

For budgeting purposes, there's an easy way to figure your total gross wages, and that is to distinguish between *work hours* and *pay hours*. Work hours are the total hours worked; in the case of our Key Grip that's 12 hours. Of his 12 hours, 8 hours are on straight time, and 4 hours are at time and a half. Those 4 hours of time and a half equals 6 *pay hours*.

How do we get that? Multiply the number of overtime hours worked (4) times the pay rate (time and a half or 1.5), 4 x 1.5 = 6, so the *total pay hours* are 8 + 6 = 14.

When you do your budget, instead of spending time calculating the time and a half pay for all your different hourly employees, do it the quick way. If you know you're budgeting for a 12-hour day (12 *work* hours), you simply multiply the person's hourly rate times 14 pay hours. In the Key Grip's case, that's $26.98 x 14 = $377.72.

In states with *no* double time, a 13-hour work day is 15.5 pay hours. A 14-hour work day is 17 pay hours.

In states *with* double time after 12 hours, a 13-hour day is 16 pay hours. A 14-hour day is 18 pay hours.

When you negotiate with your crew people, be straightforward and honest, so everyone knows what the deal is. By starting with an hourly rate, and knowing it goes to time and a half between the 8th and 12th hours worked, maybe double time after that, you've made it crystal clear.

Another thing I always say, and add to the deal memo, is that we calculate pay at quarter hours. Let's say the crew wraps at 7:10 p.m. All the gear is stowed and time cards are ready to be signed. Since we are calculating by the quarter hour, we all know that the 7 p.m.–8 p.m. hour will be divided by four, and we'll be paid as if we worked until 7:15 p.m. It's very clean this way. No misunderstandings.

Most people will not work for less than an 8-hour minimum (for unions it's standard). The exceptions are when you are hiring someone for a longer project and they'll throw in a few half-days. If it's a union shoot, review what the P&H and Vacation and Holiday rates are, and how they are applied.

Another note on double time. In states like California that mandate double time after 12 hours, there is a common but technically illegal practice you should be aware of. When booking crew, some producers try to wangle the double time out of the equation. They'll say, "Oh, by the way, we may go over 12 hours on this day or that, do you think you could waive the double time, and count extra hours as time and a half?" The crewmember, wanting the gig, will often comply. Whether you use this ploy is your business, but if you do, make sure the same rules apply to everyone.

Finally, you or the Production Coordinator should prepare a deal memo for each crewmember, reiterating the hourly wages, and the formula for paying them. The crewmember signs it, then the Producer signs it. No confusion. Standard deal memo forms are available by mail from Enterprise Printers (see Appendix).

Budget for at least 12 hours of work per day, and try to allow an extra 10% of the person's gross wages for an "overtime" contingency. Some producers reduce the overtime contingency to 5% and just routinely budget for 13- or 14-hour days. It really depends on the demands of the script or the shooting situation.

Work out what you will offer for hourly rates in the budget before you make your calls to crew, and *be consistent in your rates across the various departments*. This is important, because if you are inconsistent you'll have unhappy people on the set, or spend valuable time renegotiating rates. For example, the Gaffer's rate should be the same as the Key Grip's rate. The Best Boy Electric and Best Boy Grip rates should be the same. All Grips and Electrics should get the same. And so on. People know what the show is paying, and they can take it or not.

What do you do if you really want a particular crew person, a Key Grip for example, but your hourly rate is too low? Try sweetening the deal with a little more money on the "kit rental" (the box of supplies he brings to the job). That way, you've kept his rate the same as those on a comparable level, but he's making a bit more money for his tools and equipment. Do this only if this is someone you cannot live without, otherwise you'll be making side deals on kit rentals all over the place and leaking money for no good reason. Generally, if you can't make suitable deals within your budget, look elsewhere.

If you have negotiated your deals honestly and fairly with the above formula, you eliminate the jealousies that can occur when people in the same job level make different amounts of money. There are no secrets on the set. If there are inequities they'll be exposed before the first roll of film.

Sometimes you'll be doing a non-union shoot, and calling union members to work on it. You need to say it's non-union, because union crews are used to getting whatever the minimum rate is for that job, plus union fringes.

lATSE's fringes: Health/Retiree Health and Pension at $3.8975 per hour for every hour worked or guaranteed. Members hired by the day get an additional 7.719% of their day's pay (paid at straight time rate) for

Vacation/Holiday. Employees hired by the week already have the 7.719% factored into the weekly rate. Check your IATSE local for updates and changes.

Invoice Fees

This brings up the "invoice fee." Some crew people who usually work on big budget productions like concerts and awards shows will work non-union only if they are given an "invoice fee," which is extra money comparable to the union fringes. It is paid as a percentage (usually 20%-25%) of their gross wages. If this is the case, and you are not a union signatory, you may as well go through a union payroll service and pay the union fringes that way. Or look elsewhere for your crew. Documentary crew people do not usually ask for invoice fees.

Union vs. Non-Union: A Note of Caution

Let's say you're doing a non-union show for a large production company, and it's time to staff up. (The following situation is unlikely to happen with a smaller company or a low-budget project.) If you hire union people for your non-union show, and if the union discovers this, it can picket, and you can be pretty sure that union members will not cross the line. The union wants to become the bargaining agent for the crew, and if a certain percentage of the crew votes to have the union represent them, the producer has two choices: either sign a deal with the union, or do not sign. If the producer does not sign, all union members must leave the show (if they want to stay in the union). If you have hired union people in key positions (Gaffer, Key Grip, Sound, Camera, etc.), you'll probably be down for a day or so while you re-staff.

What to do? Try to hire non-union people, especially in key positions. How do you know if they are non-union? This part is tricky. It's actually illegal to ask a person if he or she is in the union. Why? Because in the eyes of the law it is deemed discriminatory. You can say, "This is a non-union show, do you have a problem with that?" If you're lucky, the person will volunteer that he is non-union or otherwise available. Otherwise, ask for a resume and then check to see if he works union shows.

Remember, this is unlikely to happen unless you are with a large production company doing a lot of business that the union would like to staff with its people. And please don't take the foregoing as a diatribe against unions. In fact, unions really do provide people with a decent wage and pension/health benefits, and that's to the good.

Your ability to negotiate rates that are affordable and fair have to do with your own relationships with crew members, the attraction of your project, and your production budget. If you have a multimillion-dollar budget, it's out of line to ask people to work long days for low pay. If you have a shoestring budget, you'll have to ask for favors.

Here's a checklist to have in front of you when negotiating crew rates.

1. Schedule. The number of prep and wrap days. The number of shoot days. Anticipated number of hours per day.

2. Hourly or weekly rates. Formula for overtime rates consistent with the same level jobs in other departments. No guaranteed minimum hours.

3. Kit Rentals.

4. Meals. Provided or a per diem.

5. Pre-Production/technical survey days. Rates.

6. Travel days. Rates.

7. Per diems, lodging, etc.

8. Pay day(s).

9. Payroll taxes for non-union crew. Pension/health/vacation/holiday fringes for union members.

10. Credits.

11. Profit sharing (if appropriate).

12. Deferments (if appropriate).

Let's take these points one by one:

Schedule

Discuss all "prep," "shoot," and "wrap" days as well as any holidays, breaks in the schedule, and time off. (Union crews are paid for holidays; non-union generally are not.)

Rates

Hourly or weekly rates as discussed above.

Kit Rentals

Kits contain special tools of the trade, and the production is better off renting them than buying them. Make-Up, Hair, Key Grip, Gaffer, Construction Coordinator, and many other positions have kit rentals (also called "box" rentals). Most people have standard kit fees, but if you need to sweeten the pot for someone while keeping his or her daily wage on a par with others in the same position, upping the kit rental is a way to do it.

Meals

There is a standard practice when it comes to figuring meal time. If the producer caters lunch, the minimum time is one half-hour, and it's off the work clock. If you have a "walk-away" meal, meaning that people are on their own, you must allow one hour, and only a half-hour is off the clock. We do not recommend "walk-aways" because that's exactly what happens. An hour and a half later your crew wanders back mumbling about the long lines at Taco Jack's. Generally, breakfasts are offered before the call time, or as "walking meals," meaning people munch as they work. If you have chronically late cast/crew, serving a hot breakfast before call time may be an incentive to start work on time. It also puts people in a good mood. "Second meals," meaning dinners, are counted as work time.

Catering is usually the best bet, since the crew is kept close at hand, and more focused on the shoot. For large crews, hire a catering service, and they can advise you about menus. For small crews of 5 to 15, pass around a menu from a local restaurant that delivers. Don't do what one well-known (but unnamed) producer did. The crew had been working hard for 6 hours (the usual maximum span between meals) and there was no lunch in sight. When someone finally brought this to the producer's attention, he sent an assistant out for a bag of candy bars! The crew did not revolt that day, but a lot called in "sick" the next day. We can't stress enough the value of feeding your crew well. It's worth it.

Pre-Production / Technical Survey Days

Pre-Production meetings and technical surveys (also called "tech scouts") can be anything from a minimum 8-hour call with overtime (union) to a negotiated half-day rate (non-union). These meetings and surveys prepare people for the job, and are usually well worth the expense.

Travel Days

Again, there are no set rules. Travel days can be 50% of the daily straight time rate (non-union) to an 8-hour minimum with overtime (union). The producer pays for all transportation, including taxis, limousines, airfares, and extra baggage related to the show.

Lodging/Per Diem

Lodging is arranged and paid by the producer. On overnight trips, a per diem ($39 to $55 per day) is usually paid to each crewmember to cover meals and incidentals. When lunches on the set are provided by the producer, you can either deduct the cost of lunch from the per diem, or let it slide and create some good will. By choosing to eat breakfasts and dinners at McDonald's, the crew will take home more cash. On low-budget productions, the per diem may be miniscule or non-existent, as long as the producer provides all meals.

Pay Day

Be specific on the pay schedule and stick to it. Paying people on time will quickly gain you a favorable reputation. Slow or non-payment will also earn you a reputation!

Payroll Taxes – Pension and Health

(Also see Chapter 5, 09-00 Above-the-Line Fringe, and 29-00 Below-the-Line Fringe)

To hire union employees on an official union shoot, either the production company or the payroll service must be a signatory. Consult the union rate card or the payroll service for the appropriate fringes in your state.

As an employer, you'll be paying the usual FICA, FUI, SUI, and Workers' Compensation on any employee's payroll, union or not. Check with your accountant and your union local or payroll service for up-to-date figures.

If you hire non-union people, we suggest you deduct taxes per the W-2 IRS Form completed by the employee. You can only pay on a 1099 Form (and not withhold taxes) if the person is a true Independent Contractor, which is to say he has a company and a Federal ID number, and meets the IRS criteria for Independent Contractors (search IRS websites for "Employees vs. Independent Contractors"). If you've hired someone as an independent contractor and he doesn't have a Federal ID number and he doesn't pay his taxes, or the IRS audits you and decides that this person is really doing the work of an employee, the IRS can and will go after the production company for an employee's delinquent taxes, plus the employer's contributions, plus penalties. Life is too short for that mess. If in doubt, consult an accountant or attorney about your particular project. But be aware that in your budgeting, employer contributions will add about 21% of your wages to the bottom line. For a specific rundown of these costs, see Chapter 5, 09-00 Above-the-Line Fringe, and 29-00 Below-the-Line Fringe.

Credits

Commercials, music videos, and sometimes industrials give no on-screen credit. Features and documentaries do. With above-the-line credits, and a few below-the-line, like Director of Photography, Production Designer, Composer, Production Manager, and Editor, discuss the size and placement of the credit. With crew, once the credit is determined and included in the deal memo, its size and placement is left to the producer's discretion. If credits are a puzzlement, rent a few DVDs that are like your project and write down the sequence and placement.

Profit Sharing

On most projects there probably will not be profit sharing, but if you feel someone has made a major contribution to the film, or worked for low or no wages, compensation can be enhanced by a percentage of the profits. (In order to give away percentages you must be sure your project is structured so that you can do so. Ask your lawyer.)

Deferments

Deferments are salaries that are paid later. Deferments are almost unheard of on large projects, but smaller projects that are labors of love are another story. If you are paying someone on deferment, you both should have a clear, written understanding of when the deferment is paid. Before the investors receive their money? Before the actors? After any over-budget expenses are paid first? Exactly when?

Anyone taking a deferment will appreciate this demonstration of integrity and responsibility.

Michael says, "*We recently did an infomercial that made a lot of money for the sponsor. I decided to put together the financing for our own infomercial. I went*

43

back to everyone who'd worked on the previous job and said that I'd be willing to pay their full fee (as before) or they could defer some or all of their fee for some equity in the profits from the infomercial. Everyone either deferred all or part of their fee even though they knew it was a risky proposition. This way I hoped to be able to provide more compensation for the people I work with. In addition, being able to go to investors and tell them that I already had a large part of the project paid for (from deferments) they more readily invested. The crew's deferment was treated exactly like a cash investment with crew and investors receiving their monies at the same time. I also deferred my fee figuring I couldn't ask others to do what I wouldn't do myself."

That ends the checklist for negotiating with crews. We suggest completing your budget before you do your crew deals. This way, you know what you are paying for each position, you know how much lee-way you have on kit rentals, and you've considered all the other items on the checklist. Now make your calls, and you'll find it's not really negotiating at all; it's more like staffing up with those who agree to the terms you offer. If your terms are fair, and your passion for your project high, you'll have no problem getting a crew.

Unions

Why hire union crews? Sometimes there are certain people whom you know and whose work is first rate, and you just want them. Perhaps they will not work non-union. Whether you are producing a commercial, a telefilm, or a feature, if your company is not signatory to IATSE, you can still work with union people by going through a payroll service that is a signatory (see Payroll Services below).

It's worth noting that IATSE and Teamsters both have special agreements for telefilms and some other projects. The easiest way to contact the appropriate local (there are tons of them) is through a payroll service. The DGA also has some special deals for low-budget projects that allow the production company to defer partial salaries.

For readers who wish to prepare a union budget and include all the additional rates and fringes, the names and addresses of the major unions and guilds are in the Appendix. You may also obtain current rates and the major rules and practices governing work by buying a copy of *The Labor Guide* (see Resources), which saves a lot of legwork by compiling it in one volume.

Taken as a group, the rules of the various guilds and unions are complex and overwhelming. Studied one at a time, they begin to make sense. You can understand the concerns, needs, philosophies, and restrictions inherent in each union.

For many producers, especially those with limited budgets, union rules and regulations make working with them prohibitively expensive. And the truth is, most union people will work non-union projects.

Payroll Services

A Payroll Service is a wonderful thing. The service takes your employee's completed and signed time card showing hours worked, and hourly rate, and calculates what is owed. Then they add on the requisite union fringes, if any, such as Current Health, Retirement Health, Pension, Vacation and Holiday. Finally, they issue the check, and you are free of the hassle!

Since the service also acts as the employer of record, Workers' Compensation and unemployment go through them, not you. Plus, they complete and send W-2 forms to all your employees at year's end. Fees are usually 4%-5% of your total employees' gross wages or on the entire invoice of gross wages plus fringes, depending on the company. If you can afford it, it's great headache relief.

Payroll services can act as your signatory to SAG or AFTRA for industrial/educational programs, but not for TV, features, commercials, home video, or interactive. That means if you're shooting an industrial/educational project, you can use the payroll service to pay SAG or AFTRA members without being a signatory company yourself. If you are shooting any of the other kinds of projects, your company must become signatory to legally hire those members (for a further discussion of signatory status, see Chapter 1).

To legally hire members of the DGA, WGA, and AFM (American Federation of Musicians), the production company must be a signatory. You can then hire a payroll service to handle the payroll chores, if you want.

For IATSE (which includes Teamsters) a payroll service can act as your signatory, and your non-signatory company can now use union crews. Call a payroll service for details, since there are many ifs, ands and buts and you need to customize the service to your project and your company.

Productions for Large Companies

Large companies have accounting departments with layers of approvals. And, they like to hold onto their money as long as possible to earn interest.

This can add up to slow payments that drive people crazy.

It's bad business when a crew has to wait more than 10 or 15 days to get paid — especially if they were promised prompt payments. Try to make accounting departments stick to a pre-agreed schedule, and even make it a contractual point with the company.

Below-the-Line Rates

The below-the-line rates in this book are non-union. By definition then, there are no set rates, it's all open to negotiation and industry standards. That's why we usually cite a range rather than a specific figure. The rates are loosely based on a 12-hour day, which is average for most shoots, meaning some will be 10 hours and some 14. None of the rates take into account payroll taxes or union fringes (pension, health, vacation and holiday).

Negotiating for Equipment and Services

Film labs, video post houses, equipment rental houses, catering companies and the like are all open to negotiation. If you have a lot of work for them, if you contact them during one of their slow periods, if you can offer lots of future work, or even if none of the above applies, you can ask for discounts. Be brazen — in a nice way — and you'll be surprised.

If you are not familiar with the service or equipment you seek, call around to several companies and ask for bids. Talk through the situation, and ask dumb questions — the good companies will be happy to answer them because they want your business, both now and in the future, when you know the ropes.

After you've been educated by several places and have their bids, you can compare apples to apples and start your negotiating. There's no harm in saying you have a bid for twelve dollars per person from Brown Bag Catering, and, asking if the Tastee Treat Company can do better for the same menu.

Sometimes companies will say yes to your request, but only if you pay when service is completed. Try to establish a credit line wherever you go so that you don't have to pay bills for 30 to 120 days. This way you may be able to make a little interest on the money in your bank account, boosting your assets. Weigh the costs versus the benefits.

Production Schedule

Studios or others who are financing your project will want to see a Production Schedule. Use the budget and breakdown to help forecast how long each phase will take. Again, the above-mentioned books can help.

Cash Flow Schedule

A Cash Flow Schedule projects expenses across the production schedule, and helps both the producer and the financing entity plan for the major cash transfers.

When you are producing a film or video or television show for a distributor or broadcaster you generally receive your payments on a payment schedule, never all at once. This means that you will have to know exactly how much cash is needed when. You prepare a cash flow schedule so that you can meet your needs.

Here's a tip. The usual pattern for cash transfer is one third on signature of contract, one third on start of principal photography, and one third on delivery of the master. Try to get most of the last payment at the start of post-production. With cash on hand, you can cut a much better deal with your editing facility. Otherwise, you pay them whenever the last transfer arrives, which can be 30 or even 60 days after delivery of the master.

Casting

The way features and larger productions find actors is to hire a Casting Director. These people have extensive contacts with agents, and take your script and/or character descriptions and arrange for the appropriate actors.

Casting Directors cost, but they do everything for you except make the decision. You show up at the appointed day, take a seat, sip your coffee, and watch as actor after actor performs. You can direct the actor if you want, or leave it up to the Casting Director. They'll also videotape each actor for an extra charge. At the end of the session, they'll arrange for any callbacks. They also negotiate the agreements with actors and agents, and handle SAG or AFTRA paperwork.

Casting Directors for movies and TV shows usually work by the project, and get a flat fee which is based on how much talent there is to cast, and how long it will take. Usually the producer has allotted a fixed amount in the budget — $20,000 to $40,000 is typical for a low- to mid-level feature.

For commercials, they usually hold the first session without you, and send you a video. You view the tape and sit in for the callbacks only. Commercial Casting Directors charge anywhere from $400 to $600 per day. If a Casting Director is outside your budget, however, there are some other routes.

Many scripts are written with specific professional actors, hosts, or narrators in mind. If you know who you want, simply call the Screen Actors Guild (in Los Angeles 323/954-1600) or AFTRA (in Los Angeles 323/634-8100) and ask for agency listings. From there you get the actor's agent, and you can make your offer. If you know you want a union actor, try going through the *Academy Players Directory*, a multi-volume set of books with photos of known and not-so-known actors with their agency listed. It's a trip into fantasyland just looking through the books. You can buy the books, or visit the library at the Academy of Motion Picture Arts and Sciences in Beverly Hills.

If you don't know who you want, you can call talent agencies cold and talk to the agents, asking them to send pictures and resumes. Or you can place ads for open auditions (the infamous "cattle calls" actors despise) in local trade papers read by actors (available at any good newsstand).

Or, you can join the modern age and use one of many on-line casting services. In Los Angeles, for example, there's nowcasting.com, castnet.com/casting, lacasting.com, and Breakdown Services, Ltd. (breakdownservices.com). With offices in New York, Los Angeles, and Vancouver, this casting service can get tons of actors eager to audition for your project no matter where you live.

The first step in dealing with any casting service is to identify what roles in your script you want to have professional actors audition for. A one-line role is just not going to be attractive. Next, write character descriptions for each role. Go on-line to see what others have written but beware, some are really badly done. A good description is a short paragraph designed to get actors interested in the role. Proofread. Bad grammar and misspelled words make you look sloppy and untrustworthy. If violence, nudity or sexual situations are included you must say so. Here's a sample description for a supporting role.

LAURA (29) SUPPORTING — ANY ETHNICITY

Laura is one on the nurses at the Hollywood Retirement Home. She has only been working there for a year, but already seems tired of her job. Although she is nurturing to Melvin and the other residents, her kindness can seem rehearsed and patronizing.

It's also good to write a short synopsis of your story. Show the story conflicts to make it appealing to actors. Next, just follow the service's directions for posting the character descriptions. Chances are, you'll get more responses than you can handle. Invite those actors who you want to see in person to your audition.

If you are handling the auditions yourself, you'll need to be prepared. Have a waiting area for actors where they can be greeted and sign in. Have "sides" on hand — a few pages of script the actor prepares while waiting. In the audition room, which should be spacious enough to allow movement, have a video camera and an operator. Chances are, you'll want to review some of the actors' auditions on tape. For most parts, allow about 10 to 15 minutes for each actor, and try to stay on schedule. You'll probably get exhausted saying the same thing to each actor, but keep your energy up and remember that they are there to help you achieve your vision.

When you've made your choices, always keep track of the others you liked. With low-budget productions, you never know if your actors will get a better offer and beg off. I once had a principal actor call me at 8 p.m. the night before a shoot to tell me he just got a national commercial and he wasn't showing up the next morning. I rarely get angry, but this time I lost it on the phone. My wife and daughters were staring at me from the dinner table. But after I cooled off and realized how much money he would make on residuals alone, I couldn't blame the guy. And luckily, we did have a back-up who was delighted with his sudden good fortune.

Finally, in dealing with any agent, know in advance whether it's a guild or non-guild shoot, what the tentative shoot dates are, and how much you are prepared to offer. Agents always get 10% of their client's gross salary, but you can try to fold the agent's fee into the gross, instead of adding it on top.

Actor Clearance

One final note on working with union actors. At least 12 hours before start of shooting, you or the Casting Director must call the Screen Actors Guild and verify that they are members in good standing. If they are not, you cannot employ them legally until the matter is straightened out.

Post-Production

You haven't even started shooting yet and it's time to consider post. The reason is, there are several post-production processes to use, and you have to budget for one of them.

First question: Are you shooting on film, videotape, or solid state media, like memory cards or hard drives?

Second question: Are you editing on film or nonlinear?

Third question: Is your Edited Master on film or videotape?

These are five possible combinations (simplified) for the picture path. (The audio path depends on the picture path you choose.)

A. Shoot on film. Edit on film. Master on film.
B. Shoot on film. Edit on nonlinear video (NLE). Master on film.
C. Shoot on film. Edit on nonlinear video (NLE). Master on videotape.
D. Shoot on film. Edit on film. Master on videotape.
E. Shoot on videotape (or solid state media). Edit on nonlinear video (NLE). Master on videotape. And optionally, create a film Master as well.

Let's take each one and follow its path from shooting to mastering.

A. Shoot on film. Edit on film. Master on film.
1. Production.
2. The negative is processed.
3. The negative is sorted to select circled takes (or print whole neg).
4. Circled takes are printed (and the negative is stored in a vault).
5. Dailies (Workprint) are synced with audio and screened/logged.
6. Workprint is edited/approved/Negative Pull List.
7. Negative is cut.
8. Color timing and printing into Answer Print, Printing Elements, Release Prints.

B. Shoot on film. Edit on nonlinear video (NLE). Master on film.
1. Production.
2. The negative is processed.
3. The negative is sorted to select circled takes (or go to step 4).
4. Telecine or Scanning (film is transferred to tape or digitized).
5. NLE.
6. Edit Decision List.
7. Negative Pull List.
8. Negative Cutting.
9. Color Timing/Printing Lab/Printing Elements/Release Prints.

Alternate route:
6. EDL.
7. Negative Pull List from EDL.
8. Scan Negative at 2K or 4K resolution.
9. Assemble clips per EDL in Digital Intermediate (DI).
10. DI color correction/effects.
11. Video Masters/Digital Cinema Master/Film Master.

C. Shoot on film. Edit on nonlinear video (NLE). Master on videotape.
1. Production.
2. The negative is processed.
3. The negative is sorted to select circled takes (or go to step 4).
4. Telecine or Scanning (film is transferred to tape or digitized.
5. NLE – Off-Line/On-Line Editing on same nonlinear system. Or Off-Line at lower resolution and then move media files to a higher end On-Line system for color/correction and finishing.

D. Shoot on film. Edit on film. Master on videotape.
1. Production.
2. The negative is processed.
3. The negative is sorted to select circled takes (or go to step 4).
4. Circled takes (or whole neg) are printed (and the negative is stored in a vault).
5. Dailies (Workprint) are synced with audio and screened/logged.
6. Workprint is edited/approved/Negative Pull List.
7. Negative is cut.

At this juncture, the path goes one of two ways:

A/8. Telecine (transfer to video) or Scanning (digitize).

A/9. On-Line Edit (assembly, titles, dissolves, etc.).

A/10. Video Master and Duplication.

Or:

B/8. Film Opticals (dissolves, etc.).

B/9. Timing (color correction).

B/10. Lab Processing/Answer Print.

B/11. Telecine (transfer film master to tape master).

E. Shoot on videotape (or solid state media). Edit on nonlinear video (NLE). Master on videotape.

1. Production.
2. Digitize masters into nonlinear edit system. If desired, DVD Dailies with time code or low resolution QuickTime (QT) files for paper editing.
3. Scenes selected from DVDs or QT files (paper editing).
4. NLE – Off-Line/On-Line Editing on same nonlinear system. Or Off-Line at lower resolution and then move media files to a higher end On-Line system for color/correction and finishing.

Why go through all this? Your distributor or broadcaster is clear about what format your master should be, film or tape. So you need to be clear about what format the master should be created on and what the primary distribution or broadcast mode will be before budgeting.

If you're shooting on tape and ending up on 16mm or 35mm film or a digital medium for festivals or theatrical distribution, see the section, Tape-To-Film Transfer and Digital Cinema Projection in Chapter 6, Sample Budgets.

Booking Post-Production Facilities

A big part of your budget will be post-production, so if you're not familiar with this phase, call two or three editors, post houses, and audio post houses to talk through your project and get bids on the job.

Once you've identified the post houses that you like (video and audio), put your estimated editing days on hold. Even though the editing schedule will slip and slide, at least you are on their schedule books and won't be forgotten. Keep them posted as your schedule changes.

Completion Bond

Let's say you have what's known as a negative pick-up deal for your proposed feature film (or less frequently TV or other project) where your distributor agrees to pay you an agreed sum when you *deliver* your completed film master. You take that contract to a bank or group of investors, and you borrow the money you need for production against the contract. The only hitch is, the investing group wants to be sure you'll make the film you say you'll make, on time and on budget. So they demand a completion bond (or completion guarantee).

If this is the case you must go to a completion bond company that will scrutinize you, your company, the project, your partners, and your family dog. If they agree to provide the completion bond, it gives them certain contractual rights, among them the right to monitor your production closely, and to step in if you even look like you're going over budget. "Stepping in" can mean giving you strong advice, or it can mean taking over the reins of production (which rarely happens). Should the worst occur, and the project goes belly up, the completion bond company gets stuck with repaying the investors. To protect themselves against that, they put themselves in a position of recoupment, second to the investors, just in case they can finish the film and get it to market.

The cost is usually 3-6% of the total budget, above and below-the-line. Plus, they insist that the budget contain a 10% contingency

Insurance

Just about any project that's hiring people or renting gear needs to be insured. For one thing, most equipment vendors, film permit offices, and others need proof of insurance, so it's pretty hard to produce anything without the proper insurance.

There are many insurance brokers that specialize in film and television production insurance. Make sure they are accessible to you day or night in case of emergency. And make sure they can fax or e-mail certificates of insurance to whoever needs one promptly, like within an hour or so if necessary.

The type of insurance depends on what you're doing. If you are setting up a production company you may just need liability and clerical workers compensation insurance. When you get into pre-production, send a script and a copy of the budget to the broker. Be sure and point out any stunts, special effects, animals, boats or aircraft, or hazardous shooting. You'll probably need some or all of the items in an "entertainment package" or "producer's blanket policy" such as:

Cast Insurance – covers delay due to death, injury, or sickness of principal cast members. The artist must pass a physical exam (paid for by the producer).

Negative Film and Videotape – covers loss or damage to raw and/or exposed or recorded stock.

Faulty Stock, Camera, Processing – covers loss or damage to stock caused by faulty materials or equipment.

Props, Sets, Wardrobe – covers loss or damage.

Extra Expense – covers delay due to damage of property or facilities.

Miscellaneous Equipment – covers loss or damage to equipment owned by or rented to production company.

Third Property Damage Liability – covers damage to property of others (with conditions).

Comprehensive General and Automobile Liability – required for filming on city or state roads, or any location requiring permits.

Non-Owned/Hired Car Liability – covers rented personal cars or production vehicles.

Umbrella Liability – usually a $1 million General Aggregate Limit.

Monies and Securities – covers loss of stolen cash.

Workers' Compensation – required by state law, this coverage applies to all permanent and temporary office and crew workers, and provides medical, disability or death benefits to anyone injured in the course of employment.

Guild/Union Travel Accident – necessary for any guild or union member on location.

Errors and Omissions (E&O) – covers legal liability and defense against lawsuits alleging unauthorized use of ideas, plagiarism, libel, slander and such. This coverage is usually required by distribution companies prior to release. Note that the insurance carrier (not the broker) must approve your application for this coverage. In order to do that, your attorney must have reviewed and approved the script. Allow at least a week for the insurance carrier to approve your E&O policy.

Michael says, "*When I was at Vestron Video we hired many producers to do clip compilation programs. Sometimes the cost of the E&O insurance was as much as $15,000 on a show with a budget of $75,000! It's very expensive because, regardless of the budget of the program, the insurer is taking a chance that there will not be any claims.*"

The cost of insurance depends on many factors, such as the budget of your show, whether there are stunts, travel, big stars and so on. Many producers allow 3% of the total budget as an allowance, but you can get an actual bid by calling an entertainment insurance broker and answering their questions about the show.

Locations

Scouting. Are you hiring a Location Manager to help you find locations and plan your shoot? If so, get an estimate on how much time he or she thinks it will take to do your job, and factor it into the budget. Be sure to ask about and include expenses like mileage, time to sort through and print digital photos, and video.

If you are scouting locations yourself, bring along someone familiar with production. There are lots of hidden traps here, and you need to consider things like electric power, weather, noise, neighborhood happenings (when school lets out), traffic, parking, rest rooms, eating places, light at various times of day, and so on. Here's a checklist I like to use:

Site Survey Report
Date:
1. Location description:
2. Fee:
3. Contact:
4. Address/Phone/Email:
5. Room dimensions:
6. Walls/Surface/Colors:
7. Ceiling type/Flooring:
8. Windows: (number/size/direction/coverings)
9. Interiors: Existing lighting:
10. Interior noise: AC: Intercom: Appliances: Fluorescents: Machines: Other:
11. Exterior noise: Traffic: Airplanes: Construction: School : Fire/Police: Other:

12. Power: Amperage: Breaker box location:
13. Equipment access: Stairs: Elevators: Ramps: Storage:
14. Facilities: Eating: Restrooms: Make-up: Wardrobe: Offices:
    Dressing rooms: Security: Parking:
    Actors holding area: Equipment staging area: Set dressing area:
    Water:
15. Neighbors issues:
16. Permits/Fire/Police:
17. Trash disposal:
18. Traffic closure:

Once you have a location you think you like, show it to the Director, the Sound Mixer, the Production Designer and the Director of Photography so you can plan your shots. Later, you'll do a Tech Scout with all of the above, plus, depending on the complexity of the shoot at this location, the Production Manager, Transportation Coordinator, Gaffer, Key Grip and perhaps Stunt Coordinator.

State and City Film Commissions. Many producers and location managers use a film commission's library to view photos of possible locations. They narrow down the list, and visit those that look most promising. (Some commissions' libraries are accessible on-line.) Out-of-town producers can call and discuss their needs. The commission will then send, e-mail, or fax them information about what's available. Since your show represents dollars for city or state coffers, and a boost to the local economy, most commissions will fall all over themselves trying to help.

State film commissions are usually listed among official state offices, or through the state chamber of commerce. They may also have information about support services, such as housing, catering, transportation, and so forth.

Location Services can also help you. Most have listings of homes or other sites. You go online or to their office and review photos, find places you want to visit, and have a look for yourself. Most do not charge a service fee to the producer, since they get a percentage from the homeowner. The producer just pays, and handsomely, for use of the actual location.

Location Fees. This is the money you pay to the owner of the place, and the price can be from $1 to many thousands of dollars per day. If you're hurting for money, charm your friends and their friends into loaning a location. But be advised, most professionals wouldn't even think of turning over their own house to a crew — they've seen what can happen! That means you have to be especially careful if you want to keep your friendships. We've often used "lay-out boards," 4 x 8 sheets of thin cardboard, to cover carpets and floors. We bring our own food, drinks, and toilet paper, and leave the place spotless. For larger shoots, especially through services, it's much more official. There's a contract, proof of insurance, and often strict rules about what can and cannot be done, and at what hours.

Location Permits. In many cities and counties, unless you are shooting in a bona fide studio, you need a permit — even if you are two miles up a private road in a basement. A lot of production happens without permits, because either producers don't know the rules or choose to ignore them. Call the city or county film permit office early on to get local fees, and all the rules and regulations. If you have to close streets, or have stunts or special effects to do, you may need police and fire personnel, which the permit office will tell you about.

Budgets from All Department Heads

For any large production, or where money is especially tight, ask all your department heads (Director of Photography, Key Grip, Gaffer, Art Director, Key Make-Up, etc.) to prepare department budgets. This helps everyone think through their jobs, and puts many heads together to troubleshoot. If their totals are too high, you've still got time to think up brilliant ways to do the same thing but cheaper. Some production companies insist on each department head signing off on the final department budgets.

Art Direction/Production and Set Design

This area covers anything from a stylist to help make your product shot look great to building huge sets. After you've done your script breakdown and know what you need, have conferences with your production designer to plan and budget everything from staff needs to materials and construction costs, to strike crew and cartage. As mentioned above, ask the production designer to prepare a department budget. If it's too high, you'll need to collectively sharpen your pencils.

Credit Accounts with Vendors

Many vendors will rent you equipment only if you've completed a credit application and provided proof of insurance. Having accounts around town also allows you the convenience of paying bills at the end of the month instead of C.O.D. Typical vendors are for cameras and lighting equipment, dollies, trucks, film and tape stock, props, sets and greens, wardrobe, labs, and post-production.

Production Forms

Need to purchase order books, sample contracts, release forms, call sheets and the like? Call Enterprise Printers in Hollywood 323/876-3530, or outside of California, 800/896-4444, or *www.enterpriseprinters.com.*

Purchase Orders

Some vendors won't release equipment to be charged to account without a Purchase Order, so consider using a PO when booking jobs or ordering supplies. A PO corresponds to every invoice, and thus every expense is monitored. The system prevents unauthorized purchases. All invoices can be checked off in the PO book when they come in. You can buy a PO book in any stationery store.

Check Requests

When you have to pay cash and need a check, fill out a Check Request Form. This keeps a record of who wants what for how much. It's usually signed by the Production Manager if less than $500, and by the Producer if more.

Tracking Costs

On larger productions that boast an Accountant or Auditor, the Unit Production Manager completes a Daily Production Report which records how many hours crew and cast worked, how much raw stock was used, how many people were fed, location fees, equipment used, and so on. The Accountant reviews the Production Report and calculates the expenses in each category.

How do you know if you're over or under? Since you're a really smart Producer, you already know, for example, how much overtime you've allowed for cast and crew. You can easily prorate that amount over the number of shoot days. If, after a number of days, you are consistently over on your daily allowance of overtime, or raw stock, or whatever, you know you're getting into hot water. Unless you're saving comparable sums elsewhere, it's time to cut back, which may mean a heart to heart chat with the Director.

"Hot costs," as they are sometimes called, can (and should) also be tracked weekly in a Weekly Cost Report that shows costs for each category in the budget. (For forms, see Enterprise Printers in the Resources section.)

Just because you have a Production Accountant, don't think you can slack off. As the Producer, you are responsible for tracking costs, and it'll be your backside in a sling if you come in over budget. So check the checker, and carefully review the Accountant's calculations. You may have to look hard. For instance, one Accountant we *used to* know ignored the SAG cutoff on actor's fringes (if an actor makes more than X dollars on a project, the company only has to pay Health and Welfare on the X amount, but not on anything over that amount). The result was an overpaid movie star. Imagine that.

Contact Sheet

As you begin to build your personnel for your project, start and maintain a Contact Sheet. Most producers like to organize it by Department. The list should have each and every person's name, address, e-mail address, phone numbers, cell phones, faxes, and so forth. The idea is to be able to reach anyone on the show at a moment's notice. This list (or a shortened version of it) can be circulated among all production people.

Conclusion

If you're like most producers, first assistant directors, and production managers we know, when you're not on the phone, you'll spend a good part of pre-production off in a daze somewhere, mentally chewing through every aspect of the production. This is a good thing, because you will jot down all sorts of things you would have otherwise forgotten. Your friends and family will get used to this, and eventually stop talking to you altogether. Don't worry, you're only doing your job.

chapter **3**

DEVELOPMENT/MARKETING

I have enough money to last me the rest of my life,
unless I buy something.
— Jackie Mason

Being a producer isn't just knowing how to make the movie, it's knowing how to put all the pieces together so the movie gets made. That's the front end. Then it's knowing how to market and promote the project before, during, and after it's made, so that it finds its audience. That is, after all, the whole point. Finally, you need to sell the project. This chapter is therefore a brief introduction to development and marketing, something that too many producers ignore altogether. Sales and distribution is a huge topic onto itself, but we'll also talk a bit about self-distribution.

Development

Much of a producer's time is spent pulling a would-be project together: script rewrites, attracting actors, getting financing, etc. In the studio world, it's called development. Producers tend to call it "development hell." During this long and arduous process, many hours, weeks, months and years can accrue. A great deal of money may also be spent (whether or not the movie actually gets made). In the independent world this money comes from the filmmakers, friends and family, or investors' pockets. In the studio or network/cable world, it comes from their development department.

Filmmakers often make the mistake of leaving these development costs off their budgets, probably because it's painful to think that they may have to raise this money or pay these expenses themselves. Our advice:

Consider them now, figure out what you need to spend, double or triple it, and add it to your budget. These dollars can be recouped once the film is financed.

Of course, for small projects, shorts, and videos, these expenses may be limited to phone calls and a few presentations.

For features or big documentary projects they can be rather extensive and run into the thousands, hundreds of thousands, or even millions of dollars.

Script Development
Script analysis and evaluation (by others)
Rewrites (by one or more writers)
Research Trips (location trips, research, investor presentations)
Fees to writers, co-writers, script doctors, and consultants
Photocopying
Postage, etc.
Casting Agent hire
"Pay or play" fees for actors

Presentations
Storyboards or presentation art
Key art/poster design
Still photo sessions
Trailer shoot and expenses (a mini-budget in itself)
Travel
Actors and crew fees, etc.
Preparation of breakdown and shooting schedule
Preparation of budget
Projections
Cash flow analysis
Business plan
Legal documents
Initial agreements for principals
Contracts, agreements with actors, producers, co-producers, director, etc.
Travel to markets (Cannes, AFM) and festivals
Meetings in L.A., NYC, etc.

It is not unusual for a producer to spend $50,000 to $100,000 or more developing a small, multi-million dollar budget. (The studios spend millions and sometimes never make the project.) The higher the budget, the more "names" have to be attached. This is a time-consuming process and may involve months or years of work, rewrites, etc. It could even include "pay or play" offers to the actors where they are guaranteed a fee whether or not the financing is ever fully raised, just to be "attached" to the project.

These are not only hard costs (as per the line items above), but also a vast amount of the producer's time for which he or she should be compensated in fees in the final budget. If a filmmaker is serious about making his or her livelihood from making films, they cannot self-finance the development and not get reimbursed. Otherwise they end up making the film for a fee that may be less than what they spent developing it.

Marketing

It may seem crass for us as *artists* to think this, but independent features, shorts, and documentaries are products, and like any other product, they need to be marketed and sold. Products succeed in finding their "audience" because of successful marketing and promotional campaigns. Entertainment products are no different. We must find and satisfy an audience.

There is a huge arsenal of tools available to market and promote our films and videos — from direct mail and personal sales to custom websites and trade magazine advertising. And there are many ways to get the attention of potential viewers' or buyers' eyes and ears with your film's "hooks." How, and when, do you start this whole process and decide which techniques are necessary?

The answer to the question of "when?" is now. It's possible to begin marketing and promoting your project the day you decide to make it. How do you promote something you don't have? You market your *idea* until a tangible object can take its place.

That's what the studios do with billboards, websites, previews, and magazine and newspaper articles. Why shouldn't you?

Let's look at what's included in the marketing/promotion section of an independent film budget. It really depends on what you can afford. It's great to hope that at the end of production you'll still have that little pot of money that you set aside to hire a distributor's rep, but if you really need it to pay your editor for another month or you won't finish, nobody will blame you for being a filmmaker first and a promoter second. Just keep in mind that when you do finish, those roles will reverse, and you may as well be cheerful about spending some money on the marketing, because done right, it can get your project seen. And that might help get you your next role as a filmmaker.

With that in mind, the following items are broken down into Basic and Advanced marketing and promotion expenses. Consider the Basic category a list of "must-haves." It is the least you can do to create awareness for your project with the right buyers or viewers. Consider the Advanced category as a guide describing how much time and funding the process of independent film marketing can consume. To cover all these items in detail is beyond the scope of this chapter, but to give you an idea of what some of these things cost, please see the list of Costs below.

Basic:
1. Create a promotional website
2. Solicit distributors/buyers directly with a screener and cover letter
3. Send press releases to pertinent media outlets
4. Pursue film festival screenings
5. Stage a premiere

Advanced (all of the above, plus):
1. Create a full presentation package to accompany distributor solicitations
2. Arrange distributor screenings
3. Provide an electronic media kit with downloadable photos, clips and releases on the website
4. Set up an e-commerce section on the website to sell copies of the film as well as branded film merchandise (T-shirts, hats, etc.)
5. Hire a professional on-set photographer
6. Hire a publicist
7. Hire a distribution representative
8. Create and place print ads
9. Create and place online ads
10. Promote the film to film festival staffers

11. Create and distribute marketing materials (posters, postcards, etc.) to appropriate audiences before you complete the film
12. Create and maintain a weekly film e-newsletter for appropriate audiences
13. Stage publicity stunts
14. Solicit a wide range of media for interviews and coverage
15. Self-distribution: four-walling, fulfillment, advertising, sales percentages, UPC codes, etc.

Film Marketing Line Items Costs
1. Promotional Website

a. Domain Name Registration	$15 annually
b. Site design	$500+ one-time + maintenance
c. Hosting	$200 annually
d. E-mail newsletter	$25 monthly plus fees for creation/ updating
e. Downloadable media kit	$250+
f. E-commerce store	$50 monthly plus fees for updating

2. Solicit Buyers
a. Screening copy of film on DVD $5 each
b. Cover letter – you'll need to get some letterhead and business cards printed, which can be done very cheaply yet professionally at a quick-print shop (see below for costs).
c. Postage – send all solicitations Priority Mail to potential buyers – $5 each

3. Send press releases to media
$.60 each (postage and letterhead) for those mailed.

You can also save money by distributing releases via e-mail, but check with recipient first to be sure they'll accept electronic submissions.

4. Film Festival Screenings

a. Entry fees for festival	$50-$75 each
b. Travel (if selected to screen)	$0-$500 or more depending on festival location
c. Handouts (postcards, invites)	$200

5. Premiere – staging a premiere can be done on the cheap if you are a good negotiator and can barter services (such as the rental of a theatre). Some costs to consider whether you wheel-and-deal or pay cash include:

a. Theatre rental	$500 and up
b. Digital projector rental	$100 and up
c. Advertising in local media	$200 and up
d. Searchlights and red carpet	$500 and up
e. Posters, handouts	$200 and up
f. Security	$100 and up

6. Presentation Package

a. Key Art	$250+

If you're on a budget, seek out illustrators/graphic artists at local art schools. Call the department chair and ask for referrals.

b. Photography/Prints	$100+
c. Binder	$50 (25)
d. Copies	$25

7. Stationery Package

a. Logo design	$100
b. Letterhead/envelopes	$350
c. Business cards	$50
d. Mailing labels	$50

8. Advertising/Promotion

a. Google ads	$50 (monthly PPC)
b. Print ads in targeted media	$500+

9. Professional Services

a. Photographer	$200 day plus supplies
b. Publicist	$500-$1,000 upfront retainer plus hourly/project rate

c. Distributor Representative $0-$2,000+ upfront, plus 8%-20% of sales earnings

10. Self-distribution

$50 (for initial set-up via firms like CustomFlix)

Price depends on approach. Renting theatres and placing ads to promote screenings can cost $5,000 and more per location.

11. Publicity stunts

$200+ depending on the complexity of the stunt

12. Marketing materials (depending on quantities)

a. Posters	$200+
a. Postcards	$200+
a. Newsletters	$100+

Don't forget that sometimes "invisible" costs can break the bank. Keep a close eye on the phone bill (cellular especially, and faxes), copying and paper usage, postage and mailing supplies (envelopes, padding).

Self-Distribution

If you sell or license your film to a broadcast or cable entity there may be restrictions on whether or not you can self-distribute it. If you think you can carve out self-distribution in certain markets for example, get your lawyer to negotiate the terms in your contract. If you license your film exclusively to one distribution company for all markets, then you can pack a picnic and go dream up your next film project. Hopefully, you'll be getting royalty checks in the mail. But if you plan to self-distribute your film, whether it's a feature or a documentary, let's get one thing straight from the start. Cast away all illusions that you can do it in your spare time or while you are making your next movie. This is a business and it will require your full attention.

One of the pioneers of self-distribution, Peter Broderick (*www.peterbroderick.com*), elucidates several key ideas that filmmakers can use that distinguish self-distribution from the old model. To paraphrase just a few of the items on his list:

➢ Control – The filmmaker controls the distribution process, choosing which rights to give to distribution partners and which rights to hold onto.

▸ Hybrid model – Filmmakers can split up rights, for example, licensing to a distribution company but retaining the right to make direct sales. Or retain the right to make TV/cable, VOD, airline, or educational deals.

▸ Core audiences – The filmmaker targets the core audience for the project and markets to that group. If successful, crossover to a wider audience may be possible. There are specific strategies for marketing to core audiences, including establishing relationships with organizations, cross-promotions, e-mailing lists, websites, attendance/screenings at conferences, articles in publications etc.

▸ Reducing costs – Spend less on print, TV, radio ads and use the Internet, cross-promotion, e-mail with permission, publicity.

▸ Direct sales – The model for self-distribution is to make profit margins as high as possible. Direct sales to customers via their own or partner websites achieve this.

Self-distribution is not easy. Like the settlers who braved the Oregon Trail, there are skeletons along the roadside, but there are also many who have found success. If you are contemplating it, we suggest thorough research, maybe a fulfillment house, such as Neoflix (*www.neoflix.com*), and maybe a consultant to get you on track.

Thanks to Mark Bosko for sharing his expansive knowledge of marketing in the writing of this section. A more detailed explanation (and costs) for marketing are in his book, *The Complete Independent Movie Marketing Handbook* by Mark Steven Bosko (*www.mwp.com*). Mark is also available for consulting at *mark@theboskogroup.com*.

chapter 4

HIGH DEFINITION

Film and high definition video are today's primary acquisition formats. Film's workflow for production and post is a well-worn path, but the workflow for high def looks like a jungle to all but the relative few who put in the time to understand it. There are books and web sites full of information about hi def (see *The Filmmakers Handbook* in Resources), so we won't attempt full coverage, just a few of the high points.

As you consider your project during pre-production, make your plan "soup to nuts," that is, beginning to end, script to delivery. There are many possible scenarios: you may be shooting on your own HDV camera or renting a RED, editing on your own Final Cut Pro (FCP) system or using a FCP or Avid-based post facility, going straight to DVD or the web or to a film master or digital projection. No matter what, you still need an A to Z plan, and a test of your camera and editing workflow. So ask the experts *before* you shoot a frame. This cannot be overemphasized. There are many shipwrecks on the rocks of HD workflow for foolish sailors who set forth without a map, and a little shakedown cruise around the harbor.

Before we get to the plan, let's consider some attributes of HD that are key to understanding it:

▹ Chips and pixels
▹ Frame size
▹ Aspect Ratios
▹ Frame rate
▹ Recording method
▹ Compression
▹ Bit depth
▹ Color Sampling

CHIPS AND PIXELS

Sounds like the snack bar at a high-end post house. If we peek inside a video camera, somewhere behind the lens we'll find one or more chips, called either CCDs (charged coupled devices) or CMOS (complementary metal oxide semiconductors). On the flat surface of these chips is a grid of tiny pixels, (picture elements — pix-els, get it?). One chip less than an inch in size may have millions of pixels. When light strikes these pixels, each one reads the brightness and color information in its own tiny spot in that moment in time, and creates and stores an electrical charge. The more light the more charge. In an instant, all the charges from the pixels are read, and processed into a video signal that is then recorded (oversimplifying here).

Different video formats have different numbers of pixels. Too few for your situation, and the image looks fuzzy or blocky. A sufficient number of pixels for the end use of the project — say projection in a theater — and our eyes won't even see that there are pixels. That's why we filmmakers need to know this stuff. It's not enough to just pick up a video camera and start shooting. Where will this project be shown? Under what conditions? Who is it for? What is its purpose? These questions have as much to do with our technical approach as they do with creativity and content.

To help us decide what video format is best for our project, let's look next at frame size.

FRAME SIZE

The Advanced Television Systems Committee (ATSC) is the entity responsible for defining standards like video formats. There are currently eighteen formats for digital TV broadcast, but don't worry, we're not going through all eighteen (search the web for "ATSC video formats" for the whole table). Frame size is one aspect of format. Let's start with pixels, the building blocks of the digital video image. Every image consists of rows and rows of individual pixels, square or rectangular in shape, all stacked on top of each other in a grid. These horizontal rows, or lines, are called scan lines. Look closely at your TV screen and you'll probably see them. All the pixels taken together, or you could say all the scan lines taken together, form what we call the raster image (from the Latin ras-trum, a rake, from radere, to scrape; see the grid pattern?). The number of pixels and scan lines determines the frame size.

When we say "definition," we're talking about the amount of detail in the image. Definition is measured by the number of scan lines in a frame. In NTSC territories (most of the Americas, Japan, South Korea, Taiwan, the Philippines, Burma, and some Pacific island nations and territories), the standard definition frame size is referred to as 720 by 480 (720 x 480), meaning it has 480 horizontal scan lines, and each line is 720 pixels wide. Interestingly, the pixel count is the same whether it's shot or displayed in 16:9 wide screen aspect ratio or 4:3, the old TV standard aspect ratio — the pixels themselves adjust to be shorter and fatter for 16:9, and taller and thinner for 4:3. In PAL countries (much of Europe) there are 576 scan lines, also 720 pixels wide (720 x 576).

High definition has two basic sizes, both in 16:9 aspect ratio, 720 and 1080. 720 is also known as 1280 x 720, meaning there are 720 lines of 1280 pixels per line. 1080 is also known as 1920 x 1080 — 1080 lines with 1920 pixels per line.

Beyond high definition there's 2K and 4K, sometimes called ultra high definition because their scan lines exceed 2000 and 4000 horizontal lines respectively. For example, the Silicon Imaging SI-2K camera (used to shoot much of the Oscar-winning *Slumdog Millionaire*) captures foot-age directly to disk, at either 1920 x 1080P HD or 2048 x 1152 cinema resolutions (2048 lines with 1152 pixels per line).

The 4K image is 4096 x 2160 pixels, or four times the resolution of 2K (4096 lines with 2160 pixels per line).

Most people reading this book and shooting in high def will shoot in either 720 or 1080.

ASPECT RATIOS

We've just talked about one property of the frame, its size. The oth-er property is its shape. Video and film frames are generally rectangular, but the proportions of width and height vary. The ratio of the width to the height of a picture is called the *aspect ratio*. The standard video aspect ratio is 4:3, meaning that the standard video frame has a width of 4 units and a height of 3 units. This is also expressed as 1.33:1 (divide 4 by 3).

Another common aspect ratio is 16:9, or 1.77:1, (divide 16 by 9) for high definition television. Theatrical films use 1.85:1, and widescreen films go up to 2.35:1.

Now let's consider this thing called "frame rate."

FRAME RATE

Frame rate refers to the number of images that are recorded or displayed per second. (This is not to be confused with shutter speed, which is the amount of time light gets to the sensor as each frame is captured. Standard video shutter speed is usually half the frame rate. For instance, at 24 fps, shutter speed is 1/48 second. There are exceptions. Panasonic, for instance, has cameras set to 1/60 at 24 fps. You can manually adjust shutter speeds for different effects. Talk with your DP.)

Back to frame rates. Perhaps some history will put frame rates in context. The U.S. has always controlled its electrical power to generate at 60 cycles per second, measured as hertz, or Hz, while Europe (and a great many other countries) generates at 50 Hz. In 1952, when the National Television System Committee (NTSC) was authorized by the FCC to set technical standards for the emerging black-and-white boob tube, the signal was 60 fields per second to match the 60 Hz electrical cycle.

What's a "field"? (Progressive and Interlace)

To explain, let's introduce two video *recording methods*, progressive and interlace. In the *progressive* method, identified by inserting a "p" after the frame rate, like "24p," the image from all the pixels of each frame is captured at the same moment in time, kind of like each frame in a film camera is exposed one at a time. Then there's "*interlace* scanning," or "interlace" or just "i" for short. With this method, instead of an image recording onto a full frame at a time, like in progressive video or on film, half the frame is recorded (or broadcast) at a time. This method dates back to the early days of TV, when the system was too slow to capture full frames, so they only used half the information from each frame at a time, calling each "half frame" a *field*. Each field consists of half of the horizontal video lines needed to make up the whole image for that frame. When the image is recording, it starts at the top of a field, and records only the odd numbered horizontal lines of that field, then it goes back and records the even numbered lines. When the two fields are played back one after the other, the eye perceives it as one continuous image.

Since there are *two fields for every frame*, 60 FIELDS per second can also be expressed as 30 FRAMES per second. That figure, 30fps, may sound familiar to some as the standard NTSC broadcast frame rate. And many do refer to it as such, and they are technically incorrect. History tells us why.

In 1953, color television hit the scene, but with it came a technical problem, something about color subcarrier frequencies, don't ask me. To resolve it, engineers had to lower everything by 0.1%, so the field frequency went from 60 Hz to 59.94 Hz, and the frame rate went from 30fps to 29.97fps. And that's where NTSC frame rate broadcast standards are today. In Europe, where the video standard is known as PAL, they use a field frequency of 50Hz and a frame rate of 25fps because their power system is based on 50Hz frequency alternating current rather than the 60Hz system used for North American electrical grids.

Choosing a frame rate at which to shoot used to be simple. Shooting film? 24fps. Shooting videotape? If you were in North America, it was NTSC 29.97fps, often casually referred to as 30fps. But now camera manufacturers have introduced more choices in frame rates. The good news is that this gives us a variety of "looks." The bad news is that it also gives us headaches trying to sort it out. But we'll try.

24 and 24p

There are video cameras that actually do record at 24fps, but in NTSC territories what sometimes passes for "24p" is really 23.976fps, a 0.1% slowdown that matches the NTSC frame rate of 29.97. To add to the confusion, some people round up the 23.976 and call it 23.98fps. It's good to be specific. Bottom line: know if your video camera can shoot at true 24fps or is it really 23.976p.

25p

25fps is what we used to refer to as PAL's frame rate, but increasingly the "PAL" and "NTSC" labels are falling away in favor of just referring to a field or frame rate and a progressive or interlaced recording method. PAL and NTSC are more broadcast formats. So 25p is 25 progressive frames pre second.

30p (29.97p)

As stated above, because of the 0.1% slowdown, "30p" is really shorthand for what is really 29.97 progressive fps.

50i

This stands for 50 interlaced *fields per second*.

50p

50p is 50 progressive frames per second.

60i (59.94i = 29.97fps)

Again, due to the 0.1% slowdown, 60i is shorthand for 59.94 interlaced *fields per second*. Expressed as *frames per second* it is the same as 29.97 interlaced fps.

60p (59.94p)

60p, due to the 0.1% slowdown, is really 59.94 progressive fps.

There are two flavors of 24p that we should mention, 24pN (N is for Native), and 24pA (A is for Advanced). But before we do, we should introduce one other little item, called Pulldown. Take two aspirin and read on.

Pulldown

Let's review for a second. For our purposes, there are two standard video broadcast formats in this world, PAL, at 25fps, and NTSC, at 29.97 fps. For years, film, shot at either 25fps or 24fps, was the only acquisition format around. When folks wanted to show their film on TV, they had to transfer it to video. Filmmakers aiming for broadcast in PAL countries have it easy. They can run film cameras at 25 fps, transfer to video at 25 fps, edit picture and sound at 25 fps, and broadcast at 25 fps. But filmmakers aiming for broadcast in NTSC territories encounter the dreaded monster, Pulldown.

Remember the 0.1% slowdown? Because NTSC standard television operates at 59.94 *fields* per second, also expressed as 29.97 *frames* per second, in order for film shot at 24fps to be broadcast at the 29.97 frame rate, its 24 frames must be cleverly divided and duplicated (this is the "pull-down") in the transfer to tape process (telecine) to the video standard of 29.97 fps. Read on.

If post-production needs to be done at 23.976fps, the original 24fps film footage would be telecined to video at 23.976 fps (that pull-down again). The sound is also slowed down by .01%. This slowing down, or speed variance, is the first part of Pulldown.

But if we need to edit and finish in the 29.97 video standard, we still have a problem. Even though the lower number divides neatly enough into the larger number, how do we make 23.976 film frames equal 29.97 video frames? (Sometimes you'll hear this problem stated as 24 film frames equaling 30 video frames, but we know it's good to be precise about our numbers, right?) Ever hear of "3:2 (or 2:3) Pulldown"? Take a deep breath and read on.

In the diagram below, the top row represents four frames of film shot at 24fps. When we do the 3:2 Pulldown process (aka 2:3 Pulldown, or Normal Pulldown), we'll end up at the bottom row, in 29.97fps (aka 60i fields per second). Here's what happens.

The group of four 24fps frames (and every group of four 24fps frames in the entire stream) gets converted to five frames (which is 10 fields — count all the little boxes in the bottom row) in the video stream. Frame A from the top row gets converted to Frames A1 and A2. Frame C also gets converted to two frames: C1 and C2. But Frames B and D get converted to three frames each: B1, B2, B3, and D1, D2, and D3 respectively. See the pattern? It goes 2:3:2:3, which is how the Pulldown got its name.

4 frames of original film @ 24 fps

A	B	C	D

A1	A2	B1	B2	B3	C1	C2	D1	D2	D3

5 frames (10 fields) of interlaced video Pulldown to 29.97 (aka 60i)

24pN

Now that we've endured 2:3 Pulldown, let's return to the world of HD video and specifically to the frame rate known as 24pN, or 24fps Progressive Native. 24pN means that (like 24p) the footage is shot at 23.976 fps (aka 23.98). Since that number is divisible into NTSC's broadcast frame rate of 29.97fps, there are no frames to remove in a Pulldown. But even though 24p and 24pN both record at 23.976fps, there is a crucial difference. 24pN can only be recorded to a solid state memory card (at present, a "P2" card used in Panasonic equipment). Furthermore, in 24pN, 24 frames are recorded, whereas in all of the other settings (e.g. 24p, 30p, 60p, 60i) 60 frames (actually 59.94) per second are actually recorded. For example, if the camera is set at 30p, two copies of each frame are recorded. Why is this done? As I mentioned earlier, some formats (most usually Panasonic) record ALL their video at 59.94, but insert a "flag" on each frame with frame speed information, so that upon playback, only the proper frames are automatically displayed at the designated frame rate. When 24pN is designated by the user, the system does not record all the extra frames/fields needed to make the 3:2 pulldown into a 59.94 signal. However, the system is designed to create those frames (add the 3:2 pulldown) upon playback, so that the video still appears as 24pN within the 59.94 recording system. These duplicate frames take up space, so 24pN is a setting that takes up less space on a P2 card. You can shoot longer, and use less space on a hard drive in editing.

24p Advanced

24p Advanced allows a 1:1 frame relationship for ultimate "film-out" transfers, meaning 16mm or more likely 35mm film print masters to project in theaters. You need to edit on a system capable of true 24p playback and display (as opposed to 59.94) for this to work. Unlike the 2:3:2:3 Pulldown used by film at 24fps or video at true 24p, 24p Advanced uses a 2:3:3:2 Pulldown cadence.

Do a Test, Please

We strongly suggest that you talk with your DP and your editor, in the same room at the same time, to work out the complexities of your workflow, and do a test with your camera of choice. Shoot some shots that closely resemble what you really expect to shoot. Edit in your format of choice and output to your format of choice. Know in advance what your deliverables are, like what format(s) are required, at what timings, at what frame rate, etc. The more tech specs you have up front the better. Seriously.

When to Shoot What

Here are some *very general* rules of thumb about when to shoot what format. In no way do these replace a careful and thorough review of your project's unique needs, your deliverables, a plan with your DP and Editor, and a test of your proposed workflow.

Shoot 24p (23.976)

▶ To get the "film look" on video (close to HBO movies)

▶ To stay on video and edit at 29.97

▶ If you bring in other footage that also uses 2:3 Pulldown into your timeline

▶ For DVD/Blu-ray, video

Shoot 24pN

▶ To get the "film look" on video

▶ At present, works only with Panasonic cameras using P2 Cards

▶ When you want to save space on the P2 card (shoot longer) and on hard drives

▶ When you want to master to DVD/Blu-ray or film. If you are going to broadcast use this format then edit in 720 24p/59.94. The pulldown is added in playback rather than during recording – to save space. Consult with your post people.

Shoot 24p Advanced

▶ To get a "film look" progressive DVD/Blu-ray, a progressive Quick-Time or Windows Media file, or for a master to film ("film-out"). Good for visual EFX work where you get a 1:1 relationship of each HD frame to a film frame.

Shoot 25p

To shoot in 25p, you'll need to rent or buy the 25p/50Hz version of a given camera. Remember that technically, you're shooting video for PAL broadcast territories, however, there may be reasons why shooting in 25p make sense, even if your destination is NTSC broadcast, film-out, or DVD/Blu-ray.

▶ To get the "film look" on video

▶ To get an easy path to film-out (consult with post house)

▶ To convert your 25p to 24p (23.976) during or after post to be able to deliver for NTSC DVD/Blu-ray

Shoot 30p

▶ To get the "film look" of 30p (episodic TV), but don't want 24p because maybe you have faster action to capture, and you'll go to DVD/Blu-Ray but never to film or PAL.

▶ For the web, can shoot 30p and then compress to 15p

Shoot 60p

▶ 60p (59.94) can easily be converted to 29.97 for broadcast. 720/59.94 is also an accepted delivery format for some networks.

▶ Capturing at 60p allows us to record video at a frame rate different than playback. For example, we can capture at 60p and play back at 30p, effectively slowing the video by 50%. Since the images are captured progressively — one frame at a time — image quality at the slower speed retains quality and clarity. (A downside of 60p is the extra space required for media storage.)

▶ Fast action can be captured at the highest possible quality with the least motion blur.

Shoot 60i

▶ To get the NTSC frame rate video look that we're all familiar with (news, soaps, sports).

▶ For hand-held, slow-mo, fast action (more frames = less motion blur)

▶ For quick turnaround in editing

▶ For video for broadcast

Recording Method

We already talked about the two basic video recording methods, Progressive and Interlace (see above), but there's a third method we should mention, just to make sure the water gets good and muddy. It's called *Progressive Segmented Frame* (PsF), and technically, it's not a frame rate or a video format, it's just a different way to record progressively, mostly in 24p (actually 23.976 if you're in NTSC territory) but also in 25p, 30p and others, in HD. We'll use 24PsF as our example. In 24PsF, the image is captured as one frame on the raster (where the light-sensitive pixels are) in the camera, but before it gets recorded, the progressive frame is split into two fields, each with half the horizontal lines. So just like 29.97 fps is the same as 59.94 fields per second, 24PsF is like 48 fields per second, two fields for every frame. But unlike in interlace where one field is first exposed with half the information and then the other field is exposed with half the information, in PsF both fields are captured at the same moment in time. Later, you can recombine each pair of fields to make one clean frame, which is good if you want to do a film-out.

There is no image loss in splitting a progressive capture into two fields and then recombining them into one frame later. It starts life as a progressive frame and it ends up as a progressive frame. But in the middle, where it's stored as two fields, PsF does allow you the option of editing the material as either interlaced or progressive footage. This flexibility allows PsF to be used in film-to-video transfer, for high definition mastering and for video exchange between networks.

Compression

Engineers faced a conundrum with high definition video. It inherently has tons of digital data that calls for expensive hardware, like big storage drives, fast computers and high-speed broadcast and Internet connections. On the other hand, filmmakers want high def cameras, formats and editing software that we can afford, don't give us headaches, and that we can use to show our films on everything from the web to TV to, just maybe, a movie theater. The technological answer is compression, which aims to shrink digital audio and video data and still maintain quality sound and picture.

Compression schemes are called *codecs* (*c*ompressor/*dec*ompressor), and while the topic is pretty complex (more than we'll get into here), the basic idea is simple. Video and audio signals are compressed during storage and transmission. They are decompressed when we pop the popcorn to watch and listen.

Codecs can be standardized across an entire format, like the DV codec; they can belong to one company, like the DVCPRO HD codec owned by Panasonic; they can be an audio codec like Mp3 or AAC; or even a piece of hardware, like a chip. A few common codecs you may have heard about are: MPEG-2, H.264, Avid DNxHD, Apple ProRes (currently a family of five codecs: Proxy, LT, 422, 422HQ, and 4444), JPEG2000.

Compression can happen at every point in the process from recording an image/sound to editing to broadcast. For example, one of the first places compression may occur in some formats is with Color Sampling (see below), wherein the video camera tosses out half of the color pixels, thus reducing the color data by half compared to the luminance, or brightness, data. Most of us can't see the difference. Technically, if color sampling has taken place, the video has now been compressed, but we often hear that from this point on we are dealing with *uncompressed*, or highest quality video, which is often used in finishing a project, and for that matter, in editing if you have enough storage.

There are two main compression methods to know about: Intraframe (aka I-frame) and Interframe (aka Group of Pictures or GOP).

Intraframe (within a frame)
When compressing within a frame, some video data is deleted from each single frame. Examples of formats using Intraframe compression are: DV, DVCPRO, DVCPROHD, AVC-Intra (Panasonic), DigiBeta, and HDCAM and HDCAM SR.

Interframe (between frames)
Interframe compression looks at a given sequence of frames (usually either 6 or 15) and deletes the information that is repetitive from one frame to the next. The process works by recording the first frame normally (called an *Intraframe* or *I-frame*), but after that, the codec records only what is *different* between the frame before and the frame after and so on, until the number of frames in that group of frames, or *Group of Pictures* (GOP for short) has been reached, and then it records a new Intraframe (I-frame) and then a series of frames with only the differences, and so on.

MPEG-2 and MPEG-4 are common interframe codecs, and are the basis for such formats as HDV, XDCAM, DVDs, digital satellite, and cable TV. There are different MPEG-2/MPEG-4 formats that use different length GOPs. 1080i uses the 15-frame GOP, while 720p of HDV uses a 6-frame GOP. Other video formats that are GOP compressed are: AVCHD, AVCCAM (Panasonic), XDCAM HD, XDCAM EX (Sony).

The good news about Interframe compression is that it gave us HDV and some pretty efficient compression and storage. The bad news is that, depending on what we're shooting, we may run into problems with the GOP's way of dealing with action. When nothing much happens in the shot, there's no problem with deleting what's different frame to frame, because not much is different. But when you're shooting two lightning quick samurai with their flashing swords and somersaults in the dappled light of a maple grove, a whole lot more data is different from frame to frame. The result may be those blocky digital artifacts we've come to hate.

Here's the other thing. We can't edit GOP natively. So when we put a GOP format like HDV into an edit system, it gets decompressed "behind the scenes" into an I-frame format that can be edited. All's well until we need to output and we need to change or "conform" that I-frame back into HDV. The conforming process can take many hours. If you have the time and the money, fine. But if you don't, maybe a GOP-based video format isn't the best choice for the needs of your project.

Or, maybe you should look into a work-around. One work-around (I've never tried this) is an adaptor box by Matrox called MXO, which connects to the DVI output of a Mac and gives you real-time HD-SDI from an HDV timeline with no rendering. Another work-around is to avoid editing in HDV by transcoding it into an I-frame format, like DVCPRO HD, or into an "intermediate codec" such as Apple Interme-diate Codec, which act as I-frame substitutes. Since this is not a book on editing, these are matters best discussed in depth, and tested, with your editor.

Bit depth

Bit depth in video is a measure of light, or you could say color (audio uses bit depth too — same basic idea, but measuring voltage in an audio sample). It's always expressed as a number, usually as either 8 bit or 10 bit, but it can go higher, and since it's a binary number (we're in computer land, remember) it's a power of 2, so 8 bit = 2 to the 8th power or 256 steps. 10 bit = 2 to the 10th power or 1024 steps. Steps of what? Steps between black, or no white, and maximum white. Or we could measure steps of no red to maximum red, or no green to maximum green and so on. Remember that what's being measured, say black to white, does not change. What's changing is the tool doing the measuring. To use an analogy, with 8 bit, we're using a ruler with 256 markers between every foot. With 10 bit, there are 1024 markers between every foot. 10 bit gives us more precision. Practically speaking, if we have more markers, we can measure more precisely, and then we can render and manipulate with more detail. If we can't measure it, we can't get to it.

Here's an example. If I'm shooting a movie in black and white with an 8 bit video camera, chances are I'll have few problems. Why? Because it turns out that the gray scale from black to white, at least as represented in video, can be accommodated quite well within the 256 steps of 8 bit depth. But as soon as I switch over to color, and cue my redheaded ac-tress with the sun catching the burnished highlights in her hair, the wind fluttering the folds of her many-colored dress as she stands in dappled shade with her bouquet of daffodils and pink geraniums, there are just too many colors here to be measured accurately by an 8 bit camera, at least if I expect more from my picture than a small image, like on TV or the web. If I'm projecting on a big screen, or doing any effects work with my images, or color correction, perhaps I should re-think my choice of camera and go with a format that includes 10 bit.

This doesn't mean that we should avoid 8 bit formats, just that we need to know what our goals are and whether we have the tools we need. And speaking of tools in the context of bit depth, we can take advantage of some of them to achieve our goals. We might, for example, shoot on an 8 bit HDV camera, but we can edit in say, ProRes 422, an I-frame based, 10 bit format that gives us greater precision, and then output to, say, HDCAM. This may or may not get you there, but it's a conversation, and a test, to have with your DP and your editor.

Color Sampling

Human vision is better at perceiving fine details of brightness than of color. Praise the rods and blame the cones, I guess. We have cones sensitive to red, green and blue, the primary colors that form the basis for all colors. The original video signal back in the 1930s was black and white, and it was, and still is, called *luminance*, since it was all about brightness. When color came along in the 1950s, two new signals were introduced, called *chrominance*.

Component vs composite video signals

Video formats that separate these signals are called component video, or sometimes RGB (red, green, blue) component video. Most digital video cameras of high quality use a component video signal, rather than the older, lower quality composite video, which combines color and brightness information into one signal.

Video engineers, big brains that they are, figured out that a video image still looks pretty darned good even when they throw away a bunch of the color information used to make it. Anytime we can maintain quality while reducing the quantity of data to transmit through the system, that's a good thing. When the video signal from the sensor in the camera is processed, some of the color data is thus thrown out. How much depends on the video format.

To explain all this, engineers decided on a form of color called YUV, where Y = the black and white of the image and U and V = the color parts of the image. (Later, when digital video appeared, to delineate digital color space from analog they called the digital: Y Cb Cr.)

Imagine four pixels in a row. In its purest or highest quality form, each pixel has a unique Y value (luminance), as well as a unique Cb and Cr value (color). Each pixel is fully loaded.

Y Cb Cr	Y Cb Cr	Y Cb Cr	Y Cb Cr

This is called 4:4:4 ("four-four-four") because there are four pixels each of Y, Cb and Cr. This is full color resolution. High-end 4:4:4 component color.

Now let's knock it down a notch. Let's throw away some color. Let's compress a little. What happens if we average a pair of neighbor Cb pixels and we do the same with a pair of neighbor Cr pixels? Then we get this:

Y Cb Cr	Y	Y Cb Cr	Y

This is called 4:2:2 ("four-two-two") because there are four pixels of Y, and two pixels each of Cb and Cr. This is also called *Chroma sub-sampling*. Now we half as much color resolution as brightness resolution. Is this a terrible thing? No. There are many high-quality component digital formats in 4:2:2.

Let's go down one more, to 4:1:1, in which we have four luminance samples for every one Cb and Cr, and we have one-quarter the color resolution.

Y Cb Cr	Y	Y	Y

This is the Chroma sub-sampling used in DV (NTSC). It's not recommended for green screen work or titles and effects where color resolution is more critical, but it may be perfectly fine for your project. Again, know your end use.

There are other Chroma sub-sampling scenarios as well, such as 4:2:0.

Conclusion

There isn't any such thing as the "best" video format. It all goes back to your project and its unique needs and deliverables. Will you use green screen? Do you need a fast turnaround? Will you be doing a lot of compositing or effects work? Are you headed for projection in a movie theater? The technical information presented above comes into play when you are weighing all these considerations. Chroma sub-sampling and bit depth determine how accurately you can measure color value and how well you can composite images and make effects. Knowing about codecs, GOP and I-frame, can help you understand transcoding and speed of output. Knowledge of frame size, frame rates, progressive and interlace will help you choose a "look" and narrow down the appropriate format for your project.

Here's a formula for a relatively hassle-free workflow: Work backwards. For each project that you do, start by carefully considering what formats you must deliver, where it's going to be played. Consider what special elements you'll be working with (green screen, color correction, visual effects etc.). Then, in consultation and testing with your DP and Editor, identify what format you'll be editing in. Finally, choose a format and *stick with it*. Try very hard not to change formats with different frame rates and frame sizes during that project. You'll only become depressed and be a burden to yourself and others. Onward.

chapter 5

LINE ITEMS

Little strokes fell great oaks.
       — Benjamin Franklin in *Poor Richard's Almanac*

First there are the budget *categories*, then the *line items* — the nitty-gritty details without which we have no budget at all. This chapter shakes the budget so that all the line items fall out into the daylight where we can study them.

The budget example that follows is a hybrid of film and video, loosely based on a TV movie or low-budget feature. For the scope of this book, a small feature is about as complex as we'll get. This will provide you with more than enough material for just about any project: low-budget digital feature, "no budget" digital feature, student film, music video, industrial, or documentary. This budget is therefore a master checklist to help you remember every production item in your project.

Feature film budgets distinguish between "above-the-line" and "below-the-line." "Above-the-line" refers to the producer, director, actors, script and writers, the so-called creative elements. These are also divided because "above-the-line" could vary tremendously since it is a function of expensive creative talent, where "below-the-line" figures are more stable and predictable. In many ways the word "creative" is a misnomer, since many jobs below-the-line call for equal creativity. Everything else — crew and equipment, and everything editorial — is "below-the-line." Often you'll see a third division, "Other," covering categories like Insurance, General/Administrative costs, Publicity, Festival expenses etc.

The separation is made because above-the-line people often get salaries based on their current standing in the industry, and may also get "points" (percentages) in the film's profit. This above-the-line figure is therefore based more on market conditions and the all-important hype factor than on the hard rock reality of the below-the-line, which reflects what the actual production may cost. Executives or investors can therefore readily see the differences in cost between above-the-line (talent) and below-the-line (production) costs and determine if they are getting their money's worth.

The budgets in this book for documentary, short, industrial, and so forth, retain the above/below the line format because it has now become standard. The exception is the commercial format, which is based on a design from the Association of Independent Commercial Producers (AICP).

One more note before we dive in. Occasionally, you'll see a sub-category called Desperate Measures. This was inspired by the line:

Desperate cures must be to desperate ills applied.
                    — John Dryden, English poet, c. 1687

When you're so stone broke that you must resort to Desperate Measures to complete your project, we hope these little tips will be helpful.

ABOVE-THE-LINE

01-00 Story Rights
Options
Rights
Purchases

02-00 Script
Writers' Salaries
     First Draft
     Second Draft
Polish Research
Clearance
Title Registration
Copyright
Script Copying
Script Delivery Service
Secretaries
Script Timing

Storyboards/Pre-Viz
Development
Travel and Living

03-00 Producer's Unit
Executive Producer
Producer
Associate Producer
Assistants
Secretaries
Consultants
Producer's Miscellaneous Expenses
Car Expense

04-00 Direction
Director
Assistants
Car Expense
Agency Fee

05-00 Cast
Lead Actors
Supporting Cast
Day Players
Casting Director/Staff
Casting Expenses
Choreographer
Assistant Choreographer
Secretaries
Narrator
Agency Fees
Stunt Coordinator
Stunt Players
Stunt Costs/Adjustments
Stunt Equipment
ADR/Voice Over (Actors' Fees)
Cast Overtime

06-00 Travel and Living – Producers/Director
Air Fares
Hotels Taxi/Limo
Auto
Rail
Excess Baggage
Phone
Gratuities
Per Diem

07-00 Travel and Living – Cast
Air Fares
Hotels
Taxi/Limo
Auto
Rail
Excess Baggage
Phone
Per Diem

08-00 Residuals (e.g., 2nd Run)
Writer
Director
Actors

09-00 Above-the-Line Fringe
Note: In the sample budgets, all fringes, both above- and below-the-line, are calculated *within each category* and indicated as Payroll, DGA, WGA, AFTRA, SAG, etc. We present the following laundry list so you can see all the Fringes in one place. For good measure, this list is repeated below-the-line as Line Item 29-00.

Payroll Taxes:
FICA-SS (Social Security)
FICA-HI (Medicare)
FUl (Federal Unemployment Insurance)
SUI (State Unemployment Insurance)

CREWWKCOMP (Workers' Compensation)
OFFICE WKCOMP
HANDLING FEE (Payroll Service)

Guilds/Unions:
DGA Director
SAG/AFTRA
WGA Writer
SAG/AFTRA/DGA Wk Comp
Vacation/Holiday (Union)
AFM (American Federation of Musicians)

BELOW-THE-LINE

10-00 Production Staff
Unit Production Manager
1st Assistant Directors
2nd Assistant Directors
Stage Manager
Production Coordinator
Script Supervisor
Production Auditor/Accountant
Technical Advisors
Production Assistants
Teachers/Welfare Workers
Secretaries

11-00 Extra Talent
Stand-ins
Extras
Extras Casting Fee
Extras Transportation

12-00 Sound Stage
Stage Rental
Power
Production Office

Telephone
Dressing Rooms/Shower
Make-Up
Wardrobe
Storage
Green Room
Parking

13-00 Production Design
Production Designer
Art Director
Assistants
Set Designer
Model Makers/Miniatures
Sketch Artists
Set Estimator
Purchases/Rentals
Research/Materials
Car Expense
Film

14-00 Set Construction
Construction Coordinator
Labor – Foreman and Crew
Scenic Painters
Scenic Backdrops
Greens
Purchases (Building Materials)
Rentals
Equipment
Trash Removal
Set Strike

15-00 Set Operations
First Grip (Key Grip)
Second Grip (Best Boy)
Company Grips

Boom/Dolly/Crane Grips
Grip Rentals
Crane/Dolly Rentals
Cartage
Box Rentals
Craft Service Person
Craft Service Purchases (food)
Craft Service Rentals (equipment)
Air Conditioning/Heating

16-00 Special Effects
Special Effects Person
Special Effects Assistant
Additional Labor
Special Effects – Pyrotechnical
Special Effects – Mechanical
Manufacturing Labor
Fabrication
Expendables
Rentals

17-00 Set Dressing
Set Decorator
Lead Person
Swing Gang
Additional Labor
Expendables
Purchases
Rentals
Loss and Damage
Box Rentals
Car Expense
Film

18-00 Property
Property Master
Assistant
Purchases

Rentals
Loss and Damage
Box Rentals
Car Expense
Film

19-00 Wardrobe
Costume Designer
Costumer
Additional Costumers
Expendables
Purchases
Rentals
Alteration and Repairs
Cleaning and Dyeing
Loss and Damage
Box Rentals
Car Expense
Film

20-00 Make-Up and Hair
Key Make-Up Artist
Additional Make-Up Artists
Hair Stylists
Special Make-Up Effects
Purchases
Rentals
Box Rentals Film

21-00 Electrical
Gaffer
Best Boy
Electricians
Additional Labor
Purchases
Equipment Rentals
Additional Lighting and Equipment

Generator
Driver
Fuel
Loss and Damage
Box Rentals

22-00 Camera
Director of Photography
Camera Operators
1st Assistant Camera
2nd Assistant Camera
Other Camera Assistants
Digital Imaging Technician
Still Photographer
Expendables
Camera Package Rentals (Film and Video)
Additional Equipment
Steadicam Operator and Equipment
Teleprompter/Operator
Video Assist/Operator
Helicopter/Airplane/Tyler Mounts
Underwater and Topside Photography
Video Truck (multi-camera truck)
Video Studio or Truck Crew
Motion Control
Maintenance/Loss and Damage
Box Rentals

23-00 Sound
Mixer
Boom Operator
Expendables (Batteries, etc.)
Sound Package
Sound Truck
Walkie Talkies
Radio Mics and Head Sets
Beepers

Cellular Phones
Sound Stock
Misc./Loss and Damage

24-00 Transportation
Transportation Coordinator
Transportation Captains
Drivers
Vehicle Rentals
Star Dressing Trailers
Crew Cab
Production Van
Camera Truck
Stake Bed
Set Dressing
Props
Wardrobe/Make-Up
Cast Trailer (Mobile Home/Dressing Rooms)
3-Room Cast Trailer
Production Office Trailer
Honey Wagon (Portable Toilets)
Water Truck
Gas Truck
Maxi Vans
Car Tow Trailer
Car Trailer
Camera Car
Gas and Oil
Repairs and Maintenance
Honey Wagon Pumping
Parking/Tolls

25-00 Location Expenses
Location Manager
Assistant
First Aid
Fire Officers

Security
Police
Permits
Parking
Catering Service
Crew Meals
Extras
Ice/Propane
2nd Meals
Sales Tax
Tent/Tables/Chairs
Location Office Drinks/Snacks
Location Office Supplies
Location Office Equipment
Location Office Space Rental
Location Office Telephone/Fax
Shipping and Overnight
Gratuities
Location Site Rental
Location Survey
Auto Rentals
Location Manager Assistants
Location Site Trash Removal
Miscellaneous Expenses

26-00 Picture Vehicles/Animals
Animal Trainers
Boss Wrangler
Assistant Wrangler
Wranglers
Riders/Handlers, etc.
Animals
Rentals
Veterinary Expenses
Feed/Shelter
Transportation
Picture Cars

Other Picture Vehicles
Special Equipment
Non-Performing Drivers

27-00 Film and Lab Production Film & Video
Motion Picture Raw Stock (Film – Production)
Lab – Negative Prep and Processing
Sales Tax
Videotape Stock (Production)
Solid state recording media
Hard drives
Computers/peripherals

For Editing on Film:
Film Dailies/Workprints
Sound Transfers
Projection Tests

For Editing on Videotape:
Telecine
Video Dailies
Tape Stock (Telecine)

28-00 Travel and Living – Crew
Air Fares
Hotels
Taxi
Auto
Rail
Excess Baggage
Phone
Per Diem

29-00 Below-the-Line Fringe
Payroll Taxes:
FICA-SS (Social Security)
FICA-HI (Medicare)
FUI (Federal Unemployment Insurance)

SUI (State Unemployment Insurance)
CREWWKCOMP (Workers' Compensation)
OFFICE WKCOMP
HANDLING FEE (Payroll Service)

Guilds/Unions:
DGA (Assistant Directors, Stage Managers, UPMs)
SAG/AFTRA
SAG/AFTRA/DGA Wk Comp
Vacation/Holiday (Union)
lATSE/Teamsters

30-00 Editorial
Editors
Assistant Editors

For Film Editing:
Cutting Room Rental
Purchases
Cutting Room Equipment Rental

For Video Editing:
Off-Line Editor
Off-Line Edit System
Hard drive purchase
On-Line System and Editor
Color Correction
Closed Captions

31-00 Post-Production Film and Lab/Video
For Film Editing and Mastering on Film:
Duplicate Work Prints
Negative Cutter
Develop Optical Negative
Timing (Color Correction)/Answer Prints
Inter-Positive/Inter-Negative
Check Prints
Release Prints
Master Tape/Film

Film/Tape Transfers
Standards Conversion

For Video Editing and Mastering on Video:
Videotape Masters/Safeties
Videotape Dubs and Transfers
Screening Copies

32-00 Optical Effects/Visual Effects/Digital Intermediates
Optical Effects (Film)
Optical Lab: Fades, Dissolves, etc.
Visual Effects
Visual Effects Supervisor
Pre-Visualization
Visualization Effects Editor
Matte painting
Visual EFX/CGI
Composites
Green screen stage
Other costs
Digital Intermediate

33-00 Music
Composer (All-In Package includes: Arrangers, Copyists, Musicians, Instruments, Studio, Engineers, Stock, etc.)
Licenses and Buy Outs
Music Supervisor/Clearance
Music Library

34-00 Post-Production Sound
Sound Editor
Music Editor
Dialogue Editor
Spotting for Music/Sound Effects
Music Scoring Stage
ADR
Foley
Mix

Narration Record
Other costs

On Film
Laydown
Conforming to Mag Film
Pre-Lay (Digital Work Station)
Pre-Dub
Final Dub
Printmaster
Optical Sound Transfer
Stock/Dubs/Transfers (Film)

On Video
Laydown
Edit/Pre-Lay
Mix
Layback

35-00 Titles and Graphics
Graphic Designer
Stock and Dubs
Computer-Generated Graphics
Animation

36-00 Stock Footage
Clearance Supervisor
Film and Tape Clips Licensing
Stills Rights
Artwork Rights

37-00 Insurance
Producer's Entertainment Package
Negative
Faulty Stock
Equipment
Props/Sets
Extra Expense

3rd-Party Property Damage
Office Contents
General Liability
Hired Auto
Cast Insurance
Workers' Compensation
Errors and Omissions

38-00 General and Administrative Expenses
Business License
Legal Expenses
Accounting Fees
Completion Bond
Telephone/Fax
Copying
Postage and Freight
Office Space Rental
Office Furniture
Office Equipment and Supplies
Computer Rental
Software
Transcription
Messenger/Overnight
Parking
Storage (Equipment/Supplies/Film/Tape)
Still Photographer (Equipment/Supplies/Film/Processing)
Publicity
Wrap Party
Hospitality
Production Fee

39-00 Publicity and Marketing
Publicist
Film Festival Application Fees
DVD Authoring
DVD Duplication/Replication/Packaging
Shipping/Postage

Press Kits
Still Reproduction
Travel/Lodging
Hospitality
Other

These are the basic costs which may be incurred in every budget in this book. They should cover 95% of all the items in your own budgets, so study this list to be sure you've included everything your project will require.

The next section provides a detailed description of these line items and associated costs. *Do not use our numbers! They are only guides.* **Your actual costs will vary depending on your geographic location, your skill in acquiring goods and services, and your inventiveness in solving production problems. Check with unions, guilds, and payroll services to get current rates and percentages.**

01-00 Story Rights

If you base your project on copyrighted material like a novel, a song, or a magazine article, you not only need the owner's permission, but you'll also have to pay the owner for the right to make the film version. The same applies if you are telling someone's life story, unless you are gathering material from public domain sources like court transcripts and newspaper stories, and even then, you must be careful about defamation of character.

To track down the owner of the copyright, call the publisher. If that doesn't work, and if copyright registration, renewal or transfer of ownership was after 1978, try an online search through the U.S. Copyright Office (*www.copyright.gov*). If prior to 1978 it requires a manual search. There's no charge if you go there yourself (in the Library of Congress, Washington, D.C.), or their staff will search for you at $150/hour. You can also determine whether or not a title is or has fallen into the public domain. Another option is to try a large copyright search firm like Thomson and Thomson (800) 692-8833.

Once you know who the owner is, negotiate to buy the rights or buy an option. You may want your lawyer to advise you — rights deals can be complex, and you'll want to get it right the first time.

Desperate Measures

If you really can't afford a lawyer, you can buy Film Industry Contracts, written and published by John Cones ($89.95). It contains all kinds of contracts, including an option agreement. (We make no guarantees.) Mark Litwak also has a contracts book, *Dealmaking in the Film & Television Industry*, 3rd edition (Silman-James Press) ($32.95). Or, since you're broke but willing to put in sweat equity, go to a university law library, and take notes from among the volumes of entertainment industry contracts.

An *option* gives you the exclusive right to hold the property for a specified term (usually a year or two) while you look for financing, or write script drafts, and attract stars and a director. The option agreement usually states that if the term ends with no production agreement, and if the option is not renewed, then the rights revert back to the original owner. The option payment (if any) is non-refundable. That's why a renewal clause is important. You don't want to have the project on the verge of a "green light" somewhere and then have the option expire with no renewal.

If the project goes forward, the option spells out how much money the copyright owner then gets for the rights. These agreements can be simple or complex, depending on the property and who is involved.

$$$

TV movie option for someone's life story might cost the producer anywhere from $500 on the low end to $10,000 on the high end or more if it's a famous person. When the project is made, the rights payment may be anywhere from $50,000 to $75,000 for an average TV movie (unless you're dealing with a blockbuster personality, when the sky's the limit).

Desperate Measures

Use your native eloquence and passion to convince a rights owner that your earnest efforts to get the project sold constitute sufficient consideration. Then you buy the option for a dollar (some money must change hands to make it legal). It's a perfectly valid option agreement.

Michael tells one of his option stories:

"In 1973, I optioned a 1958 best-selling Japanese book by a writer who was then Japan's leading novelist. It cost me nothing for the option itself. I held the rights for two years while I wrote several screenplay drafts, attracted some actors, and made the studio rounds with 'my property.' My option stated that if the film went into production (it never did) the author would receive $15,000 total and 5% of the producer's net profits. As it turned out, I was the third person to option the novel. The author had already received money through the various options even though a film was never made by any of us."

02-00 Script

02-01 Writer's Salaries

The writer is the unsung hero of production. When the show is a hit, audiences think the actors or narrator just made up the words on the spot. When a show flops — lousy script! In fact, dialogue is only one small part of a writer's job. Structure, theme, and overall creative treatment are even more important. Don't scrimp on the writer — get the best you can for your budget.

For budgeting, the script is the most important element in the entire production. The more work put into a detailed script, preferably a "shooting script," the more complete the budget and the greater the savings.

Our advice is to hire a writer with some experience and common sense. Writing scenes with expensive visual effects for what you know is a low-budget movie is an example of what not to do. That said, write the script unencumbered by thoughts of budgets. When you're happy with it (except you know it's too expensive), sharpen your pencil and see what you can do to save money. Can that night scene be just as effective if shot in daylight? (Saving extra lights.) Can those two scenes in the two bedrooms be shot in one bedroom? (Saving a camera setup.) Can the car chase become a foot race? If you find you've saved money but gutted the story, maybe you went too far. You be the judge.

The writer's fee will vary depending on the scale of the project and the overall budget. We give some figures below from the Writers Guild of America rate card, but don't use them without going through the WGA rate card yourself, as there are numerous ifs, ands, and buts that make every project unique.

$$$

Low Budget Original Theatrical Screenplay
including Treatment $62,642
High Budget Original Theatrical Screenplay
including Treatment $117,602

Program 60 minutes or less Network prime time
Writer's Fee: Story $13,439
               Teleplay $22,158

Program 60 minutes or less other than network prime time
High Budget ($300,000 and over)
Writer's Fee: Story $9,347
               Teleplay $16,189

Narration writing for television program 60 minutes or less.
Writer's fee: $19,169

Documentary 60 minutes or less
High Budget ($200,000 and over)
Story and Telescript: $21,043

For a short, a documentary, an industrial or an independent feature using non-WGA writing talent, these are not necessarily the figures to use. You'll need to see how much you can afford for the script, and how much the writer is willing to take. For example, a 45-minute home video might budget anywhere from $1,000 to $6,000 for the writer.

Treatments and screenplays do not necessarily have to cost an arm and a leg. It will depend on your ability as a negotiator, the perceived value of the writer, and the timeliness of the subject matter.

Desperate Measures

When a writer (non-WGA) is eager to get his or her property produced, or just get some work, you can strike a "spec" deal. This means the writer:

a) becomes your partner and gets paid an agreed sum, plus a percentage of the "back end."

b) gets paid an agreed sum at an agreed time but no percentage. Or some combination of the above.

What about the WGA? If a guild member chooses to work non-guild, it's not your problem. Just be up front about it.

Clearances (included as part of Legal in 38-00 General and Administrative)

After the screenplay has been approved on the creative side, you'll need to pass it through a legal clearance procedure to make sure you haven't inadvertently named the maniacal serial killer after the chairman of an international conglomerate. The clearance people also check on other things, like titles and place names. Consult your attorney on this, or call a clearance company and ask (one we know is Marshall/Plumb www.marshall-plumb.com).

02-08 Script Timing

For features and TV movies, the Script Supervisor reads the script and estimates the time it will play on screen. Obviously, one has this done after the script has been approved for shooting, and not while it is still in the hands of the second of nine screenwriters who will eventually rewrite it.

02-09 Storyboards/Pre-Viz

These can be anything from a director scrawling a succession of shots on a napkin to a full-blown presentation by a professional story-board artist to time spent with Previsualization software, in which, in the better programs, you can input certain camera specs, build your set, pop in your actors, and then experiment with the look of your shots in 3D so you have a pretty usable shot list. For complicated scenes (or nervous first-time directors), a storyboard or pre-viz program can really help visualize what action you want to happen when, and where to place the camera to get it on film. Many experienced directors use storyboards or pre-viz for stunts, special effects, or any potential difficulty with continuity. There are some great software programs out too. (Check The Writer's Computer Store in the Resources section.)

Producers also use boards to jazz up a pitch meeting. (Ad agencies have been doing this for years.) The pictures help convey action and feeling, and may help you make your sale.

$$$

Storyboard artists earn $1,500 to $2,500 per week, Storyboards can cost $50 and up per frame depending on complexity and whether they are in color or not.

(You may also have a creative director and artist create key art for a poster which may also be used for financing presentations. These cost $1,000 to $30,000 or more.)

03-00 Producer's Unit

03-01 Executive Producer

For smaller projects it's quite likely there won't be an executive producer. But if there is one, it's likely he or she is key to getting the project financed. Executive producers (the good ones) are people with a clear eye on the project's vision, and a hand on the phone. They have that most essential element: connections.

The executive producer often arranges financing for the project. It is his reputation for launching successful works that gets the project financed. The executive producer often hires the producer and director and oversees the project in the most fundamental way. He usually has acquired and/or developed the script or story as well.

$$$

The executive producer receives a flat fee or percentage of profits or both. For a TV movie or feature in the $3.5 million budget range, he or she could earn from $100,000 to $150,000. For a $150,000 home video budget, the executive producer can get from $10,000 to $20,000.

03-02 Producer

The producer is the one person responsible for the entire production from soup to nuts. He or she is on the project longest and oversees all elements of the production, including preparing the budget, breaking down the script, hiring the director, camera operator, crew, and actors. Producers are often "hyphenated people," such as "producer-director" or "writer-producer."

$$$

Producers can be paid a flat fee and often participate in profit sharing. Or they may prefer a weekly salary. The rates are negotiable and vary widely. A student film producer-director probably gets zip. A producer of an exercise video with a major star might get $1,500 to $2,500 a week. A low-budget feature (between $7M and $9.5M) "line producer" on location (actually a DGA job known as Unit Production Manager) gets about $5,823 a week.

If there is no executive producer, the producer packages the project (script, director, major actors). The producer handles the financing and the allotment of budget monies, negotiates the major contracts, and approves all expenditures. Sometimes a producer is hired for just part of a project.

A Line Producer, for example, oversees the pre-production and principal photography. The job ends when shooting is wrapped, plus a week or so for office clean-up. On some projects the producer also directs. Sometimes a producer and a director will work together on a project. The fees then can be fairly similar, but again, it greatly depends on the project, the reputation of the people involved, and the length of time each spends on the film.

Desperate Measures

Make the producer your partner, and defer salary to "back end," or some future point. Or pay below rate and defer the balance. This approach can apply to anyone "above-the-line" on your project, if they're game. It can work for "below-the-line" people as well, but they are usually accustomed to being paid at the end of the day. Every person and situation is different.

03-03 Associate Producer

Unfortunately, there is a lot of confusion around the title and job description of associate producer (and producer, for that matter). The title loses some of its credibility when it is indiscriminately given to relatives, girl and boy friends, and investors.

The title can be as fictitious as a fairy tale, or it can be real. When it's real, it's often a title given to the Production Manager as a perk (see Production Staff 10-00). It's also real on TV series production, where the AP can also be the Post-Production Supervisor, shepherding the project through the labyrinth of post. Since we're not dealing with episodic TV production in this book, we can skip the category.

03-06 Consultants

Consultants is a line item that covers a great number of possible contributors to the project: financial consultants, distribution consultants, historians, scientists, police experts, and medical advisors. He or she usually receives a flat fee or retainer. The consultant can be called upon at various times throughout scripting or production should the need arise.

04-00 Direction

04-01 Director

The director is the person responsible for bringing the script into reality, the person with an artistic vision — an ability to work with people and images and bring a story, concept, or idea into fruition. The director's ideas usually alter the script and its development, so if you know who the director will be, get his or her input early on in the development process.

The director is also involved in casting and often the selection of a Director of Photography, a Production Designer and Editor. The director is hired for artistic taste, ability to get the job done on budget, and to help determine the logistical approach to shooting the film or tape. He or she is a multitalented person, responsible for a wide range of responsibilities. Often the director's work continues through the editing of the film.

On smaller projects and documentaries, the director can also be the camera operator, or the writer, or even the producer. You may be able to make a flat deal with a director, or bring the director on for a specific number of days and pay on a daily basis.

Desperate Measures

If the director really wants to see the project made, or if it's a personal project, salary could be deferred until profits start rolling in. When you are starting out and producing low-budget projects, you cannot afford to pay thousands of dollars to a director (even if that's you!). DGA? Again, if a director wants to work non-guild (and plenty do!), it's not your problem.

$$$

Just for purposes of ballparking, the Directors Guild gives the following minimum rates in a few selected categories, or see *www.dga.org.*

Freelance Live and Tape Television

Dramatic non–network or network non–prime time (low budget):
60 minutes $19,292 12 days' work

Dramatic network prime time:
60 minutes $38,115 15 days' work

Film Basic Agreement — Theatrical Motion Pictures

Shorts/Documentaries:
Weekly salary $9,587
Guaranteed Prep period 2 days
Guaranteed Shoot days 1 week + 1 day
Guaranteed Cutting days 0

Low Budget Films (equal to or less than $2.5M)
Weekly salary $12,138 (discounts may apply, check DGA contract)
Guaranteed Prep period 2 weeks
Guaranteed Shoot days 10 weeks
Guaranteed Cutting days 1 week

Low Budget Films (more than $7M but less than $9.5M)
Weekly salary $14,566
Guaranteed Prep period 2 weeks
Guaranteed Shoot days 10 weeks
Guaranteed Cutting days 1 week

If the director is incorporated, with Federal ID number et al., he or she may want to do a "loan out" agreement, in which you pay his or her company directly, but not make his or her FICA, FUl, and SUI payments. Generally, however, you will pay DGA Pension and Health (currently 14.5%). If the director is not incorporated, then he or she becomes your employee, and you must pay payroll tax and DGA Pension and Health (assuming it's a DGA project).

05-00 Cast

05-01 Lead Actors and 05-02 Supporting Cast

Leading Actors and Supporting Cast are as important to the success of a film or videotape as a good script. To cast actors, refer to the section on Casting in Chapter 2. Rates can vary tremendously based on the name, experience, and perceived value of the actor. If your project is not for broadcast or theatrical release, contact SAG or AFTRA about non-broadcast rates.

$$$

These are some samples of the minimum Screen Actors Guild rates:

Theatrical and Television
Per Day	$759
Per Week	$2,634

Low-budget Theatrical Motion Picture
(total cost not exceeding $2.5 million)
Day Player	$504
Weekly Player	$1,752

These are only a few of the various rates. See the Screen Actors Guild (SAG) or AFTRA rate books online for other fees including meals, over-time, travel, night work, looping, rerun compensation, and so forth. Also check *www.sagindie.org* for several producer-friendly agreements whereby SAG actors may work on low-budget projects at reduced rates. Just allow plenty of time (weeks) to read and understand all the paperwork.

The better known an actor, the higher the rate. This could be double scale (two times the minimum) or much, much more. The more an agent can get for a client, the more he will try to charge each time, so it's worth negotiating. Because there are so many actors competing for the same jobs, you'll find prices may drop as the competition escalates.

Some agents take 10% of their actors' fees. If an actor is paid $1,000, the agent will get $100, the actor $900. Most agents will add 10% on top of the fee, so it will cost you $1,000 plus 10%, or a total of $1,100 (plus payroll taxes, and if it's a union job, then approximately 13% for Pension and Health). Be sure you understand this distinction when negotiating with agents.

110

The Guilds also make pay distinctions for what an actor does in a scene. If an actor speaks it's one rate; if he speaks five lines or less it's a cheaper rate; if he walks through a scene it's another. Be sure you understand your needs when hiring Guild actors, as it will affect the rates you will be charged.

If an actor is a "loan out" follow the same procedures as for Director, but apply the appropriate SAG or AFTRA Pension and Health.

Desperate Measures
▷ Student actors may be willing to work for free.
▷ Use non-union actors and pay below scale (say $100/day).
▷ Use union actors and pay below scale (it's the actor's choice).

05-04 Casting Director/Staff
If you can afford it, a good Casting Director takes much of the headache out of casting. (See the Casting section in Chapter 2.)

Casting Expenses
If you are handling all the casting chores yourself, you'll need a room to hold auditions, a waiting room for actors, copying of the "sides" (the script pages they'll audition with), a consumer video camera and operator, and music playback.

Dialect Coach
When an actor needs extra help with the spoken word, a dialect coach is hired. Maybe the actor speaks English with a heavy Chinese accent, and it's a problem, or maybe the actor needs to speak English with a Chinese accent. The dialect coach is the fixer.

Desperate Measures
The cheap way to get coached on dialects is to buy a booklet and audiocassette instruction packet. Samuel French Books in Los Angeles has them for about $18 (see Resources) in a variety of flavors, from Cockney accents to Australian, to French to New York. Now you can strip down to your undershirt, face yourself in the mirror, and say "You talkin' to me?" until you get it perfect.

05-06 Choreographer

If you are producing the remake of *Singin' in the Rain*, you already know what a choreographer will do for you. For the rest of us, suffice to say that if people are going to move to music, also known as dancing, you'll probably want a choreographer to bring it all together.

Some directors are terrified of staging actors, either to music or not. Some situation comedy directors even hire choreographers to help them block the action in imaginative ways. Sometimes a script will call for a character to do a "spontaneous dance," and the director may want a choreographer to make it special. Or you may have a beauty pageant that needs to be staged. So think of choreographers as more than dance designers — they can be movement designers too.

Desperate Measures

Music video producers on tight budgets often hire "choreographers" who are young people with great hip hop skills. If you can find one through a dancing school's hip hop or funk classes, you can probably get them for next to nothing. Be careful, however, since lack of experience with cameras can waste a lot of time.

$$$

Choreographers are not in any union. A reasonable pay range is $300 to $600 per 12-hour day, depending on experience. A major feature might pay $1,000 per day, and famous choreographers may command even more.

Deke's choreographer story:
"Once I produced two musical comedies for kids that were so low budget we tried to squeak by without a choreographer: We couldn't. On the first day of rehearsal, when the music played, all the actors stood around like posts. We knew we were in trouble. As a favor, a choreographer friend of the director rescued us, and even his simple moves, taught to the actors in one day, made all the difference. Lesson learned."

05-08 Narrator/Voiceover Artist

The narrator is the voice over used in documentaries, commercials, and sometimes features. Depending on the notoriety of the personality, the rates vary greatly from below scale to whatever the market will bear for well-known voices. We know one guy with a voice so deep and masculine he's always called for truck commercials. He gets $750 per hour. Commercial rates vary depending on whether the commercial is for local, regional, or national usage. Usually you must negotiate with the narrator's agent. The agent will find as many reasons as possible to ask for a high rate for his better known clients. When the commercial is aired the narrator also receives additional money through residuals (check with the Actor's Guild for rates).

$$$

Rates mostly depend on length of program. Here are some samples from the AFTRA rate card for a single program:

Announcers (10 lines or more)

Between 15 - 30 minutes $426

Between 45 - 60 minutes $762

Audition narrators when possible, either in person, or get a demo-reel from them or their agent. Many voiceover agencies have demo-reels they'll send you with dozens of voices.

Once in a while you can work "on spec" with narrators. For example, say you book a narrator to do three commercial spots. As it turns out, you also have another two spots to do but you are not sure whether the narrator will be right for the spots. To save everyone time, ask if he'll do another two spots on spec. If you or the client like and use the narration, he will get paid. If the client rejects the spot, then you're not responsible for paying for the unused reading. Agents, of course, hate this, but if you've developed a good relationship with a narrator he or she is likely to go along with it since it saves them a trip back to the studio. If the spec recording is used, call the agent and ask to be billed.

Desperate Measures

Narration for experimental films or "cause" projects has a cachet to it. Actors often do it for love and recognition. If your project has that kind of appeal, go to the biggest actor you can think of and ask if he or she will do it for minimum scale. You may be pleasantly surprised.

Models

Models are covered under the AFTRA agreement, but not SAG. Rates vary according to whether you are hiring top talent or not.

Modeling agencies have portfolios that you can go through when selecting models. They will also inform you of the various rates based on the model's experience and the type of modeling required.

05-10 Stunt Coordinator

Use top professionals to do stunts for the best, safest stunts. Getting people hurt or killed is just not acceptable.

The Coordinator is your source for everything stunt related: costs, personnel, equipment, safety. He or she breaks the script down into stunts and provides cost estimates. Stunt wisdom says to budget for at least two takes per stunt.

On the set, the Coordinator helps place cameras, and generally runs the set when cameras roll.

$$$

SAG scale for Stunt Coordinators is currently $2828 week, but good ones (don't use any other kind) get paid $3,500 to $5,500 per week. When the Coordinator actually directs the 2nd unit, he stops being paid as the Coordinator and starts getting paid as a 2nd Unit Director, a DGA position that gets $10,000/week for high-budget pictures.

05-11 Stunt Players

These are the foot soldiers of the stunt world: the men and women who leap from a helicopter over the Empire State Building and burst into a ball of falling flames.

$$$

They are covered under a SAG agreement that pays a minimum rate of $759 per day, plus what is called an *adjustment*. The adjustment is based on the degree of difficulty and danger in the stunt. For $50 you get a guy to take a fall as he runs along a rocky road. For $2,000 or so she'll turn over a flaming car, or plunge from a high rise. A fully enveloped fire burn, running, will cost you about $3,500. (If you are licensing a stunt clip from a feature film, you must negotiate with the stunt person. You may have to pay what he or she got for the original stunt.)

05-12 Stunt Costs/Adjustments

These are completely determined by the script. If you've got serious stunts, the only way to budget them is to ask a Stunt Coordinator to break it down. Just for example, let's say you want a guy to drive a car into a telephone pole. The player gets his daily 8-hour rate of $759. His adjustment might be $500. The two cars (remember, two takes) will run about $500 each. And the cost of the phone pole, its installation, and dressing with wires could easily run $1,000.

05-13 Stunt Equipment

Ditto.

05-14 ADR (Automatic Dialogue Replacement)

SAG day players (actors hired by the day for original production) receive 100% of their day rate for ADR sessions.

SAG weekly players receive 50% of the pro rata day rate for a 4-hour session. After 4 hours, they get 100% of the pro rata day rate.

06-00 Travel and Living – Producers/Director

If you are shooting with the whole company in some far-away place, you need to transport your people and house them.

06-01 Airfares

Since union actors, writers, directors, and certain crew (Directors of Photography, Production Designers) must travel first class, the Executive Producer and Producer will naturally want to travel first class as well. If you're doing a non-union show, then it's negotiable, but try and make the same deal for everyone to keep the grumbling down.

06-09 Per Diem

Per Diem for Producers and Directors on features can be in the $100 a day range. On low budget, non-union projects, if everyone is fed three squares a day, transported and sheltered, there may be no per diem at all.

07-00 Travel and Living – Cast

07-01 Air Fares

As we said above, all actors working a union show must travel first class, unless it isn't available.

07-08 Per Diem

Per Diem for a SAG actor on an overnight location is $75 per day for three meals. If the Producer provides lunch, you can deduct $15.70. If the Producer provides breakfast, you can deduct $10.50. Or you can be nice and not deduct anything. It's up to you and how close you have to shave it. For the same question with crew, see 28-00 Travel and Living – Crew.

08-00 Residuals

When commercials play, or when TV programs air after their initial run or are syndicated, or when a program enters a "Supplemental Market" (e.g. DVD release or "in-flight") or a film goes to TV, extra monies, called residuals, may be owed to actors, directors, writers, and musicians. Residuals can either be factored into a production budget (as TV movies often do for its second run), or not. Check with the distributor or studio ahead of time. If included, check with the guilds for residual rates, or consult *The Labor Guide* (see Resources).

09-00 Above-the-Line Fringe

Anyone who works for you (who is not a "loan out" from his or her own corporation) is an official "employee" in the eyes of the law. "Fringes" are what your company must contribute to appropriate government agencies and union pension/health funds on behalf of your employees. The package is also called "payroll taxes." These include:

▶ Social Security and Medicare (FICA-SS and FICA-HI) 7.65% employer's portion, and 7.65% employee's portion deducted from salary.

▶ Federal Unemployment Insurance (FUI) .8% of first $7,000 in salary.

▶ State Unemployment Insurance (SUI) adjustable by state. In California it's 6.2% on the first $7,000 in salary.

- Workers' Compensation rate is set annually by state and differs with each industry. Workers' Comp. is less for office people than for grips climbing poles to rig lights. Call your state agency to ask how much to average out for your project. Can be as low as 1.1% and as high as 7%. For purposes of illustration, let's say 4%.

- Payroll Service. If you are using a payroll service, add another 4%–5% to cover their charges.

The sum total of these adds up to 18%–23% of a person's gross salary. Your accountant, or your payroll service, can keep you abreast of any changes in the individual percentages, and can handle actual payments from your company to the respective government agencies and union funds.

In addition to the payroll taxes, union employees receive pension and health benefits. These are some current rates as examples. Call each guild, or your payroll service, to get accurate rates for your project and your geographical area.

WGA   14.5%
SAG   14.8%
AFTRA   14.5%
DGA   14.5%

For example, adding together all of the above fringes, if an Associate Producer earns $1,850 per week, add another 23% ($425.50) in payroll taxes to get the actual cost to your company – $2,275.50.

If you are paying someone from a guild, say a Director (and the person is not on a loan out from his or her own company), then you owe his or her salary, say $2,235 for four days of work, plus the payroll taxes at 23% ($514.05), plus the DGA Pension/Health at 14.5% of the salary ($324.07), for a grand total cost to you of $3,073.12.

If the person is on a loan out, then you pay the base salary of $2,235, plus the DGA Pension/Health ($324.07), (but no payroll taxes) for a total cost to you of $2,559.07.

Note: In the sample budgets in this book, all fringes are calculated as part of each category. The Above-the-Line (09-00) and Below-the-Line (29-00) Fringes are duplicated only as a laundry list to help remind you of what can be included.

10-00 Production Staff

10-01 Unit Production Manager

A good Unit Production Manager, or UPM, is the glue between all the loose ends of the production and the Producer/production company. In many cases he creates the original budget, and then spends the next weeks or months sweating bullets so that the production sticks to it. He schedules the main blocks of production, books the crew, supervises location scouts and contracts, organizes the casting process, and works with the Director and Producer to keep everything running smoothly, on schedule and on budget. Some UPMs are released after shooting, while others stay on through editing, right up to delivery of the final master. On really small productions, the Producer may have to take on the work of the UPM, but if that's the case, be aware that it's difficult to split your mind between the creative parts of your shoot, and the logistical nuts and bolts that hold it together. One part or the other will probably suffer. A UPM can also be a "Line Producer."

$$$

The pay scale for Production Managers varies, like everything else. We know one excellent PM who works a network Saturday morning live-action kid's series and makes about $2,100 per week. It helps, of course, that his job lasts for about five months.

A UPM can also join the DGA. For DGA UPMs, minimum scale for a low budget movie between $7M and $9.5M, for example, when shooting on location, is $5,823 per week, plus a production fee of $1,074 per week, plus a severance allowance of one week's pay. Check the DGA rate card for appropriate minimums and production fees for your show (*www.dga.org*).

For non-union home video productions in the $100,000 budget range, a Production Manager can earn $1,200 to $1,600 per week.

10-02 First Assistant Director

The "Velvet Fist" is an apt description of the First AD. This person keeps the set running smoothly and efficiently — always one step ahead of the next shot. He or she coordinates with all the department heads to make sure everything is ready and safe before each shot. The First AD also creates a shooting schedule for each day's work, coordinating cast and crew so that make-up, wardrobe, and rehearsal with the Director can go on while the crew is busy setting up. Every possible moment must be used to accomplish something. It helps to have a First AD with a strong voice and a commanding presence, but lacking that, respect and good rapport with all departments can also get the job done.

In television, with multi-camera shoots, the Assistant Director is usually called the Associate Director, and often sits with the Director in the control room, assisting with show timing and getting camera people ready for upcoming shots.

$$$

First ADs in the DGA are paid a minimum of $3,954 per week on movies for studio shoots (plus a production fee of $733/week), and $5,529 on location (plus a production fee of $901/week).

On any shoot where there is potential for chaos on the set — many actors, props, sets, crew, equipment, and so on — it's worth having someone function as a First AD.

On larger productions, like TV movies and theatrical features, there is also a Second Assistant Director, and even Second Second ADs. Since the First AD should not leave the set, the Second AD helps the First AD by carrying out orders off the set, like trying to pry the star out of her mobile home before panic grips the Producer and Director. The Second also handles the call sheets for the next day's cast and crew, and various other production reports. The Second Seconds are hired when there is even more potential for chaos. There must have been dozens for Ben Hur's chariot race.

$$$

The DGA scale for Second ADs is $2,650 per week in studio (plus production fee of $559/week), and $3,702 on location (plus production fee of $733/week).

10-03 Stage Manager

In multi-camera television, when the Director and Associate Director are in the control room, someone has to keep order on the set, cue performers to speak, get make-up in for touch up, make sure everything is ready for shooting, and so forth. That's the Stage Manager's job. It helps to have someone who can crack the whip pleasantly.

$$$

DGA scale for Stage Managers is $2,826 per 40-hour week for prime time programs.

10-04 Production Coordinator

The Coordinator runs the production office, and usually arrives on the first day carrying a large briefcase or box containing every production form, phone book, and restaurant guide in the city. The good ones are geniuses at knowing whom to call for anything from scenic backdrops of the Swiss Alps to iced cappuccino. They must be "buttoned up" people — very reliable, detail oriented, trustworthy, and calm under fire.

$$$

Production Coordinators are paid anywhere from $800 per week on low-budget projects to $1,200 a week on movie locations.

10-05 Script Supervisor

On movies, the Script Supervisor handles timing, which is the estimating of how long a script will play on screen. If a script is long or short, it's best to know well before shooting begins, so you can make changes inexpensively. The Script Supervisor stays close to the Director on set, marking the takes the Director wants to keep, keeping notes on what goes wrong in a take, and watching for continuity. If an actor wears an eye patch on his right eye before lunch, and on his left eye after lunch, you've got a break in continuity, and an unintentionally funny scene.

$$$

Script Supervisors make $1,200 to $1,400 per week on movies.

Desperate Measures

On very simple, low-budget, non-union projects, the position can be filled by an exceptionally bright Production Assistant at $500 or $600 per week.

10-06 Production Auditor

This person keeps track of your expenses, and produces daily and weekly cost reports. For movies, they are paid anywhere from $1,200 to $2,500 per week. Feature projects have an Assistant Auditor. If you are on your own "no-budget" project and insanely busy, we suggest hiring a bookkeeper familiar with film production to come in once a week or so to pay bills, keep accounts straight, reconcile bank statements, and generally keep you honest and sane.

10-07 Technical Advisor

When you need a true expert on the set, bring in a Technical Advisor. If you're shooting a cop movie, have a cop who really knows the ins and outs of cop reality. Maybe you should have an ex-crook also. Technical Advisors can also be brought on for safety expertise (when, for example, the script calls for underwater scenes or scenes with airplanes). Rates vary, of course, on who it is, but figure anywhere from $800 to $1,500 per week.

10-08 Production Assistants/Associates

All minor tasks not specifically assigned to other crew members are handled by the production assistants. They make petty cash purchases, are the primary "gofers" on shoots, and work on the shoot's logistical elements. This entry level position is the lowest rung on the ladder, so you often get people who think they want to work in movies but might be into serious self-delusion. You can always tell because they roll their eyes when asked to get you a cup of coffee, or worse, just stare blankly in slack-jawed amazement. "You want me to do whaaa?" Top-flight PAs are cheerful, think on their feet, and are self-motivated problem-solvers who are worth their weight in gold. Larger productions need several PAs who report to the First Assistant Director, Production Manager, and/or Producer.

$$$

Figure $100 – $125 per 12-hour day for a PA, plus mileage if they drive their own cars.

Desperate Measures

When you're too broke to hire a PA, try the local college Film/TV Department and ask for volunteer "interns," who work for the experience, and free lunch.

10-09 Studio Teacher/Welfare Worker

If you have minors on your set (under age 18), and if they are being paid, state law dictates that you hire a Teacher/Welfare worker "to care and attend to the health, safety, and morals of all minors." This is usually one person who wears the two hats of teacher and welfare worker.

There are various regulations that vary by state, but the general idea is that kids of various ages can only work specified hours, must have specific rest and recreation periods and mealtimes, must be with a parent or guardian, and, on school days, must spend specified hours being schooled. In California, for example, a baby under five months old can only "work" for twenty minutes a day, and can only be exposed to a maximum of 100 foot candles of light for 30 seconds at a time. On the other hand, a 16- or 17-year-old kid working on a non-school day does not require a teacher/welfare worker at all. In California, you need one teacher for every 10 kids on a school day, and one for every 20 kids on a non-school day. Check with a studio teacher service in your state for the local regulations.

Two other points about employing kids: permits and permits.

▶ The production company needs a permit to employ minors. In California it is obtained through the Division of Labor Standards and Enforcement (also called the Labor Commission). It is usually free, and they'll want proof that you have workers' compensation insurance.

▶ The child also needs a permit, and this is the #1 problem on the set. Parents somehow believe that all their kid needs is terminal cuteness, and they are terribly dismayed when the teacher bars them from the set and all hope of child stardom goes up in smoke. It's easy to avoid this — just tell the parents that a permit will be required from the Labor Commission.

Finally, when you are using kids in certain circumstances, in certain ways on non-school days or after-school hours and they are unpaid, you may be able to avoid hiring a teacher. Check with a Studio Teaching agency to find out if your project qualifies. Be warned, however, that should an accident happen, your liability is probably less if there is a Teacher/Welfare Worker on the set.

$$$

Typical rates:

Non-union – $200 to $225 per 12-hour day.

Union (IATSE) – approximately $260 day for 8 hours.

(Book through the local.)

11-00 Extra Talent

Extras are also called "atmosphere" because they lend authenticity to a scene. "Stand-ins" are extras who resemble specific leading actors and "stand in" while lighting is customized for the star.

Extras in the Screen Actors Guild (SAG) require minimum payments. For example:

$$$

SAG West Coast Rates

General Extras	$130 per day (8 hours)
Special Ability	$140
Dancers, Skaters, Swimmers	$302
Stand-ins	$145

There is additional compensation when the extra also supplies an extra change of clothes ($9), period wardrobe ($18), hairpiece ($18), pets ($23), camera or luggage ($5.50), car ($27), motorcycle ($35), and so forth. See Screen Actors Guild rate card or *The Labor Guide*.

11-05 Extras Casting Fee

When you need a lot of background atmosphere, like hundreds of pedestrians in an intersection, or an angry mob, or a stadium full of feverish fans, it may be time to delegate the task of casting all those people to an Extras Casting Service. There are many online. Just contact a few, describe your unique needs and they'll fill you in on their rates and services.

11-10 Extras Transportation

If you need to move your extras from location to location, not having the proper transportation at hand can slow you down and be a schedule killer. Passenger vans with drivers is one solution.

Desperate Measures

For non-union projects you could pay below scale rates, or even just coffee and doughnuts — well, maybe throw in a free lunch (some people just want to be in the movies!).

Michael says, "*That's exactly what we did for the bar scene in* Hardware Wars. *We handed out fliers asking people to show up for coffee and doughnuts at a San Francisco bar at 10 a.m. on a Sunday morning. We gave costumes to everyone when they entered and had them sign a release. We even had a friendly policemen pull people in off the streets for us when we needed more extras.*"

12-00 Sound Stage

Prices of studios and sound stages vary depending on the size, location, and equipment provided. They can be rented for months, days, or hours. Some include a complete television control room, videotape machines, audio room, video control, cameras, lights, and even crews. Others are just four lonely walls you fill with what you need. Some are on movie lots and come with soundproof walls, offices, parking for staff, crew and big production trucks, a commissary for meals, maybe even a construction shop for sets. In short, fully loaded. Others are little more than converted warehouses with tin roofs. Ever hear the sound of rain on a tin roof? It pretty much kills any hope of clean dialogue, and ADR (Automatic Dialogue Replacement) is expensive.

When you do rent a stage, be sure to ask about the little charges that can sneak up and bite you, such as power usage (some stages have no power, and you'll have to provide a generator; see 21-00 Electrical), office space, dressing, make-up and hair-dressing rooms, wardrobe room, green room, school room, eating area, tables and chairs, prop and set storage, prop and set assembly area, parking, telephone and fax, security, keys, rehearsal stage, first aid, stage manager, heating and air conditioning. (*Have you ever worked in a non-air-conditioned soundstage in L.A. in August with dancing actors dressed up in Santa's reindeer suits? Deke has. It's not pretty. Consider temperature and humidity and how it may affect your project.*)

$$$

Prices for Sound Stages vary depending on the setup.

124

▶ A fully equipped 2,400 square foot stage with video control room, three cameras, two machines, and full crew can cost from $9,000 to $14,000 for one day of shooting, depending on how many lights you use, and how much time you spend loading in your set (the day before), and striking it (the day after).

▶ A four-wall 4,700 square foot stage with three-wall hard cyc (a clean, painted background) air-conditioned, sound proofed, with limited parking, some production offices, make-up, dressing rooms and lounge can cost $525 per 10-hour prep and strike day, and $750 per 10-hour shoot day, plus power at $20 per hour, and other charges for phones, kitchen, stage manager, and whatever lights are used.

▶ A similar four-wall package for a larger stage, say 16,000 square feet, can cost $1,400 for prep and strike days, and $2,500 for pre-light and shoot days.

Desperate Measures

You can set up anywhere if all you need is a roof over your heads. Just run the studio checklist on your proposed location (adding items like toilets or honeywagons). Spend a minute standing silently — what you hear in the background is what you'll hear on your show. Is there an airport nearby? A kennel? A turkey farm?

13-00 Production Design

The "look" of your show is the domain of the Production Designer or Art Director. Big projects have both functions, the Art Director reporting to the Production Designer. Smaller ones have one or the other.

13-01 Production Designer/Art Director

He or she takes a script and, with the Director, interprets it visually, giving the set concrete detail, authenticity, and hopefully, inspiration. On low-budget projects, a Production Designer or Art Director can be employed for a wide range of jobs during pre-production and production. He or she can illustrate perspectives, scenes, set designs, and create scale models, attend to color schemes and textures, and have charge of all sets and the way they are dressed. On bigger projects, the Production

Designer's job is more conceptual, and tasks are handed to the Art Director to supervise, to the Set Designer to actually draft blueprints, to Model Makers and Estimators and so on.

Depending on your budget, the Production Designer can work every day on the set, assuring that the look of the show has the greatest visual impact. He or she is that "third" eye only concerned with how things look.

$$$

For non-union, small projects, figure $1,000 per week for someone starting out; in the range of $1,400 per week for journeyman level; and $2,500 per week and up for masters on larger projects.

Union scale for Art Directors is about $1,765 to $2,159 per week depending on experience.

Assistants' pay may range from $500 to $1,400 per week non-union, and about $1,615 per week union. Also allow for research, Polaroid, film, and car allowance, depending on the project.

13-04 Set Designer

This person is a draftsman familiar not only with sets and the requirements of cinematography and lighting, but also with the language of architects and skilled builders and craftsmen. His or her plans will be used by the Construction Coordinator and his team to build the sets.

13-05 Model Makers/Miniatures

Sometimes it helps everyone, especially the Director, to see a miniature of a set to visualize where to place actors and how best to shoot it. These are called Design/Study Models, they're made of foam core, and they can cost as little as $500 or as much as hundreds of thousands — if what you're studying is a scale model of Disneyland.

Shooting miniatures is another sort of job done by the same kind of company. If your script calls for futuristic space vehicles or submarines, or the destruction of Manhattan by a tidal wave, miniatures are one way to do it. Cost is by the project, as little as $150 for a single item or $350,000 for a space fleet.

13-06 Sketch Artist

Used by Directors and Art Directors to help visualize scenes and place cameras. Allow $1,000 to $1,500 per week.

13-07 Set Estimator

When there are so many sets and attendant costs that the Production Designer is overwhelmed, a Set Estimator is brought in to do his thing. Allow $800 to $1,100 per week.

14-00 Set Construction

There are two ways to go about Set Construction:

- Hire a Construction Coordinator who will supervise crew, purchases, rentals, equipment, cartage, strike, and disposal. Everyone will therefore be on your payroll.

- Retain a set construction company that will do it all for you, at a markup, but save you the trouble and expense of putting more people through payroll.

There is no way to enter set costs. You may be building the inside of Peter Rabbit's bunny hollow, or the entire length of Captain Nemo's *Nautilus*. That's why coordinators and construction companies exist — to give you bids.

14-01 Construction Coordinator

Allow $1,300 to $1,800 per week; plus tool rental ($750 – $850 week), and truck rental ($150 – $250 per week).

14-02 Labor

Carpenters, Painters, and Foremen are key areas for labor. Some sample weekly rates:

Foreman	$1,700 – $2,000
Painters	$1,200 – $1,700
Scenic Painters	$1,800 – $2,200
Carpenters	$1,200 – $1,700

15-00 Set Operations

The Grips and the Electricians are like eggs and bacon. They need each other. Electricians actually handle the power to the set, and with the Grips, lights get hung or set up, and shaded properly for each scene. Grips do other things too, as described below. (Electricians are in 21-00 Electrical.)

15-01 First or Key Grip

The First or Key Grip is the head of the Grip Department. In addition to working on lighting with the Electric Department, Grips handle all other rigging and setting up necessary for a shoot — like hanging scenic backdrops, setting up dolly track, blacking out a window, and so on.

$$$

Key Grips (non-union) get $300 to $450 per 12-hour day.

15-02 Second or Best Boy Grip

$250 to $350 per 12-hour day non-union.

15-03 Grips

$200 to $300 per 12-hour day.

15-04 Boom/Dolly/Crane Grips

The person who sets up booms, dollies, and cranes and works them smoothly. Sounds easy — it isn't! $250 to $300 per 12-hour day.

15-06 Grip Rentals

This line covers the miscellaneous grip equipment that may be needed — stands, scrims, apple boxes, tape and other expendables, and more. It is often included in the grip truck/lighting package (see 21-00 Electrical).

Dolly Rentals (included under "Grip Rentals")

No, this isn't an order-to-go from Radio City Music Hall. A dolly is a four-wheeled moving camera platform. Not all shoots require moving camera shots, but for that extra bit of production value, movement can bring life to an otherwise static shot. Using a dolly will take more time to set up than tripod or hand-held shots, especially if plywood or tracks need to be laid for a smooth ride.

Cranes are in this category also. They usually adopt the names of Greek gods (Zeus, Nike, Apollo). Stage cranes go up to around 19 feet. Mobile cranes (mounted on cars or trucks and equipped with power cells and batteries) can get up to 29 feet and higher. Only in rare cases will a crane be rented for most small and low-budget projects. Another device, however, called a jib, in which the camera but no operator is mounted on the end of a camera boom, can deliver certain crane-like effects for less money. Ask your DP.

There are different kinds of jibs, cranes and dollies from a few companies. Consult with the Director and the Director of Photography and agree on type of equipment, how much track, and whether you need any of the extras that come with them. Don't forget about cartage (if you do it) or delivery charge (if they do it).

$$$

Depending on what you rent, prices can go from $150 per day for a Western Dolly, to $250 a day for a Doorway Dolly. Stage cranes go from $205 to $295 per day. Local pickup/delivery can be $125 to $200. Mobile cranes are $300 to $625 per day, not including accessories or per mile charges.

15-08 Box Rentals

Lots of craftspeople have boxes or kits that they will rent to you. Key Grips may have all sorts of goodies that may be cheaper to rent than put in the Grip Package. Make-up people have make-up stuff. Gaffers have lighting stuff.

Box Rentals can also serve another useful purpose. Say you really want a certain Key Grip, but his daily rate is higher than you can pay for other Key people. (As discussed earlier, it's important to keep rates equal between the same levels of personnel in each department.) Pay him the same daily rate as other Keys, but up his pay on the Box Rental. That way you're not lying when you say all Keys are getting the same day rate. It's sneaky, but it takes care of business.

15-10 Craft Service

The "Craft" refers to the working people on a set — all the grips and electrics, camera people, props people, etc., who get real hungry and thirsty between meals and need a quick pick-me-up. So Craft Service means those who service the crafts people by having hot coffee, cold drinks, and munchies of all sorts. Even producers are welcome.

The job usually goes to a person or company for one package price that includes labor and food. Sometimes a "box rental fee" is added to cover the overhead on all the food gear like hotplates and coffee urns.

$$$

Figure $500 to $600 per week for the person (non-union), plus whatever budget for food you all agree on.

15-15 Air Conditioning/Heating

In Los Angeles, on hot summer days, you'll need air conditioning. Air Conditioning/Heating companies size the unit to suit the need. Rarely will they be asked to cool a stage higher than 8 feet above the floor (although some big stars insist on cooling the whole building so everyone is comfortable).

These companies help out in other ways too. For example, if you need to see breath for winter scenes, they'll regulate the temperature and humidity for you. Temperature can be as high as the fifties and still get "breath" with proper lighting and humidity.

Air conditioning comes by the unit ton. Figure 100 sq. ft. per ton as a starting point, than add lighting load, and the number of people. The company will get you an estimate of tonnage needed.

$$$

Prices are based on the size of units plus time and labor. A 5-ton rents for $50 per day (500 sq. ft.) An average stage unit is 8 to 10 tons at $60 to $70 per day.

Heaters are less — one furnace for a 2,000-2,500 sq. ft. stage is $65 per day. These prices do not include power and fuel.

16-00 Special Effects

These effects are mechanical, or pyrotechnic, not computer-created — anything from a shot in which a baby pulls a car door off its hinges to small gags, like squeezing a sneaker and having green slime ooze out of its heel (we did that for a shoe commercial).

Obviously costs depend on whether you're blowing up an obsolete Las Vegas hotel or doing something simple like the shoe gag.

16-01 Special Effects Person

The Key Special Effects Person works closely with the Stunt Co-ordinator to make the effects as terrific as possible, and safe for cast and crew.

$$$

Rates vary from $1,250 to $2,000 per week.

16-03 Additional Labor

If there's rigging to do before a special effect can be shot, you'll save time and money bringing in a rigging crew so all is ready by the time the rest of the company gets to the shot.

$$$

Allow $750 to $1,000 per week per person.

16-07 Fabrication

If you need just the right gizmo for your flotchet, and you're in the Mojave Desert, you'll be glad your Key Special Effects Person brought along his mobile workshop. In town, or out, give your Special Effects people enough time to fabricate what you need. Fabrication costs depend on script.

17-00 Set Dressing or Set Decoration

17-01 Set Decorator

The Set Decorator works with the Production Designer and/or Art Director to create a look for all the sets that matches the Director's and

Production Designer's vision for the movie and all its characters, their tastes, personalities, quirks and conflicts. It's materializing the themes of the movie into all the stuff with which the characters furnish their various worlds. They furnish the sets with all the stuff that makes a home a home, or an office, or a torture chamber...

$$$

Rates go from $1,250 to $1,800 per week.

17-02 Lead Person

He or she is the person in charge of the Swing Gang (see below). Rates go from $1,000 to $1,300 per week.

17-03 Swing Gang aka Set Dressers

Movers of furniture or whatever accoutrements accouter the set. $600 to $1,000 per week.

18-00 Property

Props are things actors pick up and use, as distinct from Set Dressing, which do not make it into the hands of actors.

18-01 Property Master

The Property Master purchases and rents all necessary props. On smaller shoots, he may also handle the special effects props and design special riggings.

Michael's prop story:

"Once I needed a specialty person who knew how to rig water props. The shot called for us to pour champagne into a three-glass pyramid, culminating in a champagne waterfall. I had tried this shot once without an experienced prop person, with disastrous results. In Manhattan, I found a guy known as 'Mr. Water.' 'Oh, yeah,' they'd say, 'That's a job for Mr. Water.' And sure enough, he knew everything there was to know about water — how to make it pour, how to light it, how to pump it, and how to suction it. He designed a special water rig with complicated spouts, nozzles, and pumps that made the shot work. (He was paid a flat rate plus a rental charge for the rig that he designed.)"

$$$

IATSE lists numerous classifications of "prop people," such as Prop Maker Foreman, Prop Maker Gang Boss, Special Effects Foreman, Upholsterer, Draper Foreman, Greens Foreman, and many others. See IATSE rate card for the various costs and work rules involved.

Figure from $250 - $350 per day for a Prop Master.

Box Rental might fetch $250 per week. (Get friendly with him so you can peek inside — it's a trip.)

If you use firearms or explosives you need what's called a Licensed Powder Man, who gets a 10% bonus if the explosive explodes — deliberately that is.

19-00 Wardrobe

19-01 Costume Designer

Sometimes these people are called upon to actually design clothing; other times they supervise the purchase and rental of wardrobe, and the assembly of custom clothing. In any case, you are relying on their aesthetic sense to work well with that of the Director and Production Designer. The clothes, after all, must fit the overall look of the show, like a hand in a glove.

If you producing a low budget project and are thinking of eliminating an experienced Designer, Costumer or Wardrobe Supervisor, think again. Just like Production Design and Set Decoration, how characters dress is key to how they feel about themselves and to how we perceive them. And there's a practical aspect. I once watched a scene of a couple having a conversation in a coffee shop. The wall behind them was brown. The guy's shirt was the same shade of brown. The effect of his head floating in space was unintentionally hilarious.

Sometimes Costume Designers get stuck with odd jobs. Here's Deke's Costume Designer story from a low-budget children's show:
"Humpty Dumpty had to fall off his wall, shatter into pieces, and get put together again. The Costume Designer was determined to make the gag work. She found a maker of fiberglass kayaks and had him fashion one complete egg suit, and one 'shattered' egg suit. When Humpty fell, he fell out of frame... the camera 'shook' with the impact... and then we cut to an overhead shot of poor Humpty on his

back with big eggshell fragments all about. It wasn't exactly high tech, but when I saw the little kids' faces get all worried about Humpty, I knew it had worked like a charm."

$$$

Rates go from $1,400 to $2,200 per week — unless you're the late Edith Head returned. She was the queen.

19-02 Costumers

On shows with no Designer per se, the Costumer might head the department. When there are lots of costumes, you might have a men's and a women's Costumer, each of whom would head their own divisions, hire other wardrobe people, and so forth.

$$$

Rates go from $1,000 to $1,200 per week.

19-08 – 19-12 Alterations/Repairs/Cleaning/Loss and Damage/Film

These are really separate line items, but suffice to say they can sneak up on you. If, for example, you are shooting a fistfight at the OK Corral, you may need all of the above, plus duplicates for Take 2. Let your script be your guide.

20-00 Make-Up and Hair

Whether you've got actors who just have to stand there and look gorgeous, or monsters with blood oozing from eye sockets, the Make-Up Artists and Hair Stylists are the folks who do the job. They purchase, prepare, and apply all facial and body make-up, special effect transformations, prosthetics, wigs, and hairpieces.

Since make-up is the first chore of the day for actors, get cheerful make-up artists who will send the actors out in a good mood. Seriously.

Also allow enough time. Men usually take about 15 minutes to a half hour. Women can take an hour or more. And will. No matter how hard you rap on the door.

When you have a big star, he or she may insist on a personal make-up/hair person, who usually charges twice what your regular person charges. There's not much you can do about it either, except beg for a cheaper rate.

20-01 Key Make-Up Artist

Allow from $250 to $350 per day, plus Box Rental of $30/day.

20-03 Hair Stylist

Allow the same.

20-04 Special Make-Up Effects

This line item covers everything from prosthetics (fake body parts), appliances (extra body parts, like heads that fit over your own head), gaping wounds, blood, scraped faces or knees, extra long finger nails, and so on. You need to budget for purchases, design and manufacture, and the time to apply them.

20-05 – 06-07 Make-Up/Hair Supplies

Consult your key people and budget for them.

21-00 Electrical

You'll decide what you need for lighting with your Director, Director of Photography, and Gaffer. They will discuss the creative approach, ordering every light they may need. Then you call the lighting company and make your deal for your grip truck and lighting package.

Equipment houses can recommend gaffers and grips for your production, which may eliminate hiring additional people from the rental house to watch over equipment or drive the truck. It's worth asking for these things when shopping for your equipment needs. Generally, however, the Director of Photography will have a list of favorite Gaffers and Key Grips.

21-01 Gaffer

This person heads the Electric Department, translating the requests of the Director of Photography into specific orders for renting grip and lighting equipment and setting up lights, light rigging, and all electrical functions for the set.

Consult regularly with your Gaffer (and indeed with all department heads) to troubleshoot for upcoming situations. They can alert you to potential delays, as well as the need for more or less manpower or equipment. In fact, we've found it helpful to have one or more small, informal production meetings in the course of a day, in which a few department heads gather for a few minutes to hash things out for the next few hours or the next day.

$$$

Rates for Gaffers are $300 to $450 per 10-hour day.

21-02 Best Boy

The Gaffer's first assistant. The Best Boy can also keep track of what instruments are used from a truck, so that when he returns the truck to the lighting equipment company, he makes sure you are not charged for instruments not used (if that was your deal), and not charged for any damage you did not cause. It may cost you an extra day to have him do this, but on large lighting orders it's probably worth it.

$$$

Rates go from $250 to $350 per 10-hour day.

21-03 Electricians

They rig, place, operate, and strike all the lighting gear. Rates go from $200 to $300 per day.

21-04 Additional Labor

If you have a complicated electrical setup, consider bringing in a separate crew of electricians ahead of your shoot crew. That way you virtually plug in and shoot when the time comes. The cost will more than offset what you'll pay your regular company to sit around for a few hours waiting — and losing momentum.

21-06 Equipment Rentals (Lighting /Grip Package)

Your lighting package may be a portable Omni kit for talking heads (usually comes with the camera package), a medium-size 2-ton grip truck with a full complement of small to large lights and grip gear, or a 40-foot trailer with enough candlepower to light a square dance in a cornfield.

Often you can strike a deal where a certain minimum is paid for the basic grip truck and lighting package. You are then charged an additional rate for any other equipment that you use. This way you are assured of having all the equipment you need, but you don't have to pay for it unless you use it. This does not apply to large items, like HMI lights, because an equipment house won't want to tie these up on spec. HMI's are usually charged out by the hour or by the day.

You will be asked for a certificate of insurance, which you get by calling your broker. Sometimes you can hire an "approved" freelance gaffer known by the rental house and get better rates. (If the equipment houses know that competent people will be using their gear, they know it will receive less wear and tear.)

$$$

For a 2-ton grip truck figure $250 per day (plus mileage outside a given radius); larger trucks go up to $800 or more. Then you add a per instrument charge for bigger lights. A complete lighting package for a TV movie can easily run up a $35,000 bill for three to four weeks of rentals.

21-07 Additional Lighting and Equipment

You may find that even though you rent a fully equipped studio there will still be some lights that your gaffer wants to rent. Use this line item for any miscellaneous lighting expenditures.

Additional equipment could include special riggings, dimmers, or light tents. Sometimes the camera operator will own lights that can be rented as part of his or her package at bargain basement rates.

21-08 Generator/Driver

Whenever the power needs of your lights (or other equipment, like power tools) exceed what's available, you rent a generator. The Gaffer or Best Boy will tell you what kind and size to get, and how long it will have to operate. Some are self-contained in vans, others are small or large monsters that are towed in and left, or included in a 40-foot trailer/production truck. You will need a Driver/Operator, which on small shoots may be your Best

Boy. On big shoots it will be a separate person. You'll also need fuel to feed the monsters, based on how many hours of running you expect.

$$$

▶ The smallest generators are in the 350 amps range. They can be hitched to a tow, and either delivered by the company, or picked up by someone on the production team. Average price is $335/day, plus about $30 in fuel for 10 hours of shooting.

▶ Mid-range units are 750 amps at $575/day, plus fuel at $75-$100/day.

▶ Larger units are 1,200 amps at $675 day, plus fuel at $120/day.

▶ Major features might need multiple units and/or a 2,500 amp unit pulled by a semi at $850/day plus fuel at $250/day, and an operator at $250/day.

22-00 Camera

22-01 Director of Photography

Key position — reports to the Director — translates the Director's vision into "paintings of light and shadow." DPs in film must know cameras, lenses, lights, film stock, basic editing, must match lighting and camera direction scene to scene, and must sometimes save the boss from his or her own ineptness. The same is true for the DP in digital cinematography or video, but minus the film stock. (Many DPs know film, video and digital cinematography — but ask.)

The DP's job encompasses both the physical and creative aspects of production. Vision and ability to work quickly and smoothly with others is key to the success of a production.

There are four main types of DPs:

▶ Dramatic (TV episodic, TV movies, features, commercials, music videos)

▶ Documentary/Industrial (operates the camera, works with small crew)

▶ Aerial (in charge of air-to-air and air-to-ground photography)

▶ Underwater (working alone or with full crew)

In all of the above, the DP orders the type of camera and film stock, tape or digital format, is involved with the selection of the lighting/grip package, and checks the actors (hair, make-up, costumes), sets, props, etc., for photographic consistency. The DP supervises the camera crews, lighting, sets the camera positions (with the Director), orders any special mounts (for boats, cars, planes, helicopters), and orders dollies and cranes. After shooting, the DP supervises the timing (color correction) and telecine (film to tape transfer), and screens dailies for quality control.

In pre-production, especially for narrative projects, it's wise for the Director to spend enough time with the DP to work out not only a general creative approach, a camera test (plus post-production workflow), and location surveys, but also shot lists for each scene. The shot lists should be prioritized into "must haves" and "expendables." This list must be shared with the 1st AD before he or she makes up the daily schedules.

$$$

DPs earn about $1,000 per day for TV movies and most features. For commercials and music videos the rate can vary from $750 to $3,000 per day, with $1,500 being average. For documentary work, a DP might also operate the camera for a day rate of $450 to $600 per day, which may or may not include the camera package.

Desperate Measures

There is at absolute minimum a prep day, a scout, and sometimes travel. Try to negotiate half-day rates for travel, which is pretty standard, but ask the DP to throw in some prep or scouting at no extra charge. It's worth a try.

22-02 Camera Operator

For film cameras, this person operates the camera, and is the one who looks through the camera during the shot, carrying out what the DP wants in composition, movement, and focus. He or she has many other duties, such as checking the film gate for dust, checking the film thread on new rolls, checking the F-stop, and supervising the transportation of the camera.

For video shoots when the DP is not also the Camera Operator, this person operates the video camera, setting the white balance, replacing batteries, replacing tapes or memory cards, and so forth. In studio situations, with the big cameras on moving pedestals, the Camera Operator follows the orders of the Director in the Control Room to change position, frame shots, and focus.

$$$

Rates for film Camera Operators go from $400 to $500 per 12-hour day.

Video shooters get from $300 to $450 per 12-hour day.

22-03 First Assistant Camera (Film)

The First Assistant Camera Operator is also called the Focus Puller, at least in England. In addition to following focus on shots that require it, the First AC also maintains camera reports of takes and footage used, makes sure the right film stock is in the camera, and generally hovers over the camera with the rest of the camera crew like worker bees attending the queen.

The First AC may also be a camera repair wizard, and it's not a bad idea to have someone on set who can fix the thing when it goes down.

The First AC will also need to be hired for a half to full day on each side of principal photography to check the film package, make sure that all the parts are there and that they work, and transport the equipment. There is no First AC in video.

$$$

Figure $300 to $415 per 12-hour day.

22-04 Second Assistant Camera (Film)

This person is yet another attending to the camera's every need. He or she loads film magazines, logs and labels film cans, and often works the slate or clapper.

$$$

Figure $250 to $385 per 12-hour day.

22-05 Digital Imaging Technician (DIT)

Digital cameras are so much in use, and there is so much peripheral knowledge associated with them, that this position was created to insure technical acceptability of the digital image. The DIT supervises setup, operation, troubleshooting and maintenance of digital cameras, in-camera recording, waveform monitors, monitors, recording devices, driver software, and related equipment. The DIT must also understand digital audio acquisition, timecode, and how they integrate into post environments.

$$$

The DIT is an IATSE designation, currently $385/day, $1763/week.

22-06 Still Photographer

Production stills (sets, make-up, wardrobe, continuity) are different from publicity shots. The production stills are usually shot by the respective department person. So this category is really about publicity stills.

There is a difference between shooting "documents" of the production and taking shots that can be used on posters. The former case involves a photographer who roams the set and shoots during rehearsals. For the latter case, the photographer usually sets up in a professional studio.

Then there's the question of who owns the rights. Some photographers want the rights on their own negatives so they can make money selling to magazines and newspapers. (With all the movie stars around there's good pickin's.) The producer, however, wants control of the photos to promote the film. There are various ways to work this out. Sometimes the producer owns the material, but the photographer receives money from magazine publication. However, many publicity shots from films are supplied free to the media, so the photographer would not receive any remuneration. Here the photographer may retain foreign rights if that is agreeable to all parties.

If the photographer retains some publishing rights, he or she may accept a lower day rate. After all, the photographer is being granted special access to movie stars, and may make money by selling to the publishers.

Professional still photographers have rates as varied as those of cinematographers, and are often based on experience and reputation.

$$$

To get high-quality, original work you may expect to pay $150 to $350 per 12-hour day or more for a top-notch documenting photographer, and $500 to $2,000 for a studio shoot, just for the photographer. The studio itself may be $500 to $1,000 per day. Your photographer will prepare a budget for you to include fees, studio and equipment, make-up and hair, lights, backdrops, props, film, processing, prints, and so on.

22-07 Camera Package (Film/Video/Digital)

Film Cameras

Are you shooting in 35mm or 16mm? Your Producer, Director, DP, possibly your distributor, and especially your budget will make that decision. Once made, everything you do from here on — the camera package, film stock, lab and processing, and film editing — will be affected by that choice.

In either 35mm or 16mm, your camera package will consist of a specific camera, either with sound or not ("MOS"), plus magazines, matte boxes, optical accessories, batteries, lenses, filters, heads, tripods, and the like. Your DP will make the list. Naturally the price goes up the more you add on — just like options on a new car.

Here are some rates for various cameras, just to give you some idea of prices. For larger shoots, you may want a second camera body, both as a reserve for distant location work, and for simultaneous shooting with your first camera. In the latter instance, hire a second camera operator and First AC to run it.

$$$

The rates given are by the day, but if you rent by the week, in most houses, you multiply the day rate by three, giving you seven days of shooting for the price of three. Longer term rentals give you even more leverage, so negotiate!

35mm Sound Cameras

Panavision, Arriflex, and Moviecam are three standards. We use Arriflex as examples here:

Arri 535A $600/day
Arri 435 $700/day
Arri 35 BL4S $350/day

35mm MOS Cameras
> Arri 35-3 PL $265/day
> Arri 35 IIIC PL $215/day
> Arri 35 IIC PL $120/day

16mm Sound Cameras
> Arri 16 SR3 $325/day
> Arri 16 SR2 $180/day

A TV movie or feature will budget $6,000 to $7,000 per week for an entire camera package, including lens kit and accessories — more for a second camera.

Lens Kit

Special jobs require special lenses. Most DPs will want a set of prime lenses (fixed focal lengths) and a high-quality zoom lens, plus quite possibly a super-wide angle lens. These are add-ons to the camera package. Zoom lenses fetch from $100 to $375 in 35mm, and from $75 to $150 in 16mm. Prime lenses can go from $60 to $300 in 35mm, and from $40 to $300 in 16mm.

Camera Supplies

The camera will also require expendables like camera tape, filters, canned air, packing foam, and marking pens. Figure $200 to $400 for the first day and $50 to $100 for subsequent days, which will be ample for most documentary shoots. Sometimes this equipment can be rented from the First AC or Camera Operator for greater savings, since you pay only for what is used.

Digital Video Cameras

Digital Video is a different animal. We are recording images electronically rather than on a film emulsion. We can record those images onto videotape, or onto a digital file-based media, such as a memory card, disc or hard drive.

Since the explosion of digital video there are literally hundreds of different video cameras, everything from cell phones to flip cameras to prosumer camcorders at every price point from $200 to $10,000 to professional cameras from $1,000 to $60,000 to digital single-lens-reflex (DSLR) still cameras that shoot great full HD video.

Camera manufacturers have no interest in standardizing formats, so the free-for-all continues. It's chaotic, but interesting. And for producers (particularly of lower budget, independent projects with fewer resources), be they narrative or non-fiction, it presents a problem: how do I choose what camera to use and what format to shoot on? Are some HD formats better for acquisition and editing than others?

HD Camera Formats

The answer to the last question is yes. In fact some formats are created just for editing. Let's review some of the more popular HD camera formats and see how they can work with some popular editing formats. The choice of camera format and the choice of editing format should be made with compatibility in mind. One of the first things to look at is *data transfer rates*.

One way to compare video formats is to measure the amount of data they have as the data move from point A to point B. This is called the *data transfer rate*, and the unit of measure is megabits per second (*Mbps* or *Mb/s*). It's like water through a pipe. If you have a lot of water in a big tank to get through a narrow pipe in limited time, you have a problem. Replace the narrow pipe with a wider pipe (or one with higher *bandwidth*) and voila, you have faster flow, higher *data transfer rate*, higher *throughput*.

A word about the unit of measure, megabits per second (Mb/s). Another common way of expressing data rate is megabytes per second (MB/s). Note the capital B as we move from bits to bytes. There are eight bits to a byte, so a megabyte is eight times bigger than a megabit.

Why do we care about data transfer rates?
▸ The water in the pipe is like the quantity of data. Different video formats have higher or lower rates. The size of the pipe is like the type of connection you have to your hard drive, e.g. FireWire 400, FireWire 800, SATA, SATA RAID etc. Every project has unique needs. If you have all the time in the world and you can hang out while water chokes its way through your narrow pipe, ok. But you may need a faster connection, and more storage, and the greater safety offered by RAID 5 for example. And you can calculate all this during pre-production and put it into your budget.

Data transfer rates are not the only criterion by which to assess compatibility between camera format and editing format, but the topic in depth is beyond the scope of this book. Suffice to say it warrants a talk and a test during pre-production between DP and Editor. These are some popular HD editing formats that permit excellent quality with manageable data rates:

Avid DNxHD
Apple ProRes (currently a family of five codecs: Proxy, LT, 422, 422HQ, 4444)
Cineform

Now on to HD camera formats, moving generally from more highly compressed to less compressed.

AVCHD

AVCHD is a consumer high definition digital video camera recorder format announced jointly by Panasonic and Sony. AVCHD cameras are small and inexpensive, and the picture quality is excellent for its size and price. It supports full 1920x1080 HD and 1080i, 720p and 1080p. Like HDV, it is a long GOP format and uses a strong MPEG-4 compression to get all that video into very small files. It is 8 bit depth with a 4:2:0 color space. See the full specs at *www.avchd-info.org*.

HDV

Depending on the camera you select, HDV is either a tape-based (DV) or memory card-based format that you import into your computer with FireWire or in the case of the card, directly. It supports 1440 x 1080 resolution, which is less than full HD (1920 x 1080). If you are using DV tape, yes, you must digitize all that footage in real time. On the other hand, you have tapes, hard copies of your source footage. Protect them. HDV is a long GOP (Group of Pictures) format (see Chapter 4 High Definition), which means it has some limitations when it comes to shooting or panning on fast action. It has a color space of 4:2:0, and a bit depth of 8. Talk with your DP about its strengths and weaknesses for your project.

The data transfer rate for DV is about 3.5 MB/sec, or 28 Mb/s (3.5x8). The data transfer rate via FireWire 400 is about 400 Mb/s, so DV (the water) fits inside FW400 (the pipe) with room to spare. One hour of DV video will take up about 13 GB of storage on a hard drive. (Remember to always keep about 20% of your hard drive space free for optimum function and safety.) So if you have 50 hours of documentary footage, 13 x 50 = 650 GB. You'd be wise to store that on a 1 TB drive to allow for the 20% (200 GB) of headroom, and then some.

FireWire Tip: Another thing to remember about data rate is that because FireWire is hubbed, the speed of transfer is always slowed down to roughly the rate of the lowest number. So if I plug a FW400 hard drive and a FW800 hard drive into my computer, both will sing along at the slower FW400 speed. The workaround for that is a separate card for my FW800.

There are different ways to edit HDV, each with advantages and disadvantages. The one you choose should match the needs of your project. For example, HDV can be edited in its native form, but if you have a lengthy project, the "conforming" time at the end of the process will take many hours, depending on the horsepower of your system. "Conforming" means the project needs to be recompressed to create the new GOP (Group of Pictures) structure to output to HDV. See this article by Tim Kolb for the Creative Cow called Demystifying HDV Workflows at *http://library.creativecow.net/articles/kolb_tim/demystifying_hdv.php*

There are excellent "professional" HDV cameras in the $2,500 to $18,000 range and some even higher. The difference in cost is attributed to the size of the CCD or CMOS chips, the quality of the glass in the lens, and overall quality of the lens, lens interchangeability, the variety of features, output choices, video looks, and the ergonomics.

P2/DVC ProHD/AVC-Intra 100

Panasonic makes P2, a solid state memory card for direct acquisition. Your images and sound go right onto the re-usable card. Cards come in different capacities (16GB, 32GB, 64GB), and they're expensive (over $2,000 for the 64GB). Panasonic has a newer card for less money and a shorter lifespan.

DVC ProHD is a codec used with both DVC ProHD cassette tape and with the P2 memory cards. It uses Intraframe compression (unlike HDV, which uses GOP), it has a color space of 4:2:2, and a bit depth of 8.

AVC-Intra 100 is a codec used with both DVC Pro HD cassette tape and with the P2 memory cards. It uses Intraframe compression (unlike HDV, which uses GOP), it has a color space of 4:2:2, and a bit depth of 10. It can also capture the full 1920x1080 HD raster in 1080p or 1080i systems, and the full 1280x720 in 720p systems.

146

There are a number of Panasonic cameras using the P2 format in different price ranges from $5,000 on up to the latest Varicams at $60,000.

Final Cut Pro, Media Composer, Premiere Pro and Edius all support DVC ProHD and AVC-Intra 100. Each has a data rate of 100 Mb/s, and requires storage space of 60 GB per hour of video.

Sony XDCAM

This is Sony's (and JVC's) tapeless format, which uses solid state (SxS) memory cards. The XDCAM EX supports full HD resolution — 1920x1080.

For editing, Final Cut Pro, Media Composer, Premiere Pro and Edius and Sony Vegas all support XD CAM.

Panavision Genesis

Genesis can record either to the Panavision Solid State Recorder SSR-1, or to the Sony HDCAM-SR videotape recorder in 10 bit un-compressed 4:4:4 or 4:2:2 color space.

The Red One

The Red's Super 35mm sensor provides 4K (up to 30 fps), 3K (up to 60 fps) and 2K (up to 120 fps) capture, with color space in 12 bit native RAW. It most reliably records to compact flash, using a proprietary Red CF Module. Other options are a Red Drive (RAID), and Red RAM, a solid state flash drive. Also, the Red Rocket card allows for real time rendering, a boon not only in editing, but in the ability to view dailies later the same day the footage was shot.

DSLR cameras

Both still photographers and videographers love getting HD (or sometimes "almost-HD") from the very portable Digital Single Lens Reflex (DSLR) cameras that shoot both stills and HD video. There are several on the market. Latest in the line from Canon is the EOS 7D at about $1,700. Compared to about $2,700 for Canon's 5D Mark II, this is a good deal. The 7D shoots in 24p (29.97) in 1920x1080 video. The sensor is slightly smaller than a full 35mm SLR sensor (as in the 5D), but is still five and a half times larger than 2/3" professional HD cameras.

The larger sensors provide better sensitivity to light, more clarity of image, wider lens possibilities and less depth of field, which shooters want for that cinematic look. It accepts a wide array of excellent lenses from Canon.

In HD mode, the 7D records 1920x1080 H.264 MPEG4 video at 23.98, 29.97 and 25p and 50p "PAL" format. You can also shoot 60p in 1280 x 720. File sizes give you 12 minutes of recording 24p 1080 video.

Also available is Panasonic's Lumix DMC-GH1. Technically, since the GH1 is not single-lens reflex, it's not a true DSLR camera.

The GH1 works with many lenses on the market through a series of adapters.

The format provides four times the image area of a 2/3" sensor. This means that depth of field is close to what you get with a 35mm motion picture camera, if you use good glass.

The GH1 also shoots in 24p, the best format if going for a film-out at the end of the post process. Some of the DSLR cameras out there only shoot at true 30p (not 29.97fps), and the transition from true 30p to 24p can look funky for film-out. Even so, it's necessary to shoot within exposure brackets on the GH1, avoiding overexposure and extreme motion. The images are heavily compressed, so get them as close as possible to right in the camera, since color correction isn't much of an option.

Capture can work with SD cards, which are then converted via CineForm software into ProRes 422 files ready for Final Cut Pro.

One of the benefits of any DSLR or similar camera's small size is the ability to shoot almost incognito in any location, especially in cities where crowds often gather to watch filmmaking. As these cameras become more popular, after-market products are showing up, like rigs to make shooting with such a small camera a bit more friendly.

Audio for DSLR

To date, the cameras have mini connectors, which are not ideal for the daily grind of filmmaking. For best results, record audio with a double system. One possibility is the Zoom H4n digital 4 Track sound recorder, using SD/SDHC cards with XLR inputs for the mic. Plug in headphones to monitor and sync on set with a clapboard. Then drag the audio files into your edit program and sync to the clapboard. And just because the camera is small, don't cheap out on yourself by eliminating your sound person. A good production sound Mixer will save you many headaches and dollars in post.

$$$

As stated above, retail prices for digital cameras run the gamut, from $200 to $60,000. Check out retailers on the web, like *www.bhphotovideo. com*. The larger video equipment houses usually rent a few cameras in each expense category, from prosumer to professional.

Producers and Directors agonize over camera formats, and that's okay. We suggest watching projects similar to yours that you like. Contact the production company and find out what camera they used, and ask about the editing process. You can also see a good range of products and get a lot of tech specs at *www.bhphotovideo.com*. Their prices are usually pretty good too, but definitely shop around.

The Camera Assessment Series

In 2009, the American Society of Cinematographers (ASC) and the Producers Guild of America (PGA), staged an elaborate assessment of the current generation of digital motion picture cameras and one 35mm camera. They used the following cameras — Arri D21, Panasonic HPX3700, Sony F23, Sony F35, Panavision Genesis, Thomson Viper, the RED ONE, and the Arri 435 film camera — representative of the traditional celluloid medium. These cameras were chosen because they all capture 4:4:4, 10 bit images, and deliver 4:4:4 10-bit DPX files for a digital intermediate (DI) and film-outs. The results show the various considerations that must be brought to light when selecting a camera. It's not just aesthetics, it's cost, and especially workflow in both production and post. The report, called the Camera Assessment Series (CAS), can be seen at *www.theasc.com*.

Many DP/Operators own their own equipment, and may rent it to you cheaper than an equipment house. The advantage of going through a house, however, is maintenance or camera replacement in the time it takes the guy to get back to you. If you do go through a house, the weekly rate is usually four times the daily rate. (For monthly, figure 12 rental days.) If you shoot for an entire week or longer, you can save some money. Or, for short shoots, you can rent the camera on a Friday afternoon and return it Monday morning for a one-day rate. Many rental houses will give a discount of 10% to 25% or more, especially if your camera operator or DP is a preferred or repeat customer. Always ask for the biggest discount; even if you don't get it, they'll still give you something off the original bid.

22-10 Steadicam Operator and Equipment (Film and Video)

The Steadicam is an outlandish contraption of springs, counter-weights, and shock absorbers worn by a Steadicam Operator. The camera is attached to it, and now the whole rig can walk, walk fast, run, climb or descend stairs, and generally move around all the while delivering a steady, jerk-free image.

$$$

There's a real knack to it, so Steadicam Operators get paid a bit more than an average Camera Operator — about $500 per 12-hour day or more for real athletes of the genre.

Most Operators own and maintain their own Steadicam rig, and charge around $500 to $750 per day for the equipment.

22-12 Teleprompter/Operator (Film and Video)

Direct to camera performers (such as news anchors) don't memorize lines, so teleprompters fill the bill. They are standard equipment at most TV studios, and can be fitted to any studio or field camera (even to small Mini DV or HDV), as well as a 35mm or 16mm film camera. When attached to the camera, you have a through-the-lens effect, meaning the actor or reporter reads the lines looking right at you, making you wonder how this person can be so eloquent and remember all those words.

When you want the talent to look at another person and pretend to be eloquent, the Operator places a monitor with the words just over the other person's shoulder and out of camera range.

$$$

Rates for Operator and Teleprompter run about $370 to $400 per 12-hour day. Some companies offer half-day rates as well.

22-13 Video Assist/Operator (Film)

A video tap is a piece of equipment that attaches to the film camera's reflex system, allowing you to see a video image through the lens of the film camera on a separate monitor. This is good for the Director, the

DP, other crew, and nervous advertising account execs (when they aren't schmoozing or napping) to see what's being shot. If you want, you can add digital video assist to the package, so you can play back what you've shot at variable speed frame rates. Picture and sound are usually recorded on a hard drive, or MiniDV. Agonizing over the playback of each take is a great way to waste time, so don't get suckered in.

$$$

Tap and assist systems vary on the camera type and record capability. The camera portion is supplied by the camera rental house.

Prices average around $550 for the package and $550 for the technician for a 10-hour day.

There are companies that specialize in video assist. They supply playback services, and other support equipment such as accurate slow motion video playback from a high-speed film camera.

22-14 Aerial Photography

Shooting from airplanes and helicopters requires some specialized personnel and equipment. Pilots not experienced in the precision flying needed for this job can waste your time. The pilot is also the person who will set up the aircraft, and walk you through the process, so for safety as well as professionalism, go with someone experienced in aerial photography.

You'll hear talk of the "Tyler mount" as an indispensable piece of equipment. It is a camera mount, usually rented from the camera rental house, that stabilizes the camera and reduces vibration. Tyler is one system. Wescam is another.

$$$

Figure $600 to $800 per day for the mount alone, plus the camera package (see above).

Expenses for aerial shooting vary on the camera package, the type of aircraft (jet helicopter, Cessna etc.), the experience of the pilot, and how long you shoot. Some samples:

Pilot $750 to $1,500 per 12-hour day
Camera Operator $1,000 to $1,500 per 12-hour day
Jet Ranger helicopter $1,500 for 3 hours
Cessna $100 per hour

22-15 Underwater and Topside Water Photography

Here's another specialty area for professionals only. Some underwater filming experts (Marine Coordinators) own and maintain their own film and video cameras, packages, housings, and some lights, as well as boats and dive equipment. Others are more freelance.

Michael says, "*I produced an underwater special called* Dolphin Adventures. *We had two underwater cameramen and one topside cameraman. Working underwater has its own very complex set of do's and don'ts. Because our underwater guys were highly experienced they recommended numerous shots that gave the editor tremendous coverage with which to work.*"

For topside work, Coordinators know boat behavior and can make it work the way you want for your shots. They also coordinate the water scene for safety and look. They know the various insurance rates and Coast Guard regulations.

$$$

You can spend anywhere from $2,500 to $75,000 or more for a day on or under water, but here are some sample prices:

Marine Coordinator $500 to $750 per 12-hour day
Underwater camera operators $700 to $900 per 12-hour day
Crew people add $180 to standard rates
Underwater camera package $1,000 to $1,200 per day

22-16 Motion Control

There's two kinds of motion control. In special effects work, motion control photography is a technique that enables precise repetition of camera movements controlled by computers. The images are then usually composited. In this way, you can, for instance, combine green screen with motion control shots of miniatures and composite them into a scene of a giant gorilla having his way with New York. We suggest that kind of photography go into category 32-00 Visual Effects.

The other motion control is more familiar to viewers of PBS. If you have still photos to be shot, go to a post-production house for their motion control (sometimes called Animatics) camera system, or talk with your editor about software applications. With these, you scan in your image, and the editor can clean it up (or distress it if that's what you want) digitally, and then make "camera moves" within the digital domain.

In some post houses, the motion-control camera is a contraption with a computer-run servomechanism. Its video camera points down at a table where you put your stills. The operator programs pans, zooms, and any camera moves along the still's x and y axis.

Bring in your script and actually read the narration copy that will go over the still. That helps you plan the speed of the move and what parts of the still to focus on as you move.

$$$

These cameras and operators command hefty fees, but the look is usually worth it. Expect to pay from $200 to $325/hour (includes the operator) plus stock. If you rehearse reading the copy over the stills, and make notes, you can shorten the session considerably.

22-20 Video Truck

When your show needs multiple cameras and you can't shoot in a studio with a complete camera setup, you call a video truck company. They send complete video studios on wheels to sports events, concerts, even situation comedies set up in converted warehouses. If you are shooting a concert and need multitrack audio, ask if they have a sound truck, or if they can recommend one.

Once you have a bid from a company you like, ask them to send someone over to the location with you for a technical survey. They'll help you work out how much cable to lay out, best places to load in equipment, where to put the generator, possible camera positions, and so forth.

$$$

Video trucks come in different sizes, so prices will vary. And the equipment menu is a la carte, so if you're shooting a sit-com with four cameras at $550 each, it'll be a lot less than shooting at Dodger Stadium with nine cameras. For average situations, expect to pay between $7,500 and $10,000 for a day's work.

22-25 Video Studio or Truck Crew

Whether you're in a video studio or video truck, you'll need the same crew (Director, DP, Grip and Electric crew are in their respective categories elsewhere). Here's the rundown with day rates for a 10-hour day:

Camera Operators $350 – $450

Utilities (people who pull cable and are generally useful) $250 – $300

Audio $375 – $450

Audio Assist (A-2) $300 – $375

Boom Operator (Audio) $300 – $375

Technical Director (crew chief and camera switcher) $400 – $450

Video Control (quality control of video picture) $375 – $450

Video Tape Operator (runs record machines/changes reels) $250 – $350

A few other crew people unique to video stage or video truck production:

Lighting Director $400 – $500 (reports to DP or lacking same, creates the lighting)

Associate Director (DGA) $350 – $680 (in Control Room, with Director, readies shots for Director)

Stage Manager (DGA) (readies and cues all talent) $320 – $570

Video Field Package aka "Sky Pack"

When you do not need a video truck, but you do need more than one camera, you rent a Field Package through an equipment house. This consists of your cameras (usually no more than three or four), record machines (either on-board the cameras or separate decks), possibly a field switcher so the Director can cut the show on the spot, and a video package of scopes and paintbox for quality control. For this setup, you may or may not need all of the above crew, depending on the size of your shoot. Call your video camera rental company for a bid.

Desperate Measures

If the above is too rich, you can also shoot stills by putting them on clean, black art cards with graphics spray cement, place them on an easel, and shoot them with your rental camera. The problem is, the tripod and head may not be smooth enough for really good work (remember, you're working in extreme close-up, and every camera shake will show). You can get smoother heads at slightly more expense — talk it over with your camera operator in advance. Or, do the work yourself in your editing program.

23-00 Sound

If the sound you record in the field is the sound you'll use in the master, it had better be good. Audiences tolerate lousy picture quality if the story is gripping, but they quickly become annoyed with bad sound. Feature films do a lot of ADR work (Automatic Dialogue Replacement) in audio post to correct problems with recordings in the field. Sometimes those problems are unavoidable, but a good mixer will help prevent those that are avoidable. ADR is expensive and time consuming, so save money and headaches now by heeding the advice of your Sound Mixer.

23-01 Mixer

Good ones have an uncanny ability to hear what the rest of us ignore. Background sounds like air conditioning (especially when it cuts on and off, causing havoc in editing), dripping faucets, chattering squirrels or distant school children all land on the Mixer's sensitive eardrums. Even camera noise can sometimes cause a problem. And when your Mixer says she needs to get "room tone" for every set-up, back her up and get it. Why? Because even though it means everyone on the whole set has to stand there in COMPLETE SILENCE for 30 seconds — impatient as hell — if you don't get it, guess who will be paying a sound editor to build it frame by frame at $75/hour?

$$$

Rates for Mixers average $300 to $550 per 10-hour day.

23-02 Boom Operator

These people develop amazing triceps from holding aloft a microphone attached to a "fish pole" for hours at a time. They are also good (hopefully) at keeping the mike out of the frame, yet as close as possible to the talent, and properly pointed. While the job may look easy, it requires skill and constant attention. A weak link here between the speaker's voice and the microphone can put you in a tight spot in post. Hire a good one.

On sound stages, the Boom Ops handle the mechanical Microphone Booms.

$$$

Rates average $250 to $350 per 10-hour day.

23-04 Sound Package (Film and Video)

Film

In film, the Sound Package is normally a digital recorder, such as the Sound Devices recorder 702T two-track with timecode, or 744T four-track, or the Edirol R4-Pro four-track with timecode, plus assorted microphones (including wireless radio mics), a stereo mixing panel, mic boompoles, batteries, and baffles. There may be some who still record on analog tape recorders, such as the workhorse Nagra 4.2 with timecode. Analog can be used when you are editing on film and require the 1/4-inch production sound to be transferred to Mag Film. Timecode-based systems are used when you want to transfer your film footage to videotape, and edit on a nonlinear system all the way through. The timecode machine generates timecode onto the 1/4-inch audio tape, and displays it on a "smart slate," a clapstick with a timecode window display. In the telecine transfer process, the sound and picture are synced and are timecode accurate.

Digital machines like the Fostex PD4 or FR2 transfer audio files in WAV format to the editing computer through a USB cable.

One note about recording sound on an analog machine versus a digital one, according to Fred Ginsburg, C.A.S. Ph.D., president and CEO of Equipment Emporium Inc. in Mission Hills, CA and Equipmentemporium.com. "When you record too hot on a Nagra, the audio distorts gradually. But in the digital domain, overmodulation is unacceptable and yields horrible results. On the other hand, if you record too low on a Nagra, the sound suffers from inherent tape hiss and system noise. Digital is relatively free from that problem. Therefore, when recording in digital, it is wiser to record low and allow yourself plenty of headroom in case of loud peaks. Record your reference tone around -18 to -24, and consider that your average level for normal dialog."

$$$

Nagra and similar Film Sound Packages go for around $200 to $400 per day, depending on the accessories. Analog packages should be $50 to $100 cheaper than timecode. Don't forget audio stock. Digital packages go for around $375 – $475 per day depending on accessories. Check out the Digital Feature Budget scenario at 23-04 to see what's in a typical feature audio package.

Video

In video, the Mixer records sound directly to the videotape or digital medium, so you need everything in the Film Sound Package, except the recorder. The mixer unit and other equipment can be rented through the camera house and included in the camera package, although some Mixers insist on bringing their own gear because they know they can rely on it.

If shooting MiniDV, or with any low-end HDV camera, make sure the camera has XLR audio inputs, or get a Mini-to-XLR adapter.

When pressed for money, many documentary filmmakers opt to put a shotgun mic on the camera and skip the Sound Mixer/Boom Op altogether — or worse, just use the mic that comes with the camera. Our suggestion is, if possible, do not use the camera mic. Learn about the different kinds of microphones and hire a Mixer who can also function as a Boom Operator. Good sound will actually take you further than bad sound and good picture. For some great articles on production sound, see *www.equipmentemporium.com*.

$$$

The package ranges between $50 and $200 per day, depending on specific equipment.

Sound Truck

You've just been asked to produce a Rock 'n' Roll Holiday Special for TV, so you'll want to find an audio services company that rents sound trucks. If the music is to be remixed later, you want multitrack recording capability — probably up to 48 tracks for this gig. The Mixer will mix the band, orchestra, chorus, and whatever else they throw at you. When the concert is over, you'll remix at a recording studio or post-production sound facility.

If the sound is going out live and you have no time for a remix (now or later), then you can save money because you won't need multitrack recording — only a good audio board to send the mixed stereo sound over to the video truck where it is added to the picture and beamed out to the waiting world.

$$$

Basic rate (with no travel) for a truck plus crew will be in the $5,000 per day range.

23-05-08 Walkie-Talkies/Cell Phones

Now standard issue on shoots big and small, walkies are a pain to lug around, even with belt holsters and headsets, but they are convenient. Whenever you have people spread out (and it's too far to yell), or you have to hold traffic, or cue the stampeding baboons, equip your key people.

$$$

Basic walkies go for about $8 a day, weekly at $17-24.

Cell phones currently rent for about $8/day up to $99/month and 99 cents/minute.

24-00 Transportation

Getting there is half the expense, at least for TV/cable series and movies and features. Moving everything and everyone from location to location is a formidable job. What follows is for TV/cable series and movies and features. For smaller, non-union shoots, your drivers will probably be your crew and PAs.

If you are using Teamsters on your shoot, consult the IATSE rate card job categories, work rules, and rates.

24-01 Transportation Coordinator

This person coordinates the whole enchilada, and hires the Captains and Drivers, and administrates the operation. The Captains report to him, and handle the parking, the moving of vehicles, and so forth.

$$$

Rates: $1,800 to $2,200 five-day week flat rate.

24-02 Drivers

Captains

$1,400 to $1,700 per five-day week.

Drivers

Rates vary on the type of vehicle driven. Some samples by the five-day week:

Auto/Station Wagons/Small Vans	$900 to $1,200
Forklifts/Tractors	$1,000 to $1,300
MaxiVans, Buses	$1,000 to $1,400
Camera Car Driver	$1,400 to $1,700

24-03 Transportation Equipment Rental

The Transportation Coordinator will make the truck rental deals according to your budget. If you're on your own, consult the local production guides.

Star Dressing Room

In the real old days, a nearby barn would do. Now, a mobile home or trailer is often part of the contract negotiations handled by the Casting Director. How big it is reflects the status of the star. Dressing rooms therefore range in size from huge to a shared room in the 3-Room Cast Trailer.

$$$

Some of the larger mobile homes or trailers range from $400 to $900 per week, plus towing or driving costs.

$$$

Here are some typical rates of other vehicles:

Crew Cab	$60/day
Production Van	$300/day
Camera Truck	$90/day 20'
Stake Bed	$100/day

Set Dressing 5 ton	$95/day
Set Dress Van	$65/day
Prop 5 ton	$165/day
Make-Up/Wardrobe	$300/day
Cast Trailer	$120/day
3-Room Cast Trailer	$180/day
Honeywagon (toilet)	$300/day
Gas Truck	$80/day
Maxi Van	$70/day
Water Truck	$200/day
Camera Car	$300/day

Other transportation expenses:
Gas & Oil
Repairs & Maintenance
Honeywagon pumping

25-00 Location Expenses (see Chapter 2 for more on Locations)

25-01 Location Manager

A good Location Manager, after finding the perfect places, makes the deals for the locations, gets permits, police, parking, fire, and approvals for same including those from the neighborhood. He or she also troubleshoots the location during production. The Location Manager may also need an assistant to handle the troubleshooting, while he works ahead of the shooting company to set up the next place.

$$$

Rates are $300 to $400 per 12-hour day, or $1,300 per week for low-budget projects.

25-03 First Aid

A location nurse or other qualified medical person with kit will run around $300 per 12-hour day.

25-04 Fire Officers

Local regulations may require Fire Officers on the set whenever you use any electric lights, but especially if you're using open flame or blowing anything up. Check with the local permit office for details and rates. A Fire Marshal or set Firefighter can run $500 per 12-hour day.

25-05 Security

A Watchman will cost about $100 per 12-hour day, but you and/or your sets and equipment may need 24-hour protection. On a TV/cable series and movie or feature, this figure can run into the thousands.

25-06 Police

Depending on local regulations, you may need police. In some cities they charge you, in others they don't. Check locally with the film commission or permit department. Big city rates can hover around $400 per 12-hour day.

25-07 Permits

Every big city and many small ones have Permit Departments. Since there can be many twists and turns to getting the right permit for your shoot, call them and get the local scoop while you're budgeting — not the day before cameras roll.

25-09 Catering Services

Most caterers are sensitive to the variety of palates and diets on a movie set, and most do a good job of designing a menu. A good menu, therefore, has a meat dish for those who feel cheated without a leg of something, as well as a vegetarian dish, like pasta, and a salad bar for the light eaters, veggies, and dieters.

Most services stock tables and chairs, although there may be a setup charge. You may also need tents, and even heaters if you're shooting a winter scene.

$$$

Caterers charge by the head, with average prices for a two-entree meal being from $10 to $14 per person, with a minimum of 20 or 30 people. They also charge "Server's Fees" or "Setup Fees," so ask about those.

Don't forget to budget for second meals on those days you expect to go long.

Desperate Measures

On low-budget shows, if you don't have enough people to warrant hiring a caterer, pass around the menu from a good local restaurant and have a PA take orders. Or, if it's tighter than that, say for a student film, order in a pizza.

High budget or low, don't overlook where you serve the food. People use meals as a break from the job, and an opportunity for a little fellowship, so keep them warm or cooled, as required, and away from unpleasant distractions like traffic exhaust, barking dogs, or gawking humans. Sometimes, a little quiet music from a boom box helps set the mood.

25-13 Location Office Space Rental

If you are all staying at a hotel, it may be convenient to rent an office or an extra room and have office furniture brought in, or make it part of the overall hotel deal and get the office for free. Another ploy is to rent a motor home or trailer equipped with desks, office gear, and a generator to run lights, computers, copiers, etc. Main occupants are the Production Coordinator and the Production Accountant, with room for the Producer, the UPM and a PA.

$$$

A fancy motor home or trailer decked out as an office rents for about $1,500 per week.

25-17 Location Site Rental Fees

Whether you're shooting the Brooklyn Bridge or your aunt's backyard, allow whatever is appropriate for both fees and permits. If you are going through a location service, or using a Location Manager, they'll apprise you of the likely costs. On private property, the fee might be negotiated for less on prep and wrap days than on shoot days, saving a few dollars.

The price can be anything from a barter agreement (a free DVD of the film in exchange for a few days in someone's apple orchard) to thousands of dollars. In Los Angeles, some homeowners are well used to movie companies, and actually design their homes to attract the lucrative fees. Other places in town, people have been so burned by the local tie-ups and traffic congestion that movies create that you must go through the neighborhood association, obtain signatures of neighbors, and generally pacify the natives before shooting (also see Chapter 2).

26-00 Picture Vehicles/Animals

The vehicles we see in the show — from buckboards to magic buses — are the Picture Vehicles. Animals are animals.

26-01 Animal Trainers

Boss Wrangler

He works with the Stunt Coordinator and Director to map out stunts, and otherwise handles the animal's care, feeding, transportation, shelter, tack, and working conditions. He'll prepare a budget including all of the above.

$$$

Boss Wranglers earn from $300 to $500 per 12-hour day and up in special situations.

Assistants and Wranglers earn from $200 to $300 per 12-hour day.

26-02 Animals

The cost for the critters themselves varies, as you might expect, on their level of expertise. If you want a chimp to sharpen a pencil, and he doesn't know how, you'll be charged to have the trainer teach him.

$$$

Otherwise, here are some sample rates:

Chimpanzee	$600/day
Snakes	$50 – $250/day depending on size
Zebra	$500/day
Tarantula	$50/day
Scorpion	$75/day
Flies	$300 per thousand/day
Horse	$100/day (trained is $300 and up)
Herd of cows	$200 each/day

26-03 Picture Cars

If you need a yellow taxi, armored truck, pink Ferrari, bus, cop car, limousine, or hearse, then you need a picture vehicle rental company. Costs depend on the scarcity and value of the vehicle and whether it will have to be painted, towed, driven by one of their drivers (a "non-performing driver"), and so forth. Different rates often apply for commercials, features and TV. Students should always ask for discounts.

$$$

Some sample day rates:

Contemporary police car	$250
Contemporary taxi	$250
Vintage London cab	$350
Armored car	$750
Cobra	$550

27-00 Film and Lab/Videotape Stock – Production

This category is for the production period only (see 31-00 for Post-Production Videotape/Film and Lab), and therefore includes:

▸ For film: Raw stock.

▸ For film: Lab processing and dailies.

▸ For film to tape editing: Telecine, and video dailies stock.

▸ For video: Various videotape stocks.

▸ For video: Solid state recording media/hard drives/computer peripherals

The prices quoted here are rate card, and tend to be high. As you establish relationships with stock houses, film labs, video and audio post facilities, you'll do much better. Keep shopping around, and keep asking for better prices.

27-01 Motion Picture Raw Stock

The DP decides the film stock, the amount of stock, and the brand — Kodak, Fuji, etc. Prices slip and slide frequently, and depend on quantity.

You'll be buying raw stock for both your First Unit and Additional or Second Unit cameras, and don't forget to add sales tax. When you order your film, ask them to set aside stock with the same batch and emulsion numbers.

As to 16mm vs. 35mm, it's almost always a budget decision. If you expect theatrical release, or you are shooting something that has to look the absolute best, shoot 35mm if you can afford it. Always ask for discounts.

$$$

These are some fairly typical prices for popular film stocks:

35mm

Kodak #5219	$0.58 per foot
Fuji #8573	$0.36 – 0.50 per foot

16mm

Kodak #7205	$0.34 per foot
Fuji #8672	$0.27 per foot

Desperate Measures

Film stock companies sometimes keep "short ends," "long ends," and "re-canned" film stock. Short ends are leftover reels with less than 400 feet per reel (they can be hard to use if they're too short). Long ends have 700 feet or more. Re-canned stock means they may have put the film in the magazine and changed their minds. Long ends and re-cans are used by productions big and small, but there are some possible snags.

As mothers like to say, "Don't touch that, you don't know where it's been." Insist that the film be tested. The good stock houses do this anyway, processing a strip from each can at a lab to check for density levels, scratches, fogging, and edge damage. Testing is also the only way to verify what kind of film is in the can, since cans are often mislabeled or de-labeled in the field.

Also, if you are a student, some film and tape companies provide automatic discounts. If you are a member of Independent Feature Project (IFP), American Film Institute, or the International Documentary Association, ask them about discounts for stock.

27-02 Lab – Negative Prep and Processing

Same story as raw stock — prices vary with labor and stock increases, so get quotes. These prices are rate card, so you can do better. In choosing a lab, whether a big one or a small one, go for impeccable credentials. You really don't want to reshoot hard-earned scenes.

$$$

> Typical processing costs:
>
> | | |
> |---|---|
> | 35mm | $0.12 per foot |
> | 16mm | $0.115 per foot |

27-03 Videotape Stock/Other Media (Production)

Like film, videotape stock and other media prices vary by brand and quantity. Video productions use all manner of video and media to record images and sound, from Hi8 to BetaSP to Digital Betacam (DigiBeta), MiniDV, DVCAM, DVCProHD, HDCAM, optical discs, memory cards, hard drives and more. Choosing your video stock or media depends on which camera you've selected (see 22-07 Video Cameras). Have a conversation with your Director and your DP. What camera and stock or media you use will have an effect not only on the look of the project, but on the cost, and on the method of editing, and any further post-production, like tape-to-film blow up. That's why we have emphasized throughout this book that it's smart to "backward engineer" your project before you shoot. From delivery format backwards work out all the technical details and talk with each key technical person. What are the delivery tech specs for picture and sound? How does that affect editing, color correction, graphics, audio post, up or down conversion, the Edit Decision List, other formats in editing, the frame rate, the stock used, the lighting, etc.? Work all these out beforehand, do a camera test, edit your test footage, and output it just as you plan to do it for real, and you'll catch glitches before they catch you.

These are some common videotape stocks and memory cards used for production.

BetaSP

20 min.	$8.57
30 min.	$9.00
60 min.	$18.00

Digital Betacam

22 min.	$15.34
32 min.	$30.15
64 min.	$26.22

MiniDV

60 min.	$3.40
80 min.	$8.99

DVCAM

    32 min. $9.62

    64 min. $16.49

DVCPro

    33 min. $8.37

    66 min. $11.99

DVCProHD

    126 min. $23.45

HDCAM

You get differing lengths depending on whether you shoot at 24P or 60i, so check with your Director of Photography to calculate how much stock you'll need based on which format. Also, always check to see the maximum load your camera holds. It would be embarrassing to show up on set with a box of 64's when your camera only takes 40's.

    40 min. $41.22

    64 min. $57.23

HDCAM-SR

This format is capable of recording either RGB 4:4:4 or component 4:2:2 at 440 Mb/s, providing higher bandwidth, higher bit depth, and lower compression.

    40/50 min. $72.45

Memory Cards

Panasonic P2 16GB Memory Card	$907
Panasonic P2 32GB Memory Card	$1678
Panasonic P2 64GB Memory Card	$2637
Sony SxS Pro 8GB Memory Card	$486
Sony SxS Pro 16GB Memory Card	$805
Sony PHU60K 60GB Hard Disk Drive	$975

27-04 Film Dailies

These are your workprints. Have the lab quote you up-to-date prices per foot. Don't forget to add stock costs.

    35mm (one light) $0.23 per foot

    16mm (one light) $0.21 per foot

27-05 Sound

While the film lab processes your negative and prints dailies, you take the original production sound to an audio post house to transfer the 1/4 inch audio tape to magnetic (mag) film. The Editor or assistant then syncs the mag film with the film dailies for screening.

$$$

Typical costs for transferring 1/4 inch to mag film: 35mm and 16mm costs $0.05 to $0.09 per foot. Or you can pay a stock charge of around $15 per hour.

Stock:

35mm $7 per 7 inch reel (1200 ft.)

16mm $5 per 5 inch reel (600 ft.)

If you want to have a videocassette made of your dailies, for screening purposes only, you take the mag film over to the lab, where they sync it with the workprint and do a transfer to video.

$$$

For 35mm, a video screening cassette will cost about $.05 a foot. For 16mm it's about $0.125 per foot.

27-08 Telecine

As the name implies, Telecine is the process of transferring filmed images to videotape, usually because you plan to edit on videotape or data files either all the way through to a videotape master, or you plan to edit on a nonlinear system Off-Line, then return to the film negative, conform it to the edited show, and finish the process on film, or scan the selected shots from the negative, and continue the On-Line, color correcting, and other digital manipulation in a Digital Intermediate process. From there, any number of deliverables can result, including a tape master, a film-out, or 35mm print, and digital cinema files for digital projection.

Telecine is done on expensive machines by highly trained people called "Colorists," who "color correct" your images any way you want, from a realistic, balanced look to the color-saturated look in some commercials, to the impressionism seen on music videos. A good colorist can work wonders. Be careful, however, because scene to scene color correction is like the infamous auto repair shop whose motto is, "*We're slow, but we're expensive.*"

Since telecine is so expensive, you want to use it wisely, so there are a number of approaches. Simply put, you can go:

(1) "scene to scene," meaning you'll spend upward of five hours of color correction for every one hour of shot film, getting every scene just right.

(2) "one light," meaning you run the film through telecine without any stopping for color correction. Why? Because all you want at this stage is videotape you can edit with (often called Video Dailies — and don't forget to budget for this stock). Later, you'll do the real color correction on your finished show.

(3) "best light," a cross between the two.

Which one you choose depends on how much material you have to transfer, how much time you have, how much money you have, and what your editing process is. We suggest you review all this with your editing facility and decide on a plan.

Here are some examples of how others handle the process.

▶ A commercial producer might do a one light film to tape transfer to DigiBeta, edit Off-Line on a nonlinear system, then cut the original negative into a "select reel" of all the best takes. The select reel is then transferred scene to scene, to a high-end stock like D5 or HDCAM-SR, and the commercial is finished On-Line.

▶ A TV movie or series producer might do a best light transfer to DigiBeta, and whatever the master format is (HDCAM for example). They then edit Off-Line, and go directly to On-Line using the best light HDCAM as a playback source. Now they have an edited master that is not color corrected. To get the color right, they now do a tape-to-tape color correction in Telecine. Since they are editing on HDCAM, a digital format, there is no discernible loss of picture quality by going down a generation.

By the way, in film productions, your production sound will have been recorded on a timecode recorder that puts timecode to the DAT audio tape. In Telecine, the sound is then synced to the picture for the transfer from film to tape.

For other discussions of post-production, see Chapter 2 under the subheading "Post-Production." In this chapter see Editorial (30-00), Post-Production Film and Lab (31-00), and Digital Intermediates in (32-00) Optical Effects/Digital Intermediates

$$$

Prep and Clean Negative for Telecine:
35mm and 16mm
$25 per 1,000 feet Lab Roll

Rates for Video Dailies (one light):
Budget 5:1 ratio for best-light, sync sound dailies with flex file
35mm to DigiBeta or DVCam @ $200.00 per facility hour or about
$.19 per foot
16mm to DigiBeta or DVCam @ $200.00 per facility hour or about
$.48 per foot
(Many places will have a minimum, say around $100.00. Stock is additional.)

Scene to Scene Telecine Color Correction:
35mm or 16mm to Standard Definition DigiBeta @ $300.00 – $400.00
per facility hour
35mm or 16mm to HDCAM or HDCAM-SR @ $500.00 – $700.00
per facility hour

How much time do you allow for color correction? (You can really punch a hole in your budget if you shilly-shally with this.) A starting place is to allow five hours for every one hour of show.

28-00 Travel and Living – Crew

28-01 Air Fares

Economy fare is sufficient for most crew. The exceptions are Directors of Photography and Production Designers, who are sometimes open to negotiation. Also, some contracts may demand flight insurance.

When working non-union, the issue of first-class travel becomes negotiable. For long trips, first class might be justifiable, but generally, "we'd rather see it on the screen."

Sometimes flight packages may be negotiated with airlines, and a promotional deal may be worked out. It's remarkable what a short shot of a plane taking off in your film can get you. Explore promotional tie-ins for savings on air travel.

Don't forget that humans are only one half of your travel expense. Equipment has to fly too, so allow for extra baggage and/or shipping.

28-02 Hotel

By multiplying the number of crew times the hotel day rate times the number of days, you come up with the hotel line budget. Sometimes promotions or package deals can be arranged for long stays. "It's remarkable what a short shot of the hotel can..." Never mind, you already know that one!

If you're going to be on location for a long time, say a month or more, check out renting apartments. It's probably cheaper and more like home. Try your location manager or local film commission for tips on where to look.

Gratuities

Gratuities are sometimes added to the budget. Especially when working in large cities, there will be hands out everywhere — from the doormen to the taxi drivers.

28-08 Per Diem

Meals on the set have been accounted for in Catering (25-00 Location Expenses), but what about breakfast and dinner when you're all in Calcutta? The producer can either pay all meal expenses as they occur or more frequently distribute the per diem ($50 to $60 per day per person depending on local prices) and let each person take care of his or her own meals. This way, the more frugal members of the cast and crew will go home with some pocket money and the producer will know, before the shoot, what to allot for meals.

If the producer provides all meals through catered breakfasts, lunches, and dinners, no per diem is needed, although you may want to give $10 per day for incidentals. In any case, when the producer serves a lunch, you can either deduct it from the per diem, or make for a happy crew and not deduct it. Generally, serving meals on location keeps the production more focused and moving along.

In any case, don't shortchange the crew on meals. As Confucius was so fond of saying: "A crew with an empty stomach is like a camera with no film. No food, no picture."

29-00 Below-the-Line Fringe

These folks are mostly employees (although you may have a few "loan outs" among your Line Producer, Production Designer, etc.). Once again, these are the employer contributions:

▸ Social Security and Medicare (FICA-SS and FICA-HI) 7.65%.
▸ Federal Unemployment Insurance (FUI) 0.8% of first $7,000 in salary.
▸ State Unemployment Insurance (SUI) adjustable by state. In California it's 6.2% on the first $7,000 in salary.
▸ Workers' Compensation rate is set annually by state and differs with each industry. Workers' Comp. is less for office people than for grips. Call your state agency or payroll service to ask how much to average for your project. For purposes of illustration, let's say 6%.

For Guild members, add:
▸ DGA 22.2% (ADs, Stage Managers, UPMs only–14.5% P&H + 7.719% Vac/Holiday)
▸ SAG 14.8% (Extras, Day Players, etc.)
▸ AFTRA 14.5% (Extras, Day Players)
▸ AFM 10% Pension (Theatrical/TV/Film/videotape/Industrial) $17.94 per 12-hour day for musicians. Other AFM functions are different.

For IATSE members add:
▸ Pension and Health $3.1975 per hour
   (based on straight time rate for any OT hours worked)
▸ Vacation and Holiday 7.719% on day rates based on straight time (weekly rates already include it)

For Teamsters add:
▸ Pension and Health same as IATSE

30-00 Editorial (Film and Video)

There aren't too many projects that edit straight through on film anymore, but just in case there are some diehards out there who want to learn the process, here's a slim primer.

30-01 Editor

The Editor's creative decisions, under the Director's supervision, contribute tremendously to the success of the film. The Editor (usually with an assistant) screens dailies, edits the work print into an assembly (usually while shooting continues), and later into a rough cut and a fine cut, marks the workprint for the Negative Cutter, edits the voice tracks, prepares picture loops for Automatic Dialogue Replacement (ADR, also called "looping"), checks the sync accuracy for all tracks (voice, music, and sound effects), preps and approves orders for opticals, and screens the answer print for quality control.

When no Sound Effects Editor is on the show, the Editor may also select sound effects, build the sound effects track to conform with the work print, check sync, and prepare cue sheets for sound effects dubbing.

If no Music Editor is on board, the Editor may also build the music track to conform with the work print, check sync, and prepare music cue sheets for dubbing.

On large projects there will be an entire editing team with a Music Editor, Sound Effects Editors, and perhaps others. A big-budget blockbuster film requires a veritable army of editors. On small projects an Editor with possibly an Assistant Editor can manage.

How long will editing take? For a feature, the Editor starts assembly when principal photography begins, and continues through production. There may be a finished assembly or Editor's cut within a day or two of completion of photography. If it's a DGA feature, the Director has a minimum of ten weeks to complete the Director's cut. For low-budget features (under $1.5 million), the Director has six weeks.

Scripted television shows of 30 minutes usually get edited in a couple of days. A one-hour show may go four to five days. A 90-minute show up to 15 days.

A one-hour documentary, on the other hand, can take two months, six months, or a year. Commercials and music videos are usually edited in a few days or weeks. Short films can take a week or two or more. It all hangs on the quantity of material shot, the quality of the Script Supervisor's notes, the speed of the Editor, and the ability of the Director and Editor to communicate.

If the prerequisites for editing are carefully orchestrated so the Editor isn't waiting around for sound or picture elements, the process will be cheaper and more efficient.

$$$

A Film Editor (16mm or 35mm) earns $400 to $600 per 12-hour day.

30-02 Assistant Editor

Editors usually hire their own assistants, who sync and code the dailies, break down dailies after viewing, catalogue and file each scene and take by roll number and edge numbers, mark and order opticals, book screenings, editing rooms and equipment, order dupe negatives, workprints and optical effects, and maintain a clean and orderly editing room and a cheerful attitude.

$$$

Rates go from $200 to $300 per 12-hour day.

30-05 Cutting (Editing) Room Rental (Film)

The Editor will order everything you need, including rooms, Flatbeds or Moviolas (smaller version of flatbed), benches, supplies, and so forth.

$$$

The cost of editing room equipment depends on how much you use, and whether you set up in your own office or use a facility's rooms. Here are some sample basic equipment packages for both 35mm and 16mm.

Room with Bench Setup $212/week or $850/month

Bench Setups include:
Synchronizer w/one Magnetic Head
Amp
Splicer
Two Split Reels
Two Spring Clamps

Tape Dispenser
Tightwind Attachment w/Core
Adapter
Editing Bench w/Rack and Rewinds
Trim Bin
Floor Rack
Swivel Base
Chair
Lamp

Room w/16mm 6 plate Moviola Flatbed
$312/week or $1,250/month
Room w/35mm 6 plate KEM Flatbed
$537/week or $2,150/month
Room w/35mm 6 plate Moviola Flatbed
$398/week or $1,595/month

Bench rentals are sometimes seasonal, and if they are plentiful you may find lower prices. (This is increasingly true as more and more producers are editing on video.) Or, your editor may have his own editing room and flatbed, all of which you can get for a package price, including his or her fee.

Telecine (see 27-00 Film and Lab, also discussion of different film and video editing paths in "Post-Production," Chapter 2.)

Video Editing

To begin this section, let's consider a few thoughts about nonlinear and linear editing.

Off/On-Line in one system

Whether you shoot on film, tape, memory cards, or direct to a hard drive, Off-Line editing on a nonlinear system is the standard, and the old distinction between "Off-Line" and "On-Line" has blurred because compression and storage technology has made it possible to edit everything on one system. Not that everyone does edit an entire show on one system, but it's possible. A top of the line nonlinear desktop editing system allows a producer to edit in reasonably compressed or even uncompressed video, add graphics, titles, music and sound effects, clean up audio, color correct, and output to a master of his or her choice:

HDCAM, DigiBeta, DVCam, DVD, etc. Just for the record, we strongly suggest audio post with a competent professional or facility (see 34-00 Post Production Sound).

When there is too much footage, and/or not enough storage, it's necessary to first digitize at a lower resolution for the Off-Line edit, then redigitize at highest resolution from the field tapes for the On-Line edit. But you're still in the nonlinear, digital domain.

Nonlinear Off-Line to Linear On-Line

Still, many shows choose to edit on a nonlinear Off-Line system where all the creative editing decisions are made, then take a reference copy of the Off-Line cut, the Edit Decision List (EDL), the project file, and field tapes into a traditional linear tape-to-tape On-Line system, where the show is assembled, effects added, color corrected, and then output to a master tape. For one thing, there's no time spent digitizing the field tapes into a computer. You just play them back from a videotape machine in the assembly mode you've chosen (more on that below), and assemble your show. Thus linear tape-to-tape On-Line can actually save you money compared to digitizing and then assembling on a nonlinear On-Line system. All things being equal, meaning good editors, well-maintained systems, and the nature of the work that needs to be done, the quality between a good linear On-Line and good nonlinear On-Line should be about the same. Compare the hourly rates for both, including the time spent digitizing, and judge for yourself.

Nonlinear Off-Line to Nonlinear On-Line

A third approach is to edit in a nonlinear Off-Line system, such as Final Cut Pro or Avid Media Composer, and then move to a higher end nonlinear system for On-Line, such as a higher end FCP system or Avid Symphony Nitris DX. Reasons to do this would be to take advantage of the higher end system's color correction capabilities, visual effects, layering and so on.

Post-Production Overview

We strongly suggest with this or either of the other post (and production) steps, to "backward engineer" the process in pre-production. Start with the deliverable — the master(s). What format(s) is required? What are the tech specs? All broadcasters and many festivals have tech specs. Don't wait until post to ask for them. If you don't have a buyer or a festival destination yet, at least ask your post house to prepare for those kinds of tech specs. Now work backwards. What On-Line system will best suit your project's needs? Does it have many special effects or is it straightforward live action? What are the effects? Analyze them one by one to see how much time they'll take to create. You'll work backwards to build your entire plan, and your budget. This will include your selection of camera, format, frame rate, editing platform, codec(s), and master stock. And then it should include a test run. Shoot, edit and output exactly as you intend to do it for real. Now let's look at the specific Line Items.

30-08 Off-Line Editor

Good Editors are enormously helpful in visualizing how a scene can play best, and even how an entire show can be structured (given the material that's been shot). Find one you like.

Some producers digitize their circled takes and dive right into editing. Other projects are not so structured, and the producer wants to save money in editing, and begin way off-line — in the office, creating a "paper cut."

A Note about Paper Cuts

Paper cuts spell out the proposed sequence of shots, with appropriate timecode, on paper. It's a list for the Editor to follow. They are often used with shows that are unscripted, such as documentaries.

Paper cuts begin with QuickTime files or DVD copies of everything, with timecode slaved from the field tapes burned in a window. Someone, perhaps an able PA, screens everything, and writes out what happens in each shot, including in-cues and out-cues of dialogue, with timecode. It's a laborious but essential process.

An example of a log:

12:04:06-12:04:17	Wide shot — crowded beach. Sally and Jack's yellow umbrella in center frame. Beach sounds.
12:04:21-12:05:32	MS — seagull flies in frame left — lands at water's edge — flies away as boy runs in frame right. Beach and surf sounds.

12:16:34–12:16:59	Long shot — Sally (standing) pours Jack (sitting) water from thermos into cup. Beach sounds + Director giving camera instructions.
12:17:03–12:17:12	Handheld — topless woman lies on stomach as small girl (daughter?) piles sand on her back. Girl turns to cam, stares. Beach sounds.
12:24:09 – 12:24:45	Full body shot — Sally and Jack lie on towel under umbrella. Handheld cam follows Jack — he stands, walks down beach 10 feet, then returns.

JACK: "You always do this. You always say you love me and then ask me to do something for you."

SALLY: "I do?"

JACK: "You can go get your own popsicle." Sally stands, walks past Jack and down beach. JACK: (shouts) "Get me one too."

Then it's time to assemble the paper cut, and even though you are seeing the footage, it takes a practiced eye to put it together in a way that will edit together effectively.

A paper cut can be tight or loose. A tight one means the Producer, Director, or whoever does the paper cut has a clear idea of exactly what shot will go where, and with what audio, in order to best tell the story. A loose one can be merely a sequence of interview bites that lays out the audio narrative in broad strokes. The Editor then assembles that sequence and looks for picture coverage.

Here's an example of a paper cut:

	SALLY - SOT
SALLY - SOT (sound-on-tape)	Usually Jack and I get along
Interview	great. Only lately, um, he's
Reel 3	been strange…um…kind of
03:12:56 – 03:13:09	weird…evasive.

SALLY (Audio only)
Interview
Reel 3
03:13:07–03:13:16

SALLY (Audio Only)
I think he may be seeing someone. I really do. Um... he usually is a sloppy person (LAUGHS). Well, he is. Only lately he's been cleaning up his act.

JACK
Washing the car.
Natural sound under.
Reel 6
06:13:11–06:13:29

Depending on how complicated the show, and how much footage is shot, a paper cut can be a piece of cake or a brain teaser. In either case it takes time, anywhere from a few days to weeks and weeks. It is essential to allow for this, and agree on who is to do it, and for how much money.

There are several software programs that give you multicolumn scripts and/or paper cuts, Side by Side (*www.hollyword.com*) and Final Draft (*www.finaldraft.com*).

So — back to the Off-Line Editor.

Off-Line Editing is for the creative decisions. (If you later change to an On-Line system and make major changes, the higher hourly rate can hurt.) A good Editor will suggest different ways to cut a scene, but the decision to keep trying or move on is up to you. At the end, the Editor has the project file as the master template, as well as a clean Edit Decision List (EDL) showing the time and edit code for every cut, fade, and dissolve. If you are changing to another system for On-Line, that computer file is what the On-Line Editor uses to assemble the show. If you're staying in that same system for On-Line, and you've been editing in a lower resolution, the same Editor then redigitizes the shots from the project file in highest resolution, and assembles the final show.

Or, if you've been editing in uncompressed video, there's no redigitizing necessary. The Editor just cleans up the audio and video edits, does any color correction, and you're done, or at least ready for audio post. Many producers have relationships with several favorite Editors whose work they know and trust. If you don't know any, get recommendations from other producers and directors; go meet them and see their reels.

$$$

There's a big range. Good editors a few years out of film school will work for $125/day. More experienced editors get $300 and up for a 10 hour day. There are stars, however, particularly in the feature, music video, and commercial areas, where you'll pay a premium. In Off-Line, these prices often, but not always, include the edit system. Be sure to ask.

Desperate Measures

Because Final Cut Pro and Avid Media Composer have made such inroads into schools, many film/TV students know them well. Young, accomplished editors may be willing to work for somewhere around $500/week.

30-09 Off-Line Edit System

There are three ways to go. You can edit at a post-production house, you can hire a freelance editor, rent a system, and set it up somewhere, or find an editor with his or her own equipment. The first is usually more expensive, because you are also buying the overhead (the fancy bathrooms, free snacks, and instant maintenance). On the other hand, if you do both Off-Line and On-Line at the same house, they may cut you an all-in deal that's worth it. Also, if you are a first-timer delivering for a broadcaster or even a festival, an experienced post house can show you the ropes in terms of delivery specs, proper tape labeling, and the like. It will save you headaches. The second way, renting a system and hiring an Editor, can also work, but if it's a long edit, compare the cost of rental with the cost of purchase. The third option, finding an editor with his or her own equipment, is increasingly popular. These days, there are many editors with their own systems, so that can be very cost-effective. Just do your homework and find a competent one.

What kind of Off-Line system should you choose? It depends on how sophisticated you need to get in the Off-Line process, whether you're going to stay in the same system for On-Line or move on to another system, and on your delivery format.

For example, if you shoot in DV and you intend to Off and On-Line in the same system and deliver in DV, then there are a number of systems that will suit your needs, such as Final Cut Pro, Avid Media Composer, or Adobe Premier Pro. FCP and Avid Media Composer can also output to other formats, such as BetaSP, DigiBeta or HDCAM. And with added firepower, FCP can be beefed up to be a complete Off/On-Line system.

All three will allow you to move up to other edit environments, although with FCP you need a plug-in from Automatic Duck to work in Avid.

If you know you need to change into another system for On-Line because you have visual effects and/or color correction that cannot be adequately done in your Off-Line system, then you want to make sure that your Off and On-Line systems will be compatible. Staying with the same family, such as Avid or Media 100, is safest. Just make sure that the transition from system to system is part of your pre-production test.

$$$

The following prices are for a small post house, Editor not included. The brand names mentioned are some of the current standards.

Nonlinear Off-Line Systems

▹ Avid Media Composer $2,000/week
▹ Final Cut ProHD (FCP) is often used for documentaries and low-budget features. $850/week

30-10 Nonlinear and Linear On-Line Editing (Mastering to Video)

For the picture path, this is the final stop (unless you are doing further color correction). If you are doing your On-Line in a nonlinear system, you now either continue editing in uncompressed video, or redigitize your final cuts into a system that gives the best resolution possible in uncompressed video.

If you are editing in a Linear On-Line system, you go into an edit bay as an On-Line Editor assembles your show from the project file, reference cut and EDL, using your video camera originals (field tapes), or your film-to-tape transferred video masters.

There are myriad effects we've come to expect on television shows, commercials, and music videos — layering, curls, flips, spins, wipes, boxes, supers, and so on. Video Effects in On-Line usually provide a transition from one shot or scene to another. But effects can also dress up images, putting colored boxes around them, moving the boxes around, superimposing other images, and so on. A good On-Line Editor can advise you, and tell you how much time it will take to achieve a given effect.

If you have a lot of effects, and/or if they are too complex or time-consuming for the On-Line session, go to a Graphic Artist to have the work done. Ideally, all of your graphic effects are done before On-Line, laid off to a playback tape or computer file, and brought into the On-Line session all wrapped up and pretty — ready to be dropped into the show just like any other shot. (See 35-00 Titles and Graphics.)

Rates for On-Line and Effects are by the hour. If you are in a nonlinear On-Line suite, all your video has been redigitized into the computer and you're ready to add effects that are part of the edit software. A linear On-Line suite includes a record machine, one playback machine, the Editor, and usually a Tape Operator. If you add more playback machines, any of the Digital Video Effects (DVE) available, character generator time, or extra dubs, you pay more. It's like eating at an expensive restaurant. You are prepared for the high price of the entree, but when you see how the soup, wine, dessert, and espresso doubled the price, it always makes you gulp.

That's why it's important to negotiate a good deal going in, since On-Line Editing is highly competitive. Work out what services you'll need, how many hours you expect to use (ask your Off-Line and On-Line sales person), what effects you'll use, how much character generator time you'll need (show your credits list and other on-screen verbiage to the sales person), and allow plenty for Dubs and Transfers, which includes master coded stock, and any duplicate masters (ask the sales person for an estimate).

Now you have a plan that can be compared apples to apples with several different post houses. Call a few and get bids. Try to get the rates down lower. Say you'll work nights and weekends. But always insist on a fully qualified On-Line Editor — no apprentices.

$$$

Here are some average On-Line and Effects Rates for nonlinear and linear editing (but you can beat them). Editor is included.

Nonlinear On-Line

Avid Symphony Nitris DX Finish Editing $500/hour
(Plus tape machines for digitizing @ $175 – $225/hour)

Smoke Finishing Effects Editing $1,200/hour
(Plus tape machines for digitizing)

Linear On-Line

(Rates include Editor and record machine. Source machines are charged as used.)
Mastering to D-1 $325/hour
Mastering to DigiBeta $300/hour
Mastering to D-5/HDCAM/HDCAM-SR $500/hour

(For a discussion of film and tape stock used in post-production, including masters, see the next section, 31-00 Post-Production Videotape/ Film & Lab.)

Additional On-Line Services and Digital Video Effects (DVE) with various machines range in price from $250 to $400 per hour. Character generation for identifiers and credits range from $125 to $300 per hour including operator.

31-00 Post-Production – Film and Lab/Video

This category covers the stock and processing needs in the film post path, and the digital intermediate, video stock, and video mastering line items. Let's look at the film path first.

Film

In category 27-00 Production Film & Video, your film was developed at the lab and dailies were made. The dailies are broken down by the Editor or assistant and become the Work Print, which is reworked until a fine cut is achieved. This is the film equivalent of Off-Line Editing in video where all the creative decisions are made.

31-01 Duplicate Work Prints

These are made from the Work Print, and while they used to be in black-and-white, they are now in color. When you're in Seattle, and a studio executive in NY wants to see the dailies, you make a Dupe Work Print.

A close cousin of the Dupe Work Print is the "Dirty Dupe," a black-and-white print made from the cut Work Print for the Sound Effects Editor, Music Editor, and for ADR (Automatic Dialogue Replacement, or "Looping").

35mm $0.20 - $0.30 per foot
16mm $0.20 - $0.30 per foot

31-02 Negative Cutter

Now the Work Print has been approved, the Editor has clearly marked where all optical effects are to occur, and it's time to turn it into a finished film. So off it goes to the Negative Cutter.

Working with the original camera negative is a delicate job, so don't scrimp on an amateur — you don't want a scratched or damaged negative. The Negative Cutter breaks down and catalogues the original negative and the optical or mag track, records and catalogues edge numbers of the final work print, orders necessary dupes, matches and cuts the negative to conform to the work print, and cleans and repairs the negative, as necessary. Once Optical effects have been approved, the Neg Cutter edits them into the final negative.

$$$

Rates (non-union): $550 to $850 per 1,000' reel (standard features are 10-12 reels). Allow about one day and a quarter per reel. Also budget for supplies, leader, etc. ($75 per reel).

Opticals

Opticals are the same basic effects you get in your Video On-Line and Effects (dissolves, freezes, flips, skip frames, reverse action, wipes, zooms, etc., as well as titles), except achieved through a completely different technology.

In the sequence of things, Opticals are usually ordered before the Negative Cutting. The Assistant Editor prepares a count sheet, giving precise instructions to the Opticals House. "This fade begins at this frame, lasts for three feet and ends at that frame." Then the original uncut negative is sent to the Opticals House. They make a pin-registered Interpositive for each optical effect, and use it to put the effect onto a negative. That negative is returned to the Negative Cutter to be cut into the film.

(See 32-00 Optical Effects for budget breakdown.)

31-03 Develop Optical Negative
There is one intermediate step and expense. The Optical House does the shooting but the Lab must develop the Optical Negative. Here are some prices.

$$$

35mm and 16mm $0.15 - $0.25 per foot

31-04 Answer Prints
Now that the negative has been cut, and the opticals are all included, it's time to get the colors and densities in the film looking just right. That process is achieved through the Answer Print, and is the job of the Timer. If you see colors or densities that are off, you have another Answer Print made until you get it right. Finally, you have the perfect formula for your Release Prints, but to get to the Release Print, you must make an Interpositive and an Internegative.

$$$

(If you "wet gate" the Answer Print to smooth out scratches add $0.10 per foot.)

35mm "A" roll cut negative	$.88 - $.94 per ft.
35mm "A&B" roll cut negatives	$.98 - $1.04 per ft.
16mm (from A&B rolls)	$1.05 - $1.15 per ft.

31-05 Intermediate Positive (IP)/Intermediate Negative (IN)
The IP (also called "Interpositive") is made from the original cut negative. The reason to make an IP is so you can make an IN. (Remember, we're going from negative to positive, and the only way to make a positive print you can watch is from a negative.)

Another reason for making an Interpositive is that it is the preferred element to telecine and to make the final video masters. Since the Interpositive is color balanced with the same printing lights used in the Answer Print process and is wet-gate printed, this is an ideal element from which either HD or Standard Definition video masters can be manufactured.

Now that you have an IN, you'll want to check it for any dirt, scratches, or other problems that may have cropped up. So you make a Check Print, until you're sure you have a perfect IN. It has to be perfect because that IN is what you'll use to make your Release Prints.

(Think twice before making IPs and INs or even titles until a distribution deal is worked out. You may be asked to make editorial changes and a new, expensive internegative.)

$$$

Most labs give you a break if you make the Answer Print, IP, IN, and Check Prints at their place.

Intermediate Positive
> 35mm Interpositive (from "A" roll negative) after Answer print
>> $1.05 - $1.15 per ft.
>> 16mm Interpositive (from A&B rolls) after
>> Answer print $.95 - $1.05 per ft.

Intermediate Negative
> 35mm $.90 - $.98 per ft.
> 16mm $.88 - $.97 per ft.

31-07 Release Prints

This is it. The actual prints that will journey far — illuminating darkened theaters with the brilliance of your movie magic. The Release Prints are made from two sources, a picture source (the IN or Intermediate Negative), and the sound source (the Optical Sound Track). Together, they are used to make a composite Release Print.

16mm and 35mm Release Prints can also be made from the original Negatives after the Answer Print process. However, you should use caution in the number of prints ordered. This is your original negative and repeated printing weakens splices. You can make two or three high quality prints from the originals. The cost is higher than printing from Internegatives.

35mm (A-roll)	@ $.30ft – $.40 per ft.
35mm (A&B rolls)	@ $.40ft – $.50 per ft.
16mm (A&B rolls)	@ $.40ft – $.50 per ft.

Normally, the Release Print expenses are paid by the distributor, and the more prints, the greater the lab discount. Therefore, wait until you've completed a distribution deal before ordering prints (for yourself) in quantity. You can then piggyback on the distributor's rate.

$$$

When figuring footage for the Release Prints, add 30 to 40 feet for the head and tail leader the lab will require for Release Prints, Optical Negatives, or Internegatives. A production company logo will increase the total footage as well.

35mm (from Internegative)	$.20 – $.30 per ft.
16mm (from Interneg)	$ 18 – $.25 per ft.

Lab Rush Charges

Labs are always asked to produce miracles and meet impossible deadlines. They'll do it but it costs. Rush charges can amount to 100% – 300% above standard rates. If you know that processing or printing must be done at night, on weekends or on holidays, add this line item. Avoid rush charges with proper planning. This goes for rush shipping as well.

Video

Now let's look at this category from the perspective of the film-maker who has either shot on videotape or in video media, or who has shot on film and now wants to make a telecine transfer to video.

31-12 Videotape Masters/Safeties

Months ago when you called your distributor and asked how they wanted the edited masters delivered, or read the tech specs from the cable company, you were given a tape format. They may have said HD-CAM, DigiBeta, or whatever else has been invented since this book was published. (There's a new format every Tuesday.) And don't forget to add a Safety Master, plus check your deliverables for other possible masters, such as M&E (Music and Effects — for foreign language versions), textless, closed captions etc. Your total deliverables bill can be quite high, so tally it up at the start of the project to avoid nasty surprises.

Television Standards

When an edited master is shipped to a foreign country, it needs to be converted into a different standard so their machines and televisions can read it. PAL and NTSC are two of the more common standards used around the world for recording and playing back video. Different countries use different standards, and wouldn't you know it, none is compatible with any other. NTSC is used in the U.S., and in some other countries.

PAL, used in the United Kingdom and much of Europe, displays 25 frames of video per second, compared to NTSC's 30fps, and has 625 lines of video information per frame, compared to NTSC's 525. Because its resolution is superior to NTSC, and because its frame rate is closer to film's rate of 24fps, PAL is gaining favor in the U.S. as a production and editing standard for filmmakers who intend to blow up their edited video master into 35mm film for theatrical release. (See the chapter on Tape-to-Film Blow Up.)

Here's a brief rundown of some of the most common stocks for mastering.

D-1

D-1 is a component digital tape format. Component means the video signal is split into three components — red, green, and blue. Its component status makes it a format of choice for high-end effects and graphics work, where precise colors are prized.

$$$

76-minute D-1 stock is $188 or so.

D-2

D-2 is a composite digital tape format. Composite means the red, green, and blue elements of the video signal are combined, or composited, into one signal. Because of its lower cost (lower than a component stock that is, where the RGB signals are separated), it is a format of choice for editing and broadcast.

$$$

> 64 minutes of Fuji D-2 stock is around $83.

DCVPro

This is Panasonic's digital format that meets or exceeds Beta SP. It differs from the regular DV format with higher tape speed, wider track pitch, and it uses metal particle tape compared to the metal evaporated used on regular DV.

$$$

> A 66-minute medium load of DVCPro stock is about $14. DVCProHD is Panasonic's HD entry.

$$$

> A 66-minute load of DVCPro stock is about $12.

Digital BetaCam

A popular feature of any digital format is that even several generations away from the original, there is no discernible signal loss. Compare that to BetaSP, where you really see the difference after three or four generations.

Digital Betacam (DigiBeta) is a component digital tape format of high quality that is used for production, and for mastering. It has 4 channels of audio, compared to BetaSP's 2 channels.

$$$

> 64 minutes of DigiBeta stock is around $28.

Digital Master DVCAM

Digital Master DVCAM is Sony's stock designed for MiniDV or DVCam camcorders or VTRs. They recommend it over MiniDV stock claiming it has 50% fewer visible dropouts compared to Mini-DV tape. It can be used for mastering for lower end projects.

$$$

A 64-minute load of Digital Master DVCam stock is about $18. The regular version (drop off the "Digital Master" part) is about $16 for the same length.

HDCAM

HDCAM is Sony's high definition digital tape stock.

$$$

A 40-minute load of HDCAM stock is about $35.

HDCAM SR

HDCAM SR is Sony's highest quality high definition digital tape stock.

$$$

A 40-minute load of HDCAM SR stock is about $72.

31-13 Videotape Dubs and Transfers

This is just a catch-all line item in which to put an allowance for the sundry pieces of tape that get used in post-production.

31-14 Screening Copies

These are not final DVD duplications or replications (see 39-00 Publicity and Marketing), but rather quick and dirty dubs from the editing process to be used as approval copies.

32-00 Optical Effects/Visual Effects/Digital Intermediates

This category combines old world and new world... optical effects for working exclusively in film or the digital intermediate if you capture on film or video. Let's look at optical effects first.

Optical Effects

If you captured on film, and you are editing on film, and are delivering on film, you need an Optical House for any effects like dissolves, fades, and wipes, and any text on screen, including titles and credits.

The Optical House receives the marked work print from the editor, and/or the count sheet from the editor with specific instructions for every effect. They make a pin-registered Interpositive (IP) for each optical effect, and use it to print the effect onto a negative in an optical printer. That negative is returned to the Negative Cutter to be cut into the film. Text, like titles and credits, are type set, shot on hi-con film, and composited over the IP, creating a "texted" IN.

For an average feature, the Opticals process may take two to three weeks or longer if there are changes.

$$$

There are three expenses in Opticals: the shooting of the IP, the developing of the IP, and the effects themselves. (The developing costs are covered above in category 31-00, under Develop Optical Negative.)

Shooting the IPs can run $1.60 to $2.40 per foot. If a negative has been scratched, or if you have old footage that has been mishandled, the Optical House puts the negative through a wet gate process to smooth out the defects. As a setup to the IP process, it usually runs about $100 – $150.

There are tons of effects you can order, but here is a sample menu (prices are per each effect, and are the same for 16mm and 35mm):

Dissolve	$300 - $700 (the variable is the length of the effect)
Fade	$200 - $500
Freeze Frame	$200 - $500
Repositioning	$300 - $500

(What is repositioning? Here's an example: The love scene is steamy, but in the corner of the shot we can make out the reflection of a grinning Grip in the shiny knob of the brass bed. We need to reposition the shot, and enlarge it a bit, to lose the offending leer.)

Step Printing	$300 - $500
	(Speeding up or slow motion)
Compositing text over picture	$500 per card
Text over black	$150/hour overhead camera
Artwork	$50 - $75 per card

Many Optical Houses give student discounts of 30% to 50% or better. If you're a student, ask about this.

Digital Visual Effects

Many post houses, boutique effects companies (and optical and title houses), provide digital visual effects. They're into computer generated images (CGI), main title design, traveling mattes, blue/green screen composites, high-end 3D animation and live action effects, digital compositing, and digital intermediates (DI see below).

Let's say you have an actor playing an android, and he has to unbutton his shirt, open up his rib cage, and pull a damaged chip from where the liver usually lives. That's 3D special effects. If you are planning anything like this, or any series of digital visual effects, it's imperative that you meet with the Director and the Artist and Visual Effects Supervisor doing the effect(s) during pre-production — first to see if you can afford it, and second to prepare for the shoot and for the post-production process. Visual Effects people are fond of saying that a one-hour conversation before shooting the scene can save tens of thousands of dollars in post. It's true.

The Visual Effects Supervisor will walk you through the team you'll need and the steps the team will take to get what you want and put it into a schedule and a budget.

$$$

These are the (simplified) steps you travel through to produce computer-generated effects, with some sample rates:

Inputting – film or video transfer to a storage medium.
$5 per frame for film. $225/per hour for tape.

Modeling – computer wire frame models to create 3D images.
$150/hour

Compositing – layering live action or other images with the computer images. $150/hour

Animation – making the images move over time.
$150/hour

Rendering – every frame is re-drawn by the computer.
$50/hour at about 10 minutes per frame for fairly complex work.

Output media – storage medium back to tape or film.
$2.50 – $5.00 per frame for film and
$225 per hour to tape.

Digital Intermediates

The digital intermediate, or DI for short, began as a way for projects shot on film to be scanned into a digital format on a scanner or high-resolution telecine. Once in the digital domain the images could be manipulated, color graded with superb precision, wires removed from harnesses on actors, dust removed, etc. This replaced the color timing process at the optical effects house. The end result of all this is the DI, which is used to record the movie to film and/or for a digital cinema release. Since digital cameras have become popular for shooting movies, their files have also become sources of "footage" for the DI process.

Let's step back for a second and look at why people still shoot on film, but plan for a digital intermediate. First, many directors and directors of photography argue that you get more exposure latitude and image detail on film than on available digital cameras, although many argue that the digital cameras are gaining fast. The problem is when you get that film to the lab for traditional film-to-film printing, a certain amount of that detail is lost. Enter the digital intermediate. By shooting on film and color correcting digitally, you get the best of both worlds — at least in theory.

If you've shot on a digital cinema camera, then you're going to pass through some of the stages of the DI anyway. To be successful, the DI process must be well planned and executed carefully.

There are four main stages to the process: scanning, timing/grading, color management, and film recording.

1. Scanning means translating the information from film negative into the digital domain. If you've captured on a digital cinema camera, skip this step. Before the scan, you will be asked what quality of resolution you want. Getting into all the technicalities is beyond our scope, but your goal is to get as much of the detail from the original negative as possible for what you can afford. This will translate into whether you get a "2K scan" or a "4K scan." 4k means a bit over 4000 pixels of horizontal resolution. 2k has a bit over 2000. But the vertical makes the difference. Simply put, a 4k image has four times the number of pixels than a 2k

image. Should you scan at 4k? It depends…it won't cure a soft image or a bad shot, it just captures it at a great resolution. If you need to blow up a shot to get rid of an errant boom pole in a corner of a frame, no problem. But is that reason enough to pay the added cost? Talk this all out with your DP, Director and post house.

Some people recommend scanning a cut negative on the assumption that by then all the editing choices have been made, and you won't be tempted to re-edit in the digital domain, thus blowing your budget.

Others recommend this approach: if you've edited the film off-line in video, rather than cut negative you can scan either circled takes or exact foot and frames (with 4-frame handles). This list is obtained from the final EDL from the editor. Cutting or handling the negative adds to the possibility of negative damage and dirt. Then you assemble the film digitally.

Part of the DI process is to clean up any imperfections such as camera scratches, dirt etc. You must allow for this expense. Digital Conforming costs $300 - $400 per facility hour. Allow approximately 16 - 20 hours for feature length conform. During this process, your visual effects and stock footage will also be integrated.

2. Timing/grading refers to the changes made to your images in the digital realm by the colorist and others. There are different machines on the market to effect these changes, and of course, more are being developed all the time, but what they all have in common is that they give the colorist a huge palate of colors, tints, hues, and shades with which to treat all or just part of the frame. This is where DI really shines over traditional film-to-film printing.

Digital Color correction runs $500 - $700 per facility hour. Allow 60 - 100 hours.

You can also do fixes such as remove unwanted phone poles from an exterior shot. Obviously time is money, so carelessness during production will add cost.

3. Color management is about quality control. Usually, at certain points in the process, the DI house uses a very good digital projector, rather than a monitor, to show and test the work in an environment as close to theatrical release as possible. Some houses even print tests on film and project them next to the digital projection, then watch with an eagle eye for any discrepancies.

4. Film recording is the final step. After all the color work is done in the digital realm, the information must be transferred back onto film negative. Now we're back on the traditional film track again, heading for release prints.

If a project is headed for digital cinema release, you will need a Digital Cinema Package (DCP) from your digitally color corrected files and final audio mix. These rates run $150.00 per minute. If you do not have digitally color corrected files, you may need to first create a Digital Cinema Distribution Master (DCDM). This will also cost $150.00 per minute.

Film recording runs $.75 - $1.00 per frame.

As of this writing, traditional lab work — color timing and an optical lab — is still less expensive than DI, and takes less time. On the other hand, DI can combine several budget items: color correction, titles, and standard opticals (fades and dissolves). When you add these together and compare to the traditional track, it might be worth it, especially considering DI's potential aesthetic benefits. Another advantage of DI is that color correction is done one time only. The end result is then used not only for the film version but all video or DVD versions as well.

$$$

Let's assume our feature is 90 minutes. At present, 2K scanning runs $.55 – $.75 per frame. If you've scanned in a cut negative, that's around $100,000. Circled takes would run a little more.

Digital Conforming is another $10,000 or so.

Color Correction will run around $70,000.

Film Recording will be about $110,000.

Check please. That's about $290,000.

In the DI process, since frames are frames, whether it's Super 16mm, 16mm or 35mm, the costs are the same for scanning, color correction, and record out (129,600 frames for 90 minutes).

One way some have saved is to scan at 4K to get all the resolution possible, then make 2K files from the 4K files and continue the DI with 2K. That way, you get some of the benefits of 4K resolution, and the cost savings of 2K.

Some magazine articles have mentioned a "poor man's" DI for a feature at around $75,000. The professionals with whom we spoke expressed doubt. Technology will bring prices down, but currently, expect to pay between $225,000 and $325,000 for quality work. If you do decide to go the DI route, as always, it's wise to "backward engineer" each step of your process from delivery format backwards through post to production. Consult with the DI house about their stage of the process. And do all this thinking in the budgeting phase of the project, well before shooting.

33-00 Music

This category covers the buying, licensing or creating of music, and the hiring of a Music Supervisor. The technical methods of recording and editing it are in 34-00 Post-Production Sound. There are three common ways to get music for your project:

(1) Have it composed.
(2) License pre-recorded music from a music library.
(3) Buy CDs with pre-recorded music from a buy-out music library.

33-01 Composer

A composer (preferably one with experience scoring visual media) screens your final work print (in video, it would be your On-Line edited master), and composes music directly to picture. If you get a good composer, this is the best way to go. You get the personal touch.

Costs depend on the composer's reputation, the number of musicians used, recording studio time, and total number of minutes of music needed. But you don't always need a symphony orchestra, not since the synthesizer.

The synthesizer has probably put a lot of musicians out of work, which is sad, but nonetheless it is now a permanent "player" on the scene. Many composers create the score and play all the music parts on a synthesizer. That's usually the cheapest method. If the resulting sound is too synthesized for you, composers can lay down a synthesized foundation, then bring in some musicians to sweeten the sound. A few real violins or French horns over the electronic ones can make a world of difference.

If you don't know any composers and don't really know what you can get for your budget, watch some programs, documentaries or movies whose music you like and contact the composer or production company, or call some agents who handle composers, and tell them how much you want to spend. They'll refer you to some of their clients appropriate for your show.

If you know or have been referred to some composers, ask them to bid on the music package, which may include composing, arranging and producing all necessary music, studio time, musicians, and equipment. It's called an "all-in" or a "package" deal. The composer ultimately presents you with a finished tape ready for audio post.

$$$

Some sample package budgets:

▸ A composer for a TV movie might receive $40,000 to $60,000 as a package deal.

▸ A half-hour TV show might pay as little as $3,000 to $5,000.

▸ A three-minute promotional might pay $1,500 to $2,500.

When you do a package deal with a composer, you avoid having to deal directly with the musician's union, the American Federation of Musicians (AFM). Not that they are bad people, but if you are unfamiliar with the complexities of union wages and extras, you have a steep learning curve ahead. That's why many producers like packages.

Other producers go one of three other routes:

(1) If the composer is a signatory company to the AFM, he can hire union people and take care of the union payrolls himself.

(2) If the composer is not signatory, he or she can use a payroll service that is signatory, and administrate the union payrolls through the service.

(3) The composer can hire union people, but bring them in outside of union payroll, that is, pay cash. In this last scenario, the musicians will probably want more than scale, since they are forgoing their union benefits.

Music Line Items

If for whatever reason you decide to hire the composer for creative talents only and put the rest of the music package together yourself, there are hard costs to contend with.

Composer's Fee (creative only)

Composers are outside the jurisdiction of the AFM. Fees are a negotiable amount that can be as little as $2,000 for an episode of a half-hour weekly prime time series to $100,000 for a feature if you're dealing with an established master.

Musicians

If you are working with non-union musicians, fees are negotiable, although you can get some clues by reading the American Federation of Musicians basic agreements (or see The Industry Labor Guide in the Resources section). The union work rules are complex. There are different fees for features, trailers, shorts, commercials, industrial/documentary, television, home video, and so on. Length of the program is important. Musicians who "double" (play more than one instrument) get more money. (Since it is possible to produce very different sounds by changing instruments, this is a very cost-effective way of broadening the sound landscape of the musical score.)

Figuring a union music budget requires an experienced hand. Study the AFM basic agreement or the relevant section of *The Labor Guide* to gain a basic understanding. Even then you may need help the first time. Other costs must be taken into consideration, such as leader fees, rehearsals, meal penalties, overtime, and instrument rental and cartage.

Other contractual considerations will be the publishing and auxiliary rights to the music produced (sound track and songs), which may affect the composer's and musicians' fees. A music rights lawyer should be consulted on these issues. The union commitment does not stop after the musicians walk out the door. There is a back end for musicians if the music is released as a sound track, or in foreign or other supplementary markets, and for commercials there are residual fees. Contact the music payroll service about these issues.

$$$

Some sample rates from the AFM agreement:

TV Movies and Theatrical Films
   Sideman (regular player)
   3 hours or less $262 (35 players or more)
   $301 (23 players or less)

Documentary / Industrial
>Sideman (2-hour session) $190
>Overtime after 2 hours $24/each 15 min.

Again, these are just sample rates. They don't include cartage, rental, pension, health, and other fringes. If you are putting together your own package, consult the agreement and work with someone who knows how the agreement applies to your show. Discuss it with a music payroll service (see Resources section).

Music Prep

Once the harmonic, rhythmic, and melodic structure has been established by the Composer, either the Composer or an Orchestrator/Arranger assigns the various voices (including instruments) in the form of an orchestra score. Then a Copyist produces a finished score for each musician.

$$$

Music Prep people get paid by the page, but at the beginning of a project you won't know how many pages there will be or how many musicians, so here's a rule of thumb. For an orchestra of 40 people for a 3-hour session, budget an extra 50% of the musicians' gross wages for the Music Prep folks. Adjust it later when you know what you've got.

Studio Costs

Studio costs include the room rate, the setup, piano tuning, outboard gear, tape stock, and a 2nd Engineer. (The 1st Engineer is either a staff person or a freelancer whom you will pay separately.)

$$$

Costs are $145 to $250 per hour. Try to get a flat deal (called a "lock-out") with the studio — a set number of hours for less than the combined hourly rate. Recording for commercials that only use a few hours may cost twice the usual rate, since the studio has pretty much blown the day on you.

Cartage and Rentals

This one always amazes first-time producers. In certain cities, Los Angeles and Nashville, for example, the producer must either pay cartage for some instruments, or pay the musician a set fee for bringing it in himself. For some reason, there is no cartage fee in New York City.

Cello players, for example, get $6, but percussionists with a van full of congas, bull-roarers, and slit gongs can get up to $400, as do synth players. Amps for guitars are extra, and grand pianos are way extra. (If you do need a grand piano, see if you can get the rental fee waived in exchange for a screen credit, and just pay the cartage.)

Even working non-union, musicians who play more than one instrument will expect an additional rental and playing fee, but that is small compared to what it would cost to hire additional musicians.

Synth Programming

If your composer is laying down a synth foundation, the machine needs to be programmed. This is also a handy place to hide additional creative fees to the composer (assuming he or she is actually playing the synth).

Singers

Singers are covered by the SAG and AFTRA union agreements, and are paid according to a complicated formula based on what the show is, whether they are on camera or off, whether they over-dub, if they "step out" from a group and sing solo up to 16 bars, and so on. Consult the SAG or AFTRA agreements or *The Labor Guide* (see Resources) for rates.

$$$

Some sample rates:

Television (off-camera)
4-hour session solo or duo $556/day
Overdubbing   100% of the day rate.

Payroll Service

Because music is so complicated to budget and track paperwork and residuals, there are payroll services that specialize. Their fees may be the same as for a production payroll service (4%-5% of gross payroll) or higher if they become a signatory to the AFM for you. Still, it's probably well worth it. A good service will really work with you to help get the best deals on the union contracts and keep you straight with the paperwork.

Miscellaneous

Music hard costs suffer the same slings and arrows as production hard costs, so allow for office expenses, phones, postage, messenger, and other expenses (see 38-00 General and Administrative Expenses for a master checklist).

Desperate Measures

Another route is to hire student composers and musicians from music schools who can often provide reasonable work for bottom-dollar. The student composer may well do the job for no fee (he or she gets a sample reel and a credit out of the deal) if you cover the hard costs of studios, instrument rental, cartage, tape stock, etc. Yet another way is to ask the composer for any unreleased recordings you can license directly, provided the composer owns 100% of the publishing rights (sync and master rights).

Licensing Pre-Recorded Music

Music libraries license music for a fee, based on how much music you use and in what markets it will appear. This is still called "needledrop" music, because each time the needle (remember those?) was moved on the record, it was another charge. Per "needledrop" means one continuous use of a single piece of music. You can also purchase a "production blanket," which gives you unlimited use of music within a single production. Often the fee is 4-6 times the combined needledrop price, depending on the program and the medium. In other words, negotiate.

Some libraries charge "search fees" if you use their people to search for music. In most cases, you are the searcher. You tell them what styles of music you seek, and they put you in a room with a stack of CDS and a pair of headphones. Or, you audition and even license music online.

Do not pay music license fees until after you've completed your film and know for sure what cuts you'll use. Many filmmakers mistakenly purchase music rights and then do not use the music. Finally, if you are a student filmmaker, or producing for a non-profit, ask for discounts.

$$$

Sample Needledrop Fees:

Broadcast (Free TV and Basic/Pay Cable)	$450/needledrop
Basic/Pay Cable TV only	$225
Commercial (national network + cable)	$525
Commercial (local Free TV + cable)	$175
Corporate (up to 150 copies)	$150

Production Blanket fees are usually 4-6 times the needledrop price.

33-20 Music Supervisor/Clearance

The Music Supervisor or clearance service negotiates the licensing of any music used for a project that is not originally composed. So if you want any pre-recorded music, or if you want someone to do a cover of someone else's music, or if you need to ascertain if a piece of music or its arrangement is in the public domain, enter the music supervisor. She may also handle record contracts for a soundtrack album, negotiate publishing deals for a film's music, and generally work with all parties in creating or supplying music for a project.

Do you have a scene in a club that requires pre-recorded dance music? The music supervisor works with you creatively to select the right music and then negotiates the deal.

Music clearance and negotiation is a complex end of the business that requires expertise and time. Do not leave it to last minute. If music figures prominently in your project you must get a Music Supervisor on board early in order to even have a shot at a realistic schedule and budget.

$$$

Independent feature films may budget anywhere from $1,000 to $6,000 to pay a Music Supervisor, depending on the number of songs that need to be cleared, whether these songs are major artist or indie songs, the caliber of song above and beyond who wrote or recorded it, the publishers and record labels involved, if the job requires both creative (selecting songs) or just the administrative side (clearance, licensing, cue sheets, dealing with all the politics and any other administrative tasks) and the individual music supervisor's experience.

33-40 Music Library

Some producers amass a collection of CDs from Buy-Out Libraries, and then use any music for anything anytime they want. Like the Licensing Libraries, what you get is commissioned music, mostly from synthesizers, that is organized according to the feeling of the music you want. Hence categories like "Corporate Image," "Forward Progress," and "Pensive." Single cuts have rides like, "Shopping Spree," "Cash Flow," "Japan Nights," and "Action Central News." You can find tons of them on line under "Royalty-free music."

$$$

Sample rates:

Package #1 (42 CDs of assorted styles)	$695
Package #2 (18-CD assortment)	$450
Package #3 (any 3 CDs)	$49
Package #4 (6 CDs of sound effects)	$269

Purchasing contemporary pop music by recording stars is extremely expensive and presents enormous legal problems. You must deal with the composer, the publisher, and the record company, and pay additional "reusage" fees to the musicians who performed on the original recording. Costs can run in the thousands. For a discussion of music rights, see Chapter 2.

34-00 Post-Production Sound

Because audio post is the last step in the process before mastering, some producers give it less respect, or less money, or maybe they've run out of money. In any case, it deserves full attention, and its fair share of the budget, because an inadequate sound track can ruin your project, and conversely, an inspired one can elevate your story telling to another level.

There are two sides to this coin: creative and technical. On the creative side, consult with the Sound Designer, aka Supervising Sound Editor, early in pre-production. Get his ideas about how sound can help tell the story. Why? Because it may change the way you shoot certain scenes. On the technical side, make sure there is a conversation between the Editor and the Sound Editor about how the Editor should prepare dialogue and other sound elements during the picture edit. Obviously, this little talk should occur before the picture edit begins. Good communication at this stage will save you time and money during audio post. While this seems obvious, it is missed all the time. Don't kick yourself.

First we'll follow the film path, then the video path.

Audio Post for Film

On a large production, there will be a Supervising Sound Editor to ride herd on all the post sound editors, artists and elements. On a small project, there may be just one Sound Editor. When the project is ready for audio post, there are lots of sounds to prepare: music, sound effects, dialogue, possibly dialogue replacement (ADR), Foley (sound effects), and possibly narration. Let's take each item one at a time, starting with the main positions.

34-01 Sound Editor

The Supervising Sound Editor, aka Sound Designer, works with the Director and other team members to design the overall creative and technical approach to the project for sound. This process begins in pre-production and should coordinate with picture editor. The Sound Editor may also do much of the actual editing, that is, laying out all the separate tracks, placing effects in their proper places, and preparing for the mix.

$$$

Sound Editors earn $300 to $400 per 12-hour day.

34-03 Music Editor

He or she builds the music track to conform with the work print, checks sync, and prepares music cue sheets for dubbing, and again when dubbing is finished.

$$$

Rates are $200 to $500 per 12-hour day.

34-05 Dialogue Editor

The dialogue editor assembles, synchronizes, edits, cleans up and smoothes out all the dialogue in a project. If they can use the production tracks, they will, but if any of them are unusable they replace them with alternate production tracks recorded on set or with automated dialogue replacement (ADR). ADR is recorded in post as the actors watch their performances in a sound studio and rerecord their lines. Often the dialogue editor needs to fill a track with *room tone,* which is usually a 30-second recording of the sound of the actual place, crew and actors and equipment and all, just before or after a given camera set-up. Room tone is the dialogue editor's lifeblood. A good Sound Mixer on set will always ask for room tone. A good Director will always get it and demand silence on set during the recording. Don't leave your camera set up without it.

$$$

Rates are $300 to $400 per 12-hour day.

34-10 Spotting (Music and Effects)

The Supervising Sound Editor, Music Editor, the Composer, the Director, and sometimes the Producer watch the finished picture edit of the film in what is called a "spotting session." They all talk about where music should be, and what kinds of feelings it should evoke. The Composer writes the music, and plays it for the Director and Producer in "listening sessions." Once the creative aspects of the score are approved, it is ready to be recorded on a Music Scoring Stage. The Music Editor now edits "streamers" — yellow warning stripes — onto the picture to alert the composer to upcoming tempo changes, start points ("downbeats") and such.

The Director and the Supervising Sound Editor also have a long session in which they spot for sound effects. Where should effects be and what should they sound like? What emotions are intended? As you can tell, the aural dimension is rich with possibilities to enhance the story.

After spotting for effects, the Sound Editor pulls the effects from an effects library, and/or supervises and engineers the Foley effects sessions, and syncs the effects to picture (which in video is called the "Pre-Lay").

Desperate Measures

If you can't afford to score with real musicians, then the composer writes the score, records it from synthesizer to some tape format, probably

DAT, DA-88 or Digital Audio File. You then skip the Music Scoring Stage step, and go directly to Music Pre-Lay (see below).

$$$

Spotting is usually done off a 3/4 inch, Digital Betacam or DVD with a window for timecode, so all you're paying for is people's time.

34-12 Music Scoring Stage

This is a recording studio with projection capability, so the Composer/Conductor can record the music in sync to picture. The music is recorded on multitrack tape, and/or 35mm film.

$$$

Scoring stages cost $175 to $700 per hour, depending on your budget and how elaborate you want your recording to be. An average feature score might take from five to ten days or longer to record.

34-15 Music Mix Down

After the musicians go home, the Composer and the Music Editor work with the engineer to mix the multitracks down, usually into two stereo tracks. Some Music Editors like to record the mix on a Digital Audio Workstation (DAW) such as Protools or Digital Audio Tape with timecode, and make a 4-track analog tape as a backup.

$$$

The Mix Down can happen on the same board used in the scoring session, or, less preferably, on another board. The rate is $175 to $400 per hour, depending on how "high-end" you are.

Desperate Measures

If your "orchestra" is a combo of friends, and you can't afford a scoring stage, try packing into a friend's garage recording studio rigged for video projection. Remember, if you have not recorded a synth foundation, the recording machine needs to be electronically locked to the picture; otherwise music cues will be out of sync. Consult an audio engineer at an audio sound house.

If you did record a synth foundation, and have transferred the music to a multitrack tape with timecode, you are already synced to picture, and your combo can jam along to the synth — no picture or picture lock may be needed. On the other hand your musicians lose the opportunity to put in "stings" which are musical accents that illuminate visual action.

Music Pre-Lay

The music has been mixed, and the Music Editor now needs to correctly place it to picture in a process called pre-lay. The music cues are transferred to a multitrack format which will become the playback source in the Final Dub, or Final Mix.

$$$

Pre-Lay rooms go for $140 to $275 per hour. A TV movie or low-budget feature might take up to 20 hours or so.

34-18 Automatic Dialogue Replacement (ADR) Stage

Now that the music is underway, it's time to consider ADR. Prior to booking your ADR Stage, you had a "spotting" session at your audio post house, in which you confirmed the worst: Portions of dialogue are unusable (the neighbor refused to silence his yapping yellow Chihuahua, or your lead actor just couldn't deliver that morning). You identify exactly what dialogue needs to be replaced. Your ADR Editor prepares actor's lines and cue sheets for the ADR Mixer. You now bring your actors to the ADR stage, project the film or tape, and have them try their darndest to lip sync to picture as they listen to their original lines through head-phones.

Desperate Measures

For bare bones ADR, you need a quiet place, a film loop of each scene to be looped, or a video playback, some headphones, decent micro-phones, a decent recording machine such as 1/4 inch, multitrack, DAW, or video (Beta deck or better), and the ability to lock your recording machine to your picture.

$$$

ADR rates vary from $175 to $400 per hour for one Mixer.

34-20 Foley Stage/Foley Artists

A Foley Stage is a specially designed soundproof room in which Foley Artists watch a projection of the film, and create on screen sounds that sync up with the picture. The Artists are masters at finding ingenious ways to make sounds, and include footsteps, horses walking, body punches, and a zillion other effects in their repertoire.

$$$

Foley Stages go for about $275 to $400 per hour. Foley Artists earn $350 to $425 per day. But the "Walla Crew" (true term), the people who make crowd scene sounds (like "walla walla!"), earn less, between $200 to $300 per day.

Desperate Measures

Features, TV movies, and prime time episodics Foley every footstep in the show. But you can save money by selecting only the sections that really need it. You may also use library sound effects, but be careful — the editor may spend so much time on it you would have spent the same money in Foley.

34-22 Narration Recording

Some producers like to record a rough, or "scratch" narration track during Off-Line editing, using themselves as unpaid talent. This gives you freedom to make copy changes as you go, and tailor the copy to scenes as they change.

When the cut is approved, a professional Narrator is called into the recording studio to record the final track. Some like to record to a running picture, others find this a distraction, and prefer to just record it to the producer's cues for length of each speech. We've found the latter approach to be the most successful.

To save money some producers record the Narrator with a DAT, DAW, or Nagra recorder outside the studio, but the quality may suffer from ambient sounds.

Depending on the complexity of the copy and the ability of the Narrator, figure one to three hours for a 30-minute documentary script. Take the time necessary to do the job right.

For long documentaries, calculate additional time to return to the studio to record "pick-up" lines, should re-editing become necessary. Use the same studio so the sound quality and microphones will match. Be sure your rate for a narrator includes these pick-up sessions whenever possible.

$$$

Narrators are in either SAG or AFTRA. AFTRA announcer's scale for a one-hour documentary is $499.

To record the Narrator "wild" (i.e., without a simultaneous picture) to Digital Audio Tape (DAT) in an announce booth, with Recordist and engineer, costs $175 - $300/hour, plus stock. To picture is $300/hour plus stock.

Desperate Measures

To save money some producers record the Narrator with a Nagra or comparable recorder in their shower stall, with blankets over the windows at four in the morning, but the quality may suffer from the ambient sounds of other family members snoring. A friend may also have a home recording studio that will work. But be careful, you get what you pay for.

34-24 Laydown

After all the different sound elements have been prepared, they are ready to be synced to the picture in the Pre-Lay (see Music Pre-Lay above, and Sound Editor below). The audio post house takes the approved Answer Print, which has the production sound either on an optical track attached to the print, or on mag tape, and does a *laydown*, wherein the production sound is stripped from the picture, and laid down to one track on a multitrack tape. Timecode goes to another track for reference. All the other sound elements, music, ADR, Foley, and so forth are Pre-Layed — synced to picture — on different tracks of this multitrack tape.

$$$

Laydown rates are in the neighborhood of $160 to $275 per hour.

34-26 Conforming on Mag Film

Now that you have recorded the ADR, Foley, and sound effects, Sound Editors edit them at the right place in the picture in a process called Conforming. This can be done either with mag film and a work print, or on a Digital Work Station (see below).

If you are having this done on mag film and syncing to film work prints, you can't hear any of it played together until the mix. But if you are using one of the Digital Work Stations now common in most audio post houses, you can hear it played in relation to almost everything else.

$$$

▸ When a Sound Editor works on mag film with a work print for picture, the room and equipment costs around $500 per day.

▸ Mag film stock is $80 per reel. A $4 million feature might average 60 reels ($4,800).

▸ 24-Track stock is $250 per one-hour reel. A $4 million feature can use up to 30 reels ($7,500).

34-28 Pre-Lay on Digital Work Stations

Let's say the Sound Editor wants to edit in all the sound effects. He has all the effects ready for playback (from your Foley sessions, your effects library, etc.). He now sets up a multitrack recording system, say 24 tracks. Then he goes through the show editing in all the footsteps onto one track. Next pass he'll do all the crowd cheers on another track, and so on. Then he'll edit in the ADR material on another track. He edits in everything except the music. When he's done, he has everything on the multitrack correctly placed to picture, and he has a finished picture cut on a video reference cassette with a timecode window. That 24 track will become the effects and ADR playback source in the final mix. But first, there's a Pre-Dub session.

$$$

Digital Audio Work Stations cost anywhere from $175 to $300 per hour.

34-30 Pre-Dub (Pre-Mix)

In this session, the picture is projected and the 24 track is played. Now the Mixer works with levels of the various effects, or dialogue, getting them one step closer to the final mix.

$$$

Pre-Dub sessions cost $175 to $450 per hour.

34-31 Final Dub (Mix)

In the final mix session, all your sound elements, including production dialogue and sound, ADR dialogue, narration, Foley, music, and sound effects are combined, into a stereo two track, four track (left, center, right, and surround), six track (5.1-Left , Center, Right, Left Surround, Right Surround and Sub) configuration on a new multitrack tape or mag film.

$$$

Mixing can cost anywhere from $300 to $700 per hour, depending on what equipment you use, where you mix, how many margaritas you have, and how many Mixers are in the session (big or complicated projects can use up to three Mixers).

34-32 Printmaster

Now the mixed audio on multitrack is combined, through either a Dolby or ultra-stereo matrix encoder to create the Printmaster. This element will then be used to transfer to 35mm negative for sound.

$$$

Printmasters cost from $250 to $500 per hour.

Dolby

Since great sound is the standard for home entertainment, and already exists for movie theaters, we want to include some ways producers can enhance their deliverables. Dolby Laboratories is one of several companies that has technologies that apply.

Dolby Analog

The original Dolby multichannel film sound format is still included on nearly all 35 mm film prints. This analog optical technology encodes the soundtrack into four channels: Left, Center, and Right, which play back on speakers located behind the screen, and Surround, which is heard over speakers at the sides and rear of the theatre for ambient sound and special effects. Dolby analog soundtracks now incorporate Dolby SR technology, which significantly improves the dynamic range. The analog soundtrack is still used in cinemas not equipped for digital playback. In digitally equipped theatres, it serves as a backup in case of problems with the digital track.

Dolby Digital Surround EX

At the cinema, the center-channel information contained in the Dolby Digital Surround EX soundtrack is reproduced by speakers that are placed directly behind the audience. On the film itself, the additional back surround information contained in the Surround EX soundtrack is matrix-encoded onto the regular left and right surround channels of conventional Dolby Digital 5.1 soundtracks. Even if a theater is not equipped with the extra Surround EX speakers in the rear, the information intended for it will be played through the traditional left and right surround channels.

If you want any Dolby product on your project, work at an audio post facility that has them. Otherwise, contact Dolby Laboratories for further information. See *www.dolby.com*.

There are standard contract service fees to add these technologies to your projects. The fees are usually tied to the type of project (feature, game, DVD, etc.) and to the extent of distribution (North American, worldwide etc.). Check with Dolby during the pre-production budgeting phase to plug in the right numbers, and check with the audio post facility about any extra expense for adding on the Dolby products. Also see the $5 Million Budget in this book at 34-11.

Mag Stock/Transfers

On low budget projects stay away from Mag stock — 24 track is cheaper or removable hard drives are even cheaper. Most sound edit rooms are now set up so you don't need Mag transfers. It's all done on the Digital Work Station.

34-34 Optical Sound Transfers

After the final mix, you end up with a completely mixed sound track on Mag film. The optical house shoots an optical neg of the track, which becomes the sound track for the Internegative, and ready to make release prints.

$$$

Optical Sound Transfers cost $0.35 to $0.38 per foot. An average feature will therefore be $3,500 to $4,000. There are also additional charges for Dolby, DTS and SDDS tracks.

Audio Post for Video

Audio post for video follows a similar path as film, but with different technology. The players are the same:

34-01 Sound Editor
34-03 Music Editor
34-05 Dialogue Editor

And we still begin with 34-10 Spotting for music and effects.

Then the Laydown happens (see below 34-36).

The Composer may still use a Music Scoring Stage (34-12), or maybe she'll record all the music in her own studio.

The Composer may do the Music Mix Down (34-15) herself or with the Music Editor.

The Music Editor will then get the finished music and do the music pre-lay to picture. On smaller projects, the Sound Editor will do this.

If there is a Dialogue Editor, he'll separate all the production dialogue tracks, clean them up, place them correctly in preparation for the mix, use alternate tracks from production where needed, and indicate where ADR may be needed. If there is no Dialogue Editor, the Sound Editor does this.

ADR (34-18) as needed.

Foley (34-20) as needed.

Narration (34-22) as needed.

34-36 Laydown

First you take your edited master (which has production audio on it), and go through a process called laydown, in which the audio is stripped off the videotape and put onto a multitrack audio tape. The sound is kept in sync with the picture by the master's timecode, which goes to a dedicated audio track.

34-37 Edit/Pre-Lay

The Sound Editor takes all the separate and mixed down audio elements, the dialogue, the music, sound effects, ADR, Foley, and narration, and Pre-Lays each one in its correct place relative to the picture in preparation for the final mix.

34-38 Mix

In the Mix Session, Director, Producer and the Mixer decide on the appropriate levels for each of the elements. This is a creative weaving of all the sound elements into a seamless sensory experience, and it is not always a smooth ride. There may be competing interests. Sometimes the Composer sits in, and the Sound Designer. Which element better tells the story, the hiss of the snake or the tension of the string section?

34-39 Lay-Back

When everyone agrees that the Mix is a success (given the time/budget parameters), the mixed audio is laid back to the video master. Now you have a Sweetened Edited Master, the final stop. Except you'd better make a protection copy from which you can strike any dubs. Put the Master away in a vault.

$$$

How much does all this cost? A $10 million feature may spend from $300,000 to $750,000 on audio post. A TV movie or low-budget feature ($3 million to $4 million) might spend $60,000 to $150,000 on audio post. A half-hour children's home DVD with music, dialogue, and effects could spend $3,000 to $5,000. If you have only a few elements, say music, a half-dozen sound effects, and production dialogue, you might do the same half-hour for $1,000 to $2,000.

Since audio post is often budgeted as a package "all-in" deal, first figure out exactly what you'll need and about how much you can afford, then call two or three audio post houses and get bids. Give them as much information as possible. This will help to avoid surprises.

Desperate Measures

As with video post, you can try to play one facility against another to get the bids down, but don't make up stories. All these people know each other and word quickly spreads if you're faking low quotes. If the price is still too steep, sit down with the house of your choice and work out what services you can cut to fit your budget. It is best to be honest with your facility and remember they are an extension of you. You get what you pay for and going with the lowest rate is not necessarily in your best interest.

The established audio post facility is where you'll most likely find the most qualified people, but just as in the video editing field, relatively inexpensive computers and software have provoked a revolution in audio post. Nowadays you can find many sound editors hard at work in their soundproofed garages with Pro Tools or similar software. You may not get the same range of services as you would in a facility, but you can get most everything done you need to get done. The key is finding competent talent. Remember you can buy a sharp knife but would you do your own surgery? Then again, I guess some people would. Ask other producers, and ask for a reel.

35-00 Titles and Graphics

35-01 Graphic Designer

Every graphic element you see on TV, from local news titles to Olympics openings, has been designed with computer software. When it's time to think about your opening titles and internal graphics, including any computer-made special effects, work out what you have in mind, and then meet with two or three graphic designers. Your post-production facility can recommend a few, or may even have one in-house. Get some bids, look at some reels, and go with the one who seems to grasp what you have in mind, and can do it for the money.

Projects with money can expect to see storyboards. You can make leisurely changes. Low-budget projects typically sing a different tune. Because designer time is fairly expensive, multiple drafts of a concept for a flat fee are rare. Designers and producers typically have one or two shots at getting the concept right. Good communication from the start really helps. The designer should feed back how he understood the concept. Sketches and storyboards help. The producer can react to that. Then the designer goes away and does the work, returning with the finished files — give or take a few minor changes.

Most freelance designers working on low to medium budget projects have their own computers and a good library of graphic software.
They create the files, and when approved, hand them over. You simply
drop them into your timeline in your edit.

At the other end of the spectrum are the high-end graphics houses
that do opening titles for features and TV programs, animation effects for
features and commercials, and special computer generated (CG) effects
for features.

Text Effects

All the basic PC/Mac based graphic programs, such as Photoshop
and Illustrator, have character generator capability to produce, place and
edit text. If you want to get fancier, you can go into After Effects. Again,
if you describe what text effects you seek, your designer will know what
programs to use.

Special Graphic Effects

Designers can also create or find special effects. If your script calls
for Santa to wave his hand, producing a shower of magic dust that reveals
a fully decorated Christmas tree, go to a graphics designer. But go before
you shoot, because you'll need to work out exactly how to integrate your
live action with your special effect.

There are cheap ways and expensive ways to achieve effects. These
days, plug-ins provide the "poor man's" special effects toolbox. For example, there are several that work with After Effects to give you the "magic
dust" effect. It's cheaper than having it custom designed, but since it's
available to everyone, all the "magic dust" effects start to look alike.

Whether you go custom or plug-in, ask the designer to show you
an example of the effects in the discussion stage, so you can all agree on
the look.

$$$

How much money? The more images move, the more you pay.
Some general figures can give you an idea of what to expect.

A low-budget ten-second half-hour network opening title sequence
for a reality series can run from $5,000 to $7,000. A national evening
news show open might cost $50,000 because the network's ego image is

at stake. A 45-minute home video with opening titles and a dozen simple internal graphic elements might have a $2,000 graphics budget.

Motion Control (See Motion Control in 22-16 Camera.)

A really fun (and potentially cheap) way to make title graphics is to build or use actual 3D pieces, and shoot them under a motion control camera. You can use a snorkel lens, which gets you right down among the pieces. The overall effect gives a lot of texture and 3D reality (because it is!) compared to the high cost of high-end 3D computer graphics.

One creative Graphics Designer we know was hired to design and produce an opening title sequence for a network comedy show. He built a little 3ft. x 3ft. scale model of Hometown, USA, with little streets, buildings, and storefronts. He took it to a post house with a motion control camera (@ $350/hour) and shot moves on the set with a snorkel for a couple of hours. Then he edited the footage, designed the text logo for the show, composited it over the footage, and there it was — a delightful, unique open for a total cost to the producer of $5,000.

35-04 3D Graphics and Computer-Generated Animation

While this is still pretty much the domain of the high-end graphic houses, costs are dropping all the time. There are affordable 3D graphic programs for Mac and PC and freelancers who can deliver nice looking images.

$$$

3D designers with their own studios can output the lower-end images at around $50-$75/hour.

35-05 Animation

This is such a specialized area, it's really outside our scope for this book. Suffice to say that if you want animation in your show, either standing alone or composited over live action, there are many excellent animation houses and independent artists who can work for you.

$$$

Costs are all over the map. Animators will ask: How smooth must your images move? How many backgrounds? Do the backgrounds move? Do you want shadows and reflections? Flash animation programs are plentiful and relatively cheap to produce.

Just to give you a frame of reference, the cartoon shows on Saturday morning TV have all-in budgets (producers, writers, directors, music, and all animation) of around $225,000 per half hour (actually about 22 minutes). That's around $170 per second. Prime time cartoon shows have budgets in the $400,000 to $650,000 per half hour range. That's around $300 to $500 per second — again, all-in.

As memory gets cheaper and the various platforms get more powerful, the technology will continue to decentralize, so that you'll be able to contract graphic design services for your opening titles and internal graphics from a neighbor down the street — maybe even do it yourself.

Desperate Measures

For animation, try asking at a local college or art school animation department. Or ask the chairperson of the department for exceptional graduates. We've found some great animators that way who work for very reasonable prices.

Generally, if your graphics budget really is below standard for the kind of show you're producing, go to a Graphic Designer and say, "I have $2,000 (or whatever), do you want to get creative and take on the job?" If the designer is busy, he or she will have to turn you down, but perhaps will say something like "I'm swamped now, but in two weeks I'll have time. Can you wait?"

36-00 Stock Footage

Need a shot of the Colorado State Capitol's golden dome in fresh snow? How about a close-up of a red robin eating a worm? Or World War I footage of life in the trenches? A stock footage house somewhere has your shot. If they don't, you might find one that will go out and shoot it for you, and only charge you the regular stock footage rate. (See the discussion of feature film clip clearance and stock footage in Chapter 2.)

Archive Film Clips and Stock Footage

Studios have a stock footage department where you can get generic looking shots pulled from their own movies. Or go to a stock footage library. Some have both stock and archival footage, while some specialize in one or the other. If it's contemporary sports footage you want, you'll have to go through the professional sports leagues like the NFL, the NBA and the NHL. Ask for the clip licensing departments.

$$$

Standard fees for movie studio footage average $50 per foot (on 35 mm) with a ten-foot minimum cut ($500). Stock footage libraries and archive houses usually charge by the second ($25 to $50 per second is average). They may charge you a research fee of $50 to $150 average for putting together a screening reel. Professional sports footage goes by the league. The NHL, for example, licenses hockey footage for broadcast (North American rights) at about $22 per second with a ten-second minimum. For home video rights, the same footage costs $63 per second.

Feature Film Clips. (See Chapter 2.)

36-01 Clearance Supervisor

If you have a ton of clips to license or your project depends on locating and clearing movie clips, then we suggest you check out the services of a clip clearance professional. Meet with this person early in your planning to discuss budget, because depending on what you have in mind, clips can eat you up. Some movie clips, for example, cannot be used without permission from and fees paid to the current owner of the film, the major actors in the clip, the director, and writer, any stunt people, plus the composer and musicians for any music performed and the owner of the music rights. You get the picture.

Clearance Supervisors can also advise you about:

Film and Tape Clips Licensing
Stills Rights
Artwork Rights

Look them up in the *L.A. 411 Guide* or see the Resources section.

219

37-00 Insurance

As a production company wanting to rent equipment, and insure against damage to third party's property, like locations you rent, you'll need a standard Producer's Entertainment package. To insure against anyone on your cast or crew injuring anyone from the general public during the course of your production, you'll need General Liability. To insure against any of your cast and crew getting injured, you'll need Worker's Compensation. Your distributor will probably insist on an Errors and Omissions policy as well to insure against anyone suing you or him for defamation or libel. If you have a star whose sudden disappearance or indisposition on shoot day sinks your project, you'll want Cast insurance as well. (See discussion of insurance in Chapter 2.)

$$$

Some producers allow 3% of the total budget for insurance. The safer route is to call an entertainment insurance broker and get a precise quote for your project.

38-00 General and Administrative Expenses

Inexperienced producers always seem to get stung on this one because they forget or underestimate what it costs to just show up at the office and do business. (See the discussion of Setting Up in Chapter 1, and many parallel references in Chapter 2.)

38-01 Business License

Technically, your company needs a business license to operate in your city, although many people whose offices are in the garage don't bother. The fee is based on a percentage of your company's annual gross income, and it varies by city. Call the City Clerk for an application. (See Chapter 1.)

38-02 Legal Fees

Have a heart-to-heart with your entertainment attorney about each project and what he or she estimates in fees. Some producers allow anywhere from 3% all the way up to 12% of the budget. With that kind of spread, it's better to talk it out. (See Chapter 1, "Attorney," and Chapter 2, "Legal.")

38-03 Accounting Fees

Hopefully, you have hired a Production Accountant or Bookkeeper as part of your Production Staff (budget category 10-00) to keep track of the books during and immediately after production. If you are using a Payroll Service (see Chapter 2, "Payroll Services"), you are already factoring in accounting costs for personnel into your Payroll Tax percentage. Even so, you may have accounting costs beyond those mentioned, and this is the place to put them. Many producers allow about 1% of the budget here. (See Chapter 1, "Accountant," and Chapter 2, "Tracking Costs.")

38-04 Completion Bond

Hopefully, you won't need this, but if you do, see Chapter 2, "Completion Bond."

38-05 Telephone and Fax

Estimate a monthly telephone, Internet provider and fax fee, and multiply by the number of months you'll be chained to the project. Include the basic monthly charge, connection fees, and local and long distance calls. Pre- and post-production telephone bills could be higher because of long distance calls for research and to distributors and others. Two or more lines in an office may be needed, especially during production and to accommodate other staff members.

38-06 Copying

Copies of treatments, scripts, legal contracts, releases, invoices, correspondence, and news clippings are entered here. The volume of copying will determine whether it would be worthwhile to rent a copy machine on a monthly basis as opposed to making numerous runs to the copy shop. It's usually worth the rental.

38-07 Postage and Freight

Include postage for research, promotion, mailing DVD screening copies, and distribution activities. Freight and shipping costs will be incurred if there are shoots on distant locations. Film and tape masters, equipment, scripts, cassettes, release prints, promotional materials, and a host of other unknown expenses will be included here.

38-08 Office Space Rental

Allow for Pre-Production, Production, and Post-Production, but keep track of your needs for space. In Pre-Production, for example, if your writer and researchers are working out of their homes and billing you for telephone and other expenses, you may not even need an office for a month or more, or at most, only one room. In Production, if it's local, you may need to add a room or two or three for meetings, and additional staff, like Production Coordinator, Production Manager, and Production Assistants. In Post-Production, your needs will shrink again, probably back to one office, or two if you are setting up your Off-Line Editing there as well.

38-09 Office Furniture

Some office buildings offer a furniture package, or you can rent from a rental company or visit Goodwill. Handy items are desks, filing cabinets, shelves for books and cassettes, and 8-foot tables for meetings and plenty of spread-it-out room for artwork, and so forth.

38-10 Office Equipment and Supplies

Include computer/printer rentals, computer programs, calculators, projectors, video playback/recorder and TV, and stereo/CD system. People often bring in their own computers for a show and rent them to the company for less than the cost of a standard rental.

On the supply side, what will it cost to take a grocery cart through the local office supply shop? Probably three times more than you think. It's expensive to set up a production office for the first time. Costs will depend on how many people are on your office staff.

38-11 Computer Rental

If you have to rent computers from a rental house, do the math and see if it's cheaper to buy. Sometimes your producer or coordinator or production assistants bring in their own computers. On a low-budget show, they may do it as a favor. On bigger budgets, pay them a weekly rental fee that is less than the fee you would pay to a rental house.

38-12 Software

There is some dandy production software out there. See *www.enter-tainmentpartners.com* for Budgeting and Scheduling programs. Then there are numerous script formatting, script collaborating, and storyboarding programs, plus others to make your life simpler.

For the latest hot software programs, call The Writer's Store in West Los Angeles at (310) 441-5151 or visit *www.writersstore.com*, or the venerable Enterprise Printers of Hollywood at *www.enterpriseprinters.com* or (800) 896-4444.

38-13 Transcription

Whenever you have long interviews you need to cut into pieces and edit into a show, get them transcribed — it will save your sanity many times over.

Be sure to specify whether you want the interviewer's questions transcribed or not, and whether you want a verbatim copy. Verbatim gives you all the "uh's" and "ahh's" and coughs and laughs. It's good to go with a verbatim copy because you need to know exactly what the subject is saying, and how it is said.

When you get the files back, sit down with the window dub and mark up the transcription copy with timecode in's and out's, as well as marks that tell you whether a given phrase ends at a clean edit point or not. This saves you time in off-line when you are riffling through pages of the transcript looking for just the right quote. You'll know where it is on the source reel (through your good timecode notes), and you'll know if it is a clean edit in and out.

$$$

Transcribers usually allow a 3 to 1 ratio, that is, three hours of typing for every one hour of audio. Rates are in the $30 to $40 per hour range, so one hour of audio may run you $60 - $110.

Desperate Measures

Buy or rent a transcription machine (office supply stores or eBay) and hire college students.

38-14 Messenger/Overnight

For a production office in a large city like New York or Los Angeles, it's probably more cost effective to use a messenger service than to use a production assistant's time and mileage fees on his or her car.

38-15 Parking

Is there a fee for parking on the office lot? If so, it may be worth it, especially if there is metered parking on nearby streets, or if it's dangerous for your people to get to their cars after hours.

38-16 Storage

Any project will generate countless boxes of scripts, receipts, tax statements, income statements, bank statements, financial journals, records, originals, work prints, dupes, magnetic stock, mixed music masters, narration tracks, sound effects, etc. Film or tape will need to be stored in a dust-free, safe, temperature-controlled environment. Years later, you may choose to destroy stuff you no longer need, but for the two or three years after production, keep and file everything — you'll be surprised at what you may need to retrieve.

38-17 Still Photographer

(See 22-00 Camera)

38-18 Publicity

This expense may be covered by the distributor, but if you want to send flyers or DVDs to your own list, or throw a screening party and hand out souvenirs, this is the line item.

38-19 Wrap Party

Your hard-working staff and crew deserves to bend the elbow at the show's expense, right? If you can afford it, it is nice to either bring in some pizza and beer on the last day of production, or at a later date.

38-20 Hospitality

When your distributors come to visit you'll want to take them to something nicer than Casa de Vicky's Mexican Diner.

38-21 Overhead (Production Fee)

In preparing a bid for a commercial or a client-sponsored industrial, many producers add overhead (also called the Production Fee) to represent the company's profit on the project. The fee is usually 20%-35% of the budget. If regular production expenses can be held down, then profits will be increased. If there are cost overruns, profits will be reduced — or, in the worst of situations, it will cost the production company out-of-pocket money, that is, your salary.

39-00 Publicity and Marketing

Please see Chapter 3, Development and Marketing.

Contingency

There are hundreds, if not thousands of variables involved in any project. The ability to foresee all these expenses is beyond that of most soothsayers, but that is exactly what a producer must do. It's easy to forget something. By carefully studying the script, breaking it down, and preparing the budget, and by maintaining strong control during production, a producer will come close to the estimated budget.

But when the terrain is unknown, or the script has not been fully developed, an experienced producer will add a "contingency" to the budget. How much depends on what's available: 5% is helpful, 10% is a good average, 20% is high but may be necessary if you're wading into a swamp.

Weather, changes in the script, music, recasting, reshooting, change of location, ad infinitum, conspire to push budgets upward. There will always be unforeseen expenses and a contingency comes to the rescue.

Clients and grant foundations, on the other hand, may not want to see a contingency line in the budget. They may think it is unprofessional, that it's simply the producer's way of saying, "I don't know, so I'll slop in some more money here."

Rather than showing a contingency, it can be built in (padded) into the line items. Sometimes it's necessary for a producer to make two budgets — an actual cost and a padded client budget. This way a producer can be assured that there is money for omissions, errors, and the great unknown.

The budgets in this book are "actual" budgets. They are not padded except where specified to prove a point.

The Bottom Line

Holy moley! This is the estimated total cost of the project. It's the first place a client's eye will go. The bottom line. If the total exceeds an acceptable bid, a grant application, or the amount of money a producer can raise, the production must be re-planned and the budget reduced.

What things can be eliminated? Now begins the delicate dance of deletion. But be careful here. In your zeal to get the job, you may cut too much. There is a point beyond which the show cannot be produced, at least without revising the concept (and the script). The budget cannot be too high (or the bid won't be accepted) or too low (to allow actually doing the work).

Summary

The figures quoted in this chapter, and in the next, "Sample Budgets," are based on average "book" rates in Los Angeles and New York, the two biggest production centers in the U.S. Some cities will offer lower rates, others will be higher. **It is absolutely essential that you research costs with the people and facilities where production will actually take place, and negotiate your own good deals.**

These figures are only meant to guide and assist you in the preparation of your own budgets. Hopefully, by studying the budgets that follow, you'll be able to construct your own to include all your necessary line items. If this book does nothing more than identify one oversight in your own planning, it will have been worth the price of the book.

The sample budgets that follow in this book (Chapter 6) do not have all the master list categories because most projects will not have the people, equipment, and special effects found in most major features — thank goodness!

SAMPLE BUDGETS

Few things are harder to put up with than the annoyance of a good example.
— Mark Twain, *Pudd'nhead Wilson's Calendar*

First there are the budget *categories* — the big picture. Then there are the *line items* — the nitty-gritty details without which we have no budget at all. This chapter grasps the budget and shakes it so all the line items fall out into the daylight. Now we can study them in situations that resemble real production.

Let's be clear that this chapter is for illustrative purposes only. We want to show examples of producers planning and budgeting for real world situations, albeit hypothetical ones. Please do not fall into the trap of taking a sample budget and applying it to your project lock, stock and barrel. Every project is different, and cries out for its own creative thinking and budgeting.

The sample budgets that follow may help you avoid stumbling where others have stumbled before you.

$5 MILLION FEATURE FILM BUDGET

Instructions on Downloading Budgets:

- Go to *www.mwp.com*
- Click on "Virtual Film School"
- Scroll down on menu to "Resources"
- Download Excel Spreadsheets
- Save to your desktop

$5 MILLION FEATURE FILM BUDGET

		SUMMARY BUDGET	

Fringe assumptions:

		Production:	"Skylark"
Payroll Tax	23.00%	Shoot Days:	24
WGA	14.50%	Location:	New Orleans
DGA	14.50%	Unions:	WGA, DGA, SAG
SAG	14.80%	Shoot Date:	
Overtime	10%	Exec. Producer:	
		Producer/Prod. Mgr.:	
		Director:	

01-00 Story-Rights	0	
02-00 Script	200,242	
03-00 Producers Unit	198,410	
04-00 Direction	293,015	
05-00 Cast	807,938	
06-00 Travel & Living – Producers	35,866	
07-00 Travel & Living- Cast	29,842	
TOTAL ABOVE-THE-LINE		1,565,313
10-00 Production Staff	400,070	
11-00 Extra Talent	104,618	
13-00 Production Design	45,619	
14-00 Set Construction	197,625	
15-00 Set Operations	125,989	
16-00 Special Effects	78,489	
17-00 Set Dressing	160,255	
18-00 Property	70,947	
19-00 Wardrobe	107,403	
20-00 Make-Up and Hairdressing	55,987	
21-00 Electrical	122,577	
22-00 Camera	138,557	
23-00 Sound	43,161	
24-00 Transportation	324,748	
25-00 Location Expenses	284,672	
26-00 Picture Vehicle/Animals	43,326	
27-00 Film & Lab	150,344	
28-00 Travel and Living-Crew	166,121	
TOTAL PRODUCTION		2,620,509
30-00 Editorial	136,332	
31-00 Post-Prod. Videotape/Film & Lab	5,100	
32-00 Optical Effects	150,000	
33-00 Music	85,000	
34-00 Post-Production Sound	84,750	
TOTAL POST-PRODUCTION		461,182
37-00 Insurance	85,470	
38-00 General & Administrative	101,275	
TOTAL OTHER		186,745
Total Above-the-Line		1,565,313
Total Below-the-Line		3,268,436
Total Above and Below-the-Line		4,833,749
Contingency @ 5 %		241,687
GRAND TOTAL		$5,075,437

ABOVE-THE-LINE						
	Amt.	Units	x	Rate	Sub-Total	Total
01-00 Story-Rights						
01-01 Options					0	0
01-02 Rights Purchases					0	0
				Total for 01-00			0
02-00 Script						
02-01 Writer's Salaries						
Treatment	1	Allow	1	39,957	39,957	
First Draft	1	Allow	1	39,957	39,957	
Final Draft	1	Allow	1	20,066	20,066	
Polish	1	Allow	1	13,318	13,318	
Production Bonus	1	Allow	1	20,000	20,000	133,298
02-02 Research	1	Allow	1	5,000	5,000	5,000
02-03 Title Registration	1	Allow	1	385	385	385
02-05 Script Copying	1	Allow	1	1,500	1,500	1,500
02-06 Script Delivery Service	1	Allow	1	500	500	500
02-08 Script Timing	1	Allow	1	750	750	750
02-10 Development	1	Allow	1	7,500	7,500	7,500
Payroll					139,048	31,981
WGA					133,298	19,328
				Total for 02-00			200,242
03-00 Producers Unit						
03-01 Executive Producer	1	Allow	1	175,000	175,000	175,000
03-02 Producer					0	0
03-03 Associate Producer					0	0
03-04 Assistant to Exec. Prod.	15	Weeks	1	800	12,000	12,000
03-06 Consultants	1	Allow	1	5,000	5,000	5,000
03-07 Producer's Misc. Expenses	1	Allow	1	2,500	2,500	2,500
Payroll					17,000	3,910
				Total for 03-00			198,410
04-00 Direction						
04-01 Director	1	Allow	1	250,000	250,000	250,000
04-02 Assistant	10	Weeks	1	550	5,500	5,500
Payroll					5,500	1,265
DGA					250,000	36,250
				Total for 04-00			293,015
05-00 Cast						
05-01 Lead Actors						
Role of Frances	1	Allow	1	250,000	250,000	
Role of Skylark	1	Allow	1	200,000	200,000	450,000
05-02 Supporting Cast (6 day weeks)						
Role of Harry	2	Weeks	1	3,750	7,500	
Role of Edna	2	Weeks	1	4,000	8,000	
Role of Sheriff Rizzoli	1.4	Weeks	1	3,000	4,200	
Role of Hoot	1	Week	1	2,500	2,500	
Role of Charlene	1	Week	1	2,500	2,500	
Role of Lady Jane	1	Week	1	2,500	2,500	27,200
05-03 Day Players (Includes agency fees at 10%)						
Role of Balthazar	3	Days	1	750	2,250	
Role of Rudnick	2	Days	1	725	1,450	
Role of Shorty	3	Days	1	725	2,175	
Role of Soda Jerk	1	Day	1	695	695	
Role of Waitress #1	1	Day	1	695	695	
Role of Waitress #2	1	Day	1	695	695	
Role of Wilty	1	Day	1	695	695	
Role of Ruth	1	Day	1	695	695	
Role of Man in Car	1	Day	1	695	695	
Role of Dispatcher	1	Day	1	695	695	
Role of Cleaning Lady	1	Day	1	695	695	

$5 MILLION FEATURE FILM BUDGET (CONTINUED)

	Amt.	Units	x	Rate	Sub-Total	Total	
Role of Plumber	1	Day	1	695	695	12,130	
05-04 Casting Director/Staff - L.A.	1	Allow	1	25,000	25,000	25,000	
Casting - New Orleans	1	Allow	1	10,000	10,000	10,000	
05-05 Casting Expenses	1	Allow	1	1,000	1,000	1,000	
05-06 Choreographer	2	Weeks	1	2,200	4,400	4,400	
05-07 Assistants (Choreographer)	1	Week	1	850	850	850	
05-10 Stunt Coordinator	3	Weeks	1	3,500	10,500	10,500	
05-11 Stunt Players (6 day weeks)	1.4	Weeks	4	2,588	14,493	14,493	
	20	Mandays	1	695	13,900	13,900	
05-12 Stunt Costs/Adjustments	1	Allow	1	5,000	5,000	5,000	
05-13 Stunt Equipment	1	Allow	1	2,500	2,500	2,500	
05-14 ADR (Actors' fees)	1	Allow	1	10,000	10,000	10,000	
05-15 Cast Overtime	1	Allow	1	15,000	15,000	15,000	
Payroll					545,080	125,368	
SAG					544,573	80,597	
				Total for 05-00			807,938
06-00 Travel & Living – Producers/Director							
06-01 Airfares - LA - New Orleans	2	1st	1	2,008	4,016	4,016	
06-02 Hotel (incl. 4 wks prep Dir + Prod)	60	Nights	2	125	15,000	15,000	
06-03 Taxi/Limo	1	Allow	1	500	500	500	
06-04 Auto	2	Months	2	800	3,200	3,200	
06-05 Rail					0	0	
06-06 Excess Baggage					0	0	
06-07 Phone	1	Allow	1	850	850	850	
06-08 Gratuities	1	Allow	1	300	300	300	
06-09 Per Diem	60	Days	2	100	12,000	12,000	
				Total for 06-00			35,866
07-00 Travel & Living- Cast							
07-01 Airfares							
Role of Frances	1	1st	1	2,008	2,008	2,008	
Role of Skylark	1	1st	1	2,008	2,008	2,008	
Role of Harry	1	1st	1	2,008	2,008	2,008	
Role of Edna	1	1st	1	2,008	2,008	2,008	
07-02 Hotels							
Role of Frances	26	Nights	1	125	3,250	3,250	
Role of Skylark	26	Nights	1	125	3,250	3,250	
Role of Harry	16	Nights	1	125	2,000	2,000	
Role of Edna	16	Nights	1	125	2,000	2,000	
07-03 Taxi/Limo	1	Allow	1	750	750	750	
07-04 Auto	32	Days	2	45	2,880	2,880	
07-05 Rail					0	0	
07-06 Excess Baggage					0	0	
07-07 Phone					0	0	
07-08 Per Diem	32	Days	4	60	7,680	7,680	
				Total for 07-00			29,842

	Amt.	Units	x	Rate	Sub-Total	Total
BELOW-THE-LINE						
10-00 Production Staff						
10-01 UPM/Line Producer						
Prep/Travel	7	Weeks	1	6,355	44,485	
Shoot	4	Weeks	1	6,355	25,420	
Wrap	3	Weeks	1	6,355	19,065	
Severance	1	Allow	1	6,355	6,355	95,325
10-02 Assistant Directors						
First AD						
Prep/Travel	3.4	Weeks	1	5,094	17,320	
Shoot (Incl. 6th day)	4	Weeks	1	5,094	20,376	
Prod. Fee (shoot days)	24	Days	1	166	3,984	
Severance	1	Allow	1	5,094	5,094	
Overtime Allow	12	Days	1	450	5,400	52,174
Second AD						
Prep/Travel	1.8	Weeks	1	3,411	6,140	
Shoot (Incl. 6th day)	4	Weeks	1	3,411	13,644	
Prod. Fee	24	Days	1	135	3,240	
Severance	1	Allow	1	3,411	3,411	
Overtime Allow	24	Days	1	350	8,400	34,835
10-04 Production Coordinator						
Prep/Travel	6	Weeks	1	1,200	7,200	
Shoot	4	Weeks	1	1,200	4,800	
Wrap	2	Weeks	1	1,200	2,400	14,400
Ass't Coord.						
Prep	6	Weeks	1	750	4,500	
Shoot	4	Weeks	1	750	3,000	
Wrap	1	Week	1	750	750	8,250
10-05 Script Supervisor						
Prep	5	Days	12	21	1,286	
Shoot	20	Days	14	21	6,000	
Saturdays Worked	4	Days	18	21	1,543	
Wrap	3	Days	12	21	771	
2nd Camera Days	8	Days	1	40	320	
Overtime	1	Allow		9,921	992	10,913
10-06 Production Auditor/Accountant						
Prep/Travel	7	Weeks	1	2,100	14,700	
Shoot	4	Weeks	1	2,100	8,400	
Wrap	4	Weeks	1	2,100	8,400	
Post-Production	7	Weeks	1	800	5,600	37,100
Assistant Auditor						
Prep/Travel	6	Weeks	1	1,300	7,800	
Shoot	4	Weeks	1	1,300	5,200	
Wrap	4	Weeks	1	1,300	5,200	18,200
10-07 Technical Advisors	1	Flat	1	15,000	15,000	15,000
10-08 Production Assistants						
Office PA						
Prep	30	Days	12	7	2,574	
Shoot	20	Days	14	7	2,002	
Wrap	10	Days	12	7	858	
Saturdays Worked	9	Days	12	7	772	
Overtime	1	Allow	1	5,434	543	6,750
Set PA #1						
Prep	3	Days	12	7	257	
Shoot	20	Days	14	7	2,002	
Saturdays Worked	4	Days	18	7	515	
Overtime	1	Allow	1	2,774	277	3,052
Set PA #2						
Shoot	20	Days	14	7	2,002	
Saturdays Worked	4	Days	18	7	515	
Overtime	1	Allow	1	2,517	252	2,768
10-09 Teachers/Welfare Workers	4	Weeks	1	1,250	5,000	5,000
10-10 Secretaries					0	0

$5 MILLION FEATURE FILM BUDGET (CONTINUED)

	Amt.	Units	x	Rate	Sub-Total	Total	
Payroll					303,766	69,866	
DGA					182,333	26,438	
				Total for 10-00			400,070
11-00 - Extra Talent							
11-01 Stand-ins @ 12 hr. days	24	Days	4	133	12,768	12,768	
11-02 Extras (non-SAG)	300	Extras	14	8	34,146	34,146	
11-03 Extras Casting Fee @ 10%	1	Allow	1	46,914	4,691	46,914	
Payroll					46,914	10,790	
No SAG extras rep in N.O.							
				Total for 11-00			104,618
13-00 Production Design							
13-01 Production Designer							
Prep/Travel	6	Weeks	1	2,750	16,500		
Shoot	4	Weeks	1	2,750	11,000	27,500	
13-03 Assistants							
Assistant #1 Prep/Travel	30	Days	12	9	3,344		
Shoot	20	Days	14	9	2,601		
Overtime	1	Allow	1	5,946	595	6,540	
13-07 Purchases/Rentals	1	Allow	1	1,000	1,000	1,000	
13-08 Research/Materials	1	Allow	1	500	500	500	
13-09 Car Expense	10	Weeks	1	150	1,500	1,500	
13-10 Digital camera	1	Allow	1	750	750	750	
Payroll					34,040	7,829	
				Total for 13-00			45,619
14-00 Set Construction							
14-01 Construction Coordinator							
Prep	20	Days	12	25	6,000		
Shoot	20	Days	14	25	7,000		
Saturdays Worked	4	Days	18	25	1,800		
Overtime	1	Allow	1	14,800	1,480	16,280	
14-02 Labor - Foreman							
Prep	20	Days	12	21	5,143		
Shoot	20	Days	14	21	6,000		
Saturdays Worked	4	Days	18	21	1,543		
Overtime	1	Allow	1	12,687	1,269	13,955	
Labor - Crew	1	Allow	1	50,000	50,000	50,000	
14-03 Scenic Painters							
Lead Scenic Painter							
Prep	10	Days	12	21	2,572		
Shoot	20	Days	14	21	6,000		
Saturdays Worked	4	Days	18	21	1,543		
Overtime	1	Allow	1	10,115	1,011	11,126	
Labor - Painters	1	Allow	1	25,000	25,000	25,000	
14-05 Greens	1	Allow	1	5,000	5,000	5,000	
14-06 Purchases (Bldg materials)	1	Allow	1	25,000	25,000	25,000	
14-07 Rentals (Tools/Paint kit)	1	Allow	1	7,500	7,500	7,500	
14-08 Equipment	1	Allow	1	12,000	12,000	12,000	
14-09 Set Strike	1	Allow	1	5,000	5,000	5,000	
Payroll					116,362	26,763	
				Total for 14-00			197,625
15-00 Set Operations							
15-01 First Grip							
Prep/Travel	7	Days	14	25	2,450		
Shoot	20	Days	14	25	7,000		
Saturdays worked	4	Days	18	25	1,800		
Wrap	1	Day	14	25	350		
Overtime	1	Allow	1	11,600	1,160	12,760	

	Amt.	Units	x	Rate	Sub-Total	Total
15-02 Second Grip (Best Boy)						
Prep	5	Days	14	22	1,540	
Shoot	20	Days	14	22	6,160	
Saturdays worked	4	Days	18	22	1,584	
Wrap	1	Day	14	22	308	
Overtime	1	Allow	1	9,592	959	10,551
15-03 Other Grips						
Grip #1						
Prep	4	Days	14	21	1,176	
Shoot	20	Days	14	21	5,880	
Saturdays worked	4	Days	18	21	1,512	
Wrap	1	Day	14	21	294	
Overtime	1	Allow	14	8,862	886	9,748
Grip #2						
Prep	4	Days	14	21	1,176	
Shoot	20	Days	14	21	5,880	
Saturdays worked	4	Days	18	21	1,512	
Wrap	1	Day	14	21	294	
Overtime	1	Allow	14	8,862	886	9,748
Grip #3						
Prep	4	Days	14	21	1,176	
Shoot	20	Days	14	21	5,880	
Saturdays worked	4	Days	18	21	1,512	
Wrap	1	Day	14	21	294	
Overtime	1	Allow	14	8,862	886	9,748
Additional Grips	40	Mandays	14	16	8,999	
Overtime	1	Allow	3	8,999	900	9,899
15-04 Dolly Grip						
Prep	1	Day	14	23	322	
Shoot	20	Days	14	23	6,440	
Saturdays worked	4	Days	18	23	1,656	
Overtime	1	Allow	1	8,418	842	9,260
15-05 Craft Service						
Prep	4	Days	14	13	720	
Shoot	20	Days	14	13	3,598	
Saturdays worked	4	Days	18	13	925	
Wrap	2	Days	14	13	360	
Overtime	1	Allow	1	5,603	560	6,163
Purchases	24	Days	1	275	6,600	6,600
Rentals	1	Allow	1	500	500	500
15-06 Grip Rentals						
Package	4	Weeks	1	1,250	5,000	
Dollies	4	Weeks	1	1,250	5,000	
Cranes (incl. Driver)	2	Days	1	1,000	2,000	
Add'l Equip.	1	Allow	1	2,000	2,000	14,000
15-07 Grip Expendables	1	Allow	1	7,500	7,500	7,500
15-08 Box Rentals						
Key Grip	4	Weeks	1	250	1,000	1,000
Craft Service	4	Weeks	1	150	600	600
Payroll				77,878	17,912	17,912
			Total for 15-00			125,989
16-00 Special Effects						
16-01 Special Effects Person						
Prep/Travel	12	Days	12	25	3,600	
Shoot	20	Days	14	25	7,000	
Saturdays Worked	4	Days	18	25	1,800	
Overtime	1	Allow	1	12,400	1,240	13,640
16-02 SFX Ass't	20	Days	14	21	6,000	
Saturdays Worked	4	Days	18	21	1,543	
Overtime	1	Allow	1	7,543	754	8,298
16-03 Additional Labor						
Shoot	100	Mandays	14	18	24,990	
Saturdays Worked	20	Mandays	18	18	6,426	

$5 MILLION FEATURE FILM BUDGET (CONTINUED)

	Amt.	Units	x	Rate	Sub-Total	Total	
Overtime	1	Allow	1	31,416	3,142	34,558	
16-06 Manufacturing Labor	1	Allow	1	1,500	1,500	1,500	
16-07 Fabrication	1	Allow	1	1,000	1,000	1,000	
16-08 Expendables	1	Allow	1	5,500	5,500	5,500	
16-09 Rentals	1	Allow	1	1,000	1,000	1,000	
Payroll				56,495	12,994	12,994	
				Total for 16-00			78,489
17-00 Set Dressing							
17-01 Set Decorator							
Prep/Travel	17	Days	14	25	5,950		
Shoot	20	Days	14	25	7,000		
Saturdays Worked	4	Days	18	25	1,800		
Wrap	5	Days	14	25	1,750		
Overtime				16,500	1,650	18,150	
17-02 Lead Man							
Prep/Travel	17	Days	14	21	5,100		
Shoot	20	Days	14	21	6,000		
Saturdays Worked	4	Days	18	21	1,543		
Wrap	5	Days	14	21	1,500		
Overtime				14,144	1,414	15,558	
17-03 Swing Gang							
Swing Gang #1							
Prep	10	Days	14	18	2,499		
Shoot	20	Days	14	18	4,998		
Saturdays Worked	4	Days	18	18	1,285		
Wrap	5	Days	14	18	1,250		
Overtime				10,032	1,003	11,035	
Swing Gang #2							
Prep	10	Days	14	18	2,499		
Shoot	20	Days	14	18	4,998		
Saturdays Worked	4	Days	18	18	1,285		
Wrap	5	Days	14	18	1,250		
Overtime				10,032	1,003	11,035	
Swing Gang #3							
Prep	10	Days	14	18	2,499		
Shoot	20	Days	14	18	4,998		
Saturdays Worked	4	Days	18	18	1,285		
Wrap	5	Days	14	18	1,250		
Overtime				10,032	1,003	11,035	
17-04 Additional Labor	1	Allow	1	1,400	1,400	1,400	
On-Set Dresser (Shoot)	20	Days	14	16	4,500		
Saturdays Worked	4	Days	18	16	1,157		
Overtime				5,657	566	6,222	
17-05 Expendables	1	Allow	1	1,500	1,500	1,500	
17-06 Purchases	1	Allow	1	25,000	25,000	25,000	
17-07 Rentals	1	Allow	1	35,000	35,000	35,000	
17-08 Loss & Damage	1	Allow	1	1,500	1,500	1,500	
17-09 Box Rentals					0	0	
Set Decorator	8	Weeks	1	200	1,600	1,600	
Lead Person	8	Weeks	1	150	1,200	1,200	
17-10 Car Expense							
Set Decorator	8	Weeks	1	150	1,200	1,200	
Lead Person	8	Weeks	1	150	1,200	1,200	
17-11 Film	1	Allow	1	500	500	500	
Payroll				74,435	17,120	17,120	
				Total for 17-00			160,255

	Amt.	Units	x	Rate	Sub-Total	Total	
18-00 Property							
18-01 Property Master							
Prep/Travel	22	Days	14	25	7,700		
Shoot	20	Days	14	25	7,000		
Saturdays Worked	4	Days	18	25	1,800		
Wrap	5	Days	14	25	1,750		
Overtime				18,250	1,825	20,075	
18-02 Assistant							
Prep	20	Days	14	21	6,000		
Shoot	20	Days	14	21	6,000		
Saturdays Worked	4	Days	18	21	1,543		
Wrap	5	Days	14	21	1,500		
Overtime				15,044	1,504	16,548	
18-03 Purchases	1	Allow	1	10,000	10,000	10,000	
18-04 Rentals	1	Allow	1	10,000	10,000	10,000	
18-05 Loss & Damage	1	Allow	1	2,000	2,000	2,000	
18-06 Box Rentals							
Prop Master	4	Weeks	1	250	1,000	1,000	
18-07 Car Expense							
Prop Master	9	Weeks	1	150	1,350	1,350	
Assistant	7	Weeks	1	150	1,050	1,050	
18-08 Film	1	Allow	1	500	500	500	
Payroll				36,623	8,423	8,423	
				Total for 18-00			70,947
19-00 Wardrobe							
19-01 Costume Designer (6 day flat)							
Prep/Travel	4	Weeks	1	2,250	9,000		
Shoot	4	Weeks	1	2,250	9,000		
Wrap	1	Week	1	2,250	2,250	20,250	
19-02 Costumer							
Prep/Travel	17	Days	14	18	4,251		
Shoot	20	Days	14	18	5,001		
Saturdays Worked	4	Days	18	18	1,286		
Wrap	5	Days	14	18	1,250		
Overtime	1	Allow	1	11,788	1,179	12,966	
19-03 Additional Costumer							
Prep	15	Days	14	18	3,751		
Shoot	20	Days	14	18	5,001		
Saturdays Worked	4	Days	18	18	1,286		
Wrap	5	Days	14	18	1,250		
Overtime	1	Allow	1	11,288	1,129	12,416	
Additional Costumers (Shoot)	15	Mandays	14	18	3,751		
Overtime	1	Allow	1	3,751	375	4,126	
19-04 Expendables	1	Allow	1	500	500	500	
19-05 Purchases	1	Allow	1	10,000	10,000	10,000	
19-06 Rentals	1	Allow	1	25,000	25,000	25,000	
19-07 Alteration & Repairs	1	Allow	1	3,000	3,000	3,000	
19-08 Cleaning & Dyeing	1	Allow	1	3,000	3,000	3,000	
19-09 Loss & Damage	1	Allow	1	1,500	1,500	1,500	
19-10 Box Rentals							
Costume Designer	9	Weeks	1	150	1,350	1,350	
19-11 Car Expense					0	0	
Costume Designer	9	Weeks	1	150	1,350	1,350	
19-12 Film	1	Allow	1	500	500	500	
Payroll				49,758	11,444	11,444	
				Total for 19-00			107,403

$5 MILLION FEATURE FILM BUDGET (CONTINUED)

	Amt.	Units	x	Rate	Sub-Total	Total
20-00 Make-Up and Hairdressing						
20-01 Key Make-Up Artist						
Prep/Travel	4	Days	14	25	1,400	
Shoot	20	Days	14	25	7,000	
Saturdays Worked	4	Days	18	25	1,800	
Wrap	1	Days	14	25	350	
Overtime	1	Allow	1	10,550	1,055	11,605
20-02 Additional Make-Up Artist	15	Days	14	21	4,500	
Saturdays Worked	4	Days	18	21	1,543	
Overtime	1	Allow	1	6,043	604	8,053
20-03 Hair Stylist						
Prep/Travel	7	Days	14	25	2,450	
Shoot	20	Days	14	25	7,000	
Saturdays Worked	4	Days	18	25	1,800	
Wrap	1	Days	14	25	350	
Overtime	1	Allow	1	11,600	1,160	12,760
Additional Hair Stylist	15	Days	14	21	4,500	
Saturdays Worked	4	Days	18	21	1,543	
Overtime	1	Allow	1	6,043	604	8,158
20-05 Purchases	1	Allow	1	2,000	2,000	2,000
20-06 Rentals	4	Weeks	1	250	1,000	1,000
20-07 Box Rentals						
Key Make-Up	24	Days	1	30	720	720
Add'l Make-Up	19	Days	1	30	570	570
Hair Stylist	24	Days	1	30	720	720
Add'l Hair	19	Days	1	30	570	570
20-08 Film	1	Allow	1	500	500	500
Payroll				40,575	9,332	9,332
Total for 20-00						55,987
21-00 Electrical						
21-01 Gaffer						
Prep/Travel	7	Days	14	25	2,450	
Shoot	20	Days	14	25	7,000	
Saturdays Worked	4	Days	18	25	1,800	
Wrap/Travel	1	Days	14	25	350	
Overtime	1	Allow	1	11,600	1,160	12,760
21-02 Best Boy						
Prep	5	Days	14	22	1,540	
Shoot	20	Days	14	22	6,160	
Saturdays Worked	4	Days	18	22	1,584	
Wrap	1	Days	14	22	308	
Overtime	1	Allow	1	9,592	959	10,551
21-03 Electrics						
Electric #1						
Prep	4	Days	14	21	1,176	
Shoot	20	Days	14	21	5,880	
Saturdays Worked	4	Days	18	21	1,512	
Wrap	1	Days	14	21	294	
Overtime	1	Allow	1	8,862	886	9,748
Electric #2						
Prep	4	Days	14	21	1,176	
Shoot	20	Days	14	21	5,880	
Saturdays Worked	4	Days	18	21	1,512	
Wrap	1	Days	14	21	294	
Overtime	1	Allow	1	8,862	886	9,748
Electric #3						
Prep	4	Days	14	21	1,176	
Shoot	20	Days	14	21	5,880	
Saturdays Worked	4	Days	18	21	1,512	
Wrap	1	Days	14	21	294	
Overtime	1	Allow	1	8,862	886	9,748
21-04 Additional Labor	30	Mandays	14	21	8,820	

	Amt.	Units	x	Rate	Sub-Total	Total
Overtime	1	Allow	1	8,820	882	9,702
21-05 Purchases	1	Allow	1	7,000	7,000	7,000
21-06 Rentals	4	Weeks	1	5,500	22,000	22,000
Add'l Equip.	1	Allow	1	5,000	5,000	5,000
Condors	1	Allow	1	7,000	7,000	7,000
Additional Generator	1	Allow	1	2,000	2,000	2,000
21-09 Loss & Damage	1	Allow	1	2,000	2,000	2,000
21-10 Box Rentals						
Gaffer	4	Weeks	1	250	1,000	1,000
Payroll				62,258	14,319	14,319
				Total for 21-00		122,577
22-00 Camera						
22-01 Director of Photography/OP						
Prep/Travel	7	Days	1	1,200	8,400	
Shoot	4	Weeks	1	7,200	28,800	37,200
22-02 Camera Operator (B Cam)						
Prep/Travel	2	Days	12	35	840	
Shoot	8	Days	14	35	3,920	
Saturdays Worked	2	Days	18	35	1,260	
Overtime	1	Allow	1	5,180	518	6,538
22-03 1st Ass't Camera						
Prep/Travel	4	Days	14	30	1,680	
Shoot	20	Days	14	30	8,400	
Saturdays Worked	4	Days	18	30	2,160	
Wrap	2	Days	14	30	840	
Overtime	1	Allow	1	13,080	1,308	14,388
B Cam 1st Ass't	10	Days	14	30	4,200	
Saturdays Worked	2	Days	18	30	1,080	
Overtime	1	Allow	1	5,280	528	5,808
22-04 2nd Ass't Camera						
Prep	2	Days	14	23	644	
Shoot	20	Days	14	23	6,440	
Saturdays Worked	4	Days	18	23	1,656	
Wrap	2	Days	14	23	644	
Overtime	1	Allow	1	9,384	938	10,322
B Cam 2nd Ass't	10	Days	14	23	3,220	
Saturdays Worked	2	Days	18	23	828	
Overtime	1	Allow	1	4,048	405	4,453
22-05 Still Photographer	1	Week	1	1,500	1,500	1,500
22-06 Expendables	1	Allow	1	1,200	1,200	1,200
22-07 Camera Package Rental	4	Weeks	1	7,000	28,000	28,000
22-10 Additional Equipment	1	Allow	1	5,000	5,000	5,000
22-11 Steadicam Operator & Equip.	2	Days	1	1,500	3,000	3,000
22-17 Maintenance/Loss & Damage	1	Allow	1	1,500	1,500	1,500
22-18 Box Rentals						
1st Ass't Cam	4	Weeks	1	300	1,200	1,200
Payroll				80,209	18,448	18,448
				Total for 22-00		138,557
23-00 Sound						
23-01 Mixer						
Prep	2	Days	14	25	700	
Shoot	20	Days	14	25	7,000	
Saturdays Worked	4	Days	18	25	1,800	
Wrap/Travel	2	Days	14	25	700	
Overtime	1	Allow	1	10,200	1,020	11,220
23-02 Boom Operator						
Shoot	20	Days	14	21	6,000	
Saturdays Worked	4	Days	18	21	1,543	
Overtime	1	Allow	1	7,543	754	9,318

	Amt.	Units	x	Rate	Sub-Total	Total	
23-03 Expendables (Batteries, etc)	1	Allow	1	1,500	1,500	1,500	
23-04 Sound Package	4	Weeks	1	1,900	7,600	7,600	
23-05 Walkie Talkies	4	Weeks	25	20	2,000	2,000	
23-06 Radio Mics & Head Sets	4	Weeks	5	15	300	300	
23-08 Cellular Phones/Service	1	Allow	1	5,000	5,000	5,000	
23-10 Misc. / Loss & Damage	1	Allow	1	1,500	1,500	1,500	
Payroll				20,538	4,724	4,724	
				Total for 23-00			43,161
24-00 Transportation							
24-01 Transportation Coordinator (6 day flat)							
	6	Weeks	1	2,500	15,000	15,000	
24-02 Drivers							
Captain							
Prep	10	Days	10	19	1,900		
Shoot	20	Days	18	19	6,840		
Saturdays Worked	4	Days	21	19	1,596		
Wrap	5	Days	18	19	1,710	12,046	
Star Trailer Drivers							
Driver #1							
Prep	1	Day	10	19	190		
Shoot	20	Days	18	19	6,840		
Saturdays Worked	4	Days	21	19	1,596		
Wrap	1	Day	18	19	342	8,968	
Driver #2							
Prep	1	Day	10	19	190		
Shoot	20	Days	18	19	6,840		
Saturdays Worked	4	Days	21	19	1,596		
Wrap	1	Day	18	19	342	8,968	
Production Van Driver							
Prep	3	Days	10	19	570		
Shoot	20	Days	18	19	6,840		
Saturdays Worked	4	Days	21	19	1,596		
Wrap	2	Days	18	19	684	9,690	
Camera Truck Driver							
Prep	3	Days	10	19	570		
Shoot	20	Days	18	19	6,840		
Saturdays Worked	4	Days	21	19	1,596		
Wrap	2	Days	18	19	684	9,690	
Stakebed Driver (Construction)							
Shoot	5	Days	18	19	1,710	1,710	
Set Dressing Driver							
Prep	10	Days	10	19	1,900		
Shoot	20	Days	18	19	6,840		
Saturdays Worked	4	Days	21	19	1,596		
Wrap	5	Days	18	19	1,710	12,046	
Second Set Dressing 5 Ton	10	Days	18	19	3,420	3,420	
Props Driver							
Prep	6	Days	10	19	1,140		
Shoot	20	Days	18	19	6,840		
Saturdays Worked	4	Days	21	19	1,596		
Wrap	5	Days	18	19	1,710	11,286	
Make-Up/Wardrobe Driver							
Prep	6	Days	10	19	1,140		
Shoot	20	Days	18	19	6,840		
Saturdays Worked	4	Days	21	19	1,596		
Wrap	5	Days	18	19	1,710	11,286	
Prod. Office Trailer Driver							
Prep	1	Days	10	19	190		
Shoot	20	Days	18	19	6,840		
Saturdays Worked	4	Days	21	19	1,596		
Wrap	1	Days	18	19	342	8,968	
Honeywagon Driver							

		Amt.	Units	x	Rate	Sub-Total	Total	
	Shoot	20	Days	18	19	6,840		
	Saturdays Worked	4	Days	21	19	1,596		
	Wrap	2	Days	18	19	684	9,120	
Maxi Van #1	Driver							
	Prep	6	Days	10	18	1,080		
	Shoot	20	Days	18	18	6,480		
	Saturdays Worked	4	Days	21	18	1,512	9,072	
Maxi Van #2	Driver							
	Prep	6	Days	10	18	1,080		
	Shoot	20	Days	18	18	6,480		
	Saturdays Worked	4	Days	21	18	1,512	9,072	
Car Carrier		10	Days	18	19	3,420	3,420	
Insert Car (car to car cam platform)		2	Days	18	19	684	684	
Water Truck Driver		4	Days	18	19	1,368	1,368	
Caterer	Shoot	20	Days	18	19	6,840		
	Saturdays Worked	4	Days	21	19	1,596	8,436	
Caterer Ass't	Shoot	20	Days	18	18	6,480		
	Saturdays Worked	4	Days	21	18	1,512	9,588	
Additional Drivers		1	Allow	1	3,500	3,500	3,500	
24-03 Equipment Rental								
Star Dressing Trailers		4	Weeks	2	475	3,800	3,800	
Crew Cab		38	Days	1	60	2,280	2,280	
Production Van (40' w/ 2 gennies)		27	Days	1	300	8,100	8,100	
Camera Truck		25	Days	1	100	2,500	2,500	
Stake Bed		7	Days	1	90	630	630	
Set Dressing 5 Ton		34	Days	1	95	3,230	3,230	
Add'l Set Dressing 5 Ton		14	Days	1	95	1,330	1,330	
Set Dress Van		34	Days	1	65	2,210	2,210	
Props 5 Ton		39	Days	1	95	3,705	3,705	
Wardrobe/Make-Up		35	Days	1	300	10,500	10,500	
Crew Stake Bed		28	Days	1	90	2,520	2,520	
Prod. Office Trailer		25	Days	1	120	3,000	3,000	
Honeywagon (Portable Toilets)		25	Days	1	300	7,500	7,500	
Water Truck		24	Days	1	200	4,800	4,800	
Gas Truck		24	Days	1	80	1,920	1,920	
Maxi Vans		30	Days	2	70	4,200	4,200	
Car Tow Trailer		10	Days	1	70	700	700	
Car Trailer		10	Days	1	70	700	700	
Camera Car		3	Days	1	300	900	900	
24-04 Gas & Oil		1	Allow	1	12,000	12,000	12,000	
24-05 Repairs & Maintenance		1	Allow	1	3,500	3,500	3,500	
24-06 Honeywagon Pumping		1	Allow	1	500	500	500	
24-07 Miscellaneous		1	Allow	1	5,000	5,000	5,000	
	Teamster Fringes:							
	P&H - 6,400 hrs. @ $3.20					20,480	20,480	20,480	
	V&H @ 7.719%					12,917	12,917	12,917	
	Payroll					167,338	38,488	38,488	
					Total for 24-00			324,748
25-00 Location Expenses								
25-01 Location Manager								
	(6 day flat)	11	Weeks	1	2,150	23,650	23,650	
25-02 Assistants (6 day flats)								
	Assistant Location Mgr.	7	Weeks	1	1,800	12,600	12,600	
	Local Contact Person	4	Weeks	1	1,000	4,000	4,000	
25-03 First Aid		4	Weeks	1	1,400	5,600	5,600	
25-04 Fire Officers								
	Shoot	24	Days	1	400	9,600	9,600	
25-05 Security		1	Allow	1	18,000	18,000	18,000	
25-06 Police		24	Days	1	400	9,600	9,600	
	Additional Police	1	Allow	1	4,000	4,000	4,000	
25-07 Permits		1	Allow	1	2,500	2,500	2,500	
25-08 Parking		1	Allow	1	7,500	7,500	7,500	

$5 MILLION FEATURE FILM BUDGET (CONTINUED)

	Amt.	Units	x	Rate	Sub-Total	Total
25-09 Catering Service						
Crew Meals	24	Days	80	13	24,000	24,000
Extras	300	Meals	1	13	3,900	3,900
Ice/Propane	4	Weeks	1	300	1,200	1,200
2nd Meals	13	Days	1	500	6,500	6,500
Sales Tax	1	Allow	1	3,050	3,050	3,050
Tent	1	Allow	1	1,500	1,500	1,500
25-10 Location Office Drinks/Snacks	12	Weeks	1	200	2,400	2,400
25-11 Location Office Supplies	1	Allow	1	2,500	2,500	2,500
25-12 Location Office Equipment	1	Allow	1	3,000	3,000	3,000
25-13 Location Office Space Rental	2.5	Months	1	4,000	10,000	10,000
24-14 Location Office Telephone/Fax	1	Allow	1	15,000	15,000	15,000
25-15 Shipping & Overnight	1	Allow	1	1,500	1,500	1,500
25-16 Gratuities	1	Allow	1	2,000	2,000	2,000
25-17 Location Site Rental						
Shoot	24	Days	1	3,500	84,000	84,000
25-18 Location Survey	1	Allow	1	2,000	2,000	2,000
Photos/Film	1	Allow	1	750	750	750
25-19 Auto Rentals						
Location Manager	12	Weeks	1	250	3,000	3,000
Assistants	2	Weeks	1	150	300	300
25-20 Miscellaneous Expenses						
Mileage/DGA/SAG/Crew	1	Allow	1	1,000	1,000	1,000
Payroll				87,050	20,022	20,022
				Total for 25-00			284,672
26-00 Picture Vehicles/Animals						
26-01 Animal Trainers						
Boss Wrangler	3	Weeks	1	1,700	5,100	5,100
Assistant Wrangler	3	Weeks	1	1,200	3,600	3,600
Wranglers	1	Week	5	1,000	5,000	5,000
Riders/Handlers, etc	1	Day	20	125	2,500	2,500
26-02 Animals						
Horses	1	Allow	1	8,000	8,000	8,000
Veterinary Expenses	1	Allow	1	500	500	500
Feed/Shelter	1	Allow	1	1,200	1,200	1,200
Transportation	1	Allow	1	5,000	5,000	5,000
26-03 Picture Cars						
Sheriff Rizzoli's Car	1.4	Weeks	1	500	700	700
Frances' Car	3	Weeks	1	500	1,500	1,500
Skylark's Car	3	Weeks	1	500	1,500	1,500
Background Cars	1	Allow	1	5,000	5,000	5,000
Payroll				16,200	3,726	3,726
				Total for 26-00			43,326
27-00 Film & Lab - Production						
27-01 Raw Stock (Film-Production)	6000	Ft.	24	0	66,240	
Second Camera	2000	Ft.	10	0	9,200	
Sales Tax	1	Allow	1	75,440	6,224	81,664
27-02 Lab-Negative Prep & Process	164,000	Ft.	1	0	19,680	19,680
27-03 Telecine	1	Allow	1	49,000	49,000	49,000
27-04 Digital Dailies (incl. in Telecine)			1	0	0	0
				Total for 27-00			150,344

	Amt.	Units	x	Rate	Sub-Total	Total	
28-00 Travel and Living-Crew							
28-01 Airfares-LA-New Orleans-RT	24	Fares	1	489	11,736	11,736	
DP/Cam Op/1stAC/Gaffer/Key Grip							
Key Make-Up/Key Hair/Costume Des.							
Costumer/Props/Set Dec./Swing Lead/							
Spec. Efx/Prod. Des./Ass't Prod. Des.							
Tech Adv./Auditor/Ass't Auditor/Editor/Ass't Ed.							
Prod. Coord/1st AD/2nd AD/UPM							
28-02 Hotels	1031	Nites	1	100	103,100	103,100	
28-03 Taxi	1	Allow	1	1,500	1,500	1,500	
28-04 Auto - UPM	64	Days	1	35	2,240	2,240	
28-05 Rail					0	0	
28-06 Excess Baggage	1	Allow	1	2,500	2,500	2,500	
28-08 Per Diem	1001	Days	1	45	45,045	45,045	
				Total for 28-00			166,121
30-00 Editorial							
30-01 Editor - Shoot/Post	16	Weeks	1	2,400	38,400	38,400	
Post-Production Supervisor	8	Weeks	1	2,400	19,200	57,600	
30-02 Assistant Editor - Shoot/Post	16	Weeks	1	1,300	20,800	20,800	
30-06 Purchases	1	Allow	1	1,500	1,500	1,500	
Payroll				78,400	18,032	18,032	
				Total for 30-00			136,332
31-00 Post-Prod. Film & Lab/Videotape							
31-02 Negative Pull selects for DI	12	Reels	1	350	4,200	4,200	
Supplies	12	Reels	1	75	900	900	
				Total for 31-00			5,100
32-00 Digital Intermediate							
32-10 Digital Intermediate 2K scan	1	Allow	1	150,000	150,000	150,000	
				Total for 32-00			150,000
33-00 Music							
33-01 Composer	1	Allow	1	85,000	85,000	85,000	
(All-In Package includes: Arrangers, Copyists,							
...Musicians, Instruments)							
				Total for 33-00			85,000
34-00 Post-Production Sound							
34-01 Sound Editor	6	Weeks	1	2,000	12,000	12,000	
34-03 Music Editor	1.2	Weeks	1	2,000	2,400	2,400	
34-04 Dialogue Editor	2	Weeks	1	2,000	4,000	4,000	
34-05 Spotting for Music/Sound FX	24	Hours	1	45	1,080	1,080	
34-06 Music Scoring Stage	6	Days	1	1,400	8,400	8,400	
34-07 Music Mix Down	2	Days	1	1,400	2,800	2,800	
34-08 ADR (Studio/Editor)	2	Days	1	1,400	2,800	2,800	
34-09 Foley (Stage/Editor)	7	Days	1	2,200	15,400	15,400	
34-09 Foley (Artists)	7	Days	2	350	4,900	4,900	
34-10 Mix	45	Hours	1	250	11,250	11,250	
34-11 Printmaster + M&E	8	Hours	1	300	2,400	2,400	
34-11 Dolby Printmaster Digital + SR	1	Allow	1	8,000	8,000	8,000	
34-12 Optical Sound Transfer	12000	Ft.	1	0	4,320	4,320	
34-13 Stock/Dubs/Transfers (Film)	1	Allow	1	5,000	5,000	5,000	
				Total for 34-00			84,750
37-00 Insurance							

$5 MILLION FEATURE FILM BUDGET (CONTINUED)

	Amt.	Units	x	Rate	Sub-Total	Total
(Allow 3% of Below-the-Line)	1	Allow	1	2,848,999	85,470	85,470
37-01 Producers Entertainment Pckg.						
Negative					0	0
Faulty Stock					0	0
Equipment					0	0
Props/Sets					0	0
Extra Expense					0	0
3rd Party Property Damage					0	0
Office Contents					0	0
37-02 General Liability					0	0
37-03 Hired Auto					0	0
37-04 Cast Insurance					0	0
37-05 Workers Compensation					0	0
37-06 Errors & Omissions					0	0
				Total for 37-00		85,470
38-00 General & Administrative Expenses						
38-02 Legal	1	Allow	1	45,000	45,000	45,000
38-03 Accounting fees	1	Allow	1	5,000	5,000	5,000
38-05 Telephone/Fax	1	Allow	1	10,000	10,000	10,000
38-06 Copying	1	Allow	1	1,500	1,500	1,500
38-07 Postage & Freight	1	Allow	1	1,000	1,000	1,000
38-08 Office Space Rental	1	Allow	1	12,000	12,000	12,000
38-09 Office Furniture	1	Allow	1	2,000	2,000	2,000
38-10 Office Equipment & Supplies	1	Allow	1	5,000	5,000	5,000
38-11 Computer Rental						
Line Producer	14	Weeks	1	125	1,750	
First AD	7	Weeks	1	125	875	
Prod. Coordinator	12	Weeks	1	125	1,500	
Prod. Accountant	22	Weeks	1	125	2,750	
Office	8	Months	1	350	2,800	
Printers	8	Months	1	350	2,800	12,475
38-12 Software	1	Allow	1	1,500	1,500	1,500
38-14 Messenger/Overnight	1	Allow	1	1,000	1,000	1,000
38-15 Parking	1	Allow	1	800	800	800
38-16 Storage	1	Allow	1	1,500	1,500	1,500
38-19 Wrap Party	1	Allow	1	2,500	2,500	2,500
				Total for 38-00		101,275
Contingency @ 5%					241,687	241,687
GRAND TOTAL						$5,075,437
Total Above-the-Line						1,565,313
Total Below-the-Line						3,268,436
Total Above and Below-the-Line						4,833,749
				Check budget totals	5,075,437	5,075,437

$5 MILLION
FEATURE FILM BUDGET

01-00 Story Rights

This movie is not based on a book, or on anyone's life story. It's an original screenplay based on an idea by the Executive Producer, who jotted it down on the back of an envelope as he stood in a line at the unemployment office.

02-00 Script

The Executive Producer interested an investor in the idea, who put up the money to hire a respected but unproduced screenwriter.

02-01 Writer's Salaries

The Writer was paid WGA scale for the treatment through the polish, and negotiated a production bonus for himself (not required by the WGA) that pays him an additional $20,000 should the picture go into production.

02-02 Research

The Writer also convinced the Executive Producer to allow this line item for the purchase of books, and several trips to New Orleans to research background for the story, which takes place in the 1960s.

02-03 Title Registration

A legal fee paid to a clearance house to make sure there was no conflict with using the title.

02-08 Script Timing

Usually the script is timed after it has been approved for production, but in this case the script was long, and knowing that this might be a strike against him in getting a production deal, the Executive Producer wanted to know how long the movie would play as part of his pitch to the studio.

02-10 Development

The Executive Producer ran up a travel bill on his credit cards trying to get investors. This is his way of getting the money back.

03-00 Producers Unit

03-01 Executive Producer

His fee for the production period of the picture. He also has a "back end" deal to share profits with the investor, providing if there are any after the studio earns its production and promotion money back and takes its profit. But that's another book.

03-02 Producer

The Executive Producer has managed to do all the deal-making himself — that is, with no other "Producer" partners. He hires a Line Producer (10-01) to actually produce the movie, and the Editor to both edit and supervise post-production.

03-03 Associate Producer

Sometimes the Associate Producer is the Post-Production Supervisor, but in this case, the Executive Producer has hired the Editor to handle the post. So there is no AP on this one.

03-04 Assistant to the Executive Producer

This person helps the Executive Producer get through the days of pre-production, production, and half of post-production. The Executive wanted to keep him on until the end but had to cut somewhere, and post is quiet compared to production.

03-06 Consultants

This is a slop category. In this case, the Executive Producer had extensive production meetings with an established Producer who could not work on the project, but accepted an "honorarium" for his production advice.

03-07 Producer's Miscellaneous

Another slop category for unexpected expenses.

04-00 Direction

04-01 Director

The Executive Producer and the studio have selected a reasonably seasoned Director of low to medium budget films. He is paid over the DGA scale, and there is no payroll tax applied because his company is receiving the checks.

The Director is on location with the Executive Producer, Producer, and Location Manager a full five weeks before cameras roll. After the 24 days of shooting (and four days off), the Director will return to L.A., and, after a short break in which the Editor assembles the first rough cut, will spend the next two months creating the "Director's Cut." After that he plans a vacation in Majorca with his three children from his ex-wife, and his current companion.

05-00 Cast

05-01 Lead Actors

These rates are way over-scale, but these are the stars. SAG pension and health rates are at a given percentage (currently 14.8%), but if an actor earns over $200,000 in any single film, anything over that figure is not subject to the P&H. You can add it into the budget anyway, to create a secret pocket of cash for a rainy day, but check the actor's check requests to make sure you're not overpaying. Also, check with SAG for any changes to those rates or rules.

05-02 Supporting Cast

The roles of Harry and Edna are played by actors flying in from Los Angeles, so their pay for a 6-day week is calculated on a special formula. Check with SAG to figure out what your formula is, because there are several "ifs," "ands," and "buts."

Similarly, because the other supporting players are local people, their pay is calculated differently from Harry and Edna's.

In this case, the actors playing Harry, Edna, and Sheriff Rizzoli are paid over-scale. Their fee includes a 10% agency fee. The other supporting cast players are local people, working a 6-day week, at SAG scale, plus an agency fee.

Note: This may be the first time you've encountered weeks with decimal points (Sheriff Rizzoli). This notation is often used for people who are hired by flat weekly rates. When a person is hired for one or more 5-day weeks plus a partial week, the partial week is divided into tenths. So one week and one day is shown as 1.2 weeks. A week plus 2 days is 1.4 weeks. A week plus 3 days is 1.6 weeks. And a week plus 4 days is 1.8 weeks. This makes budgeting simpler because you just multiply by the weekly rate instead of having to stop and figure out what the day rate is.

05-03 Day Players

The actors playing Balthazar, Rudnick, and Shorty are local character actors paid over-scale, plus agency fee. The rest of the Day Players are paid SAG scale plus agency fee.

05-04 Casting Director

This is a package price based on the number of cast, and the time allowed for the casting process. The price includes fees for the Casting Director and staff, room rental for auditions, video camera and stock to tape auditions, and other administrative costs of doing all of the actor's SAG paperwork. The lion's share goes to an L.A.-based Casting Director to handle the principal parts. The rest goes to a New Orleans–based person for the smaller parts.

05-05 Casting Expenses

An extra allowance is provided for copying of scripts, overnight delivery, and so on.

05-06 Choreographer

A Choreographer and one assistant are on board to stage a barn dance scene, and a steamy dance sequence between the two stars in a roadside honky-tonk.

05-10 Stunt Coordinator

Since the stunts in this picture are pretty run of the mill as stunts go (mostly fighting and falling), the Stunt Coordinator is only on for 3 weeks total. This includes all his prep time, which occurs during pre-production because the stunt scenes are near the start of the shoot. This rate is for 6-day weeks.

05-11 Stunt Players

Since only some of the stunt work is regular, only four stunt players are on weekly contracts (6-day weeks). The others are budgeted in a more general way as "man days" (a measure of how much labor is required to perform a task), because they are called in on an "as needed" basis.

05-12 Stunt Costs/Adjustments

"Adjustments" are the extra monies stunt people get for doing what they do. This line is only $5,000 because the stunts are pretty basic. More dangerous stunts get higher adjustments.

05-13 Stunt Equipment

This figure is what the Stunt Coordinator has budgeted for some special rigging, padding, and so on, needed to pull off the fight.

05-14 ADR

Since we have no idea how much ADR work there will be by the picture's end, this is a reasonable allowance.

05-15 Cast Overtime

Another reasonable allowance.

06-00 Travel and Living — Producers

06-01 Air Fares

Two first-class fares and free champagne for the Executive Producer and the Director. Everyone else gets salted nuts.

06-02 Hotels

The Executive Producer and the Director are at the location for about one month of prep and one month of shoot.

06-09 Per Diem

Daily expenses for the Executive Producer and the Director.

07-00 Travel and Living — Cast

07-01 Air Fare

First-class fares are standard for SAG players.

07-02 Hotels

The two stars are on location for practically all of the shoot period; "Harry" and "Edna" for a little over half of the period.

07-08 Per Diem

Daily expense allowances are part of the SAG agreement for players on location. The locals don't score here.

10-00 Production Staff

10-01 UPM/Line Producer

The Unit Production Manager/Line Producer (who will naturally prefer the latter title) is a nuts-and-bolts, up-through-the-ranks person with years of experience and know-how. This rate is the DGA scale for UPMs on location. It also includes his DGA production fee.

During the prep phase on location, the Line Producer checks in frequently with the head of each department, asking them to reassess their budgets in view of the Director's creative choices for specific setups and action. If any department budgets get too high, it's up to the Line

Producer to either rob some other department, or confer with the Director to reduce costs.

His life span on the project is only through production and three weeks of cleaning up. Then he looks for work again.

10-02 1st AD/2nd AD

The 1st AD is on location with the Director from the start of prep through the shoot. The 2nd AD joins up about two weeks before the shoot. Payments for both are DGA scale for locations on a 6-day (Saturday included) shoot schedule. Also included on a separate line are the DGA "production fees" which are payable for every day cameras roll. 1st and 2nd ADs can be paid a "production fee" for prep days as well, at the Line Producer's discretion. This Line Producer opted not to, and made that clear at the outset.

10-04 Production Coordinator/Assistant Coordinator

On for almost the same prep, shoot and wrap time as the Line Producer, the Coordinators are essential in getting the myriad production elements ready. Payments are in the industry standard ranges for this level of budget, for a 6-day shoot schedule.

10-05 Script Supervisor

The Script Supervisor needs five days to get the script ready for shooting, and thereafter will be on hand for every frame of film shot.

Also, there are eight days when the Script Supervisor will keep camera notes for two cameras, and he or she gets a "bump" or extra money for those days.

Note: If you are reading this budget from top to bottom, this is the first time you'll come across an hourly wage. The formula for paying people by the hour goes like this: The number in the times box (marked with an x at the top of the budget page) refers to the number of pay hours a person works. For this picture, the budget is calculated on a 12 work-hour day. So why enter the number 14 in most of the shoot lines? Because it represents pay hours, not hours worked. If a person works 12 hours, 8 of those hours are paid at straight time, and 4 hours are paid at time and a half (1.5). Four hours multiplied by 1.5 = 6 pay hours. So the total pay hours is the sum of 8 plus 6, or 14 pay hours.

The next number, for example with the Script Supervisor ($21.43), represents the person's hourly rate.

"Prep" and "Wrap" line items are self-explanatory, and vary according to the demands of each job. "Shoot" and "Saturdays Worked" need an explanation.

This is a 4-week, or 24-day shoot. Monday through Friday are straight time for 8 hours, and time and a half for 4 hours, which is 12 work hours per day, or 14 pay hours. Saturdays are also worked at a 12-hour day, but Saturdays are paid at time and a half. Twelve hours multiplied by 1.5 = 18 pay hours. That's why the number 18 sits in the "Saturdays Worked" box.

10-06 Production Accountant/Assistant

The Auditors or Accountants come on during prep to set up the books and handle payroll for all prep personnel. They are most active during the shoot period as they pay bills, payroll, and prepare daily and weekly Cost Reports that tell the Line Producer and the studio how much the picture is behind schedule and over budget.

10-07 Technical Advisor

An expert in law enforcement techniques is on hand during the shoot to keep Sheriff Rizzoli (and the Director) honest in the depiction of police methods of the 1960s.

10-08 Production Assistants

The Office PA is another indispensable person in the production chain of command. He or she, and the Set PAs, help on the set, reporting to the ADs. They must be bright, energetic, cheerful, efficient, and cheap.

10-09 Teacher/Welfare Worker

As the schedule turns out, there will be kids on the set during almost all of the shoot period. There are fewer than 10 at any given time, however, so only one Teacher/Welfare Worker is required. Also, since this is a summer time shoot, and the kids are on vacation, no school time is required, only daily periods of R&R.

11-00 Extra Talent

11-01 Stand-Ins
There is no SAG Extras agreement for the location, New Orleans, but this was figured on SAG minimums anyway, since these people will be on set for 12 hours a day during the entire shooting period.

11-02 Extras
There is one big barn dance scene that will employ 100 extras for one day. They will be required to stomp their feet and clap as two of the stars do a star turn. These are SAG rates, even though SAG does not represent extras in New Orleans. In some places, it's possible to get away with paying less, but not in New Orleans. The Line Producer does save a little by not paying SAG pension and health.

11-03 Extras Casting Fee
All the headaches of calling and organizing 300 people, and doing their paperwork, are handed off to an Extras casting agency for a 10% charge of Extras' salaries.

13-00 Production Design

13-01 Production Designer
The Production Designer must be on hand during prep to scout, help select, and design for all the locations. He or she is on a weekly (6-day) flat. The 1960s period look has to be resurrected for everything.

13-10 Digital camera
This is the first of many departments that requires stills. They help in pre-production when the department head cannot lay eyes on the real thing. And they help in continuity during shooting, when something or someone has to be reconstructed more than once.

14-00 Set Construction

14-01 Construction Coordinator
For this picture, about one month is required to build the sets

needed to start shooting. Sets needed later in production will be built after shooting begins. The Construction Coordinator works with the Production Designer on the plans, then gets the construction crew and painters in gear to get the sets ready on time.

Note: As a department head, the Coordinator gets the same rate, $25 per hour, as other similar department heads, such as Set Dressing, Set Operations, Property, and Electric. Their assistants and workers also get paid on a par with those in other departments. Consistency in the rate of pay keeps grumbling and jealousy about money in check.

14-02 Labor

The Foreman is a man with experience, knowledge of local deals, and good contacts for local crew. Based on conversations with the Production Designer and Construction Coordinator, an allowance of $50,000 is set aside for construction crew.

14-03 Scenic Painters

The Lead Scenic Painter is the Foreman to the painting crew. Like the Construction Foreman, this man knows local deals and crew contacts.

14-05 Greens

This is a fairly average allowance for plants, shrubbery, and the like, but there isn't all that much call in the script for action in and around the bushes. The Greens will also be used to mask an atrocious pink porch that the homeowner will not allow to be repainted — something about his wife spending three months to get the pink the exact right shade.

14-09 Set Strike

It's always unbelievable how much time, money, and effort go into making sets look perfect, sometimes for just one shot, only to have them taken apart and destroyed a day later. This line item covers the cost of taking sets apart and hauling them off to storage warehouses or city dumps.

15-00 Set Operations

15-01 Key Grip

The Key Grip needs some prep time on location to pick a crew, and scout the locations to get a sense of the equipment and pre-rigging needs. This person is being flown in from L.A. because it's an important position and the Line Producer wanted someone he had worked with before.

15-02 Best Boy Grip

Once in New Orleans, the Key Grip and the Line Producer bring on a Second Grip to assist with prep and shoot.

15-03 Other Grips

The three other Grips who will work the whole shoot are local as well, and probably known to the Second Grip as reliable people. An allowance of 40 man-days has been provided for extra Grips needed for pre-rig, striking, and additional heavy days.

15-04 Dolly Grips

Prep time is allowed for these specialized Grips to check out the dolly.

15-05 Craft Service

Because the crew needs coffee and donuts (and eggs, toast, bacon, cereal) at the crack of dawn, and coffee to stay awake at night, these necessary people are often first on and last off the set. An ample overtime allowance is provided. At $275 per day for purchases, there's a healthy sampling of good food on the table, including hot "walking meals" for breakfast when needed.

15-06 Grip Rentals

During the prep period, the Director of Photography, Director, and Line Producer determine what cranes and dollies, along with standard grip equipment, will be needed to get the shots that will keep the story visually interesting. Then the equipment is ordered well in advance. Sometimes the shooting schedule changes, and specific equipment, like a big crane for example, may not be available. That's why good Line Producers, especially on location, have backup plans that include knowing where to get what they need.

16-00 Special Effects

16-01 Special Effects Person
This is another key person who flies in from L.A., in this case to have about 10 days prep time on location to survey the camera setups and troubleshoot any technical and safety problems that might come up to ruin his gags or get someone hurt.

He'll also have to time to pre-rig an effect involving Rain Birds (rain storm sprinklers), and huge fans that simulate a windstorm that blows two kids and a horse across an outdoor square dance platform. Fun.

16-02 SFX Assistant
This is a local guy who will also provide a mobile effects shop to fabricate or repair needed items on the spot (provided for in 16-09).

16-03 Additional Labor
One hundred man-days are allowed for extra help in setting up the windstorm shot, a few car scrapes, and sundry other effects.

16-06/16-07/16-08 Manufacturing Labor/Fabrication/Expendables
These categories cover all the special rigging and materials needed to achieve the effects. The Special Effects Person has been key in estimating the cost of all this.

17-00 Set Dressing

17-01 Set Decorator
Working closely with the Production Designer, the Set Decorator arrives for three weeks of prep to scour New Orleans for the right period furniture, drapery, and other house and office accouterments that will make the scenes look right out of the 1960s.

17-02 Lead Man

The Lead Man is someone who has worked often with the Set Decorator. He works ahead of (i.e., "leads") the shoot unit, and is in charge of propping locations, handling returns, and generally running the Swing Gang.

He and the Set Decorator scour New Orleans, often in separate cars (17-10), as well as hire the Swing Gang (17-03) who will physically move everything into place on the sets, hang the curtains and the lights, lay the carpet, and then take it all away when the shot is done.

17-06/17-07 Purchases and Rentals

Together, there's $60,000 to buy all the carpet set dressing used on the film. Anything that can be resold will be resold.

18-00 Property

18-01 Property Master

This is another fly-in from L.A., about four weeks prior to shooting. There are lots of props to buy and rent for this picture, including four antique blunderbuss muskets that must fire. The Prop Master also has a powder license to legally handle the firearms.

18-02 Property Assistant

This is a local person who knows where things can be found, and will help with buying and renting props.

19-00 Wardrobe

19-01 Costume Designer

The Designer works on a 6-day flat week, and flies in from L.A. for 4 weeks of prep. She works with the Director and Production Designer to make sure the styles and colors of the costumes blend in with the overall look of the film. Most of the 1960s fashions will be rented, but quite a few will be bought, made from scratch, or adjusted from contemporary clothing (19-05 and 19-06). The Costumer (19-02) and Additional Costumer (19-03), a local person, help do the adjustments. Lead and Supporting cast members are fitted well in advance, and all costumes are approved by the Director.

19-03 Additional Costumers
Fifteen man-days are allowed for more costumers to clothe certain extras for special business in the barn dance scene, and in several street scenes.

20-00 Make-Up and Hairdressing

20-01 Key Make-Up Artist
The Key Make-Up Artist has already had a discussion with the Director about the look of the actors. Since this is a realistic picture with no special make-up effects, it wasn't a very long conversation.

The Key Make-Up has two days to travel (one each way), like everyone else, and two days to check out any special setups, and gather any needed supplies.

The Line Producer, being the think-ahead kind of person that he is, heard through the grapevine that the actress playing "Edna" typically takes two and a half to three hours for regular make-up. He therefore worked with the 1st AD, who sets call times, to allow for that little glitch in the schedule.

20-02 Additional Make-Up Artist
Six days of the 24-day schedule are scenes that can be handled by the Key Make-Up alone, but the other 18 need help.

20-03 Hair Stylist
The Hair Stylist has three more days prep than the Key Make-Up — remember, this is the '60s when hair was king. The character of "Skylark" has a rich mane of long hippie hair, but the actor just got off a picture in which he played a combat Marine. The answer is a wig, of course, which requires a bit more prep time each shoot day (Rentals 20-06). Other characters also sport long hair, but they've managed to grow their own.

20-04 Additional Hair Stylist
Same as the Additional Make-Up.

21-00 Electrical

21-01 Gaffer

The Gaffer is another key person who has been hired by the Director of Photography. They have a long relationship of working together, and the Gaffer usually second-guesses the DP. In addition, he tells good jokes, and since the DP is also operating the camera on this one, the stress level might be a little higher.

The Gaffer flies in for a week of prep on location, which involves a tech scout for each scene, hiring crew, conferring with the DP and the Key Grip for special equipment or crew needs, securing the right lighting equipment, and hiring the Best Boy and three local Electrics who will be the core team of his department.

21-02 Best Boy

The Best Boy is a New Orleans man with a good professional reputation and a recipe for a killer gumbo. He comes on for the same prep period as the Gaffer, and assists in running the crew and keeping track of all the lighting inventory.

21-03 Electrics

These three come on for 4 days of prep, during which they prepare and check all the lighting equipment, organize the truck, and do some prerigging for the first day's shoot.

21-04 Additional Labor

Thirty man-days have been allowed for the several setups that will require extra lights. The first is the now famous barn dance/windstorm scene, which requires substantial pre-wiring since it's a night shoot with water all over the place.

21-05 Purchases

This money covers the various "expendables" in the lighting budget, such as gels, black wrap, tape, replacement bulbs, and so forth.

21-06 Rentals

This is the basic lighting equipment package, which the Gaffer and the Line Producer have assembled per the instructions of the DP and within the limits of the overall budget. It comes from a New Orleans supplier, in a 40-foot production trailer truck with twin generators.

There is also Additional Equipment, Condors (crane-like devices that get lights up in the air and hold a man in a basket to adjust them), and an Additional Generator. These are for the barn dance night shoot, and for several other less elaborate night shoots.

22-00 Camera

22-01 Director of Photography/Operator

The DP and the Director are old collaborators who work well together. On this shoot he will also operate the A camera. He arrives on location for 5 days of prep, and walks through each proposed setup with the Director and the Gaffer. He is on a 6-day per week flat.

22-02 Camera Operator (B Cam)

A second camera will be used for 10 days of the 24 days of shooting, but 2 of those 10 days will be with a Steadicam Operator (22-11). The B Camera Operator flies in from L.A. with no more than an afternoon of prep before his 8 days of shooting. As a specialist, his rate is higher than the $25 per hour paid to Keys and most department heads.

22-03 1st Assistant Camera

This is another specialist whom the DP relies on to pull focus, change lenses, and set f-stops. He also knows how to repair the camera for minor problems, which can be especially handy on location.

The 1st AC arrives on location for 2 days of prep, and checks out the two cameras, lenses, magazines, and other attachments very carefully to make sure no schlock equipment gets on the set. He'll also make sure the right film is on hand, and the film loading room is shipshape.

The B Camera 1st AC is local, shows up on his first shoot day, and works for 10 days, 2 of which are assisting the Steadicam Operator.

22-04 2nd Assistant Camera

The 2nd ACs load magazines, make sure can labels are accurate, handle the clapboard or slate, and generally help the others on the camera crew. Both of these assistants are local.

The 2nd AC for the A camera has 2 days of prep, working right alongside the 1st AC. Similarly, the 2nd AC for the B camera sticks with the 1st AC for the B camera, working 10 days, 2 of which are with the Steadicam Operator.

22-05 Still Photographer

The Line Producer wanted to have a still photographer on hand for the whole period, but decided he couldn't afford it. So the one week in which the movie's stars and supporting cast are all working is the week the still photographer shows up for production and promotion stills. She's a good shooter from New Orleans.

22-07 Camera Package Rental

The DP orders one Arriflex 535A with lenses as the A camera package, and an Arriflex 535B (camera body only) as the B camera. It will also act as a reserve camera in case of major trouble. The lens package consists of Zeiss Standard Speed PL Primes, and includes 16mm, 24mm, 32mm, 50mm, 85mm, and 100mm, plus one 500mm telephoto. The entire package, with magazines, filters, accessories, and batteries, comes to $7,000 per week.

22-10 Additional Equipment

This account allows for extra rentals for things that come up in the course of shooting, like a special camera rig for a difficult shot.

22-11 Steadicam Operator and Equipment

This is a local man who rents himself and his harness out as a package for $1,500 per day. The Director wants a moving camera look for some of the square dance scenes, and several others. Two days' work.

23-00 Sound

23-01 Mixer

The Mixer and the Boom Operator are actually a local couple who rent themselves and their sound package. In the one day of prep, the Mixer checks equipment and loads it into the camera/sound truck.

23-02 Boom Operator

The Boom Op shows up on the first shoot day with her "fish pole" (the mike boom), and her strong arms.

23-04 Sound Package

Since this film is being edited on videotape, a portable machine, such as a Fostex PD-4. or a Nagra 4STC timecode recorder is used to record sound. Since the sound package will be rented for four weeks, the Mixer gives about a 33% discount.

A basic sound package for theatrical production (courtesy of production sound guru Fred Ginsburg at *www.equipmentemporium.com*):

▶ Mackie mixer with at least 4 XLR mic inputs, 48vPhantom, 3-band EQ, and Aux sends ($35)

▶ Sound Devices recorder 702T two-track with timecode, or 744T four-track, or the Edirol R4-Pro four-track with timecode ($80 – $100 plus $25 – $40 for a timecode slate)

▶ Inverter and 12v battery pack ($30)

▶ Two – three condenser shotgun mics ($20 to $40 each)

▶ Shockmounts for each shotgun mic ($5)

▶ Windscreen (e.g. Equalizer or full zeppelin system $8-$15)

▶ One or two boompoles, 12-foot min. ($10)

▶ Dynamic handheld mic ($10)

▶ Lavaliers (e.g. MT830, AT899, ECM77 – $10) (Omni lavs for interviews)

▶ Proximity lavaliers (e.g. Countryman B3, ECM44 – $10)

▶ Two wireless units (e.g. Lectronsonics, Sony or Audio Technica 1800 series – $35 to $50)

▶ Assortment of mic cables, including 30's, 50's ($2 each)

▶ Headphones for sound mixer and boom op ($5)

▶ Duplex cable to connect to boom operator ($10)

▶ Portable cart ($10)

$495 total rental price/day

23-05 Walkie Talkies

Everybody wants a walkie, it seems, from the Line Producer to the Crafts Services person. While they can be a pain in the neck to lug around, they can also save a lot of walking and serious yelling. A relatively cheap convenience.

23-08 Cell Phones/Service
The cell phones are expensive but worth it.

24-00 Transportation

24-01 Transportation Coordinator
A competent Coordinator is a glorious thing. This man is a local with years of experience. He knows how to help the production team analyze the schedule and break out all the transportation needs.

24-02 Drivers
The Captain is the first lieutenant to the Coordinator.

There are 18 drivers on this shoot. Some prep for merely a day, which means they check out the truck and drive it to the first location. Others, like the Props or Set Dressing Drivers, have up to 10 days of prep, during which time they run all over town picking up the various items ordered by the Production Designer, Set Decorator, Costume Designer, and so on.

Drivers get 18 pay hours per average day, because they work 14 hours to everyone else's 12. They're on the set an hour prior and off the set an hour later.

24-03 Equipment Rentals
The vehicles list itself is a monument to careful planning. Every day of the shoot has been mapped out according to vehicle needs. In as many cases as possible, trailers have been rented instead of trucks. This means a Crew Cab or Maxi Van can haul the trailer to its place, then unhook and do other things.

25-00 Location Expenses

25-01 Location Manager
The Location Manager agrees to an 11-week deal on a weekly flat fee that includes Saturdays during production and as needed during prep.

A full seven weeks before production begins, she starts scouting. She takes tons of pictures and video (25-18 Location Survey) and sends them back to the Executive Producer, Line Producer, and Director in Los Angeles. They spend hours on the phone with her, going through all the details: Several property owners are balking at the size of the crew; a special fire permit is required for one scene; the seasonal rains may interrupt some shooting; tide charts show that the schedule must be adjusted to shoot during low tide; a holiday occurs that will cause traffic jams on the day a company move is planned.

Two weeks later, now five weeks before production, the Director, Executive Producer, and Line Producer show up in New Orleans to finalize all the locations.

In addition to locations for shooting, the Location Manager also helps the Line Producer select and make deals for housing for cast and crew. In this case, a pleasant, nearby hotel lowered its rates sufficiently to accommodate everyone. It could not, however, provide any production office space, which was a blow to the Line Producer who likes to roll out of bed and crawl to his desk in the morning. (See Production Office Space Rental 25-13.)

25-02 Assistants

The Assistant Location Manager joins up for three weeks of prep, to help the Location Manager get all the location paperwork and permits in shape. She stays on for the whole shoot.

The Local Contact Person is one Melville Oliver Bollineaux, a retired local politician whom residents call "Righteous Mel." He knows every alley, bog and bayou in 50 miles, and half the people too. Best of all, he is a master in the art of southern sweet talk, and will probably save the company thousands of dollars in grief.

25-03 First Aid

A local nurse is on hand each shooting day for anything from cuts and bruises to worse. She has good connections to local doctors, hospitals, and ambulance services.

25-04 Fire Officers

A county ordinance says a fire officer must be on hand for all shooting.

25-05 Security

This is a fairly healthy allowance for security guards, but production vehicles and parked crew cars need protection during all shooting, gear needs to be guarded during meals, and several nights the trucks will be left in remote areas. It's good insurance.

25-06 Police

A county ordinance says a police officer must be on hand for all shooting. Additional police will be used for traffic and crowd control during some shooting on city streets.

25-07 Permits

The $2,500 goes to the city and county.

25-08 Parking

This estimate is probably high, but the Line Producer stuck it in as cash for a rainy day.

25-09 Catering Service

The Location Manager has recommended Frank's Finger Lickin' Kitchen to cater the shoot meals. Frank agrees to $13 a head, which includes a vegetarian and a meat entree for each meal, plus choice of two salads, side dishes, drinks, and dessert. That price also includes servers, and table and chair setup and strike. It also includes a "walking breakfast" of hot food that the crew eats without a formal sit down. The tent is separate, as is the lunch for the 300 extras, and 2nd meals for the estimated 13 days when the shoot will go over the estimated 12 hours a day.

25-13 Location Office Space Rental

Home base for the production office is found at an office building two blocks from the hotel. It's a bit pricey for the neighborhood, but convenient.

25-17 Location Site Rental

This $3,500 per day is an average cost that includes prep and strike days. There's a house in the French Quarter that's going to run $5,000 per day for 5 days. But at the other extreme, there's a field and forest property in a remote section of the county that will only cost $750 per day for 4 days.

25-18 Location Survey

All those pictures and video and various expenses the Location Manager incurred while surveying are paid back to her here.

25-20 Miscellaneous Expenses

Mileage for DGA, SAG, and crew (.44/mile) is reimbursements for local people who drive their own cars to the far-flung reaches of the county for the field and stream stuff.

26-00 Picture Vehicles/Animals

26-01 Animal Trainers

The Boss Wrangler and the Assistant Wrangler come on for a week of prep to walk through the scenes with horses, including the big dance scene in which 20 extra horses will be used. A nearby rancher agrees to feed and keep the horses for the two weeks they're needed, and even throws in horse trailers to get them to and from the set each day for a reasonable fee.

The five Wranglers come on for the second week, and the 20 Riders/ Handlers come on for the day of the dance scene.

26-02 Animals

Regular horses go for about $150 per day, but the horses for the stars and supporting cast are naturally better looking and better trained than most, and go for $300 per day. One little break — the Boss Wrangler was able to negotiate a half-day rate for horses with a day off from shooting.

26-03 Picture Cars

The three main picture cars are 1960s vintage, and cherry, so they have to be trailered to every location. The background cars are just that, and can be driven on the short hops. For the one long hop back into the city, a larger car trailer will be used.

27-00 Film and Lab – Production

27-01 Raw Stock

The A camera is budgeted for 6,000 feet of film a day. That's about 1 hour and 7 minutes of exposed film per day, or about 26 hours and 40 minutes total for the 24-day schedule. If the finished movie is 2 hours, as expected, that's about a 13:1 ratio.

The B camera is estimated to shoot 2,000 feet per day (about 22 minutes), for 10 days, for a total of about 3 hours and 42 minutes. That brings the grand total ratio to about 15:1.

The stock prices were negotiated at .46 per foot from a Los Angeles supplier.

27-02 Lab – Negative Prep and Process

Negative will be developed at .12 per foot from an L.A. lab.

27-03/27-04 Telecine and Digital Dailies

Telecine is the transfer of the 35mm negative to videotape and digital files. "Dailies" are a film print, videotape, DVD or digital file of the footage shot during the day. Some people call them "rushes" because films labs "rush" to develop and print the film overnight and get it back to the production the next day.

This is the usual workflow: shoot film each day, a lab processes the film overnight (27-02), and makes a best-light telecine master of the footage. The telecine master can be both on videotape (say on HD-CAM-SR) and in digital file format. From this master come the "digital dailies," and depending on various factors, the dailies can be in various formats, such as DVCam, DVD, or QuickTime files.

Different people need to watch dailies; Directors use dailies to check actor performances, framing and overall look, DPs and Camera Crew check lighting, color and focus, Producers just check because that's what producers do, and they make sure we're on schedule and budget, Studio Executives check to see how the picture is looking, actor performance and overall quality level, and Editors may need dailies as a source of video/audio to ingest into a non linear editing system to begin the editing process.

You can actually watch digital dailies in a number of ways. You can stream them online, or download them, with access via a private network. Some crews on remote locations use a satellite dish to establish an Internet connection. Maybe the Director wants hers on DVD so she can watch it in her hotel suite at night. The Editor may want his as digital files, or on high quality tape.

Digital dailies come with software, which allows us to annotate the video with information (called metadata) like circled takes, camera settings, or other notes useful for editors or colorists.

28-00 Travel and Living - Crew

28-01 Airfares

All airfares Los Angeles to New Orleans and return are coach (this is a non-union shoot). The personnel flying from L.A. includes all production department heads with the exception of Sound, Set Construction, and Transportation. That is: Camera, Electric, Set Operations, Make-Up and Hair, Wardrobe, Props, Set Dressing, Special Effects, Production Design, Production, and Editing. These departments are considered so essential to the Director's creative concept for the picture that they should be headed by people whose work the Director and/or Line Producer knows — hence all of them come from L.A. The other people flying in are in turn key to the effectiveness of the department heads.

There are 24 fares in all, each arriving according to the timetable for prep established by the Line Producer.

28-02 Hotels

The total number of weeks in the hotel, including prep and shoot time, is obviously different for different people. Each one is calculated, and the total is given as 143 weeks, or 1,001 room/nights. With visitors and studio people dropping in, the Line Producer allows another 30 room/nights, bringing the total to 1,031 room/nights.

DP	5 weeks
Cam Op B	2 weeks
1st AC	5 weeks
Gaffer	5 weeks
Key Grip	5 weeks

Key Make-Up	5 weeks
Key Hair	5 weeks
Costume Designer	6 weeks
Costumer	5 weeks
Property Master	7 weeks
Set Decorator	6 weeks
Swing Lead	6 weeks
Special Effects	5 weeks
Production Designer	7 weeks
Asst. Prod. Designer	6 weeks
Technical Advisor	7 weeks
Auditor	9 weeks
Asst. Auditor	9 weeks
Production Coordinator	9 weeks
1st AD	7 weeks
2nd AD	6 weeks
Line Producer/UPM	9 weeks
Editor	4 weeks
Asst. Editor	4 weeks
	144 weeks

28-08 Per Diem

The same formula applies to Per Diem – 1,001 man-days at $50 each.

30-00 Editorial

30-01 Editor

The production is working with a post-production house in Hollywood for both the picture and audio stages of the project. Here's on overview of the workflow: Film will be overnighted to L.A., and processed the next day at a lab. The post house then takes the original negative and does a "best light" telecine transfer to HDCAM-SR tape and QuickTime (QT) files, also making any additional digital dailies as described above. The Editor loads the QT files into Final Cut and with input from the Director, edits the Off-Line, or "creative" cut. Once the picture cut is done, it is considered "locked," and goes to audio post. Simultaneously, the picture cut now goes to one of two places, either

On-Line, or digital intermediate (DI). An On-Line is pretty much as assembly of the Off-Line, using the Edit Decision List (EDL) and program file as a guide, and the pulling the actual shots from the best light HDCAM-SR telecine transfer. Color correction would also happen in the On-Line. On-Line rates run anywhere from $350-650/hour.

For this picture, they're using a DI process, which is more elaborate and expensive. Since there is opportunity for plenty of digital manipulation in a DI, one would not choose it unless you had planned for it, or run into some production problems that the DI could solve, like removing wires from the harness holding the stunt actor 20 feet in the air as he "jumps" over the herd of horses rumbling beneath him. Here they again take the EDL and project file from the Off-Line edit as a guide, and incorporate the On-Line into the DI process — that is, they assemble the movie. Instead of using the HDCAM-SR as a source, however, they use the selected scenes ("selects") from the original film negative, and scan those into digital files. After the picture is manipulated, and color corrected, they go to the deliverables stage, which includes a film-out, where 35mm prints and/or digital cinema files are made for projection (for more on Tape to Film and Digital Cinema, see Sample Budget #5, Tape-to-Film Transfer/Digital Cinema Projection). Information about this workflow is courtesy of Jim Hardy, at HTV/illuminate, a high quality full service post-production house in Hollywood (www.htvinc.net).

Both the Editor and the Assistant Editor (30-02) fly in at the start of production to set up an editing room where they can download Quick-Time files of the dailies and begin assembly of the film itself. When the shoot is over, they fly home to L.A., and set up shop at the post house to continue. With a little luck, the film is assembled soon after the shoot, and ready for the Director to make his cut.

The Editor edits for 12 weeks after returning to L.A., cutting the Director's idea of the movie, then making fixes with respect to the studio's and the Executive Producer's notes.

As the picture gets closer to being "locked," and then is actually locked, the Post-Production Sound process begins (34-00), and the Sound Editor, Composer, Music Editor, and Dialogue Editor come on board.

31-00 Post-Production Film and Lab

31-02 Negative Pulls

A Negative Cutter uses the EDL as a guide to pull the selected shots (selects) out of the original negative and assemble them onto reels ready for scanning in the DI process.

32-00 Digital Intermediate

32-10 Digital Intermediate

The 35mm negative selects are scanned into data files. Now the EDL and program file from the Off-Line are brought in to guide in the "conforming" or On-Line process, to conform the scanned files to exactly match the hard creative work that the Editor and Director put into the EDL. Once the picture is assembled, digital manipulation and color correction is done. At the end of that process, the picture is ready for the post audio Layback, in which the final mixed audio is layed back to the edited picture master.

33-00 Music

33-01 Composer

The Executive Producer made a package deal with the Composer to supply all the music. So now it's the Composer's job to write the music — with the approval of the Director and the Executive Producer, of course — and have it performed. All that for $85,000. (The recording and mixing are part of the Post Sound process. See 34-00.)

34-00 Post-Production Sound

The team is working with a post audio facility and because the Post Supervisor is a crackerjack Editor and savvy guy, he contacted the Sound Editor to review how the audio tracks should be laid out in the picture edit. And of course they had this conversation before the picture edit even started. Why? Unfortunately, some picture editors pay no attention to how they handle the dialogue, music and effects tracks, figuring, "Oh, the Sound guy will take care of all that stuff." Then the Sound Editor inherits a mess that takes many days to sort out, and guess who pays for it? You!

In this case, the Sound Editor gets dialogue, music and effects on discrete tracks, all nicely organized and documented just like they talked about. He gets an OMF file of the edit timeline and a movie file to sync up to it.

34-01 Sound Editor

The sound editor supervises the sound team during audio post, and does most of the editing, other than dialogue and music. He lays out all the separate tracks in Pro Tools, places effects in their proper places, and prepares for the mix.

$$$

$75/hour

34-03 Music Editor

The Music Editor sits with the Composer, Director, and Producer to spot the film for music. She attends the scoring session, in which the music is recorded, and then edits the music track to the picture. That process takes about six weeks.

34-04 Dialogue Editor

The dialogue editor assembles, synchronizes, edits, cleans up and smoothes out all the dialogue. If she can use the production tracks, she will, but if any of them are unusable she replaces them with alternate production tracks recorded on set or with automated dialogue replacement (ADR).

$$$

$50/hour, and 10 days, or $5,000. Note that the production sound mixer recorded room tone at the end of nearly every camera set-up. It probably saved the Dialogue Editor three days of constructing it frame by frame, or nearly $1,500.

34-05 Spotting

The Director, Producer, and Sound Editor watch and listen to the movie for sound effects and trouble spots, like dialogue replacement. The Sound Editor then selects the sounds and positions them in the right places. This spotting session is repeated with the Composer and Music Editor to spot for music cues. Each session takes a few hours.

34-06 Music Scoring Stage

The Composer has been working on the music since the first rough cut or before and playing pieces for the Director during the picture cut. Its finished when Post Sound is underway. Then it takes two weeks for the Arranger and the Copyist to prepare it for the orchestra to play. Finally, with the film projected and the orchestra cued up, the scoring session begins. Over six days, the Composer, working with the Music Editor and the Recording Mixer, records the music to multitrack tape.

34-07 Music Mix Down

Over the next two days, the Composer, Music Editor, and Recording Engineer mix the multitrack down to three stereo tracks.

34-08 ADR

The two actors playing "Frances" and "Skylark" need to come in for ADR for two days. Luckily they were both in L.A. at the time.

$$$

$175/hour for the Sound Editor and the studio.

34-09 Foley

Two Foley artists come in to do a complete pass. (This process is done after the Dialogue Edit.) It takes seven days.

$$$

$275/hour for the Sound Editor and the Foley Stage. $350/day for each artist.

When a picture is likely to have overseas distribution (not this one) and foreign language dubbing, distributors want a "Foley-filled M&E." Sometimes, sound effects are recorded on the set along with the dialogue, and used in the final mix — say when an actor slams a door. That sound is part of the dialogue track, and when that track is eliminated for the dubbing, there goes the door slam with it. An extra Foley session replaces all sounds tied to dialogue.

34-10 Mix

The Producer, Director, Composer, and Editor gather for the Mix. All the sound elements have been placed in the correct positions, and now the Mixer will apply his artistry to weave their levels in just the right way to tell the story, as the team argues in the background. About 45 hours later, the mix is done, and it's time for Dolby (see Digital Feature Budget Post Production Sound at 34-16).

Thanks to Doug Greenfield at Dolby Labs for generously supplying us with the following information about the Dolby process. For further info, check out www.Dolby.com.

34-11 Printmaster

Assuming you're going with Dolby, when the mixers complete the mix, a Dolby engineer typically comes in for the Printmaster pass to operate the Dolby recorder, and assure that the sound track survives intact through the Optical Sound Negative phase.

In the printmaster session, the various Pre-Dub masters are summed together one more time to a 6-track "Printing master." Dolby records this into their proprietary digital recorder, to the Dolby Digital MO (magneto optical) disc, a high density storage media. It looks like a CD-sized floppy in a plastic enclosure to avoid contamination. The Dolby Digital MO is configured L (left), R (right), C (Center), LFE (Low Frequency Effects or Subwoofer), LS (Left Surround), RS (Right Surround). This is also known as the 6-track format, or the 5.1, (5 full-range audio channels with the LFE or Sub channel or Subwoofer being limited to 0.1% of the audio spectrum). Engineers point out that while ".1" channel convention does indicate a limited bandwidth channel, in fact, the Dolby DMU recorder records a bandwidth of nearly three octaves (25 Hz to 120 Hz) for the LFE or Subwoofer channel. So the figure is more like 30% on a logarithmic (per octave) scale.

Simultaneously, a secondary, backup recording is made, to another digital media, typically ProTools.

When the 6-track pass is completed, the Dolby Stereo mix is created. From the same individual Pre-Dub masters, the Dolby recorder creates the 2-track master, also recorded to the MO. This is the analog track on the film, which every theater in the world can play. Digital playback is optional, or an add-on.

In this format, the stereo surrounds are combined to a single mono track or channel, and the LFE or Sub is either discarded or mixed back into the Center channel. These 4 channels (L,C,R,S) then get matrix encoded (some sort of magic) into 2 channels (Left total, Right total, or Lt, Rt) and Dolby SR noise reduction is applied. It is this 2-track master that also appears on VHS tapes, broadcast, etc. The matrix-encoded 2-track master, also known as the Lt/Rt (for left total, right total) master, is recorded and monitored with consideration for the headroom limitations inherent in the SVA (stereo variable area) soundtrack on 35 mm film. This master, SR-decoded, was appropriate for the linear tracks on videocassettes. With the advent of DVD, a separate Lt/Rt master, allowing up to 20 dB of headroom (compared to the 6 to 8 dB of headroom for the SVA optical soundtrack master), was, and is, often recorded. In the theater, a Dolby processor either plays the 6-track digital, or decodes the 2 tracks on film back to the 4 channels (L,C,R,S) in the auditorium. At home, Dolby Pro-Logic will get you 4-channel audio (L,C,R,S). Dolby Digital is the 5.1 or 6-track mix.

$$$

8 hours is allowed for the services of the post house engineer.

For this project, the distributor wants worldwide distribution but an initial rollout of only 50 prints, so the contract service fee they pay to Dolby for these technologies and trademarks, as well as for the services of a Dolby engineer during certain phases of the mix, is $8,000 for the Dolby Digital and Dolby SR. The basic Dolby Motion Picture Service Agreement (MPSA) fee for feature films mixed in North America with no restrictions on distribution or number of prints, is currently $11,000. The MPSA fee for feature films mixed in North America for worldwide distribution, with a maximum of 50 prints, is $8,000. The MPSA for feature films mixed in North America, for distribution in North America only, with a maximum of 50 prints, is $5,000. This last MPSA fee is known as the "festival license." Dolby allows 16 hours for the services of the Dolby consultant for the standard agreement, and 8 hours for the two limited release MPSAs.

The result is the print master encoded with Dolby Digital and Dolby SR, which give the sound track that "surround sound" feeling in theaters equipped with both digital and analog playback systems.

34-12 Optical Sound Transfer

This MO is used to shoot the Optical Track Negative (OTN), which will include SR-D and Lt (Left total) and Rt (Right total) analogue. The "SR" in SR-D refers to the Dolby noise reduction process added to the analog 2 track. The "D" refers to the digital 6-channel mix. If additional formats are also required, i.e. Dolby competitors SDDS and DTS, these elements can also be shot at the same time as the Dolby Track. However, they must be delivered on separate formats and also have approval from the companies prior to shooting the OTN. Four formats on one negative are called a quad-optical negative track, SR-D, SDDS, DTS, and analog.

After the negative is shot, the OTN and the Inter-Negative (IN) are married together to create a 35mm composite print. Now everyone can kick back and smoke a big fat Cohiba.

$$$

To shoot a 35mm Optical Track Negative is .32 to .47 cents per foot. But we have two more budget categories to go through.

37-00 Insurance

37-01 Producers Entertainment Package

The insurance for this film wasn't a big problem because there really wasn't anything extraordinary about the production.

37-02 – 37-06 General Liability, Hired Auto, Cast Insurance, Workers' Compensation, E&O

The stunts were not life-threatening, all the cast showed up healthy and sober, and since it was an original story, there wasn't anyone to sue the studio or the production company because they were libeled.

The 3% of below-the-line formula was applied for insurance.

38-00 General and Administrative Expenses

38-02 Legal

The $45,000 allowance is based on a rule-of-thumb applying about 1% to 1.5% of the budget total, above- and below-the-line. For this picture, it does the trick, because everything went fairly smoothly. The attorney prepared standard contracts for the Director, star talent, and department heads, as well as location and production/distribution agreements.

38-03 Accounting Fees

After the show is wrapped, and the production auditors have gone on to other projects, there will be accounting to do, not only for un-finished stuff that trickles in, but for tax preparation as well. This is an allowance for that time.

38-05 Telephone and Fax

This line item covers phone bills for the home base production office in L.A., and therefore includes all the calls during development of the project, and during post-production. Calls during production came from the line item in the Location Expenses category.

38-11 Computer Rental

The Line Producer, 1st AD, Coordinator, and Accountant all brought their laptops to the party, and were compensated at $125 per week. The office computer and printers were budgeted as rentals, but the Line Producer suggested that for the same money they could own the equipment. The Executive Producer agreed, and that's what they did.

38-12 Software

This allowance permits the production team to buy several copies of a computerized budgeting and scheduling program for use on location and at the home office.

38-19 Wrap Party

Requires no explanation. A good time was had by all.

DOCUMENTARY VIDEO BUDGET

Instructions on Downloading Budgets:

▸ Go to *www.mwp.com*
▸ Click on "Virtual Film School"
▸ Scroll down on menu to "Resources"
▸ Download Excel Spreadsheets
▸ Save to your desktop

DOCUMENTARY VIDEO BUDGET

Fringe assumptions:		Production:	
Payroll Tax	23%	Length:	30 min.
Overtime	10%	Format:	Video (P2)
		Prep:	4 weeks
		Shoot:	9 days
		Post:	6 weeks (Off/On-Line Nonlinear to DigiBeta/Internet
		Unions:	None

SUMMARY BUDGET		
02-00 Script	4,680	
03-00 Producers Unit	25,600	
04-00 Direction	12,300	
05-00 Cast	554	
TOTAL ABOVE-THE-LINE		43,134
10-00 Production Staff	13,284	
15-00 Set Operations	531	
21-00 Electrical	4,853	
22-00 Camera	9,151	
23-00 Sound	3,965	
24-00 Transportation	495	
25-00 Location Expenses	936	
27-00 Stock - Production	1,400	
TOTAL PRODUCTION		34,614
30-00 Editorial	13,042	
33-00 Music	2,000	
34-00 Post-Production Sound	4,900	
35-00 Titles & Graphics	2,400	
TOTAL POST-PRODUCTION		22,342
37-00 Insurance	5,700	
38-00 General & Administrative	4,350	
TOTAL OTHER		10,050
Total Above-the-Line		43,134
Total Below-the-Line		67,006
Total Above and Below-the-Line		110,140
Contingency @ 10 %		11,014
GRAND TOTAL		$121,154

ABOVE-THE-LINE	Amount	Units	x	Rate	Sub-Total	Total	
02-00 Script							
02-01 Writer Salaries (non-union)	1	Flat	1	3,500	3,500	3,500	
02-03 Title Registration	1	Allow	1	375	375	375	
Payroll				3,500	805	805	
				Total for 02-00			4,680
03-00 Producers Unit							
03-02 Producer	1	Flat	1	20,000	20,000	20,000	
03-06 Consultants	1	Allow	1	1,000	1,000	1,000	
Payroll				20,000	4,600	4,600	
				Total for 03-00			25,600
04-00 Direction							
04-01 Director (non-union)	1	Flat	1	10,000	10,000	10,000	
Payroll				10,000	2,300	2,300	
				Total for 04-00			12,300
05-00 Cast							
05-08 Narrator (non-union)	1	Day	1	450	450	450	
Payroll				450	104	104	
				Total for 05-00			554
BELOW-THE-LINE							
10-00 Production Staff							
10-01 Unit Production Manager	6	Weeks	1	800	4,800	4,800	
Prep: 4 weeks							
Shoot: 1 week							
Wrap: 1 week							
10-08 Production Assistant	10	Weeks	1	550	5,500	5,500	
Prep: 4 weeks							
Shoot: 1 week							
Wrap: 5 weeks							
Runner	1	Week	1	500	500	500	
Payroll				10,800	2,484	2,484	
				Total for 10-00			13,284
15-00 Set Operations							
15-01 First Grip							
Shoot	1	Day	14	25	350		
15-05 Craft Service (PA)							
Purchases	7	Days	1	50	350	350	
Rentals	1	Allow	1	100	100	100	
Payroll				350	81	81	
				Total for 15-00			531
21-00 Electrical							
21-01 Gaffer							
Prep	1	Day	10	25	250		
Shoot (12 hrs.)	7	Days	14	25	2,450		
Overtime				2,700	270	2,970	
21-06 Equip. Rental							

	Light/Grip Pckg	7 Days	1	100	700	700	
	Extra Package	1 Day	1	500	500	500	
	Payroll			2,970	683	683	
			Total for 21-00				4,853
22-00 Camera							
22-01 Director of Photography/Op.							
	Scout	1 Day	12	$32.14	386		
	Shoot (12 hrs.)	9 Days	14	$32.14	4,050		
	Overtime			4,435	444	4,879	
22-07 Camera Pckg Rentals (Video)		7 Days	1	450	3,150	3,150	
	Payroll			4,879	1,122	1,122	
			Total for 22-00				9,151
23-00 Sound							
23-01 Mixer	Shoot (12 hrs.)	7 Days	1	350	2,450		
	Overtime			2,450	245	2,695	
23-03 Expendables (Batteries, etc)		1 Allow	1	150	150	150	
23-06 Radio Mics		5 Days	2	50	500	500	
	Payroll			2,695	620	620	
			Total for 23-00				3,965
24-00 Transportation							
24-03 Production Van		9 Days	1	55	495	495	
			Total for 24-00				495
25-00 Location Expenses							
25-06 Catering Service							
Crew Meals (6 crew + 4 guests)		6 Lunch	12	13	936	936	
			Total for 25-00				936
27-00 Stock - Production							
28-03 P2 card rental - 64Gb		2 Cards	1	300	600	600	
28-04 Hard drive purchase		2 drives	1	400	800	800	
			Total for 27-00				1,400
30-00 Editorial							
30-08 Editor		5 Weeks	1	1,500	7,500	7,500	
30-09 Off/On-Line Edit System		5 Weeks	1	500	2,500	2,500	
30-09 HDMI card		1 card	1	200	200	200	
30-12 Transcription QTs (incl in editing)							
30-13 DVD Screening Copies		20 DVD	1	35	700	700	
30-14 Video Masters/Safeties/Textless					0	0	
	DigiBeta Master	1 Tape	1	21	21	21	
	DigiBeta Protection	1 Tape	1	21	21	21	
	DigiBeta deck rental	1 day	1	375	375	375	
	Payroll			7,500	1,725	1,725	
			Total for 30-00				13,042
33-00 Music							
33-01 Composer		1 Allow	1	2,000	2,000	2,000	
(All-In Package includes: Arrangers, Copyists,					0	0	
...Musicians, Instruments, Studio,					0	0	
Engineers, Stock, etc)					0	0	
			Total for 33-00				2,000
34-00 Post-Production Sound							

34-01 Spotting for Music/Sound Efx	3	Hours	1	75	225	225
34-05 Narration Record	1	Hour	1	175	175	175
34-14 Laydown	1	Hour	1	175	175	175
34-15 Pre-Lay	24	Hours	1	75	1,800	1,800
34-16 Mix	10	Hours	1	175	1,750	1,750
34-17 Layback	1	Hour	1	375	375	375
34-18 Stock/Dubs/Transfers (Video)	1	Allow	1	400	400	400
			Total for 34-00			4,900
35-00 Titles & Graphics						
35-01 Graphic Design & Workstation	1	Allow	1	2,000	2,000	2,000
35-02 Stocks and Dubs	1	Allow	1	400	400	400
			Total for 35-00			2,400
37-00 Insurance						
37-01 Producers Entertainment Pckg	1	Allow	1	2,000	2,000	2,000
Negative					0	0
Faulty Stock					0	0
Equipment					0	0
Props/Sets					0	0
Extra Expense					0	0
3rd Party Property Damage					0	0
Office Contents					0	0
37-02 General Liability (Included)					0	0
37-03 Hired Auto					0	0
37-04 Cast Insurance					0	0
37-05 Workers Compensation	1	Allow	1	1,200	1,200	1,200
37-06 Errors & Omissions	1	Allow	1	2,500	2,500	2,500
			Total for 37-00			5,700
					0	
38-00 General & Administrative Expenses					0	
38-02 Legal	1	Allow	1	1,500	1,500	1,500
38-03 Accounting fees	1	Allow	1	500	500	500
38-05 Telephone/FAX	1	Allow	1	500	500	500
38-06 Copying	1	Allow	1	125	125	125
38-07 Postage & Freight	1	Allow	1	200	200	200
38-08 Office Space Rental				0	0	0
38-09 Ofice Furniture				0	0	0
38-10 Office Equipment & Supplies	1	Allow	1	200	200	200
38-11 Computer Rental	1	Allow	1	0	0	0
38-13 Transcription (5 hrs x 3)	15	Hours	1	25	375	375
38-14 Messenger/Overnight	1	Allow	1	125	125	125
38-15 Parking	1	Allow	1	100	100	100
38-16 Storage	1	Allow	1	150	150	150
38-17 Still Photographer	1	Allow	1	250	250	250
Equip./Supplies/Film/Processing	1	Allow	1	125	125	125
38-18 Publicity	1	Allow	1	0	0	0
38-20 Hospitality	1	Allow	1	200	200	200
38-21 Production Fee	1	Allow	1	0	0	0
			Total for 38-00			4,350
Contingency @ 10%					11,014	11,014
GRAND TOTAL						$121,154
Total Above-the-Line						43,134
Total Below-the-Line						67,006
Total Above and Below-the-Line						110,140
			Check budget totals		121,154	121,154

283

DOCUMENTARY VIDEO BUDGET

Overview

This is a 30-minute documentary program shot locally on the Panasonic HPX-170 (P2). It has vérité footage (following people in real life), interviews, footage that complements and illustrates the interviews and vérité, sometimes called "B-Roll," and a narrator that holds it all together.

The producer aims for a cable or broadcast pickup, but the likelihood of them buying rights for a single program is slim, so he is designing it for Internet release as well, even if it means splitting it into shorter segments.

Pre-Production: 4 weeks
Shoot: 7 days of vérité/interviews/B-roll
Edit: 4 weeks
Additional B roll: 2 days
Final Edit: 1 week
Audio Post: 1 week

02-00 Script

02-01 Writer's Salaries

The writer is actually the producer paying himself a little extra money, but putting it in another category to make it look better.

The "script" is the narration, which will be written in its final draft form only when the editing is finishing up.

Does this mean the producer has no idea where he is heading? No. He has spent much time even before pre-production figuring out what the program is about (in research), what its flow will be, and what ideas will hold it together. He has written all this in his proposal and treatment (see this general process mapped out in Ch. 2 Preproduction, Pre-Production for Non-Fiction Films).

During editing, he will record himself reading the first draft narration copy in a "scratch track." As editing proceeds, the producer/writer will see and hear how the copy works, and make changes as the show evolves. When it's just right, he'll have a professional narrator come in to make it sound wonderful.

02-03 Title Registration

Since the producer wants this to air on a broadcast or cable network, and on the Internet, he wants to make sure its title hasn't been used before. The investment here will protect him from having to pay more to change the title later on. His attorney will recommend a tide clearance house.

03-00 Producer's Unit

03-02 Producer

The producer is paying himself a flat for 14 weeks of work, not even counting all the time he put in writing the proposal, doing research, and pitching the project. It's a low rate, even throwing in the writing fee, but what can he say — this is his first big project, it's a labor of love, and he's got to hold costs down.

03-06 Consultants

Several people have kindly spent a lot of time helping the producer shape his ideas for the show, and this is a modest payback. Since it's going out in five different checks at $200 each, he's decided not to count it as payroll.

04-00 Direction

04-01 Director

You may be wondering why a straightforward documentary needs a Director. Couldn't the Director of Photography/Camera Operator set up the lighting and handle the creative aspects of the Director's job? In this case, probably so, but the Producer has made a strategic decision to hire an experienced Director anyway because:

(a) It's his first big project (he's nervous as hell) and he figures he'll be busy enough handling production, writing, and listening to the content of the interviews undistracted by how it all looks.

(b) He wants the B-Roll to be visually exciting, and he doesn't think he has enough experience to shoot it the way he imagines it.

(c) His deal with the Director includes sitting in on some of the editing. He'll use the Director's experience to help structure the flow of the story.

Chances are good that after this project, the Producer will have the confidence to direct and produce, and depend on the DP/Operator for beautiful cinematography, and on the Editor for good structure and flow. Depending on the complexity of the next project and the budget, he may even lose the Production Manager.

05-00 Cast

05-01 Narrator
The Producer has found a Narrator who is a member of a union but has agreed to work non-union for this show.

10-00 Production Staff

10-01 Production Manager
The Producer wants to concentrate on the content of the show, and on what the Director is doing, to make sure everything lives up to the vision he had in mind. That's why he's hired a Production Manager to help guide the project through pre-production, and shooting. The Producer can give orders, and leave all the details to the PM and the Production Assistant. The PM is hired on a weekly flat that includes the 7 days of shooting as one week.

On the scout for the shoot, the PM considers practicalities like where the nearest bathroom is at each camera setup, where the nearest power source is, crew parking, whether the carts carrying the gear will be able to get from point A to B, where the nearest grocery and hardware stores are, nearest telephones, fax machines, and so forth. Always thinking ahead.

The PM is on for a week after shooting to pay all the bills, make sure all equipment gets returned, and all other production details are neatly put to bed. This way, the Producer can get to work on the "paper cut" right away.

10-07 Production Assistant

The PA is on for the same pre-production period as the PM, and will assist the PM during that phase. Additionally, the PA will stay for five weeks after shooting to help clean up, and assist the Producer in getting the editing process rolling. The Producer wants to keep the PA on for the entire post process, mainly to hold the fort at the office, but can't afford it.

The most important function of the PA during the shoot is handling the P2 cards, and uploads. P2 is a completely file-based, tapeless system. Video data is recorded onto the P2 cards. When a card is full, the DP hands it to the PA, who uploads it via a card slot to a laptop, which is connected to two external hard drives for backup. As soon as the PA verifies that the data is securely uploaded and backed up, he deletes the data on the P2 card, and its ready for another round of data capture. The PA is on a weekly flat, which includes the 7 straight days of shooting as one week.

Since the PA is occupied with the P2 uploading, a Runner is hired for the week. Runners, also known as "go-fers," are the lowest rung on the ladder. They are usually bright, young people looking to get a start in the business. Typically under-paid, they are nonetheless indispensable. The Runner is paid $500 flat.

15-00 Set Operations

15-01 First Grip

The Grip is needed for the night shoot only.

Remember that the number in the multiplication ("x") column, in this case 14, refers to *pay hours*. Fourteen pay hours translates into 12 hours of work. See Chapter 2, Pre-Production, for a discussion on why using pay hours is more accurate, and less prone to confusion, than the often used shorthand of "$350 per day."

15-05 Craft Service

The PA and the Runner, along with their other duties, have the responsibility of keeping the crew lubricated and energized with plenty of water, juice, and munchies for the long days outdoors. Even with a crew as relatively small as seven (Producer, Director, Production Manager, Camera Operator, Sound, Gaffer, and PA, plus interview subjects), they'll easily go through a bag of groceries a day. Since they'll be moving around, they put the cooler on a cart, so all they have has to do is wheel the craft service to the next setup.

21-00 Electrical

21-01 Gaffer

The prep day for a Gaffer is unusual for a relatively simple documentary like this, but there is a reason. One of the shoot days includes a night scene that requires pulling together some extra lights. Thus the prep day. The Gaffer is paid at the same rate as the Grip, since both are experienced people who usually work bigger shows.

21-06 Light Package

The package used everyday includes a standard Omni kit, plus three pieces of 4x8 foam core, a hard/soft gold shiny board, a hard/soft silver shiny board, a 4x4 silk, 6 C-stands, and an assortment of sandbags, apple boxes, and so on.

For the night shoot, the Director, DP, and the Gaffer assemble a package that is delivered to the site. It includes one 2K, six 1Ks, a 12x12 silk, two hi-roller stands, and an assortment of sandbags, cable, apple boxes, and quad boxes. Since they'll be shooting near a swimming pool, they throw in four ground fault receptacles, which automatically shut off all power if a light hits the water. Nobody fries on this shoot.

22-00 Camera

22-01 Director of Photography

The DP/Camera Operator scouts the locations with the Director, Producer, and Production Manager. They consider how the sunlight will be at different times of day, how the sound ambience may affect them, and generally try to get the best angles on what they plan to shoot. He is paid an hourly rate that adds up to about $450 for 12 hours worked — a pretty good deal for the Producer. Ideally, a documentary Producer seeks a DP/Operator with his or her own camera and basic equipment, such as tripod and perhaps a simple lighting package. Not only is this efficient because the DP knows her own gear and presumably takes good care of it, but its also usually cost effective for the Producer. Most DPs will package themselves and their gear for less than what a Producer would pay for them separately. In this case, however, the DP is "in between" cameras, so the Producer must rent.

22-07 Camera Rentals

The camera is a Panasonic HPX-170. The package includes a tripod, a set of filters, batteries and charger, plus a shotgun mike, two hard wire lavalier microphones, fishpole, and mixer. Radio mikes (wire-less) are extra (see 23-00 Sound). They shoot in DVCPRO HD.

The package is rented by the day, but since the main shoot goes for 7 days straight, the rental house does not charge for the weekend.

23-00 Sound

The Mixer gets the best sound he can by properly placing mikes, and by listening carefully during shooting for any sound pollution. Passing airplanes, trucks, passionate conversationalists, air conditioning units, and cats and dogs all qualify. It's one of the joys of exterior shooting.

23-06 Radio Mikes

Some of the shooting will be done on people walking at some distance from the camera, so wireless mikes are needed. They are rented at the same "7 days for 5" rate as the camera package.

25-00 Equipment Rental

25-02 Production Van
A mini-van with the back seats removed carries the camera package, the daily light package, the cooler (up front in case of spillage), and sundries.

26-00 Location Expenses

26-06 Catering Service
One of the things the PM did on the scout was pick up menus from nearby restaurants that deliver. A couple hours before lunch, everyone agrees on one restaurant, and the PA gets orders.

28-00 Stock-Production

28-03 P2 Card Rental
Two 64 Gb cards are rented. Each card records 64 minutes with the DVCProHD codec. The Producer estimates recording about 3-4 hours of material per day.

30-00 Editorial

The overall plan is for the Editor to transfer the interviews to QuickTime movies with timecode window burn, have a transcription company transcribe them, and then the Producer can do a paper cut (see *A Note About Paper Cuts* in Ch. 5 Line Items at 30-08 Off-Line Editor). While the Producer is doing the paper cut, the Editor will start to assemble the vérité footage. The Producer will hand a preliminary edit list of the interviews to the editor, who will cut it together. Then they will fine tune the vérité footage, the interviews, and intercut all that with the B-roll footage shot at the time. Then, the Producer will have two days to shoot any additional B roll they need to cover holes in the edit. They'll have one final week after that to lock and clean up the picture before audio post.

30-08 Editor

The off-line editing takes four weeks. The Editor is experienced in documentary work, meaning he looks for interesting coverage for talking heads as well as good "natural sound" sequences where the camera has captured people in action and we see it unfold. He is paid on a weekly flat.

30-09 Off/On Line Edit System

The Editor provides his own Final Cut Pro (FCP) system, deck, hard drive storage, monitors, the whole rig, for $500/week. He transfers the MXF (P2) files from the hard drive into his system. He will edit at highest resolution, and color correct in FCP. The final output will be to DigiBeta, for which they will have to rent a deck for a day.

The Editor has installed a Blackmagic Design Intensity Pro card into his Mac Pro (with Quad-Core Intel Xeon processors). The cost of the card is only $200, and it allows him to drive an HD calibrated broadcast monitor for playback of the edited sequences. This is very helpful for both editing and color correction. (For editors with projectors and surround sound audio systems, the Intensity Pro card's HDMI/audio outputs can also be used to connect, so you can see your project on a larger screen direct from the computer.)

30-12 Transcription QTs

The interviews will be transcribed so the Producer can review them on paper and actually edit sequences together that may not have happened in real time. Here, the Editor uses FCP to create QuickTime (QT) videos from the P2 card footage, reading the timecode (TC) from the MXF (P2) files or regenerating the TC if necessary and burning an upper or lower window into the picture. Many transcription companies want you to upload your QT (or MPEG-4, H.264, or WM9) files to their FTP sites on the web, and give you instructions to compress the files into a lower resolution. The Editor also sends the QT files with the window burn to the Producer. When the transcriptions are complete, he can open up his laptop, watch the QT movies on one side of the screen, and follow along with the written text on the other side. This is important, because sometimes in looking at the text, you might think there's a perfect edit point, but when you listen to the speaker, you realize that she inflects in an odd way, or doesn't stop talking.

30-13 DVD Screening Copies

When all is said and done, the Producer has 20 DVD copies duplicated — 19 to show to potential distributors, and one for his mom.

30-14 Video Masters

The master will be to a DigiBeta, a preferred format for broadcast/cable companies. A protection master is made as well. A DigiBeta deck is rented for a day. The Editor also encodes the program to MP4 with H.264 video and AAC audio, which is compatible with video iPods, iPhone and Apple TV, and prepares it for launch on the Internet. (For a handy and inexpensive booklet on encoding recipes, see *www.proappstips.com/EncodingRecipes*.)

34-00 Music

34-01 Composer

Once the picture is locked, that does it for the picture side of the equation. Music and sound effects are next.

The Producer finds a Composer with a sophisticated home studio, and makes a flat deal. The money is so-so for a 30-minute score that requires quite a bit of music, so the Composer wants to do it entirely on his synthesizer. The Producer persuades the Composer to bring in some friends to play some acoustic instruments over the synth bed, to liven up the music. Seeing possible future business with this Producer, the Composer agrees. They sit down together to spot the show. Two days later the Composer has some musical ideas ready for playback.

A week later, the Composer turns in a DAT cassette with the score, all synced to the locked cut and ready for mixing with the sound effects and production sound (dialogue and natural sounds).

35-00 Post-Production Sound

The Producer calls around to a few audio post facilities. Some are busy. Some are expensive. He finds one with a good reputation, willing to do the show for the budget.

35-01 Spotting for Music/Sound Effects

The music part has already happened, so the Producer sits with a Sound Editor and spots for effects. The effects are not complicated, so this session lasts only three hours.

35-05 Narration Record

The Producer knows from the off-line scratch narration exactly how long each piece of narration must be. He makes a deal with a voice-over artist to do the track. They set up in an announce booth at the post audio house and lay it down, careful to stay within the timings now dictated by the final cut.

35-14 Laydown

The DigiBeta Master is brought to the audio post house, where the production audio is stripped off to tape.

35-15 Pre-Lay

The Sound Editor takes all the sound effects and narration, and places them at the right points in the show onto another piece of tape. All the production audio, meaning the talking and other sounds recorded in the real world, is cleaned up, and every edit is checked.

35-16 Mix

The playback sources (production sound, music, sound effects, and narration) are now mixed together into what will be the final stereo sound track of the show. The Producer, Director, and Mixer spend one long day mixing the whole show.

35-17 Layback

The mixed audio is now laid back to the original DigiBeta Master, and the show is complete. Finite. The Producer heaves a great sigh of relief, and is first in line the next day at the unemployment office.

36-00 Titles and Graphics

(This is kind of an anti-climax, because graphics actually take place during the edit process.)

36-01 Graphic Design and Workstation

The Producer and the Director want a simple but nice opening title sequence for the show, some transition graphics that will serve as the visual equivalent of chapter headings, and some bumpers to get into and out of commercial breaks.

The Producer wants to work with a freelance Graphic Designer who works out of her own office. A design plan is worked out that can be done for the money.

When the graphics are done, they are dropped into the edit.

37-00 Insurance

The Producer has contact with a broker who handles all kinds of entertainment insurance packages, from movies to home videos. This is a simple shoot, no crazy stunts, no travel, no star cast to worry about not showing up. Even the E&O is simple because no previously published or produced materials are being used, so no one can be libeled.

38-00 General and Administrative Expenses

Most of the G&A lines are self-explanatory. They cover the running of the production office. Only three require any review:

38-02 Legal

The only legal activity so far is reviewing contracts sand deal memos for cast and crew. The Producer hopes to have a little bit left in this line to apply to a review of his first distribution contract.

38-03 Accounting

The Producer has found a bookkeeper who keeps track of all accounts, pays all bills and payroll, and prepares end-of-the-year tax forms for all employees.

38-13 Transcription

The Producer allows 3-5 hours of transcription time for every one hour of material to transcribe, at $30 per hour (but always check your local rates). So that usually comes out to about $90 - $120 for every hour of video. If you have cross talk, heavy accents, or bad audio, allow more time.

38-17 Still Photographer

The Producer bites the bullet on this one. A still photographer is an expensive line for this show, but since some of the interview subjects may not be available after the show is finished, he decides to bring in the photographer for some publicity stills that will help stir up excitement later.

DIGITAL
FEATURE BUDGET

Instructions on Downloading Budgets:

- ▷ Go to *www.mwp.com*
- ▷ Click on "Virtual Film School"
- ▷ Scroll down on menu to "Resources"
- ▷ Download Excel Spreadsheets
- ▷ Save to your desktop

DIGITAL FEATURE BUDGET

					Production	VariCam 720p DVCPro-HD tape	
Fringe assumptions:						Off-Line:	Non-linear
Payroll Tax	23%					On-Line	Non-linear to HDCAM
SAG	15%						
Agency Fees	10%						
SUMMARY BUDGET							
02-00 Script						2,480	
03-00 Producers Unit						4,000	
04-00 Direction						2,000	
05-00 Cast						15,032	
		TOTAL ABOVE-THE-LINE					23,512
10-00 Production Staff						23,900	
11-00 Extra Talent						1,380	
13-00 Production Design						6,120	
15-00 Set Operations						5,900	
17-00 Set Dressing						3,200	
18-00 Property						325	
19-00 Wardrobe						3,300	
20-00 Make-Up and Hairdressing						2,300	
21-00 Electrical						9,151	
22-00 Camera						29,200	
23-00 Sound						9,675	
24-00 Transportation						1,175	
25-00 Location Expenses						10,735	
		TOTAL PRODUCTION					112,665
30-00 Editorial						40,265	
33-00 Music						2,500	
34-00 Post Production Sound						21,580	
35-00 Titles						1,200	
		TOTAL POST-PRODUCTION					67,092
37-00 Insurance						8,250	
38-00 General & Administrative						3,975	
		TOTAL OTHER					8,250
Total Above-The-Line							23,512
Total Below-The-Line							191,982
Total Above and Below-the-Line							215,495
Contingency @ 5 %							10,775
	GRAND TOTAL						$226,270

ABOVE-THE-LINE		Amount	Units	x	Rate	Sub-Total	Total	
02-00 Script								
02-01 Writer's Salary								
Final Draft						2,000	2,000	
02-02 Research						0	0	
02-03 Clearance						0	0	
02-04 Copyright Registration						30	30	
02-05 Script Copying						200	200	
02-08 Script Timing						250	250	
					Total for 02-00			2,480
03-00 Producers Unit								
03-01 Executive Producer						0	0	
03-02 Producer						4,000	4,000	
					Total for 03-00			4,000
04-00 Direction								
04-01 Director						2,000	2,000	
					Total for 04-00			2,000
05-00 Cast								
05-01 Lead Actors								
	Role of Toby	15	Days	1	75	1,125		
	Role of Eileen	15	Days	1	75	1,125		
	Overtime @1.5	2	Hours	2	844	844	3,094	
05-02 Supporting Cast								
	Role of Ralph	10	Days	1	75	750		
	Role of Sarah	10	Days	1	75	750		
	Overtime @1.5	2	Hours	2	563	563	2,063	
	Role of PeeWee	5	Days	1	75	375		
	Role of Snort	5	Days	1	75	375		
	Overtime	2	Hours	2	281	281	1,031	
05-03 Day Players								
	Role of the Widow	3	Days	1	75	225		
	Overtime	2	Hours	1	84	84	309	
	Role of Taxi Driver	2	Days	1	100	200		
	Overtime	2	Hours	1	75	75	359	
	Role of Henry	1	Day	1	100	100		
	Role of Foxy Lady	1	Day	1	100	100		
	Role of Waiter #1	1	Day	1	100	100		
	Role of Waiter #2	1	Day	1	100	100		
	Role of Waiter #3	1	Day	1	100	100		
	Role of Mama Po Po	1	Day	1	100	100		
	Role of Papa Po Po	1	Day	1	100	100	1,284	
	Overtime	2	Hours	7	525	525	725	
	Payroll						2,039	
	SAG						1,241	
	Agency Fee						887	
05-04 Casting Director/Staff						0	0	
05-14 ADR (Actor's fees)		1	Allow	1	2,000	2,000	2,000	
					Total for 05-00			15,032
BELOW-THE-LINE								

10-00 Production Staff							
10-01 Unit Production Manager							
	Prep	3	Weeks	1	700	2,100	
	Shoot	3	Weeks	1	775	2,325	
	Wrap	1	Week	1	700	700	5,125
10-02 First Assistant Director							
	Prep	1	Day	1	150	150	
	Shoot	3	Weeks	1	750	2,250	7,525
10-04 Production Coordinator							
	Prep	1	Week	1	500	500	
	Shoot	3	Weeks	1	600	1,800	2,300
10-05 Script Supervisor (PA)							
	Prep	1	Week	1	700	700	
	Shoot	3	Weeks	1	750	2,250	
	Wrap	1	Week	1	700	700	5,950
10-06 Production Auditor/Accountant						0	0
10-08 Production Assistants							
	PA #1 Prep	2	Weeks	1	300	600	
	PA #1 Shoot	3	Weeks	1	300	900	
	PA #1 Wrap	1	Week	1	300	300	
	PA #2 Prep	1	Week	1	300	300	
	PA #2 Shoot	3	Weeks	1	300	900	3,000
					Total for 10-00		23,900
11-00 - Extra Talent							
11-02 Extras		1	Day	20	60	1,200	1,200
11-03 Extras Casting Fee		1	Allow	1	1,200	1,200	180
					Total for 11-00		1,380
13-00 Production Design							
13-01 Production Designer							
	Prep	3	Weeks	1	750	2,250	
	Shoot	3	Weeks	1	800	2,400	4,650
13-03 Assistants							
	Prep	1	Week	1	300	300	
	Shoot	3	Weeks	1	300	900	
	Wrap	2	Days	1	60	120	1,320
13-08 Research/Materials		1	Allow	1	75	75	75
13-10 Digital camera expense		1	Allow	1	75	75	75
					Total for 13-00		6,120
15-00 Set Operations							
15-01 First Grip							
	Prep	2	Days	1	125	250	
	Shoot	3	Weeks	1	625	1,875	2,125
15-02 Second Grip (Best Boy)							
	Prep	2	Days	1	100	200	
	Shoot	3	Weeks	1	575	1,725	
	Wrap	1	Day	1	100	100	2,025
15-05 Craft Service							
	Prep	1	Day	1	50	50	
	Shoot	3	Weeks	1	200	600	650
Purchases		15	Days	1	50	750	750
Rentals						0	0
15-06 Grip Rentals (see Elect.)					0	0	0
15-07 Grip Expendables		1	Allow	1	350	350	350
15-08 Box Rentals						0	0

					Total for 15-00			5,900
17-00 Set Dressing								
17-06 Purchases		1	Allow	1	2,500	2,500	2,500	
17-07 Rentals		1	Allow	1	350	350	350	
17-08 Loss & Damage		1	Allow	1	350	350	350	
					Total for 17-00			3,200
18-00 Property								
18-01 Property Master (See PA)						0	0	
18-03 Purchases		1	Allow	1	200	200	200	
18-04 Rentals		1	Allow	1	125	125	125	
					Total for 18-00			325
19-00 Wardrobe								
19-01 Costume Designer								
	Prep	1	Week	1	500	500		
	Shoot	3	Weeks	1	500	1,500		
	Wrap	1	Day	1	100	100	2,100	
19-04 Expendables		1	Allow	1	100	100	100	
19-05 Purchases						0	0	
19-06 Rentals		1	Allow	1	850	850	850	
19-08 Cleaning & Dyeing		1	Allow	1	250	250	250	
19-09 Loss & Damage						0	0	
					Total for 19-00			3,300
20-00 Make-Up and Hairdressing								
20-01 Key Make-Up Artist								
	Shoot	3	Weeks	1	500	1,500	1,500	
20-02 Additional Make-Up Artists						0	0	
	Shoot	1	Week	1	500	500	500	
20-06 Purchases		20	Days	1	15	300	300	
					Total for 20-00			2,300
21-00 Electrical								
21-01 Gaffer								
	Prep	2	Days	1	125	250		
	Shoot	3	Weeks	1	625	1,875	2,125	
21-02 Best Boy								
	Prep	2	Days	1	100	200		
	Shoot	3	Weeks	1	575	1,725		
	Wrap	1	Day	1	100	100	2,025	
21-06 Grip/Lighting Truck		3	Weeks	1	750	2,250		
	KinoFlos	3	Weeks	1	667	2,001		
	HMI pars	1	Day	2	125	250	4,501	
21-10 Box Rentals						0	0	
21-11 Lighting Expendables		1	Allow	1	500	500	500	
					Total for 21-00			9,151
22-00 Camera								
22-01 Director of Photography								
	Prep	3	Days	1	125	375	375	
	Shoot	3	Weeks	1	800	2,400	2,775	
22-03 First Camera Assistant		3	Weeks	1	500	1,500	1,500	
22-04 Digital Imaging Tech		3	Weeks	1	750	2,250	2,250	
22-05 Still Photographer						0	0	
22-06 Expendables		1	Allow	1	250	250	250	

DIGITAL FEATURE BUDGET (CONTINUED)

22-07 Camera Pckg (VariCam)		9	Days	1	900	8,100	8,100	
22-10 Basic Pckge Plus								
	Tripod/Monitors						0	
	Lenses/Filters						0	
	Follow focus						0	
	Paintbox etc.						0	
	Total pckge:	9	days	1	1,550	13,950	13,950	
					Total for 22-00			29,200
23-00 Sound								
23-01 Mixer								
	Prep	1	Day	1	100	100	100	
	Shoot	3	Weeks	1	750	2,250	2,350	
23-02 Boom Operator		3	Weeks	1	575	1,725	1,725	
23-03 Expendables (Batteries, etc.)		1	Allow	1	150	150	150	
23-04 Sound Package		12	Days	1	395	4,740	4,740	
23-05 Walkie Talkies		3	Weeks	10	12	360	360	
23-08 Cellular phone bills		1	Allow	1	250	250	250	
					Total for 23-00			9,675
24-00 Transportation								
24-03 Equipment Rental								
Production Van		2	Weeks	1	300	600	600	
Cube Truck		1	Week	1	325	325	325	
24-04 Gas & Oil		1	Allow	1	250	250	250	
					Total for 24-00			1,175
25-00 Location Expenses								
25-07 Permits		1	Allow	1	1,170	1,170	1,170	
25-08 Parking		1	Allow	1	75	75	75	
25-09 Catering Service								
Crew Meals		15	Days	30	12	5,400	5,400	
Extras		1	Day	20	12	240	240	
2nd Meals		15	Days	30	7	3,150	3,150	
25-15 Shipping & Overnight		1	Allow	1	200	200	200	
25-17 Location Site Rental		10	Days	1	50	500	500	
					Total for 25-00			10,735
27-00 Videotape Stock - Production								
27-03	DVCProHD (46's)	91	Units	1	63	5,733	5,733	
	Sales Tax (.0825%)					473	473	
	VHS (time code dailies	91	Hours	1	1	91	91	
	Sales Tax (.0825%)					8	8	
					Total for 27-00			6,304
30-00 Editorial								
30-08 Off-Line Editor		10	Weeks	1	2,000	20,000	20,000	
30-09 Off-Line Edit System		10	Weeks	1	1,000	10,000	10,000	
30-10 On-Line System & Editor		16	Hours	1	600	9,600	9,600	
30-12 Videotape Stock/Dubs		1	Allow	1	250	250	250	
30-13 Screening Copies (VHS)		1	Allow	1	100	100	100	
30-14 Video Masters/Safeties		3	units	1	105	315	315	
					Total for 30-00			40,265
31-00 Post-Production Videotape								
31-10 HD to DVCam (w/DV stock)		91	Cassette	1	17	1,547	1,547	
					Total for 31-00			1,547

33-00 Music							
33-01 Composer	1	Allow	1	2,500	2,500	2,500	
(All-In Package includes: Arrangers, Copyists,							
...Musicians, Instruments, Studio,							
Engineers, Stock, etc.)							
				Total for 33-00			2,500
34-00 Post Production Sound							
34-01 Sound Editor	150	Hours	1	35	5,250	5,250	
34-05 Spotting	10	Hours	1	35	350	350	
34-08 Dialogue Editor	100	Hours	1	30	3,000	3,000	
34-10 ADR	10	Hours	1	175	1,750	1,750	
34-12 Foley (Sound Editor/Stage)	8	Hours	1	275	2,200	2,200	
34-12 Foley Artist	8	Hours	1	35	280	280	
34-16 Mix	30	Hours	1	125	3,750	3,750	
34-20 Dolby Contract Svce fee							
Dolby Digital + SR	1	Allow	1	5,000	5,000	5,000	
				Total for 34-00			21,580
35-00 Titles							
35-01 Designer & Workstation	1	Allow	1	1,200	1,200	1,200	
				Total for 34-00			1,200
37-00 Insurance							
37-01 Producers Entertainment Packa	1	Allow	1	5,000	5,000	5,000	
Negative					0	0	
Faulty Stock					0	0	
Equipment					0	0	
Props/Sets					0	0	
Extra Expense					0	0	
3rd Party Property Damage					0	0	
Office Contents					0	0	
37-02 General Liability	1	Allow	1	1,750	1,750	1,750	
37-03 Hired Non-Owned Auto					0	0	
37-05 Workers Compensation	1	Allow	1	1,500	1,500	1,500	
37-06 Errors & Omissions	1	Allow	1	0	0	0	
				Total for 37-00			8,250
					0		
38-00 General & Administrative Expenses					0		
38-01 Business License	1	Allow	1	800	800	800	
38-02 Legal	1	Allow	1	1,500	1,500	1,500	
38-03 Accounting fees	1	Allow	1	500	500	500	
38-04 Completion Bond					0	0	
38-05 Telephone/FAX	1	Allow	1	600	600	600	
38-06 Copying	1	Allow	1	100	100	100	
38-07 Postage & Freight	1	Allow	1	100	100	100	
38-08 Office Space Rental					0	0	
38-09 Office Furniture					0	0	
38-10 Office Equipment & Supplies	1	Allow	1	150	150	150	
38-11 Computer Rental					0	0	
38-12 Software					0	0	
38-13 Transcription					0	0	
38-14 Messenger/Overnight	1	Allow	1	100	100	100	
38-15 Parking	1	Allow	1	50	50	50	
38-16 Storage (Equip./Supplies/Film/Tape)					0	0	
38-17 Still Photographer					0	0	
Equip./Supplies/Film/Processing					0	0	

38-18 Publicity					0	0	
38-19 Wrap Party	1	Allow	1	75	75	75	
38-20 Hospitality					0	0	
				Total for 38-00			3,975
Contingency @ 5%						10,775	10,775
	GRAND TOTAL						$226,270
Total Above-The-Line							23,512
Total Below-The-Line							191,982
Total Above and Below-the-Line							215,495
				Check budget totals	226,270	226,270	

DIGITAL FEATURE BUDGET

Digital Feature

This is a straightforward, character-driven story that will be shot on High Definition (HD) on a Panasonic VariCam to DVCPro-HD tape, edited in a non-linear editing suite, mastered to HDCAM, and ultimately transferred to 35mm film in a separate budget (See the chapter on Tape-to-Film Transfer).

This picture must be shot on a tight schedule. The Producer is paying professionals less than normal, and if she's shooting on a loose schedule, and key people in her cast or crew get offered a higher paying gig, guess what? They're gone and she's scrambling to replace them in the middle of shooting. She decides on a three-week schedule with weekends off for rest — 15 shoot days. Furthermore, she carefully plans to keep the shoot days limited to 10 hours.

Deferments

To entice professionals to work on her picture for little up-front money, the Producer asks them to defer a large percent of their salaries, and offers Points, in the movie (see Points below).

They all know that the chances of ever getting paid their deferments, much less points, is probably nil. On the other hand, it's a chance to work with a good script, interesting people, and to be creative on a low budget. For some of them, it's also an opportunity to step up the ladder, and enhance their resumes.

Here's the deal the Producer offers on deferments. She asks everyone (except actors — that comes later) if they will defer most of their salary. She tells them the salary she has already put into her budget. That's a number she knows she cannot exceed. Then she negotiates the deferment based on what the person would normally receive for a 15-day shoot. That total figure, minus the earned salary, is the amount of the deferment.

For example, if a Gaffer normally earns $400 for a 10-hour day, then a 15-day shoot, with no overtime, plus 2 days of prep, would give him $6,800. The Producer is offering $125 a day. The 17 days comes to $2,125. So the amount of the deferment is the difference between the two, or $4,675. Time cards and daily production reports make sure there are no disagreements in the amount of hours worked. At the end, the deal is modified as needed if the Gaffer worked more hours.

When do people get their deferments? The Producer does a standard Deal Memo with each and every crew member. It includes this sentence:

DEFERRED RATE: $ (agreed amount) to be paid at sale of film.

All deferments shall be paid *pari passu* after investors' recoupment of capital contribution plus 10%.

This means that if and when the film is sold, the first dollars that come to the Producer (after the distribution company has taken its cut) go to the investors. When they have recouped their initial investment plus 10% interest, then everyone else who is owed deferred salary starts to get paid *pari passu*. Pari passu is a legal term meaning everyone is equal and will be paid without preference. If there's $50,000 in profit, after the investors get their share, then that $50,000 is divided in equal shares among the rest according to a percentage of the deferred amount.

Here's how that works. The Producer adds up the total of the deferred salaries, lets say it's $150,000. If there is $50,000 in profit, that amounts to one third, or 33% of the total deferred amount. Each person gets paid 33% of their deferred salary.

Hopefully, there will be sufficient profit that everyone gets their full deferred salary.

Points

The deal the Producer made with her investors is that if and when money comes to the Producer from the distribution company, that money goes first to the investors until they recoup their investment plus 10%. If there is more profit then the deferments get paid, including deferments to the Producer and the Writer/Director. If there is more profit after that, then each dollar that comes to the Producer is split between the Producer's production company and the investors. What's a fair split? It's up to the parties to figure that out, but generally, the Producer should not receive less than 50%.

The Producer isn't getting rich yet. In order to attract the best professionals she could to the project, she offered some of them Points. What's a Point? A Point is 1% of something — and she is very careful to say what that something is. This is what's in her deal memo:

DEFERRED POINTS: 1 point shall be given to Contractor of Producer's net.

The "Contractor" is the Gaffer or the Director of Photography, etc. The something from which she will give 1 point is "Producer's net." That's key, because half the profit is already going to the investors. What she has done to avoid confusion is convert her 50% of the total profit into 100% of "Producer's net" profit. That way it's easy to figure out the points given to her crew. One point equals 1% of what the Producer actually receives, or another way of saying the same thing is one point equals a half of 1% of the film's net proceeds (before the investors receive their cut).

In this instance, the Producer offers 1 point to each of the Department Heads or key people (UPM, Production Designer, First Grip, Costume Designer, Key Make-Up, Gaffer, Director of Photography, Mixer, and Composer) and 5 points as an aggregate to the rest of the crew, to be shared equally. The Writer/ Director and the Producer agree to split the remaining Producer's net 50/50.

Giving everyone a stake in the project makes people work harder and pay attention to the quality of the product. It also creates a happier work environment.

The actors are covered under the SAG agreement to receive more money if there are profits, and the post-production houses get almost normal rates, although sometimes Points deals can be made with them to keep post costs lower.

02-00 Script

02-01 Writer's Salary

The Writer is also the Director, and gets $2,000 for the script and $2,000 for directing. She agrees to a deferment of $100,000 in total fees. Only $96,000 to go!

02-03 Clearance

The Producer opts not to do clearance because she feels that the script is free of any potentially litigious material. Many times, insurance companies won't provide Errors and Omissions (E&O) insurance without script clearance. (See Clearance 02-03 in the Digital "No Budget" Feature.)

In most cases, however, producers should send a completed script to a professional clearance service like Marshall/Plumb (*www.marshall-plumb.com*). Clearance can be expensive ($1,500-$3,000), but they'll tell you if your blood-sucking villain has the same name as the president of Toyota.

This Producer is figuring on clearing the film after it's been made, although there is a risk that some re-cutting or even re-shooting might be necessary if a company or person balks or wants too much money.

02-04 Copyright Registration

In order to become signatory to the Screen Actors Guild (SAG) (which this Producer wants to do for reasons to be explained soon), a production company must show chain of title on the script to prove there are no liens against it. To establish title, the Producer registers the script at *www. copyright.gov* (get the "how-to" pdf file at *www.copyright.gov/circs/circ45.pdf*). If the writer has already registered the copyright in his own name, and the producer has bought the script, then the writer must do an Assignment of Rights to make the film the legal property of the production company. The Producer wants to have the right to exploit the script in perpetuity for all media worldwide. The copyright itself still belongs to the writer.

Note: Also consider registration with the Writers Guild of America (see Appendix under Trade Associations). You need not be a member, and it only costs about $30. It's not ironclad protection against someone stealing the idea, but it's useful if there's ever an arbitration.

02-05 Script Copying

You've got 50 people needing a 120-page script. Find a bargain copying service.

02-08 Script Timing

The Script Supervisor times the script a week before the shoot. It's important to know how long the movie is, because if scenes are playing faster or slower than timed, the Director should know. It can affect pacing and rhythm of the entire picture.

03-00 Producers Unit

03-01 Executive Producer

None. The Producer did the deals, formed the company, and raised the money.

03-02 Producer

This Producer has experience, but wants to spend much other time watching performances and shooting. So she hires an experienced Production Manager (see 10-01).

(If you don't have experience as a Line Producer or Production Manager, hire a good one. There are too many pitfalls to risk losing your or anyone else's money.)

$$$

The Producer pays herself $4,000 up front (the same as the Writer/Director), plus a deferment of $96,000, also the same as the Writer/Director.

04-00 Direction

04-01 Director

The other $2,000 for the Writer/Director is here (See 02-01 for her total deal).

05-00 Cast

05-01 Lead Actors
05-02 Supporting Cast
05-03 Day Players

This is a non-union shoot with one exception: all the actors are members of SAG. The Producer and Director both feel that SAG members are generally better, more experienced actors.

As SAG members, they must be paid according to the signatory agreement the production company makes with the guild. In this case, this picture qualifies for SAG'S Ultra-Low Budget Agreement, which stipulates that the total budget must be less than $200,000, and the picture must be shot entirely in the U.S. This allows the production company to hire any willing SAG member to work for $100/day.

The Producer is entitled exhibition only in festivals and in motion picture theaters, but not on basic cable or television. Any distribution in any medium beyond that requires more money to the actors, payable according to whatever SAG agreement applies.

There is a danger here for the Producer. When she sells the film she must remember to negotiate enough to pay the actors what they are due.

It's extremely important to understand the precise terms of whatever SAG agreement a producer is signing. SAG actors have the right, for example, to re-negotiate certain terms after a film is sold. There are ways for producers to protect themselves (being generous with deferments and points is one), but it would be wise for an inexperienced producer to consult with someone who's been around the block a few times.

If the money is there, some producers like to ante up and pay the regular SAG minimums up front, just so they don't have to deal with negotiating later on if the film is sold.

SAG members must be paid their standard pension and health package (currently 14.8%) and the Producer adds an agency fee of 10%.

Since the actors are now technically "employees," they also get the usual package of Social Security and Medicare at 7.65%, Federal Unemployment Insurance at .8%, State Unemployment Insurance (CA @ 5.4%), Workers' Compensation Insurance (CA illustration @4%). Since payroll for actors can be tricky, she hires a payroll service to handle their checks (5%). She allows a total of 23% of the actors' payroll, which covers the employee package plus the payroll service fee.

Note: Before budgeting, call a payroll service and get current percentages for all of the above.

If the Producer were to hire a well-known actor, even at scale, there may be hidden costs that often come with hiring stars. This can range from a separate "Star" trailer, to special accommodations, limos, specified personal assistants, hair and make-up people who do not work at scale, etc., etc. Look before you leap.

All above-the-line people (Writer, Director, Producer, and over-scale Actors) need a separate contract. All others, including department heads, crew, and production team, are hired as Independent Contractors so the production company does not have to pay fringes. The company does issue a 1099 tax form at the end of the year, and the IRS can hold the production company responsible if the Independent Contractor does not pay his or her taxes. Most deal memos include a paragraph that states that the person agrees to pay all taxes. It's not ironclad protection, but it might help if the company gets audited.

The only addition to all of the above is the allowance for overtime. The SAG agreement permits an actor to work an 8-hour day; after that, it's overtime at time and a half for the 9th and 10th hour, and double time for the 11th and 12th hour. Since the rest of the shooting day is planned at 10 hours, the Producer allows for two hours of OT for all the actors, except the Extras.

05-04 Casting Director/Staff

No money! The Producer sets up the auditions in the rec room of her church, and she and the Writer/Director sit through many nights of cold readings.

05-14 ADR

This money is to pay actors who come in for ADR. There are always times when the audio ambiance (dogs, kids, garbage trucks, leaf blowers, buzz saws — the usual suspects) intrudes on the actors' dialogue.

If at all possible, stay away from noisy locations. You'll pay dearly for it in post.

10-00 Production Staff

10-01 Unit Production Manager

The Producer hires an experienced UPM and brings him in three weeks prior to shooting to handle making locations deals, crew and equipment deals, getting SAG paperwork in on time, creating schedules, and just making sure that all the details the Producer has set up will actually work.

The UPM will stay for one week of wrap to make sure all the crew and SAG paperwork is done properly, all equipment is returned on time, any loss and damage is handled, etc.

$$$

The UPM agrees to defer most of his salary and work for $775/week during the shoot, and only $700/week for prep and wrap, well below his usual rate of $1800/week.

10-02 First Assistant Director

The First AD keeps track of what or who we're waiting for, what's needed right now to keep things moving forward, and what we need to do to get everything done that's on the daily schedule.

The First AD also signs actors out when they leave the set so there's no confusion about hours worked. (Usually a 2nd AD function on bigger films.)

He also does the Daily Production Report, which is considered the legal document of what happens every day. It includes time in and out for everyone, anything that delayed shooting, injuries, what equipment was used, what scenes were shot, the number of set-ups, when lunch was, the weather, etc. (For standardized Daily Production Reports, see *www.enterpriseprinters.com*.)

The Producer brings him on one day ahead of shooting to check the schedules.

$$$

He agrees to work for $750/week and defer his usual rate of $1,500/week.

10-04 Production Coordinator

An experienced person, she is brought on one week prior to shooting (usually 4-5 weeks prior on bigger budget films). She makes sure crew deal memos get signed, she works with the UPM to order equipment, and get it picked up.

During production, she backs up the UPM to make sure everything that's supposed to happen actually does.

$$$

She works for $500/week and defers her usual rate of $850/week.

10-05 Script Supervisor

Her notes will either help in post or cause nightmares. She keeps track of all takes and time code, noting the circled takes, pointing out if anything is missed, and also tracks continuity. Experience helps.

$$$

She works for $700/week for one week of prep and wrap, and $750/week during shooting, deferring her usual rate of $1200/week.

10-06 Production Auditor/Accountant

Here, this job is done by the Producer. There is, however, money (under 38-00 General & Administrative Expenses) for a bookkeeper two times a week. All the Department heads did a budget as part of their prep, and the UPM constantly updates the budget to keep track of expenses on a daily basis.

10-08 Production Assistants

Two willing and cheerful PAs (is there any other kind?) are hired. PA #1 is hired for two weeks of prep to help in the office and make runs. He also stays on for a week of wrap. Another PA is hired for the shoot.

One of the PAs responsibilities on the set is to maintain the craft service table.

$$$

They work for the incredibly cheap price of $300/week, deferring regular rates of $625/week.

11-00 Extra Talent

11-02 Extras

The extras are non–union at $60/day. (SAG says that under the Ultra Low Budget Agreement, the producer can hire non–union extras.)

There are no stand–ins during lighting, the actors are generally happy to do it or the 1st AD taps an idle crew member.

On this shoot, the Extras, unlike the SAG actors, are not paid through a payroll service. They are given cash or checks.

11-03 Extras Casting Fee

The best way to get extras (union or not) is through an extras casting service, which goes through the weary task of contacting all the extras, giving them the call time information, wardrobe notes, and so on.

Generally, these services charge about 15% of the total gross payroll.

13-00 Production Design

13-01 Production Designer

The Production Designer has an eye for color and style at a bargain basement price.

Usually, there are set dressers and prop people, but this is low–budget, so the Production Designer, plus one assistant, does it all. Occasionally a PA will be dispatched to pick up needed items or lend a hand.

With few exceptions, most of the locations are shot as is, but dressed with deft accents.

$$$

She agrees to a weekly of $800, and only $750/week during the three weeks of prep, deferring the rest.

13-03 Assistants

The Assistant is an up-and-coming, ambitious young person who gets a Set Decorator credit, good for the resume.

13-10 Digital camera expense

Snapshots are printed to show to the Director for approval.

15-00 Set Operations

15-01 First Grip

The First Grip's prep time is two days, in which he meets with the Gaffer and the DP, surveys the locations, and checks the equipment list.

15-02 Second Grip

The Best Boy Grip preps along with the First Grip, and stays an extra day for wrap to make sure all the equipment gets returned.

15-05 Craft Service

One of the PAs handles the grocery shopping (at the local discount market), borrowing the coffee um, extension cord, 8-foot table, plastic cover, etc.

15-07 Grip Expendables

Shiny Board, color correction gels, diffusion, foam core, duct tape, colored tape, markers, layout board to protect the floors, a tool here and there.

17-00 Set Dressing

17-06 Purchases

$2,500 is allowed for various fabrics, paint, duvatene, a table setting, a stuffed fox, etc.

17-07 Rentals

They need to rent a mock-up of a throne from the French court circa 1700.

17-08 Loss and Damage

Hopefully not used.

18-00 Property

18-01 Property Master

A beleaguered PA takes on this responsibility. Not recommended except in dire financial straits.

18-03 Purchases

Various props, including 40 squirt guns and a dozen Roman candles.

18-04 Rentals

For the broadswords in the fight scene at the July 4th BBQ.

19-00 Wardrobe

19-01 Costume Designer

An experienced Wardrobe Supervisor gets a "Designer" credit. One week prep allows him to root through the actors' closets and do a frantic mix and match for every scene.

The one day of wrap he returns his rentals and eats lunch at Pink's on La Brea (killer chili dogs).

19-04 Expendables

Needles and thread, etc.

19-06 Rentals

For renting WWI German Army helmets, ladies' swimsuits from the 1950s, and a magnificent rooster costume.

19-08 Cleaning and Dyeing

Plenty of cleaning every day (actors sweat under those lights).

20-00 Make-up and Hairdressing

20-01 Key Make-up Artist

The Make-Up Artist also does hair — an important thing to ask for in low-budget projects.

$$$

$500/week is low for her, but it's a fun project and she keeps working. Her deferred amount is based on her usual rate of $400/day.

20-02 Additional Make-up Artists

On selected days, another Make-Up/Hair person comes in to help.

20-06 Purchases
Make-up and supplies.

21-00 Electrical

21-01 Gaffer
The Gaffer is a Best Boy who gets his first Gaffer credit here. He and the Key Grip always get equal money, as do the Grip and Lighting Best Boys.

The Gaffer meets with the Key Grip and the DP, for two days of Tech Scouting and prep, so all equipment is ready for the first set-up.

This picture now has a crew of two Grips and two Electrics, including the Gaffer and Key Grip ("2 and 2"). A bigger budget crew would start with a "4 and 4."

21-02 Best Boy
As above.

21-06 Grip/Lighting Truck
A small grip/lighting truck for $750/week is a good deal. It's got an assortment of tweenies, 1Ks and 2Ks, some other smaller lights, some small dollies, and grip gear.

The DP also rents two 1200 pars for a night scene ($125 each), and most importantly, some Kino Flos, to give a soft ambiance. They're used a lot.

Note: All the lights above plug into AC and are fast and easy to use. If you can get by without a generator, you avoid the cost and hassle, plus an almost guaranteed visit by the fire marshall.

The Producer kicks in $100 to the home owners to help on the electric bills.

21-11 Lighting Expendables
Color gels, tape, etc.

22-00 Camera

Shoot on film or video? Video is cheaper — not just the raw stock, but you don't have to process it either, and it's faster to edit — and they're dealing with a tight budget. They decide to shoot on video.

The ultimate goal is to create an HD Edited Master that will be transferred to 35mm for theatrical release (see the chapter on Tape-to-Film Transfer). Even though the Producer will spend close to $39,000 on the transfer, she's figuring the cost will still be lower than shooting on film.

Shooting for a Tape-to-Film Transfer
There are some shooting considerations to keep in mind when you know you'll have a tape-to-film transfer. For a more complete list, please see the chapter, Tape-to-Film Transfer.

▶ Use the best camera you can afford.

▶ Consider PAL format over NTSC. PAL has more lines of resolution and a shooting rate of 25 frames per second (fps) which is closer to film's 24fps.

▶ Pay attention to the aspect ratio (See this discussion in the chapter on Tape-to-Film Transfer).

▶ Use normal electronic shutter speed, not faster or slower.

▶ Don't up the gain on the camera, it only causes visual "noise." Instead, pump more light into the scene.

▶ Don't sharpen the detail on the camera, it will only increase the sharp video look on the film.

▶ Check with the company doing your transfer about how well (or poorly) their process deals with hand-held movement and fast action in the frame.

▶ Check to see how well their process handles computer effects done in editing.

▶ Make some tests where you replicate the shooting and lighting conditions and styles that you want to use. It may cost some time and a little money, but you'll get much better results. Talk with the company you're using for the tape-to-film transfer for details. (For more shooting hints, see the chapter, Tape-to-Film Transfer.)

22-01 Director of Photography

This is this DP's first feature credit, although he's had plenty of experience in shorts, music videos, and commercials.

$$$

He works for $800/week because of that credit, and also because he wants the experience of shooting video for a tape-to-film blow up.

22-03 First Camera Assistant

A First AC is brought on primarily to focus, also to label, prep camera, load, unload, keep track of the camera logs, and slate the shots.

22-04 Digital Imaging Technician

This position is responsible for setup, operation and maintenance of the HD cameras and all the related gear and software. He works for $750 week and a deferment rate of $1800/week, all well below his usual (union) rates, but it's payback.

22-07 Camera Package Rental

Two HD camera packages are considered, the Cine-Alta Sony HDW F900R and the Panasonic AJ-HDC27 VariCam. There are good things to be said for both, but the Panasonic is less expensive. They get a Basic Package Plus, and the company agrees to a 3-day week, so the 15-day shooting period, or 3 weeks, is reduced to 9 billable days for a total of $13,950.

Panasonic 720p VariCam Package:
Camera Body
1 – HD ENG Zoom Lens
1 – Zoom Control
1 – Color HD Monitor
1 – Power Supply
1 – Quick Release Plate
4 – Batteries
1 – Battery Charger
1 – Sachtler Video 20 Head, Tripod, Spreader
 $ 900.00/Day

Basic Package Plus:
1 – Abakus Extension Eyepiece with Leveling Rod
1 – 6mm T1.5 Canon EJ HD Lens
1 – AJA HDSI Downconverter
1 – RCU EC-3 Paintbox
1 – Astro HD 6" On-Board Monitor
1 – Block Battery
1 – 4 Stage Mattebox
1 – Sunshade
1 – Chrosziel Follow Focus
1 – 138mm Pola
1 – Set of ND Filters
1 – Set of Black Promist Filters
1 – Baby Tripod, Hi-Hat
2 – BNC Cables
   $ 1,550.00/Day

23-00 Sound

23-01 Mixer

The Mixer is an experienced sound man. He preps for one day, meeting with the DP and visiting the locations to check for sound problems and make sure he has the right gear.

$$$

He agrees to a way low rate of $750/week, and a deferment rate of $1750/week.

23-02 Boom Operator

He's an experienced Boom Op (no mics in the frame, please) and works for $575/week on a deferred rate of $1200/week.

23-03 Expendables

Batteries, etc.

23-04 Sound Package

The Mixer puts together a basic sound package such as the one described below. The separate recorder is not needed since they are recording sound straight to video. Average daily rental prices are in parentheses.

The following comes courtesy of Fred Ginsburg, Ph.D., and can be found at *www.equipmentemporium.com*, along with other valuable audio information.

A basic sound package for theatrical production starts with a decent mixing panel such as a Mackie offering at least 4 XLR mic inputs with 48vPhantom, 3-band EQ, and Aux sends (for feeding the boom operator) ($35). One should also have a portable cart to set it up on ($10). AC is usually available on sets, but remote locations may require an invertor and a 12v battery pack ($30).

At least two or three condenser shotgun mics ($20-$40 each). The AT4073a is an excellent, general purpose short shotgun. The AT4071a is a condenser full shotgun, ideal for exteriors. The AT4051a or AT4041 are short range but extremely low echo — perfect for tight interior shots. Exterior conditions will call for a good windscreen, such as an Equalizer or full zeppelin system ($8-$15).

At least one good dynamic handheld mic, for loud sound effects and also for narration ($10).

One or two boompoles, at least 12 footers ($10 each). Make sure there are suitable shockmounts for each shotgun mic, such as the AT8415 or KSM ($5 each). (Zeppelins include their own mounts.)

Lavaliers worn on the body also work as "plant" mics, meaning you can plant them strategically around the set to pick up audio where the actors will be. Plant mics require an open sound with good reach, such as the MT830, AT899, and ECM77. Open sounding mics also cut better with overhead miking.

Proximity lavaliers such as the Countryman B3 and the ECM44 are useful for isolating actors from background noise or other actors ($10).

At least two good wireless units, such as the Lectronsonics, Sony or Audio Technica 1800 series ($35-50 each).

An assortment of mic cables, including 30 footers and some 50's ($2 each). Use a duplex cable to connect to the boom operator ($10).

Professional headphones for the sound mixer and boomperson ($5 each).

If you are going to bring a recorder for double system recording, the type of recorder that you should bring is dependent on the budget and the style of post-production. Standard choices include Sound Devices recorder 702T two-track with timecode, or 744T four-track, or the Edirol R4-Pro four-track with timecode ($80 – $100 plus $25 – $40 for a timecode slate).

23-05 Walkie Talkies

Very handy for communication between grip truck and set, and for AD, PAs, Grips, and Electrics.

23-08 Cellular Phone Bill

The phones at the houses where shooting is happening will be turned off, so cell phones (on vibrate) are a necessity.

24-00 Transportation

24-03 Equipment Rental

A van is rented just prior to shooting for pickups, a few days during the shoot for company moves, and a day after for returns.

Note: It's easy to get fouled up with transportation logistics — conflicts between departmental needs (Electric needs a light and Art needs a sofa). On bigger films, each department has its own vehicle. Smaller guys need to be sharp and figure it all out.

The Art Department needs a larger cube truck to haul some furniture.

25-00 Location Expenses

25-07 Permits

Some low-budget producers shoot without permits. All it takes is one irate neighbor to call the cops who will ask to see your permit. There goes an entire day of shooting.

Exception: The Producer, Director, DP/Sound/PA, and two actors go to a neighborhood cafe where they have already obtained the owner's permission, and a signed location release. If they get caught, there's only an hour gone, not the whole day, and they'll try again at another cafe.

The Coordinator pulls the permits. (Find someone who knows the ropes in the permit office — there are many tricks to the trade.)

25-09 Catering

A well-fed crew is a happy crew. The Producer gets a good deal at $12 a head. Second meals, when needed, are take-out from decent local restaurants.

25-17 Location Site Rental

There are only three principal locations, and for this budget and schedule, that's just fine. Company moves take way too much time.

Two of the sites are in homes owned by the Producer and the Writer/Director, which are free.

The third location is a friend's house where the shooting will be for the bulk of the schedule, 10 days. The friend, perhaps under the influence of a hallucinogen, agrees to a fee of $50/day. He'll never do that again.

27-00 Videotape Stock – Production

27-03 Videotape Stock – Production

The price for a large size DVCProHD (32 minute record time) assumes she buys all production and post videotape from the same place. Bulk discounts. About $24 each.

30-00 Editorial

The Producer knows that she can edit off-line less expensively by renting a nonlinear system, or finding an editor with his or her own system, but she wants an established facility. She knows it provides a greater possibility for a smooth transition from off-line to on-line, and good overall technical support. Plus she chooses a facility with a good audio bay, so transitions between picture and sound will likely be smoother.

She figures 8 weeks to cut the picture and 2 weeks to tweak the fine points. At the end of the 10 weeks, the picture will be redigitized and reassembled in a top-of-the-line editing system with uncompressed video. Here's how it plays out:

30-08 Off-Line Editor

The edit facility has an editor who has worked on numerous features.

$$$

He's hired at $40/hour. (The Producer has no deferment deals from here on out, with the exception of the Composer.)

30-09 Off-Line Edit System

The facility has an Avid Media Composer system and agrees to a weekly rate of $1,000.

The DVCProHD camera masters are down converted to DVCam with slaved time code for editing (see 31-00 Post-Production Videotape below).

Time code DVD dailies are made for the Producer and Director. They make a "select" list from all the footage and from the circled takes. This process knocks down the ratio of footage now in consideration to about 4:1.

The Off-Line Editor digitizes the select list from the DVCam dubs into the system.

30-10 On-Line Editing

When all the editing is done Off-Line, the picture is considered "locked." Now the Producer and Director move into a different editing bay for the On-Line. In this case, it's an Avid Nitris DX Editor system. The Editor now takes the HD camera masters, and digitizes only the final shots from the project file and the Edit Decision List (EDL) into the Nitris system.

$$$

The Editor and system cost $600/hour, and they'll be here for two 8-hour days, so that's $9600.

The actual assembly of the final cut will take several hours. The bulk of the time in this bay is spent in the highly subjective process of color correction. Fortunately, this is a straightforward relationship story with a realistic look shot in few locations, so there's no forcing the limits of color to achieve startling effects.

30-12 Videotape Stock/Dubs

This is a slop category for any pieces of stock the Editor may need to transfer onto or from something else.

30-13 Screening Copies (DVD)

This allows for maybe 10 or so DVD screening copies of the Edited Master.

30-14 Video Masters/Safeties

The main expense here is the HDCAM Masters and Safety Masters. The Producer decides to make:

1 Edited Master

1 Safety Edited Master

1 Edited Master with separate Music and Effects track.

She also gets the Final Edit List burned onto a CD, and carefully stores all her camera masters in a cool, dry, safe place.

The HDCAM stock is $105 for a 124-minute. (See the section on Reel Breaks in the chapter on Tape-to-Film Transfer.)

31-00 Post-Production Videotape

31-10 HD Down Convert

The DVCProHD camera masters are transferred to DVCam. Why go that expensive step? To preserve the quality of the camera masters, to transfer the timecode accurately to the down converted medium, in this case DVCam, and to save considerable money by not having a DVCProHD deck for weeks on end in the Off-Line.

33-00 Music

33-01 Composer

The Producer makes a deal with a composer to do the score using a combination of synthesized and real musicians (including a great trio of female back-up singers) to keep costs down. The composer receives a copy of the locked picture with visible timecode, and goes to work. Her fee is "all-in," meaning she pays for the whole enchilada — musicians, the recording studio, etc. — and makes a small profit. She delivers the final score on time code DAT, divided into the specific music cues that have been agreed to. Each cue will be correctly positioned in the Off-Line bay, and mixed with the dialogue and sound effects in the Mix of the Post-Production Sound process.

The Composer agrees to an all-in fee of $2,500, and a deferment of $10,000. Plus she keeps the publishing rights to her music, just in case she can make a hit single out of one of the tracks.

34-00 Post-Production Sound

The Producer has decided to work with a small post audio facility who will give her a good rate. Since the HDCAM edited master will be transferred to 35mm film, a mix for theatrical release is needed. The Producer has opted to work with Dolby Laboratories to make the theatrical mix. She could have chosen others, such as DTS (Digital Theater Systems), or SDDS (Sony), who are competitors of Dolby, but her ex-boyfriend (they're still friends) is an audio engineer and he likes Dolby. Here are the basic steps in this feature's audio post.

34-01 Sound Editor

The sound editor carefully digitizes the audio into ProTools, avoiding any overmodulation or distortion. He supervises the post audio process and, in this case, because it's low budget, does most of the work. This means laying out all the separate tracks, placing effects in their proper places, and preparing for and doing the mix. He checks every single cut to make sure the sound across it is quiet. This has been done in the video edit to catch all the major glitches, but most edit rooms are not equipped with the speakers and acoustics to do quality sound work. The next step is Spotting.

$$$

The facility gives the Sound Editor's services at $35/hour, a good rate.

34-05 Spotting

The Director, Producer, and Sound Editor watch and listen to the movie for needed sound effects and any trouble spots, like dialogue replacement. Sound effects make the picture realistic, like car doors, traffic, birds, barking dogs, restaurant sounds, etc. The Sound Editor then selects the sounds and positions them in all the right places. As he goes, he's also setting the levels relatively in place in preparation for the mix. This spotting session is repeated with the Composer to spot for music cues. Each session takes a few hours. On this production, the Sound Editor will lay in the music cues.

34-08 Dialogue Editor

A dialogue editor is brought in to assemble, synchronize, edit, clean up and smooth out all the dialogue. If she can use the production tracks, she will, but if any of them are unusable she replaces them with alternate production tracks recorded on set or with automated dialogue replacement (ADR).

$$$

The facility gives the Dialogue Editor's services at $30/hour, and it takes 10 days, or $3,000, but at the end, the dialogue track is clean as a whistle. One reason: the production sound mixer was diligent about recording room tone at the end of nearly every camera set-up. It probably saved the Dialogue Editor three days of constructing it frame by frame, or nearly $1,000.

34-10 ADR

Two actors are in for ADR. It takes a day to get their lines right.

$$$

$175/hour for the Sound Editor and the studio.

34-12 Foley

A Foley artist comes in to do a cloth pass and some walking on various surfaces. (This process is done after the Dialogue Edit.)

$$$

$275/hour for the Sound Editor and the Foley Stage. $350/day for the artist.

The following does not apply with this picture, but when a picture is likely to have overseas distribution and foreign language dubbing, some distributors want what's called a "Foley-filled M&E." Sometimes, sound effects are recorded on the set along with the dialogue, and used in the final mix — say, when an actor slams a door. That sound is part of the dialogue track, and when that track is eliminated for the dubbing, there goes the door slam with it. An extra Foley session replaces all sounds tied to dialogue.

34-16 Mix

The Producer knows that 30 hours of mix may be on the slim side, but she's counting on it being a straightforward relationship picture with mostly dialogue and simple sound effects.

The music has been prepared by the Composer on timecode DAT (or as a ProTools session if both Composer and Sound Editor are in ProTools). All the music cues have been carefully positioned according to time code to fit picture exactly.

Dolby

This is where Dolby enters the scene. For the Dolby Digital the-atrical mix the sound house mixes in a 5.1 format. The 5.1 means 5 full range channels (Left, Center, Right behind the screen, Left Surround [left back + left wall] Right Surround [right back + right wall]), plus a sub-woofer channel, the .1 (because it is limited to 0.1% of the audio spectrum). Engineers point out that while ".1" channel convention does indicate a limited bandwidth channel, in fact, the Dolby DMU recorder records a bandwidth of nearly three octaves (25 Hz to 120 Hz) for the LFE or Subwoofer channel. So the figure is more like 30% on a logarithmic (per octave) scale. This is what gives us that "surround sound" experience. (If they were also doing a mix for TV and home entertainment they would tailor the mix a bit, perhaps limit the dynamic range somewhat, but otherwise pretty much stick with the original mix.) HD broadcast and some Cable networks provide this 5.1 audio.

Note: Dolby also has Dolby Digital Surround EX, which creates Left wall, Back wall, Right wall (3 surround channels) making it, in effect, 6.1. You might consider this if your movie has discrete sound effects that should come from selected speakers in the theater, like that weird electric slurring sound the Vicadanian ray gun makes when it turns your brains to mush. EX allows "cleaner" pans from the screen to the back, or overhead of the audience, and a truer sense of something "behind" the audience.

34-17 Layback

The mixing team, with the Dolby engineer along to guarantee the Dolby goes okay, lay down the mixed tracks. The final 6-track mix is recorded to the Dolby DMU (Dolby's proprietary recorder) on a Magneto Optical (MO) disc, a 2.3 gig storage media. A Dolby Stereo 2-track mix is also created and recorded. The MO is delivered to the optical sound track camera and the sound negative is shot from the MO. The sound negative gets "married to" the picture negative and the composite print is created.

34-20 Dolby Contract Service Fee

For this project, since the producer does not yet have a distribution agreement, she opts for the minimal Dolby agreement. Known as the "festival license," Dolby has a limited release Motion Picture Service Agreement (MPSA) for distribution in North America, with a maximum of 50 prints. The fee for this MPSA is $5,000. This includes the Dolby Digital soundtrack, as well as the SR-encoded Lt/Rt soundtrack.

Dolby aligns the mix stages to industry standards, and briefly checks that at the mastering session. They provide the proprietary recorder (the DMU), the MO, and insure that the mix they capture can and will survive the optical camera and composite printing process, so that the final product, in the real world, reflects the mix created in the studio environment.

It should be noted that the above is just a scenario. When we spoke with Dolby, they wanted us to tell you that fees and services vary, depending on distribution, and formats and the specs of your specific project. Also, if you are a first-time filmmaker, tell Dolby; they want to do all they can to establish good relationships. Dolby is a great resource for answering questions, so ask before you leap.

The Dolby Digital standard contract service fee is currently $11,000 with no limitations on distribution territories or number of prints. This includes the print master, and royalty free trademark application. Most major studios include it, and the list of independents is growing.

35-00 Titles

The opening title sequence is simple, but even though most of it was done in the Off-Line Edit, some additional effects need to be added, so the Producer works with a Graphic Artist in After Effects.

The closing credits are all white type on black background, and are done in the On-Line session.

37-00 Insurance

The Producer's Entertainment Package ($5,000) is a standard package that includes faulty stock, equipment damage, third-party property damage, and office contents.

Workers' Comp insurance was part of the SAG package, but the crew needs coverage also.

General Liability is required by vendors renting equipment, usually for $1 million.

Errors and Omissions will be required by the distributor, but the Producer is figuring she'll pay for it later, hopefully as part of the sale.

38-00 General & Administrative Expenses

38-01 Business License

Every time the Producer starts a film she starts a new company specifically for that film and only that film — so that her exposure to lawsuits is limited. An LLC requires an Operating Agreement, which means a lawyer has to do it. The good news is she can clone 90% from her previous agreements, so his fee is minimal.

38-02 Legal

The lawyer checks the Operating Agreement, any thorny deal memos that may come up, and any proposed distribution agreements.

38-03 Accounting Fees

This is the twice-a-week Bookkeeper.

38-20 Wrap Party

They won't be taking the cast and crew to Disneyland on $75, but at least everyone can have a few good pulls on some bottles of beer and dig into the pile of ribs from the rib joint down the block. For vegetarians the PAs have cooked a mountain of pasta with marinara sauce. The Caterer was invited to the party, and brought along a chocolate cake. Now it's off to the Tape-to-Film Transfer, and then Sundance!

DIGITAL
"NO BUDGET" FEATURE

Instructions on Downloading Budgets:

- ▶ Go to *www.mwp.com*
- ▶ Click on "Virtual Film School"
- ▶ Scroll down on menu to "Resources"
- ▶ Download Excel Spreadsheets
- ▶ Save to your desktop

DIGITAL "NO BUDGET" FEATURE

						Production:	EX-3		
Fringe assumptions:						Off/On-Line:	Non-linear to DigiBeta		
Payroll Tax	0%								
SAG	0%								
Agency Fees	0%								
SUMMARY BUDGET									
02-00 Script							115		
03-00 Producers Unit							0		
04-00 Direction							0		
05-00 Cast							0		
		TOTAL ABOVE-THE-LINE							115
10-00 Production Staff							0		
11-00 Extra Talent							0		
13-00 Production Design							0		
15-00 Set Operations							340		
17-00 Set Dressing							100		
18-00 Property							50		
19-00 Wardrobe							25		
20-00 Make-Up and Hairdressing							84		
21-00 Electrical							1,200		
22-00 Camera							9,500		
23-00 Sound							2,954		
24-00 Transportation							100		
25-00 Location Expenses							1,260		
		TOTAL PRODUCTION							15,613
30-00 Editorial							15,453		
33-00 Music							150		
34-00 Post Production Sound							12,050		
		TOTAL POST-PRODUCTION							27,653
37-00 Insurance							0		
38-00 General & Administrative							225		
		TOTAL OTHER							0
Total Above-The-Line									115
Total Below-The-Line									44,682
Total Above and Below-the-Line									44,797
Contingency @ 5 %									2,240
	GRAND TOTAL								$47,037

	Amount	Units	x	Rate	Sub-Total	Total
ABOVE-THE-LINE						
02-00 Script						
02-01 Writer's Salary						
Final Draft					0	0
02-02 Research					0	0
02-03 Clearance	1	Allow	1	40	40	40
02-04 Copyright Registration					0	0
02-05 Script Copying	1	Allow	1	75	75	75
02-08 Script Timing					0	0
				Total for 02-00		115
03-00 Producers Unit						
03-01 Executive Producer					0	0
03-02 Producer					0	0
				Total for 03-00		0
04-00 Direction						
04-01 Director					0	0
				Total for 04-00		0
05-00 Cast						
05-01 Lead Actors						
Role of Olaf	12	Days	1	0	0	
Role of Thoren	12	Days	1	0	0	0
05-02 Supporting Cast						
Role of Kara	12	Days	1	0	0	
Role of Paul	12	Days	1	0	0	
Role of Luf the Gamble	8	Days	1	0	0	
Role of Ulu the Snake	8	Days	1	0	0	0
05-03 Day Players						
Role of the Waxman	3	Days	1	0	0	
Role of Chauffer	2	Days	1	0	0	
Role of Sky	1	Day	1	0	0	
Role of Janitor	1	Day	1	0	0	
05-04 Casting Director/Staff					0	
05-14 Looping (Actor's fees)					0	
				Total for 05-00		0
BELOW-THE-LINE						
10-00 Production Staff						
10-01 Unit Production Manager						
Prep	1	Week	1	0	0	
Shoot	12	Days	1	0	0	
Wrap	3	Days	1	0	0	0
10-03 1st AD						
Prep	1	Week	1	0	0	
Shoot	12	Days	1	0	0	

	Wrap	2	Days	1	0	0	0
10-05 Script Supervisor (PA)							
	Prep	1	Week	1	0	0	
	Shoot	12	Days	1	0	0	
	Wrap	3	Days	1	0	0	0
10-06 Production Auditor/Accountant						0	0
10-08 Production Assistants							
	PA #1 Prep	1	Week	1	0	0	
	PA #1 Shoot	12	Days	1	0	0	
	PA #1 Wrap	3	Days	1	0	0	
	PA #2 Shoot	12	Days	1	0	0	0
	PA #3 Shoot (Media)	12	Days	1	0	0	0
					Total for 10-00		0
11-00 - Extra Talent							
11-02 Extras							
					Total for 11-00		0
13-00 Production Design							
13-01 Production Designer							
	Prep	1	Week	1	0	0	
	Shoot	12	Days	1	0	0	0
13-10 Digital camera	1	Allow	1	0	0	0	
					Total for 13-00		0
15-00 Set Operations							
15-01 First Grip							
	Prep	2	Days	1	0	0	
	Shoot	12	Days	1	0	0	
15-02 Second Grip (Best Boy)							
	Shoot	12	Days	1	0	0	
15-05 Craft Service							
	Prep	1	Day	1	0	0	
	Shoot	12	Days	1	0	0	0
Purchases		12	Days	1	20	240	240
Rentals						0	0
15-06 Grip Rentals (see Elect.)					0	0	0
15-07 Grip Expendables	1	Allow	1	100	100	100	
15-08 Box Rentals						0	0
					Total for 15-00		340
17-00 Set Dressing							
17-06 Purchases	1	Allow	1	0	0	0	
17-07 Rentals	1	Allow	1	100	100	100	
17-08 Loss & Damage	1	Allow	1	0	0	0	
					Total for 17-00		100
18-00 Property							
18-01 Property Master						0	0
18-03 Purchases	1	Allow	1	50	50	50	
18-04 Rentals					0	0	0
					Total for 18-00		50
19-00 Wardrobe							

19-01 Costume Designer							
	Prep	1	Week	1	0	0	
	Shoot	12	Days	1	0	0	
	Wrap	1	Day	1	0	0	
19-04 Expendables		1	Allow	1	25	25	25
19-05 Purchases						0	0
19-06 Rentals		1	Allow	1	0	0	0
19-08 Cleaning & Dyeing		1	Allow	1	0	0	0
19-09 Loss & Damage						0	0
					Total for 19-00		25
20-00 Make-Up and Hairdressing							
20-01 Key Make-Up Artist							
	Shoot	12	Days	1	0	0	0
20-02 Additional Make-Up Artists						0	0
	Shoot				0	0	0
20-06 Purchases		12	Days	1	7	84	84
					Total for 20-00		84
21-00 Electrical							
21-01 Gaffer							
	Prep	2	Days	1	0	0	
	Shoot	12	Days	1	0	0	
21-02 Best Boy							
	Shoot	12	Days	1	0	0	
21-06 Grip/Lighting Truck		1	Flat	1	1,000	1,000	1,000
21-10 Box Rentals						0	0
21-11 Lighting Expendables		1	Allow	1	200	200	200
					Total for 21-00		1,200
22-00 Camera							
22-01 Director of Photography							
	Prep	3	Days	1	0	0	
	Shoot	12	Days	1	0	0	0
22-05 Still Photographer						0	0
22-06 Expendables		1	Allow	1	200	200	200
22-07 Camera Pckg (Sony EX-3)		1	Flat	1	4,000	4,000	4,000
22-07 Lens Pckg (Sony EX-3)		4	Days	1	850	3,400	3,400
22-10 Additional Equipment						0	0
	Field monitor	2	Weeks	1	250	500	500
	Hard drives	4	Allow	1	350	1,400	1,400
					Total for 22-00		9,500
23-00 Sound							
23-01 Mixer							
	Prep	1	Day	1	0	0	
	Shoot	12	Days	1	0	0	0
23-02 Boom Operator		12	Days	1	0	0	0
23-03 Expendables (Batteries, etc.)		1	Allow	1	150	150	150
23-04 Sound Package		12	Days	1	217	2,604	2,604
23-05 Walkie Talkies		2	Weeks	10	5	100	100
23-08 Cellular phone bills		1	Allow	1	100	100	100
					Total for 23-00		2,954
24-00 Transportation							
24-03 Equipment Rental							
Production Van		4	Weeks	1	0	0	0
24-04 Gas & Oil		1	Allow	1	100	100	100

				Total for 24-00			100
25-00 Location Expenses							
25-07 Permits	1	Allow	1	585	585	585	
25-08 Parking				0	0	0	
25-09 Catering Service							
Crew Meals				0	0	0	
2nd Meals	6	Days	20	5	600	600	
25-15 Shipping & Overnight	1	Allow	1	75	75	75	
25-17 Location Site Rental				0	0	0	
				Total for 25-00			1,260
27-00 Video Memory Cards - Production							
27-03 Memory cards (16GB SxS)	2	Cards	1	550	1,100	1,100	
Tax @.0825				91	91	91	
				Total for 27-00			1,191
30-00 Editorial							
30-08 Off/On-Line Editor/System	10	Weeks	1	1,500	15,000	15,000	
30-13 Screening Copies (DVD)	1	Allow	1	100	100	100	
30-14 Video Masters/Safeties	3	Cassettes	1	51	153	153	
DigiBeta deck	1	Day	1	200	200	200	
				Total for 30-00			15,453
33-00 Music							
33-01 Composer	1	Allow	1	150	150	150	
(All-In Package includes: Arrangers, Copyists,					0	0	
...Musicians, Instruments, Studio,					0	0	
Engineers, Stock, etc.)					0	0	
				Total for 33-00			150
34-00 Post Production Sound							
34-01 Sound Editor	120	Hours	1	35	4,200	4,200	
34-05 Spotting (Incl)			1		0	0	
34-10 ADR	8	Hours	1	175	1,400	1,400	
34-12 Foley Editor/Stage	8	Hours	1	275	2,200	2,200	
34-12 Foley Artist	1	Day	1	350	350	350	
34-16 Mix	24	Hours	1	150	3,600	3,600	
34-17 Layback	4	Hours	1	75	300	300	
				Total for 34-00			12,050
35-00 Titles	0			0	0	0	
				Total for 35-00			0
37-00 Insurance							
37-01 Producers Entertainment Package				0	0	0	
Negative					0	0	
Faulty Stock					0	0	
Equipment					0	0	
Props/Sets					0	0	
Extra Expense					0	0	
3rd Party Property Damage					0	0	
Office Contents					0	0	
37-02 General Liability					0	0	
37-03 Hired Auto					0	0	
37-05 Workers Compensation	1	Allow	1	0	0	0	
37-06 Errors & Omissions	1	Allow	1	0	0	0	
				Total for 37-00			0
					0		

38-00 General & Administrative Expenses						0	
38-01 Business License						0	0
38-02 Legal	1	Allow	1	0	0	0	
38-03 Accounting fees	1	Allow	1	0	0	0	
38-04 Completion Bond						0	0
38-05 Telephone/FAX	1	Allow	1	100	100	100	
38-06 Copying	1	Allow	1	25	25	25	
38-07 Postage & Freight	1	Allow	1	25	25	25	
38-08 Office Space Rental						0	0
38-09 Office Furniture						0	0
38-10 Office Equipment & Supplies	1	Allow	1	25	25	25	
38-11 Computer Rental						0	0
38-12 Software						0	0
38-13 Transcription						0	0
38-14 Messenger/Overnight	1	Allow	1	25	25	25	
38-15 Parking	1	Allow	1	0	0	0	
38-16 Storage (Equip./Supplies/Film/Tape)						0	0
38-17 Still Photographer						0	0
Equip./Supplies/Film/Processing						0	0
38-18 Publicity						0	0
38-19 Wrap Party	1	Allow	1	25	25	25	
38-20 Hospitality						0	0
				Total for 38-00			225
Contingency @ 5%						2,240	2,240
GRAND TOTAL							$47,037
Total Above-The-Line							115
Total Below-The-Line							44,682
Total Above and Below-the-Line							44,797
				Check budget totals		47,037	47,037

DIGITAL
"NO BUDGET" FEATURE

The Producer/Director is a guy with some experience producing and directing documentaries for local television. He wants to make a feature movie of a script written by a friend. His determination will be well-tested. And, he'll also have to wangle thousands of dollars' worth of free equipment and labor, and get his hands on about $47,000 in hard cash.

This chapter in his life will last about three months. He will eat, sleep and breathe this movie, kissing his incredibly understanding wife and children goodbye every morning, and returning home every night to the warm bosom of his family, who never once resent that Daddy is asleep ten minutes after dinner.

On the other hand, he will test his mettle as a filmmaker and a human being. And he will join in a grand enterprise with comrades of more or less equal commitment and talent.

02-00 Script

The Writer has several unproduced feature scripts under his belt, and has learned the hard way how to structure a good story and create memorable characters. What's encouraging about this script, from a standpoint of shooting on the cheap, is that:

1) It's a simple character-driven story. No car chases, no scenes with more than 10 extras, no special effects.
2) It's a local story: local landscapes, homes, and streets. No travel.
3) It has a small cast.
4) Its sets are homes or places that already exist. No construction. Little or no furniture, backdrops, or prop rentals.

5) Wardrobe comes from actors' closets, or is borrowed.

6) No special make-up effects.

7) Lighting is simple and straightforward; no elaborate set-ups.

02-01 Writer's Salary

There is none. But if the movie gets sold, then the Writer, along with every-one else, gets some money based on the Producer's Agreement.

The Agreement

He asks cast and crew to defer salaries. Since some have never worked on a film before, and have no idea what they would earn, he negotiates the deferment based on non-union industry standards for 12 days of work. A basic day rate is established for each person. In the case of the Producer/Director, Writer, and the Composer, a flat fee is negotiated.

The 1st AD keeps daily production reports, which are signed by each person to make sure there are no disagreements in the amount of hours and days worked. At the end, the deal is modified as needed if someone worked more or fewer days.

The Producer does a standard Agreement with everyone. It includes this sentence:

DEFERRED RATE: $ (*agreed amount*) to be paid at sale of film. All deferments shall be paid pari passu after investors' recoupment of capital contribution plus 10%.

This means that if and when the film is sold, the first dollars that come to the Producer (after the distribution company has taken its cut) go to the investors. In this case, the Investors are members of the Producer's family. When the Investors have recouped their initial investment plus 10% interest, then everyone else who is owed deferred salary starts to get paid *pari passu*. Pari passu is a legal term meaning everyone is equal and will be paid without preference. If there's $50,000 in profit, after the investors get their share, then that $50,000 is divided in equal shares among the rest according to a percent-age of the deferred amount.

So the Producer adds up the total of the deferred salaries, let's say it's $150,000. If there is $50,000 in profit, that amounts to one third, or 33% of the total deferred amount. Each person gets paid 33% of their deferred salary.

342

Hopefully, there will a profit and everyone will get their full deferred salary.

Points

If there is more profit after that, then each dollar that comes to the Producer is split between the Producer's production company and the investors 50/50. It's up to the producer and investors to figure out a fair split, but generally, in our opinion, a producer should not get less than 50%.

Now you might think that the Producer is getting rich. Not quite. As part of the Agreement, the Producer offers Points. What's a Point? A Point is 1% of something, and the Producer is very careful to say what that something is. This is what's in the Agreement:

DEFERRED POINTS: 1 point (or fewer or more depending) shall be given to Contractor of Producer's net.

The "Contractor" is the Independent Contractor with whom he has made the Agreement, i.e., the actor or Gaffer or Writer or Director of Photography, etc. The something from which he will give points is "Producer's net." That's key, because half the profit is already going to the investors. So what he has done to avoid any confusion is convert his 50% of the total profit into 100% of "Producer's net" profit. That way it's easy to figure out the points given to his cast and crew. One point equals one percent of what the Producer actually receives, or another way of saying the same thing is one point equals a half of 1% of the film's net proceeds (before the investors receive their cut).

In this instance, the Producer offers 1 point to everyone in the cast and crew who worked the 12 days, fractions of points for those who worked fewer days, and 2 points to the Unit Production Manager, 1st AD, Director of Photography and the Sound Mixer, because they are professionals. Other Points are saved if needed for post-production.

The Producer includes a paragraph in the Agreement that gives him sole discretion in deciding whether or not to continue the project at any time.

If things start to fall apart big time, for whatever reason, even the weather, then he has to be able to pull the plug. After all, he's got borrowed money to pay back with interest.

Giving everyone a stake in the project makes people work harder and pay attention to quality. It also creates a happier work environment.

02-03 Clearance

He doesn't have the $1,200 or so it would take for legal clearance of the script, so he does an "item by item clearance." He carefully reviews the script to make sure there are no business names, products or trademarks that will be featured — everything is fictional. Then he reviews the character names. All are first names only. That's good, except for one character whose first and last names are used in connection with a bank robbery. That could be a problem if there actually is someone by that name who robbed a bank or who is in prison. He contacts the clearance company, and for $25 an item, plus expenses, pays only $40 for clearance. It's not ideal, but it'll get them to a distribution company with at least some credibility. (For a more complete discussion of Clearance, see 02-03 in the chapter on Digital Feature Budget.)

For a scene shot in a convenience store, the Producer makes sure that no products or brand names are recognizable. He turns cans around on shelves, or makes sure they are in the deep background. He asks the DP to create a shallow depth of field in one shot so a beer sign in the background is out of focus.

02-04 Copyright Registration

Nothing for now, but if the Producer gets distribution, he may set up a company just for this movie, and register the copyright (in the Writer's name) to show that the script has a clean "chain of title." (For more on legal items, see the Resources section under Books.)

The other kind of "Registration" is with the Writers Guild of America. You needn't be a member, it only costs about $30 to register a script, and at least it establishes that so and so wrote this script at this time. It's not iron clad, but it's a small protection against someone stealing the idea.

02-06 Script Copying

No copy store in town gives him free copying for a screen credit, so he finds the cheapest place in town.

02-08 Script Timing

He reads through the script several times scene by scene with a stopwatch, reciting the lines and including all the pauses and time for action. When he's found the right pace for each scene, he marks the script. If during shooting the scenes are coming in a lot faster or slower, that's a flag. He'll need to consider whether his interpretation was wrong during the timing, or if he needs to make changes now in the shooting.

03-00 Producer's Unit

03-02 Producer

No money up front. He only profits if the film is sold, along with everyone else.

04-00 Director's Unit

04-01 Director

(See Producer.)

05-00 Cast

The Producer is fortunate — he lives in a city where there are many actors, both professional and amateur. In two weeks, he finds his cast from college theater departments, community theaters, and from among the professional ranks. Professionals who are union members (SAG or AFTRA) are not supposed to work on non-union projects, but if they choose to, it's their decision, and does not affect the Producer. He just says up front that this is a non-union gig.

Rehearsals are in the evenings, about three weeks prior to the shoot.

Note: If this were a short film, instead of a feature-length project, the Producer might use only Screen Actors Guild (SAG) actors. Typically, he might find they are more professional and maybe more talented. SAG has a "Short Film Agreement," which permits production companies to become signatory to SAG (no fee), and use willing SAG actors for totally deferred salaries. However, the Producer may show the film only at festivals. (See *www.sagindie.org* for this and other SAG agreements.)

If and when the film is sold, the Producer must negotiate compensation with the actors, and get their consent, before any further distribution can happen. It's critical to understand the precise terms of whatever SAG agreement a producer signs. SAG actors have the right, for example, to re-negotiate certain terms after a film is sold. There are ways for producers to protect themselves (being generous with deferments and points is one), but it would be wise for an inexperienced producer to consult with a producer who's been around the block.

05-04 Casting Director/Staff

The Producer puts out the word for auditions (held in the conference room of a friend's company), and he and the Writer hold auditions. Four days later they have their cast.

05-14 ADR

Any Automatic Dialogue Replacement (ADR) time will be added to actors' deferment Agreements.

10-00 Production Staff

10-01 Unit Manager

The Producer/Director finds an agreeable colleague, a fellow producer no less, who has never done a feature, but who has worked up the production ranks, and knows the ropes. His experience counts in creating realistic schedules, scouting and securing locations, finding crew and equipment, and mothering less experienced crew.

Schedule

The Producer, 1st AD, and the UPM do a scene by scene "break down" of the script: who is in each scene, where it's shot, what time of day, what equipment is needed, what crew, etc. They figure it can be shot in 12 days — just about right for an all-volunteer cast and crew. Much longer and other obligations call.

They ask cast and crew to write down when, over the next 12 days, they can commit to shooting, then map a shooting schedule based on availability. They also must match personal schedules with script requirements, like scenes shot at sunset, a night scene, and a bicycle chase that rips through a park at sunrise.

The UPM helps out a day here and there, then comes on full-time for a week of prep, the 12 days of shooting, and three days of wrap.

10-03 1st AD

The Producer finds a 1st AD who has actually worked on features before, and it will turn out to be the best staff decision he makes. This guy's experience about how to organize a daily schedule and find short-cuts to getting shots is invaluable.

10-05 Script Supervisor

Script Supervisors can save headaches by taking scrupulous notes. What take are we on? What's the timecode? Which take did we like? How far did the actor get before the nice doggie barked and spoiled the shot? Didn't Kara have a freshly lit cigar in her right hand just before Olaf slapped her? Or was it her left hand?

This inexperienced Script Supervisor comes on for a week of prep to read and time the script, sit in on the last rehearsals, and get familiar with the locations. After shooting, he stays on for three days to try to tidy up his script notes.

10-06 Production Auditor/Accountant

The Producer's mom's friend is a bookkeeper. She comes in twice a week in exchange for washing her car three times.

10-08 Production Assistants

The Producer finds some college and high school students through film and theater departments.

The First PA comes on for a week of prep, and stays for three days of wrap to make returns, and clean up after the shoot. The Second PA comes on for the shoot only.

The third PA comes on for the shoot and is assigned the key position of Media Assistant. During the shoot there is a consistent workflow that must be followed. She begins by labeling each of the two 16GB SxS memory cards, like 001 and 002. This little step can avoid confusion on set when, for example, you've dropped the card with the footage on it and its next to a bunch of clean cards. The label and the log you keep, tell you what's what. The PA offloads one card, makes sure the files were transferred (by spot checking a random sampling of clips) and they're backed up on two portable hard drives, erases it, and then hands it back to the camera crew for re-use. She uses a MacBook Pro and two

FireWire drives. Back at the hotel room or office, she transfers all the footage for the day onto two different full size drives, one for the Editor and Producer, and the other for backup. For extra security, some like to transfer the footage to an online storage site as well. Not a bad idea. Now the portable drives can be erased and they're ready for the next day's shoot.

11-00 Extras

The script calls for 20 Extras to provide atmosphere for several scenes: diners in a restaurant, joggers during the sunrise bicycle chase, pedestrians, and riders on a bus. The Producer casts them from among those who auditioned unsuccessfully for the larger parts.

13-00 Production Design

The production design is pretty much "as is." Even so, there is furniture to swap out, different color drapery to hang, a coat of paint here and there, and a few necessary items from the thrift store. Why have a Production Designer? With all the craziness of production, it's necessary to have one person whose eyes are on "the look."

13-01 Production Designer

This is an interior design student at a local college, who wants to try her hand at a feature. The small touches she adds make a big difference. In addition to the above, she adds a plant here, a draped orange scarf there. She tilts a lampshade at a crazy angle to add a droll touch to a scene with an uptight professor.

She also handles Set Dressing, and Props.

The Production Designer preps for a week and becomes familiar with the script, watches the actors rehearse, checks the locations, makes out her scene by scene lists for set dressing and props, and gathers what she needs. Returns after the shoot will be handled by the PA.

13-10 Digital Camera

A borrowed digital camera keeps a hot set intact from day to day. Was the blue coffee cup on the right arm of the sofa? Was the rug rolled up?

15-00 Set Operations

15-01 First Grip

The First and Second Grips, as well as the Gaffer and Best Boy, are all college students with about two years of student productions under their belts.

The First Grip and the Gaffer both come on for two days of prep, checking out the locations with the DP and Director, getting the expendables, and checking out the gear.

15-05 Craft Service

The Producer has worked the local grocers for free snack food and drinks. One store provides fresh fruits and vegetables every day, and a case of bottled water. Packaged foods, like chips, cookies, breads, bagels, peanut butter and jelly, etc. are bought at the discount market.

15-07 Grip Expendables

Layout board to protect the floors, duct tape, colored tapes, markers, a tool here and there.

17-00 Set Dressing

The Production Designer is ingenious at raiding the homes of friends for special items. She scores a six-foot-tall African fertility statue that is so intimidating it makes it into a scene watching over Thoren and Kara smooching.

17-07 Rentals

The only rental is a suit of (fake) armor.

18-00 Property

Again, this job falls to the Production Designer.

18-03 Purchases

Goldfish for an aquarium scene. The pet store said no to a loan.

19-00 Wardrobe

19-01 Costume Designer

The Producer's fashion-mad friend reads the script, discusses wardrobe with the Producer/Director, and spends prep week in the actors' closets, mixing and matching outfits.

19-04 Expendables

Needles and thread, etc.

20-00 Make-Up and Hairdressing

20-01 Key Make-Up Artist

She's a student at a cosmetology school, adept at both hair and make-up. The Producer/Director briefs her on the cast's skin tones, complexions, hair, and any special needs. Make-up on the shoot is extremely simple, in many cases when time is short, it's just powder and a comb-out.

20-06 Purchases

Foundation, powder, and lipstick.

21-00 Electrical

21-01 Gaffer

College students as described under 15-01.

21-02 Best Boy

College students as described under 15-01.

21-06 Grip/Lighting Truck

The Producer/Director and the DP score a grip/lighting truck with two 1Ks, 2 650s, a 300 Arri, and 3 soft boxes, plus reflectors and assorted grip gear including a small dolly and track for a flat of $1,000 for the 12 days. Ordinarily, that would have cost twice that. Plus, they got 2 HMI pars for two nights, normally $125/day each. The lighting company gets a screen credit featuring their company logo.

The HMIs, 1Ks and 650s are good because they plug into AC: no generator needed. The danger, of course, is that they'll overload the circuits and constantly trip the breakers. That's why the DP goes on the scout, checks out the breaker box and outlets, and figures out how many amps will be needed per circuit per set-up. The soft boxes are used constantly because they set up quickly and give even, soft light.

21-11 Lighting Expendables
Gels, diffusion, black wrap, foam core tape, etc.

22-00 Camera

22-01 Director of Photography
The DP is a professional news and documentary camera operator curious about working in drama.

He takes time to become familiar with the Sony EX-3 being used here (See 22-07 Camera Package).

With a 12-day shoot, and a script that's almost 100 pages, that's about 8 pages a day! That means about one hour for every setup of camera and lights. Dolly moves are probably out. Too much setup time. Complicated lighting is out. Soft boxes are in.

Exterior lighting will be reflectors, with silks overhead for smaller scenes to cut down contrast and soften the look.

The plan is to shoot master shots first, then move in for two and three shots, then singles, starting with a larger area and working smaller and smaller.

22-05 Still Photographer
Publicity stills will be needed if the movie gets any play. A photographer friend agrees to donate services and even pay for the film and processing. The Producer makes a mental note to invite him over for some vegetable lasagna, a family favorite.

22-07 Camera Package
Finding the right HD camera takes some searching through the literature and the web sites, and talking with other veterans of the HD

wars. The Producer and the DP choose the Sony EX-3. Here are a few of the reasons why:

- Included in the package is a ½-inch lens adaptor to allow use of other 1/2-inch lenses, plus the ability to use other optional lens adaptors for 2/3-inch, cinema-style and digital SLR lenses.
- It has multiple frame rate recording such as 59.94i, 50i, and native 23.98P, as well as being 1080i/720P switchable
- The camera has two memory card slots, allowing a pair of 16 GB SxS PRO memory cards to record up to 140 minutes of HD footage.
- With its semi-shoulder mount, it's easily adaptable to hand-held work, which is important for this shoot.

The Producer rents the EX-3 package for 12 consecutive days at $500/day at a 34% discount, or about $4,000. He also rents a lens package at $850/day for 4 days.

22-10 Additional Equipment

A 16:9 field monitor cabled to the camera provides the Director and Script Supervisor needed on set viewing. Two portable hard drives are purchased as back-up for the media on set, and two larger drives to contain the media before editing begins, one master and one backup.

Oh yes, and the bean bag, a large bag filled with a few pounds of plastic beads. Just plop it down, settle the camera into the beans, and you have an instant camera mount.

23-00 Sound

23-01 Mixer

The Sound Mixer is an experienced documentary colleague of the DP who agrees to do the shoot just to experience working with actors.

He comes in one day ahead to check out the sound package and practice with the rookie Boom Operator.

23-02 Boom Operator

The Boom Op is a college film/TV student.

23-04 Sound Package

The basic sound package for video production (also see the Digital Feature Budget at 23-04):

▶ Mackie mixer with at least 4 XLR mic inputs, 48vPhantom, 3-band EQ, and Aux sends ($35)

▶ Two - three condenser shotgun mics ($20 to $40 each)

▶ Shockmounts for each shotgun mic ($5)

▶ Windscreen (e.g. Equalizer or full zeppelin system $8-$15)

▶ One or two boompoles, 12 foot min. ($10)

▶ Dynamic handheld mic ($10)

▶ Lavaliers (e.g. MT830, AT899, ECM77 - $10) (Omni lavs for interviews)

▶ Proximity lavaliers (e.g. Countryman B3, ECM44 - $10)

▶ Two wireless units (e.g. Lectronsonics, Sony or Audio Technica 1800 series - $35 to $50)

▶ Assortment of mic cables, including 30's, 50's ($2 each)

▶ Headphones for sound mixer and boom op ($5)

▶ Duplex cable to connect to boom operator ($10)

▶ Portable cart ($10)

$290 total rental price/day. The rental company agrees to a 25% discount.

23-05 Walkie Talkies

The rental house throws in 10 walkies for the nominal price of $100.

23-08 Cellular Phone Bill

Unfortunately, the phone company doesn't wheel and deal. $100 is budgeted.

24-00 Transportation

24-03 Equipment Rental

One of the PAs owns a pickup. The Producer owns a mini-van. Everyone pitches in with wheels when needed.

24-04 Gas & Oil

It's only fair to reimburse some gas money. $100 allowed.

25-00 Location Expenses

25-07 Permits

"Permits? We don't need no stinking permits! We're guerrilla film-makers!"

Imagine the scene: cars parked all up and down the block for several days in a row, neighbors who can't put their garbage cans out on garbage day. Driveways that get accidentally blocked. The neighborhood frustration mounts, until someone calls the cops, who ask to see your permit. There goes the day.

Shooting without a permit may have its place when it's a very small crew and they're doing run and gun shooting on the street. If the cops come, they shoo you away and you find another street. But that's not this movie.

The UPM pulls the permits from the permit office. Police and fire safety officers are waived because there's no traffic interruption and no generator.

(Permit fees vary widely, so check your local office.)

25-09 Catering Service

Catering is provided by the "Oh Boy! It's Brown Bag Lunch Time Co." Everyone brings their own and trades snacks, just like in 4th grade.

The Producer can't quell the pangs of guilt, however, when everyone is still working past dinner time. He gets some free pizzas from Luigi's down the street, but then Luigi says "Basta!!" and the Producer has to pay for the remaining six days' worth.

25-17 Location Site Rental

The Producer has cajoled friends to give up their homes for shooting. Cost: Three perfectly good friendships.

27-00 Video memory cards – Production

27-03 Video memory cards

The Producer figures they'll shoot about 4 hours' worth of footage for each of the 12 days. So that's two 16 GB SxS PRO memory cards to record up to 140 minutes (2 hours 20 minutes) of HD footage. After each card is uploaded into the computer it is erased and ready to record new footage.

30-00 Editorial

The Producer considers buying a turnkey editing system, and learning how to edit himself, but he's a little short with the money. With the new systems running anywhere from $5,000 to $15,000 (including computer, display, presentation monitor, speakers, drives, and software), he can't squeeze it in. He also knows that becoming adept at editing will take time, and he wants to get this project finished.

If he had it all to do over again, he would probably start learning to edit any way he could. Then he'd save up for his own system. Finally, he'd make his movie and edit it himself. Come to think of it, that's not a bad plan for the next one.

In any case, now it's time to get serious about editing. He begins to talk with his other filmmaking friends, and friends of friends, asking around for an editor with his own system who might be interested in cutting a feature.

30-01 Off-/On-Line Editor and System

For $1,500/week, the Editor agrees to work for the 10 weeks he and the Producer figure it will take to off-line and on-line the picture.

(The Producer was lucky to find this Editor. For budgeting purposes, it would be wise to allow $2,000/week and up.)

The Editor has Final Cut Pro, a wide screen display, a calibrated HD monitor that will allow them to see fairly accurate color and clarity of the final images, small but decent speakers, and several terabytes of RAID 5 storage.

Remember the inexperienced Script Supervisor? The Producer realizes he can't always tell which take is circled by looking at the script notes.

The old workflow for edit prep might have the Editor transferring all the masters to a set of timecode DVDs, so the Producer/Director could review all the footage, make script notes of which takes and parts of takes he wants to work with. Instead, the Editor sets up a simple Final Cut workstation for the Producer, and using the Sony FCP Logging plugin, the footage is loaded into the Log & Transfer window so he can mark and label clips to his heart's content. This way, he gets to sift through all the takes, prioritize them, and become familiar with the footage. This material gets handed to the Editor on a separate drive. The Editor copies/pastes all the bins/clips into the new project, links to the Raid system and editing is ready to begin.

FYI: another workflow might make use of a device called the Drobo. This little box holds four SATA drives of any size. The Drobo provides RAID-5 backup protection, meaning that if one drive should fail, the footage is automatically backed up. After each day's shoot, the clips are transferred from the cards to the drives in the Drobo using Sony Clip Browser, a free download. Then the Editor creates a new project in FCP, importing the clips from the Drobo and converting them to Quick-Time so FCP will be happy. Now editing can begin with the security of knowing that the original clips are still in the Drobo, should disaster occur. Some people add an extra layer of security by transferring the original clips in the Drobo to LTO tapes — not a bad idea.

The Sony XDCam/EX-1 or EX-3 footage has one trade-off: it's saved in MPEG-2, which is a long GOP format (see Chapter 4 High Definition). Briefly, long GOP (Group of Pictures) can be explained by describing what it isn't. In a frame of film, all the information, or data, that you need to know about that image is contained in that single frame. Certain forms of video, called *intraframe*, compress data in a similar way. Long GOP is an *interframe* compression, in which the data that would have been in a single frame is in a *group* of frames. The first frame of the group has the most data, and succeeding frames have the rest of the data to complete the picture. This creates a problem in editing, because the system, in this case Final Cut, has to recreate the missing full frames of video. Whenever you add a transition or other effect, FCP's message pops up, "Conforming MPEG-2 Video." FCP is creating new frames and then you must render. It's a slow process. There are ways around this.

One way is to edit in a ProRes timeline for whatever frame rate and size the source footage was in. The only problem with this method is that everything must be rendered eventually, and that will take some time. Nonetheless, this is the method that the Editor and Producer agree upon. The Off-Line takes about nine weeks.

When the cut is done, and the picture is locked, the Editor makes a DVD copy with visible timecode, and gets it to the Composer (see 33-00 Music).

While the Composer is working away, the Editor cleans up the audio as much as possible before going off to Post-Production Sound (34-00).

For the final lay-off to the DigiBeta masters, the Producer has to rent a DigiBeta deck. The Producer got this deal by asking an edit facility to let him do the lay-off between midnight and 6am on a Saturday night, when the DigiBeta machine was not normally in use. Cost: $200.

One producer actually made a deal with a dubbing house to schlep his computer and drives over on a slow weekend, hook them up and go directly into the DigiBeta deck. They charged him about $150. Labor intensive but not a bad price.

30-13 Screening Copies (DVD)

The Producer makes a few copies to show to potential distributors, his mom, and his wife and kids.

30-14 Video Masters/Safeties

The expense is the DigiBeta Master, the Safety Master, and the separate M&E (Music and Effects) Master. The Producer decides to do an M&E because it's so much easier to do now while the movie is in the edit system. The M&E will be used if the movie is ever dubbed into foreign languages. (There are audio considerations for M&Es as well. See 34-16 Mix.)

The DigiBeta stock is $51 for a 94-minute, and he needs three.

The Producer also gets the Final Edit List burned onto a CD, and carefully stores all the camera masters and clones in a cool, dry, safe place.

Now the picture is ready for sound.

34-00 Post-Production Sound

Part of the master plan is to take the edited master on DigiBeta and make a blow up to 35mm film. But that's later, maybe much later. This will mean a mix for theatrical release that is different from a mix for television. (For a discussion of theatrical mixes and the Dolby process, see 34-00 Post-Production Sound in the chapter on the Digital Feature.) The Producer is working with a small post audio facility.

34-01 Sound Editor

The sound editor digitizes the audio into ProTools, avoiding any overmodulation or distortion. He supervises the post audio process and, because this is low budget, does most of the work. He lays out the separate tracks, places effects in their proper places, and prepares the mix. He checks every single cut to make sure the sound across it is quiet. This has been done in the video edit to catch all the major glitches, but most edit rooms are not equipped with the speakers and acoustics to do quality sound work.

The next step is Spotting.

34-05 Spotting

What sound effects should be used? Where should they go? The Director, Producer, and Sound Editor watch and listen to the movie for sound effects and trouble spots, like dialogue replacement. The Sound Editor selects the sounds and positions them in all the right places. As he goes, he's also setting the levels relatively in place in preparation for the mix. This spotting session is repeated with the Composer to spot for music cues. Each session takes a few hours, but is included in the overall deal. On this production, the Sound Editor will lay in the music cues.

34-08 Dialogue Editor

Normally, a dialogue editor is brought in to assemble, synchronize, edit, clean up and smooth out all the dialogue, but on this project, low budget as it is, the Sound Editor does this chore. If he can use the production tracks, he will, but if any of them are unusable he replaces them with alternate production tracks recorded on set or with automated dialogue replacement (ADR). It's part of his Sound Editor hours.

34-10 ADR

Two of the actors are brought in for ADR for a day.

$$$

$175/hour for the Sound Editor and the studio.

34-12 – Foley

A Foley artist also comes in to do some walking on various surfaces. (This process is actually done after the Dialogue Edit.)

$$$

$275/hour for the Sound Editor and the Foley Stage. $350/day for the artist.

(For a discussion on post-sound needs for foreign distribution see 34-04 ADR & Foley in the chapter on the Digital Feature.)

34-16 Mix

The mix is fun; it's when everything comes together — all the sounds and dialogue and the music.

The music has been prepared by the Composer on timecode DAT (or as a ProTools session if both Composer and Sound Editor are in Pro-Tools). All the music cues have been carefully positioned according to timecode to fit picture exactly.

34-17 Layback

The mixing team lays back all the mixed sound to the three Digi-Beta Masters. The Producer heaves a big sigh of relief, goes into a quiet bar, and orders a cold beer, where he ponders the meaning of life.

35-00 Titles

The opening title sequence is done in the Off-/On-Line Edit — simple images and simple text.

The closing credits are all white type on black background, and are done in the On-Line session. The tape-to-film company recommends bringing the credits on and off, rather than a roll, for a smoother effect in 35mm.

37-00 Insurance

37-01 Producers Entertainment Package

The standard Entertainment Package includes a number of items, but the key ones the Producer is concerned about are: Faulty stock, Equipment, and third-party property damage. (He calls Laurie Beale at Gary Krouse Insurance, 818/407-5300.)

The cost of the policy without cast insurance is $1,750. With cast insurance it's $3,250.

It gives him a sick feeling in his stomach, but he just can't afford it this time around. He declines insurance. He's flying without a net.

This means he puts down a $5,000 damage deposit for the camera and sound gear on his credit card. Oh well.

37-02 General Liability

The GL for $1 million is normally necessary to rent equipment, and to secure some locations, but in this case there isn't any heavy equipment. A short-term policy for up to nine months is $1,750. Sorry. Too rich for his blood.

37-03 Hired Non-Owned Auto

The Producer takes out insurance through the truck rental company.

37-05 Workers' Compensation

Workers' Comp is based on payroll. There isn't any payroll on this project, and while that doesn't let the Producer off the hook in case of an accident, yes, he is liable, he declines the Workers' Comp as well, and keeps a watchful eye over everyone. Zero accidents!

37-06 Errors and Omissions

When there is a deal for distribution, and the picture is about to see the light of day, that's when there is exposure, and the Producer and Distributor need to be insured for libel and slander. Cost is about $4,500 per year. E&O insurance probably won't be given without Clearance (See 02-03 Clearance).

38-00 General & Administrative Expenses

38-01 Business License

Under normal circumstances, where more money was available, the Producer would start a new company specifically for every film, so exposure to lawsuits is limited. An LLC or even a DBA does the trick. The mandatory state fee for the LLC is $800 in CA, but the paperwork he gets for $25. An LLC requires an Operating Agreement, which means a lawyer has to do it. The good news is he can clone 90% from his previous agreements, so the fee is minimal. But for this picture — zilch.

38-02 Legal

A lawyer friend of the family looks over the Agreements with cast and crew for free.

38-03 Accounting Fees

This is the friendly Bookkeeper.

38-20 Wrap Party

$25 buys a few six packs and a piñata so everyone can hit something. Shooting is over!!

When the picture is all posted, the Producer throws a screening party for cast and crew, preferably after the drinking.

TAPE-TO-FILM TRANSFER AND DIGITAL CINEMA PROJECTION

Tape-to-Film Transfer

Even though digital video cameras are continuously improving in image resolution, 35mm film is still highly desired as an acquisition format. But for a filmmaker on a budget, film can hurt, while video can make things possible. But what do you do when it's time to show your film in a movie theater and all you have is a DigiBeta or HD master? That's when you're glad there's such a thing as a Tape-to-Film Transfer. That's also when you're kicking yourself that you didn't start preparing for it in pre-production. You'll see why as you read on.

If money were no object, many producers would still shoot in 35mm. It looks great, and it's what's distributed to and projected in most movie theaters, although Digital Cinema (projection from a Digital Master file) is gaining fast. But the beauty of tape-to-film is that video allows you to capture image at a lower cost than film, which means you've saved some money *on the front end*. Then, when you've finished your edit, you can decide if it's good enough to spend the hunk of cash you'll need for tape-to-film transfer. It's often the difference between wishing you could make a movie if only you had the money, and actually doing it because with digital filmmaking, it's affordable.

We're assuming here that you want to show your finished product in movie theaters, where you'll need a transfer from an HD digital master, a standard definition videotape master, or a digital file, to 35mm and/or Digital Cinema projection. In addition to 35mm film and Digital Cinema Masters, the final images and sound can be delivered on other formats, including:

▶ Videotape (e.g. D5, D1, HDCAM-SR etc. for subsequent conversion to NTSC, PAL, DVD)

▶ Hard drives

Let's note too the growing trend to shoot and edit digitally, manipulate the image digitally with color correction, CGI, and compositing as needed, and then project digitally via a Digital Cinema Master, leaving film out of the process entirely.

There are several methods of tape-to-film transfer, and each has its supporters (and detractors). Plus, new technologies are cropping up. It's a dynamic field, and the filmmaker should take the time to research the various possibilities, meet the people at different companies, and most importantly, go see their work. Ask to screen examples of projects as similar as possible to yours in shooting style, lighting, and camera equipment. Compare prices, service, and whether or not you get to keep your negative and optical print. Ask for client references. How do former clients feel about the company's service, billing and technical expertise? In short, you're about to spend a lot of money, so become an expert.

Types of Tape-to-Film Transfers

The technology is moving fast, but at present, laser technology is preferred for obtaining the widest color gamut and contrast range. The laser system has a red, green, blue (RGB) laser and writes RGB lines across the film. For more information, check the list at the end of this section for a few companies that do tape-to-film transfers.

$$$

Prices vary from house to house, but generally, on the ARRI (a German company that makes a laser recorder), a 90-minute feature film will run about $37,000, or about $411/minute.

Let's look into some of the considerations we need to keep in mind when planning, shooting, and editing for a tape-to-film transfer.

Aspect ratio

Aspect ratio is the relationship between the width and height of a picture. Standard television pictures are squareish, and have an aspect ratio that is referred to as 1.33:1. That number, just in case you were curious, is achieved by dividing the width of the picture by its height. Standard television has a ratio of 4 units wide by 3 units tall, or 4:3. This ratio is then presented as 1.33:1 because 4 divided by 3 is 1.33. So the aspect ratio of standard TV is 1.33 to 1, expressed as 1.33:1.

Digital televisions, and High Definition (HD) TVs, have a wider screen with a ratio of 16:9 (1.78:1). Most 35mm movies are slightly more rectangular, and have an aspect ratio of 1.85:1.

The point of all this is that once the final format is decided (standard TV, 16:9 TV, 16mm, 35mm, etc.), the Producer, Director, and DP have to agree on how to compose the shots to best fit the aspect ratio of the final format.

If shots were composed with 35mm (1.85:1) in mind, and care was taken to stay within Safe Action limits, then only a little bit (less than 5%) of the top and bottom on the screen will be cropped when the video is transferred to 35mm. If, however, the picture was shot with full screen video in mind (4:3, or 1.33:1), it will either have to fit inside a wider aspect ratio, and there will be black borders on the left and right sides, or the house can enlarge the video frame to fill the movie screen aspect ratio, and crop the image to fit. In the latter scenario, blowing up a smaller piece of the image results in decreased resolution, plus about 26% of the image may be lost. Most DPs and Directors hate to see that much of their hard work get degraded and lopped off.

16:9 Cameras

Most DPs recommend shooting in useable 16:9 cameras. We say "useable" because some cameras don't have true 16:9, they use a 4:3 chip with a 16:9 switch, so even though you're shooting in a 16:9 aspect ratio, you're not gaining any resolution, in fact, with some cameras, you're losing some. There are, however, true 16:9 professional cameras, and anamorphic lenses for 4:3 prosumer cameras, which can be attached to the 4:3 camera to compress the image optically into the 4:3 format (but the video must be played on a 16:9 monitor or the image will look squished).

Ask your transfer house if they've had problems with specific cameras. If you have the time and money, test a few of the different cameras you may be considering with transfers to 35mm.

Letterbox

It is possible to compose shots for 35mm, that is, shoot with a 16:9 camera, and then play that image on a 4:3 monitor, but then the image is "letterboxed." Letterbox puts the 16:9 image in the 4:3 format by placing black bands across the top and bottom. Letterboxing is quite common nowadays — but obviously the 16:9 image is most accurately watched on a 16x9 sized monitor that has 16:9 capability.

Many festivals require "video screeners" that are "letterbox" versions of your film. This version plays the 16x9 image on a 4:3 television screen with black borders on the top and bottom of the TV monitor. On the other hand, plenty of festivals now screen digital movies. Maybe it boils down to where you want your movie seen, in the digital screening room or on the silver screen.

Choosing the Tape-to-Film Transfer Company

Before you shoot, check a few prospective companies. Ask to look at films that are comparable to your project. Ask what equipment was used in shooting and what systems were used in the transfer. Compare current prices and service (ask whether you get your negative and optical print as part of the deal). Get and check out recommendations. Allow plenty of time for this process; there's a lot of money involved, and after all your hard work, you'll want to sit in a movie theater and know that you did all you could to get the best picture quality possible.

After you've made your decision, get their specs and suggestions for what will work best for your shoot with their particular method. And then do some tests.

Shooting for a Tape-to-Film Transfer

There are some shooting considerations to keep in mind when you know you'll have, or might have, a tape-to-film transfer. Most, but not all tape-to-film transfer companies recommend these specifications, so check with your company for details.

▸ First, use the best camera you can afford, and become thoroughly familiar with it before shooting begins. (This is only a rule of thumb. Some filmmakers may choose a lower end camera for aesthetic reasons.)

▸ Some video formats do better than others when crossing over to film. Here's a list of formats in ascending order: SVHS, Hi8, BetaSP, MII, DVCPro25, DVCam, DV, Digital8, D1, D5, DCT, DigiBeta, DVCPro50, Digital S, BetaSX, IMX, HDCam, DVCProHD, HD-CAM-SR.

▶ Then there are the digital file based formats, like P2 and SxS. With file-based formats, it can be trickier to determine quality. That's because the file name — e.g. "P2" — is just a wrapper for the data inside. The data itself could be high resolution or very compressed. It's important, therefore, that you have your files verified with a facility before you shoot your movie to determine their viability for film-out.

▶ Shooting in progressive scan? Be sure to check with your Editor and tape-to-film houses. Some are set up to handle it well. Others are not.

▶ Most transfer houses recommend 24p for shooting. Most prosumer and professional cameras now shoot in some type of 24fps. If you plan on a film-out, you need to shoot in this mode. If you also have video deliverables, you can always convert the 24fps to 30fps and/ or 25fps.

▶ If you're shooting in 16:9, have a 16:9 monitor on the set with an underscan feature.

▶ Use high resolution monitors to verify focus.

▶ Avoid using such camera functions as automatic focus, electronic zoom and electronic stabilizers as they may cause artifacts during capture.

▶ Filters can affect digital images, so test them prior to principal photography.

▶ Consider using a PAL format. The difference between PAL and NTSC is especially noted in the lower-end cameras. PAL is particularly helpful in films with lots of fast action. Many filmmakers prefer PAL format over NTSC because it has more lines of resolution and a shooting rate of 25 fps which is closer to film's 24 fps. The problem with PAL for North American filmmakers has been the scarcity of the gear, not only cameras but decks as well, although the situation has improved. Most editing systems are switchable between PAL and NTSC. And some transfer companies charge less to transfer PAL-based projects. One word of caution, shooting in PAL in the U.S. where everything is 60HZ can cause a strobing effect when shooting in natural light if the shutter speed is set incorrectly.

▶ Pay attention to the aspect ratio (see discussion above).

▶ Use normal electronic shutter speed, not faster or slower, unless for a desired aesthetic.

▶ Don't up the gain on the camera, it only causes visual "noise." Instead, pump more light into the scene, or if you can't do that, use a more sensitive camera.

▶ Don't sharpen the detail on the camera, it will only increase the sharp video look on the film.

▶ If you decide to use filtration on the front of the lens, test extensively. On some digital capture cameras a ¼ pro-mist can turn into a ½ pro-mist.

▶ Finally, make some tests where you replicate the shooting and lighting conditions and styles that you want to use. Take the test all the way through color correction, to include the final look of the film. And don't just shoot charts, shoot interiors, exteriors, make-up etc. It may cost some time and a little money, but you'll get much better results. Talk with the company you're using for the tape-to-film transfer for details. One transfer company expert with whom we spoke said, "The test is the single most important gift filmmakers can give themselves before beginning production. You will have different questions after a test. You may decide to change the camera you're using. Or change the shooting technique, or the lighting. Review the entire process from capture through editorial. Camera technology moves fast and there have been instances where the editorial systems have not caught up to the camera technology."

Video Treatment Processes

There are several video treatment processes that can make your video look more like film. Probably the best known of these is a company in southern California called FILMLOOK Inc. (*www.Filmlook.com*). Typically, these processes create the motion characteristics and gray scale of film, and can even simulate the grain of film. If the picture has been shot according to their suggested specs, the result will look better, and in many cases it gets pretty close to the look of film. The process is done before you have a color-corrected edited master on video. Some basic color correction is done as part of the process, or they can run Da Vinci 2K color correction simultaneously with the process. Again, if you are considering this process, get the recommended shooting specs before you shoot.

Be warned, however, that if you plan to do a tape-to-film transfer, do not use your video treated master; you'll get a film with visible video artifacts. Instead, create two masters (preferably on DigiBeta or HD-CAM), one for tape-to-film, and another for FILMLOOK, or whoever you choose.

$$$

The prices for FILMLOOK are charged by the running minute or by the hour depending on whether Da Vinci color correction is used. See their website at *www.Filmlook.com* for current rates.

If you want to save money and if time is not too much of an issue, you might want to do video treatment on a computer using one of several software programs. Adobe After Effects can do it. So can the DigiEffects Cinelook plug in.

Reel breaks

Reel breaks are the places in the movie where the projectionist may have to start the next reel of your film. (Some splice all the reels together and run it through one projector.) Generally, when you screen your movie, you must supply the theater with the separate 35mm reels. A 90-minute feature can go onto four 20-minute 35mm reels and one 10-minute 35mm reel — or some such breakdown. Film is manufactured in 20-minute reels (2,000 ft).

So how should you deliver your video master to the tape-to-film company for transfer? Ask them before you edit. Some companies want you to make individual videocassettes that match the exact length of each 35mm camera reel, with audio and visual sync points at the top. Others will do that for you, but you'll need to tell them at what timecode you want your 35mm reel breaks.

The rule of thumb is: *reel breaks should be at picture breaks and sound breaks.* Overlapping dialogue, music, or sound effects at a reel break will be noticed. Silence is golden. If possible, make it at a simple transition, like a cut between scenes where the outgoing scene has a slight pause at the end, and it's okay if we miss a half second of the incoming scene. But don't make the break during a fade up or fade out to black.

Sound

Some tape-to-film companies accept the sound as mixed onto

the edited master, while others want it separately, on timecode DAT or DA88/98, properly synced to picture. In any case, the mix should be a "theatrical mix," meaning it is made for use in movie theaters, not on television or home video, which has different requirements. Discuss what kind of mix you need with your Sound Editor or Mixer. (For a discussion of a theatrical mix, please see the Digital Feature Budget, 34-00 Post-Production Sound.)

We've heard transfer experts complain that some people don't put a "2 pop" onto all the picture and sound elements for sync, at both head and tail of each reel. A 2 pop is a countdown to 2 on the picture and a pop or beep sound that lasts 1/24th of a second, 2 seconds before action starts. Mixers in Post know this, but sometimes need reminders.

Also note if you have a Dolby SRD track you will need to contact Dolby for Licensing schedules and fees. A Dolby rep comes to your sound house and "blesses" the track with reel breaks comparing them to the picture. Upon approval, your sound house will make the MO disk from which you have your Optical Track Negative made. This will also accompany your picture elements to the transfer house to make any other deliverables that require the Dolby process.

Conclusion

We think it's fair to say that given a clean, well-lit piece of video, most of these higher-end technologies can give the filmmaker an excellent quality tape-to-film transfer. So like the golfers say, "It ain't the clubs, baby, it's the Tiger Woods swinging 'em." In technical terms, the quality of standard definition video (meaning everything but High Definition) is much lower than the ability of the machines to transfer. Consequently, the manipulation of the image and the machine works best with skilled and talented people. The moral of the story is: meet the people, see their work, and test.

Digital Capture / Digital Out

As digital technology improves, and as costs play a key role, especially for independent producers, another workflow has become popular: digital capture to digital intermediate for color grading and effects to digital finish. The digital finish may be in lieu of making a film negative (or "film-out") until such time as the producer gets a distribution deal that requires it. A digital finish, with digital files prepared to specs for

Digital Cinema Projection (see below for more on that), is now accepted by the Academy of Motion Picture Arts and Sciences for possible Oscar nomination. This workflow is usually a more affordable option than a traditional film-out.

For more information check with:

- ▶ EFILM in Hollywood, CA, (323) 463-7041 *www.efilm.com*
- ▶ Cineric in New York, NY (212) 586-4822 *www.cineric.com*
- ▶ FotoKem in Burbank, CA (818) 846-3102 *www.fotokem.com*
- ▶ IVC Digital Film Center, Burbank, CA (818) 569-4949 *www.ivchd.com*

Tape-to-Film Transfer Sequence and Expense

What follows is a case study of one Producer's journey through tape-to-film transfer. She's the same Producer depicted in the Digital Feature Budget chapter.

During her pre-production phase, the Producer carefully researches and compares the tape-to-film processes and prices, and chooses the company she wants to use. Her decision is partly based on the willingness of the staff to work with her to get the look she and the Director want.

She, the Director, and the Director of Photography have chosen to work with the Panasonic AJ-HDC27 VariCam camera. It shoots in 16:9 aspect ratio, at 1280x720 progressive at a capture rate of 24fps (which is variable, but in this case, they have no plans to use the variable feature). It uses DVCProHD large size cassettes which have 32-minute record times.

The DP and Director meet with the tape-to-film company to see examples of footage similar to what theirs will be, talk about the limits of dolly shots, pans, or any moving camera shots, and review the shooting specs that will give them the best possible 35mm picture. These include using normal shutter speed, no extra gain, no extra detail, and no computer effects.

Shooting in 16:9 gives an aspect ratio that transfers better than standard 4:3, because the film equivalent of 16:9 is 1.78:1, which is very close to 35mm's 1.85:1. In composing their shots, they'll stay within the safe action area, and will not crowd the top and bottom of the frame, because they know that the height of the 16:9 image is slightly taller than 35mm and will therefore be lost in the transfer. (The width of the two images is the same.)

The next step is to shoot some tests. The DP makes sure he is completely familiar with the camera. The Producer, Director and DP set up some scenes that typify the conditions and style of the picture, including exteriors, interiors, close-ups, medium shots, etc. Ideally, she tests before the official shooting schedule begins, or if that's not possible, at the top of the schedule. She also tells the actors and crew that these are camera tests, and that certain scenes may need re-shooting. They only need to shoot two to three minutes of tests, at a cost of about $500 for 35mm. In this case, the company will credit that back to her when she pays for the final transfer. Again, service is important when dealing with filmmakers. The companies just want to avoid people who test and test and then never show up for the party.

Now that everyone is satisfied that they can get the look they want, and that it will show up as a thing of beauty on 35mm, the team goes off to shoot and edit the picture. The Post Sound edit is equalized for a theatrical mix in Dolby SR and Dolby Digital (see this discussion in the Digital Feature Budget 34-00 Post-Production Sound).

There was one thing that happened during the shoot. The Director wanted a dolly shot tracking an actor running next to a building. The building was only about three feet from the actor, and when the Director looked at the shot, it strobed a bit. They took the tape into their transfer company and analyzed how to reshoot to make the shot work with no strobing, which would have shown up in the transfer. Another example of good service.

During On-Line editing, they are careful to follow their transfer company's advice to not crush blacks or whites, but work with gamma levels (grays) instead. The Producer is also following advice by working in an editing system where the video signal is uncompressed and component.

In the Post Sound, after the picture is mixed and laid back to the HDCAM master, a copy of the sound track, synced to picture, is laid off to DA98.

Before they lay it off to the HDCAM master, however, they check with the transfer company to see how they want the video, in one piece, or already broken into reel breaks. If in one piece, then the company needs to know the timecode of where the Producer wants the reel breaks to occur. For 35mm, the reel breaks should be roughly every 18 to 20 minutes, and not where there's music, overlapping dialogue, or in the middle of an actor's sentence.

Up to this point, all the expenses are included in the Producer's original budget (see Digital Film Budget). Now she heads into Tape-to-Film territory, and she's ready to spend some serious money.

She takes her sound track on DA98, and goes to a lab, where she has an optical sound track negative made.

As part of her Post-Production Sound budget, she had Dolby SR and Dolby Digital put on a sound neg. Printing and sound negative costs are variable from lab to lab but for the same time length, she budgets $5K for optical sound negative and $7K for first (and sometimes second) prints.

$$$

Cost: $5,000 – $7,000

She then delivers her HDCAM Master to the tape-to-film transfer company. They do the transfer, and she now has a 35mm (silent) negative and a one-light print to check it.

$$$

Cost: $22,000

She goes back to the lab, where they sync the optical sound track negative to the 35mm.

$$$

Cost: $190 for 5 reels

She also has a magnetic sound track made to test the sync.

$$$

Cost: $1,500

Now she asks the lab to make an Answer Print, which she and the Director color correct scene to scene. The final step — the lab makes the Composite Print.

$$$

Cost: .35 cents per foot, or about $3,000

Additional Release Prints will cost about $1,600 each.

Her total expense is $38,700, or about $430/minute. She owns all her elements, and she's done and ready for Sundance!

Note: Prices vary widely for both lab work and tape-to-film transfer. Some companies say to figure on about $35,000 out the door, others say $50,000 or even $80,000. Some require the sound on a separate element, such as DA98, others take your edited master on DigiBeta, HDCAM, or DV-CAM or whatever, and strip the sound off themselves or go through a lab. It's the Wild West. We suggest you check out the different companies, take the tours, see their films, get their bids, and then make up your mind.

Digital Cinema Projection

We can now go to the movies and watch trailers, shorts, ads, and entire features completely in a digital format. Digital cinema uses digital technology to distribute and project movies. A movie can arrive at a theater on hard drives, optical disks or via satellite, and projected on a digital projector instead of a conventional film projector.

First, a little history. Back in 2002, the major Hollywood studios foresaw the emergence of digital cinema, and wisely realized that if warring formats and standards were unleashed, everyone would probably lose money. So they jointly formed the Digital Cinema Initiative, or DCI, to establish a standard open architecture for digital cinema systems.

Now let's say you've shot your project on film and you want to make it available for digital cinema projection, or you've shot it on video and here you are with a DigiBeta or HDCAM master and you want to get it ready for digital cinema projection. What are the steps in the workflow? In either case, film or video, you must begin the process with your movie in a digital file format, because you will be creating a deliverable called a Digital Cinema Package (DCP). The specific type of elements in a DCP are defined by the DCI group, and you can reference *www.dcimovies.com* for the current DCP specification.

To see how we get to the Digital Cinema Package, let's review the process of production and post.

Most features that are digitally projected are shot on 35mm film, processed, then scanned at 2K (2048x1080) or 4K (4096x2160) resolution into their next incarnation, the digital intermediate, where they now exist in a digital format. Most features that have originated on digital video and are digitally projected have been shot at 1920x1080 HD resolution using high-end cameras like the Sony CineAlta, Panavision Genesis, or Thomson Viper. Other cameras like the Red One can record 4K RAW. In any case, these pictures already exist in a digital format.

In post-production, there can be different workflows, even within a given medium, like film or digital video. That said, here's a possible scenario. In the film workflow, the film that ran through the camera is processed and scanned into digital files on a scanner or high-resolution telecine. In the digital workflow, the data files from the digital camera are normally converted to whatever file format works best for the editing platform being used and the final deliverables. After the creative work of editing, all of the files are "conformed" to match the editor's edit list. Then the movie is color corrected. Finally, a digital intermediate is made to record the motion picture to film and/or for the digital cinema release.

If the next step is digital cinema release, a digital master needs to be made. Do not attempt this at home. Go to a professional individual or post facility that can create your DCP. When the sound, picture, and data elements have been completed (please see below for a more comprehensive technical explanation), they are assembled into a *Digital Cinema Distribution Master* (DCDM), which contains all of the digital material needed for projection. The images and sound are then compressed, encrypted, and packaged to form the Digital Cinema Package (DCP).

Motion JPEG 2000 (sometimes referred to as MJ2 or MJP2) is the leading digital cinema standard for storage, distribution and projection.

What you just read is the shorthand version for technical dummies like me. Thanks to Sean Romano, VP of Operations at Deluxe Digital Cinema in Hollywood (*www.bydeluxe.com/services_digital_initiatives.php*), what follows is a more comprehensive version for those interested in the technical details. Take it away, Sean.

Let's start with an overview of what components comprise the DCP. Specifically, there are: the image files (a jpeg2000 frame sequence), audio files (individual broadcast wav tracks), select coordination files (such as the ASSETMAP, VOLINDEX, and CPL), as well as any ancillary data elements (such as subtitle files). The DCI specification was also designed with a fairly robust security element; as such, any DCP can be encrypted during its creation. The workflow used to create the elements referenced above is commonly referred to as the Digital Cinema Mastering process.

Image Files

During the Digital Cinema Mastering process a technically savvy post-production facility and/or individual will most commonly start with the compression of the image files into the jpeg2000 file format from a DCDM (Digital Cinema Distribution Master) sequence that has been rendered in the XYZ color space. In DCI-approved Digital Cinema Playback systems, the jpeg2000 image essence is generally played back at 24fps and falls into one of the following four image resolutions:

▶ Flat 2K –   1998x1080
▶ Scope 2K – 2048x858
▶ Flat 4K –   3996x2160
▶ Scope 4K – 4096x1716

The specification does allow for alternate frame rates (most notably 48fps for 3D or Stereoscopic display); however, currently 24fps is the most widely supported. Once the compression has been completed, it is now time to create the material exchange format (MXF) file that is made up of the newly created jpeg2000 file sequence. If encryption has been requested, than it is applied during the MXF track generation. If multiple sequences are required, this process can be repeated, creating multiple MXF elements related to the image essence of the DCP.

Audio Files

In the DCP the audio components also must be presented as an MXF file or series of MXF files, and are required to meet strict guidelines. The audio element type must be a broadcast wav file or series of broadcast wav files that run at 24fps (this is the current practice as the DCI specification does allow for different frame rates as the technology advances) and match the duration of the jpeg2000 frames/MXF track listed above. If encryption has been requested, than it is applied during the MXF track generation. Also, if multiple audio sequences are required this process can be repeated to allow for multiple MXF elements.

Once the audio and image essences have been converted into their required formats, the digital cinema mastering personnel will now create a series of files related to the playback and tracking of the assets involved with the DCP. These files are represented by the following elements:

▶ CPL (Composition Playlist)
▶ Assetmap
▶ Volume Index
▶ PKL (Packing List)

Each of these components represents a different aspect of how a Digital Cinema Playback system recognizes and subsequently plays back a given DCP. The most important element listed above is the CPL or Composition Playlist, as it is the file that designates which image and audio files are authorized for playback as well as how those files are to be presented. All of the files in this category are written in the open source file format known as eXtensible Markup Language or XML. The remaining files (Assetmap, Volume Index, and PKL) are designed to track the DCP assets (CPL, image MXF tracks, audio MXF tracks) for Digital Cinema Playback systems.

The last steps in the Digital Cinema Mastering process are an evaluation of the completed DCP and the creation of a master element. All "sign-off" DCP evaluations are typically done in two stages. The first is a technical evaluation by the Digital Cinema mastering personnel and the second is a separate evaluation with any personnel directly related to production of the project. If the content has been encrypted the Digital Cinema Mastering personnel will need to be involved with the creation of the unlock codes (KDM — key delivery messages) related to the playback or subsequent re-distribution of the material in question. Once a DCP has been approved (by both the Digital Cinema Mastering personnel and the designated project personnel) an archive or "output" element is created. This new element (typically an external USB hard drive) can then become a source that all of the necessary delivery media can be derived from.

INDUSTRIAL/CORPORATE BUDGET

Instructions on Downloading Budgets:

- Go to *www.mwp.com*
- Click on "Virtual Film School"
- Scroll down on menu to "Resources"
- Download Excel Spreadsheets
- Save to your desktop

INDUSTRIAL/CORPORATE BUDGET

Fringe assumptions:			INDUSTRIAL BUDGET	
Payroll Tax	23%		Shoot Days:	2
WGA	14%		Location:	Local
DGA	13%		Unions:	AFTRA
SAG	14%		Production:	Super 16mm film
AFTRA	12%			HPX-170 (P2)
Agency Fees	10%		Off-Line:	Non-linear - 5 days
			On-Line	Non-linear - 12 hrs. to D2

SUMMARY BUDGET

02-00 Script	2,460	
03-00 Producers Unit	7,700	
04-00 Direction	0	
05-00 Cast	1,416	
TOTAL ABOVE-THE-LINE		11,576
10-00 Production Staff	1,661	
13-00 Production Design	2,844	
14-00 Set Construction	2,000	
15-00 Set Operations	4,302	
16-00 Special Effects	750	
19-00 Wardrobe	2,032	
20-00 Make-Up and Hairdressing	461	
21-00 Electrical	3,652	
22-00 Camera	8,799	
23-00 Sound	619	
24-00 Transportation	660	
25-00 Location Expenses	2,700	
27-00 Film & Lab	3,565	
TOTAL PRODUCTION		34,044
30-00 Editorial	6,310	
33-00 Music	2,000	
34-00 Post-Production Sound	3,070	
35-00 Titles & Graphics	2,500	
36-00 Stock Footage	2,700	
TOTAL POST-PRODUCTION		16,580
37-00 Insurance	0	
38-00 General & Administrative	0	
TOTAL OTHER		0
Total Above-the-Line		11,576
Total Below-the-Line		50,624
Total Above and Below-the-Line		62,200
Contingency @ 10 %		6,220
GRAND TOTAL		$68,420

	Amount	Units	x	Rate	Sub-Total	Total
02-00 Script						
02-01 Writer's Salaries	5	Days	1	400	2,000	2,000
Payroll				2,000	460	460
				Total for 02-00		2,460
03-00 Producers Unit						
03-02 Producer	14	Days	1	500	7,000	7,000
Payroll				7,000	700	700
				Total for 03-00		7,700
04-00 Direction						
04-01 Director					0	0
				Total for 04-00		0
05-00 Cast						
05-01 Lead Actors						
Basketball star					0	0
Scientist	1	Day	1	380	380	380
Narrator (2x scale)	1	Hour	1	622	622	622
Agency fee @ 10%	1	Allow	1	622	62	62
Payroll				1,002	230	230
AFTRA				1,002	121	121
				Total for 05-00		1,416

	Amount	Units	x	Rate	Sub-Total	Total
10-00 Production Staff						
10-08 Production Assistants						
Set PA	8	Days	1	150	1,200	1,200
PA/Script	1	Day	1	150	150	150
Payroll				1,350	311	311
				Total for 10-00		1,661
13-00 Production Design						
13-02 Art Director						
Prep	3	Days	1	325	975	
Shoot	2	Days	1	325	650	1,625
13-03 Assistant						
Prep	3	Days	1	125	375	
Shoot	2	Days	1	125	250	
Wrap	0.5	Day	1	125	63	688
Payroll				2,313	532	532
				Total for 13-00		2,844
14-00 Set Construction						
14-06 Purchases (Bldg. materials)	1	Allow	1	1,000	1,000	1,000

14-07 Rentals (Greens/drapery etc.)	1 Allow	1	1,000	1,000	1,000	
			Total for 14-00			2,000
15-00 Set Operations						
15-01 First Grip						
Prod. shot Shoot	1 Day	12	25	300		
Talent Shoot	1 Day	12	25	300	600	
15-02 Second Grip (Best Boy)						
Prod. shot Shoot	1 Day	12	22	264		
Talent Shoot	1 Day	12	22	264	528	
15-04 Dolly Grip						
Prod. shot Shoot	1 Day	12	22	264		
Talent Shoot	1 Day	12	22	264	528	
15-05 Craft Service						
Prep	1 Day	6	13	78		
Shoot	2 Days	12	13	312	390	
Purchases	2 Days	1	100	200	200	
15-06 Grip Rentals						
Package	2 Days	1	250	500	500	
Dolly	2 Days	1	250	500	500	
Cartage	1 Allow	1	75	75	75	
Smoke cracker	1 Day	1	200	200	200	
15-07 Grip Expendables	1 Allow	1	200	200	200	
15-08 Box Rentals				0	0	
Key Grip	2 Days	1	30	60	60	
Craft Service	2 Days	1	25	50	50	
Payroll			2,046	471	471	
			Total for 15-00			4,302
16-00 Special Effects						
16-05 Special Effects-Squishy Shoe	1 Allow	1	750	750	750	
			Total for 16-00			750
19-00 Wardrobe						
19-01 Stylist						
Prep (shoes/wardrobe)	2 Days	1	350	700		
Shoot	2 Days	1	350	700	1,400	
19-04 Expendables	1 Allow	1	50	50	50	
19-05 Purchases	1 Allow	1	100	100	100	
19-10 Box Rentals	2 Days	1	30	60	160	
Payroll			1,400	322	322	
			Total for 19-00			2,032
20-00 Make-Up and Hairdressing						
20-01 Key Make-Up Artist	1 Day	1	350	350	350	
20-07 Box Rentals	1 Day	1	30	30	30	
Payroll			350	81	81	
			Total for 20-00			461
21-00 Electrical						
21-01 Gaffer						
Prod. shot Shoot	1 Day	12	25	300		
Talent Shoot	1 Day	12	25	300	600	
21-02 Best Boy						

Item	Qty	Unit	X	Rate	Amount	Subtotal	Total
Prod. shot Shoot	1	Day	12	22	264		
Talent Shoot/Wrap	1	Day	14	22	308	572	
21-05 Purchases	1	Allow	1	350	350	350	
21-06 Equipment Rentals	2	Days	1	900	1,800	1,800	
21-10 Box Rentals							
Gaffer	2	Days	1	30	60	60	
Payroll					1,172	270	270
Total for 21-00							3,652
22-00 Camera							
22-01 Director/DP/Op							
Prod. Shot: Prep	1	Day	1	1,000	1,000		
Shoot	1	Day	1	2,000	2,000		
Invoice fee @ 10%	1	Allow	1	300	300	3,300	
Talent Shoot: DP/Op							
Prep	1	Day	1	450	450		
Shoot	1	Day	1	750	750	1,200	
22-03 1st Asst. Camera							
Prep	1	Day	6	30	180		
Shoot	1	Day	12	30	360	540	
22-06 Expendables	1	Allow	1	250	250	250	
22-07 Camera Package Rental							
Prod. Shot: Arri 16SR2 (MOS)	1	Day	1	200	200		
Prime lense set	1	Day	1	250	250		
Cam. accessories	1	Day	1	450	450	900	
Talent shoot: HMC-150 Pckge.	1	Day	1	200	200	200	
22-12 Teleprompter/Operator	1	Day	1	450	450	450	
22-13 Video Assist/Operator	1	Day	1	800	800	800	
Payroll					5,040	1,159	1,159
Total for 22-00							8,799
23-00 Sound							
23-01 Mixer							
Talent Shoot:	1	Day	12	25	300	300	
23-03 Expendables (Batteries, etc)	1	Allow	1	100	100	100	
23-04 Sound Pkg (Incl. w/cam pkg)						0	0
23-06 Radio Mikes	1	Allow	1	150	150	150	
Payroll					300	69	69
Total for 23-00							619
24-00 Transportation							
24-03 Equipment Rental							
Production Van	4	Days	1	65	260	260	
Set Dressing	4	Days	1	75	300	300	
24-04 Gas & Oil	1	Allow	1	100	100	100	
Total for 24-00							660
25-00 Location Expenses							
25-09 Catering Service							
Crew Meals (2 days)	25	Meals	2	12	600	600	
Tent/Tables/Chairs	1	Allow	1	100	100	100	
25-17 Location Site Rental							
Gym	2	Days	1	1,000	2,000	2,000	
Total for 25-00							2,700

27-00 Film & Lab - Production							
27-01 Raw Stock (Film-Production)	3200	Feet	1	$0.46	1,472		
Sales Tax	1	Allow	1	1,472	121	1,593	
27-02 Lab-Negative Prep & Proc.	3200	Feet	1	$0.12	368	368	
27-03 Memory cards - Production							
P2 cards - 32GB	2	Cards	1	70	140	140	
27-08 Telecine (sc. to sc.-circled takes @ 5:1)							
	4	Hours	1	350	1,400	1,400	
27-09 DBeta Tape Stock (1 hr.)	1	Allow	1	64	64	64	
DVCam stock	1	Allow	1	30	30	30	
				Total for 27-00			3,565
30-00 Editorial							
30-08 Off-Line Editor	5	Days	1	300	1,500	1,500	
30-09 Off-Line Editing System							
Non-linear	5	Days	1	150	750	750	
30-10 On-Line System & Editor	12	Hours	1	300	3,600	3,600	
D2 Record/D2+BSP playback							
30-12 Videotape Dubs/Stock & Transfers							
Prod. shot: D2 to BetaSP	1	Allow	1	70	70	70	
Misc.	1	Allow	1	100	100	100	
30-13 Screening Copies (DVD)	10	disks	1	12	120	120	
30-14 Video Masters/Safeties/Textless							
D2 Edit Master-10:00	1	Cass.	1	85	85	85	
D2 Safety (textless)	1	Cass.	1	85	85	85	
				Total for 30-00			6,310
33-00 Music							
33-01 Composer	1	Allow	1	2,000	2,000	2,000	
(All-In Package includes: Arrangers, Copyists,					0	0	
...Musicians, Instruments, Studio,					0	0	
Engineers, Stock, etc)					0	0	
				Total for 33-00			2,000
34-00 Post-Production Sound							
34-01 Sound Editor	30	Hours	1	40	1,200	1,200	
34-05 Spotting	3	Hours	1	40	120	120	
34-05 Narration Record	2	Hours	1	125	250	250	
34-08 Dialogue Edit (Included above)			1		0	0	
34-16 Mix	5	Hours	1	250	1,250	1,250	
34-17 Layback	0.5	Hour	1	200	100	100	
34-18 Stock/Dubs/Transfers (Video)	1	Allow	1	150	150	150	
				Total for 34-00			3,070
35-00 Titles & Graphics							
35-01 Graphic Designer & Workstation							
Package	1	Allow	1	2,500	2,500	2,500	
				Total for 35-00			2,500
36-00 Stock Footage							
36-01 Film and Tape Clips Licensing	60	Seconds	1	45	2,700	2,700	
				Total for 36-00			2,700
37-00 Insurance							
37-01 Producers Entertainment Package					0	0	

Negative		0	0
Faulty Stock		0	0
Equipment		0	0
Props/Sets		0	0
Extra Expense		0	0
3rd Party Property Damage		0	0
Office Contents		0	0
37-02 General Liability		0	0
37-03 Hired Auto		0	0
37-04 Cast Insurance		0	0
37-05 Workers Compensation		0	0
37-06 Errors & Omissions		0	0
	Total for 37-00		0
		0	
38-00 General & Administrative Expenses		0	
38-02 Legal		0	0
38-03 Accounting fees		0	0
38-05 Telephone/Fax		0	0
38-06 Copying		0	0
38-07 Postage & Freight		0	0
38-08 Office Space Rental		0	0
38-09 Ofice Furniture		0	0
38-10 Office Equipment & Supplies		0	0
38-11 Computer Rental		0	0
38-12 Software		0	0
38-14 Messenger/Overnight		0	0
38-15 Parking		0	0
	Total for 38-00		0
Contingency @ 10%		6,220	6,220
GRAND TOTAL			$68,420
Total Above-the-Line			11,576
Total Below-the-Line			50,624
Total Above and Below-the-Line			62,200
	Check budget totals	68,450	68,420

INDUSTRIAL/CORPORATE BUDGET

Overview

Industrial films and videos can be the sorriest little projects you ever laid eyes on. Or they can be artistic, interesting, and well budgeted. Some are for training (*Service, Maintenance, and Assembly of Rear-Axle Components*). Others are for sales or promotions to the public (*Beauti-Control – Cosmetics for your everyday*).

Whatever the project, the producer must ask the client, "What's the point?" Or, put a bit more delicately, "Who are we trying to reach, and what do we want to have happen?" Surprisingly, many companies are fuzzy on this, and you as the expert communicator get to help clarify and focus.

If the client's first question to you is, "How much for a 15-minute video?" you know you're dealing with a neophyte. It's like asking an architect, "How much for a house?"

Since a 15-minute video can be a talking head, shot in real time, and unedited (a few hundred bucks), or an extravaganza of live action, computer graphics, and original score (many thousands), it's a good idea to agree beforehand on the general amount of money a company wants to spend. You wouldn't want to be like the architect who spends weeks designing a mansion for a client who can only afford a tree house.

Once you know what the point of the piece is, and roughly how much the client wants to spend, you can finalize your deal on paper and start scripting.

This sample industrial budget is for an athletic shoe company that will introduce a new line of basketball shoes. The eight-minute video will be shown on DVD players in the back rooms of retail shoe stores, and appear on the company's website. The audience is salespeople, mostly young men in their twenties, who want to be entertained as they learn three or four key selling points they can use on customers.

02-00 Script

02-01 Writer's Salary

The Writer/Producer is hired to take the company's existing research and sales materials, and conjure up a concept that will drive the sales points home to the audience. He negotiates a day rate, which is smart, because several people in different departments must approve the script, and there may be twists and turns, even reversals, in the conceptual approach.

The approved script calls for two days of shooting. The first day is the product shot, in which the shoe is shot on Super 16mm film in a number of situations in a gym. The second day is a comic scene between a basketball star under contract with the company, and an actor playing a scientist. This is shot on HD video. There is also stock footage and graphics intercut.

03-00 Producer's Unit

03-02 Producer

The Producer negotiates a flat day rate here as well. He estimates four days of prep, two shoot days, five days of nonlinear off-line editing, two days of nonlinear on-line, and three days of audio post. In truth, some of the prep time overlaps into his writing time.

His flat rate means he gets that rate no matter how many hours he may work in a day beyond a minimum of 8 to 10. It also means he'll be directing the one day of talent shooting for no extra money.

04-00 Direction

As mentioned, the Producer directs the talent day shoot. The product shot is directed by the Director of Photography and supervised by the Producer.

05-00 Cast

05-01 Lead Actors

The basketball star is under contract with the company to appear in a specified number of promotionals and commercials, so his salary does not appear in this budget.

The actor playing the scientist is an AFTRA member (this is the only guild to which this company is signatory), and he receives day scale for non-broadcast.

The Producer finds him by calling a number of agents and asking for auditions. The auditions are taped on a little consumer HDV camera somebody has in the department, so company officials may approve the casting.

10-00 Production Staff

10-08 Production Assistants

It would be helpful to have a Unit Production Manager or Associate Producer for a few days to help pull everything together, especially on the talent shoot day when the producer will be busy directing. But the company gets kind of cheap when it comes to staff.

They insist on hiring a PA who knows their operation, and can almost do the work of a UPM for a PA's pay. This person, the Set PA, is hired for 8 days (5 days prep, 2 days shoot, 1 day wrap).

A Script PA is hired for the talent shoot day to be a Script Supervisor. She takes timecode notes, tracks all takes with the script, and watches for continuity. Had it been a more complicated shoot, the Producer would have insisted on a professional Script Supervisor, but he figures he can scrape by with a competent PA.

13-00 Production Design

13-02 Art Director

An Art Director is hired to make both the product shot and the talent shoot look great. The location for both is a gymnasium at a local private school, chosen because it has one wall of gracefully arched windows that will look good in the background.

The Art Director meets with the Director of Photography and the Producer to discuss both shoot days.

The product shot is easier because it's all in close-sup, meaning everything in the background is out of focus. They agree on a plan to place an 8x10 panel of translucent material, a shoji screen of rice paper on a wood lattice, about 30 feet back from the shoe, and light it from behind. A smoke machine gives atmosphere to the scene, and other lights create shafts of light through the smoke and illuminate the shoe.

A second product shot places the shoe on a Greek style pedestal, with drapery in the background.

The talent shoot is tougher because these two guys, one of whom is almost seven feet tall, are having a conversation in this huge, empty gymnasium, and the company doesn't want to light the whole place. In the scene, the scientist interrupts the star's practice by wheeling in a teacher's desk, a student's desk/chair, and a blackboard for an unlikely science lesson.

The set and lighting problem is solved by using several translucent "wild walls" placed at strategic points in the background and lit from behind. The arched windows are lit from outside (since the sun refuses to stay in one place during the shoot). Careful camera placement and lens selection lets the team get the best of the gymnasium setting without having to light the whole room.

It's a good example of how collaboration between Writer, Director, Art Director, and Director of Photography can get a great look for not a whole lot of money.

13-03 Assistant
The Art Director's Assistant helps throughout the prep and shoot, and is assigned the half day wrap (returning rented materials), on his lower rate.

14-00 Set Construction

14-06 Purchases
The wild walls need to be built, plus sundries purchased. The Art Director and Assistant do the labor.

14-07 Rentals
The greens, pedestals, drapery, and classroom furniture are rental items. They would ordinarily go into a Set Dressing budget, but to keep the Art Department's expenses in one category, they are placed here.

15-00 Set Operations

15-01 First Grip and 15-02 Second Grip
Key and Best Boy Grips show up on shoot days to help with lighting setups, dolly setup, and assist the Art Department. The "12" refers to

the number of pay hours. Twelve pay hours is equal to 10 hours actually worked. Lunch is one half-hour, catered, and off the clock.

15-04 Dolly Grip

A dolly is used each shoot day for tracking shots. The Dolly Grip sets up and operates the dolly.

15-05 Craft Service

The Craft Service person preps for a half day, buying groceries, and works for 2 days. The grocery bill is $100 per day.

15-06 Grip Rentals

The Grip Package includes all the C-stands, camera flags, sand bags, and Hi-Roller stands that the Electric Department needs to position and focus lights both inside and outside the building.

The smoke machine also comes out of this budget.

The dolly is a Fisher 10 that is picked up and delivered by the dolly company.

15-07 Grip Expendables

This is the tape, black wrap and other items purchased by the Grip Department for the shoot. Some producers make it a habit to claim what's left over at the end of the shoot for the production company, since it is technically owned by the company. If you've got the storage space, it's a good idea, since the stuff adds up.

16-00 Special Effects

16-05 Special Effects Package

A special prop is needed for the talent shoot. A competitor's shoe (the brand name is masked) is rigged so that a vile green jelly will squish out from the heel when the basketball star squeezes it. A special effects company charges $750 to rig up two shoes that can be refilled for multiple takes.

19-00 Wardrobe

19-01 Stylist

A Costume Designer is replaced by a Stylist for this shoot. She gathers the wardrobe together for the basketball star, and the white lab coat for the scientist.

Most importantly, however, she coordinates with the company about the shoes. The shoe, after all, is the "hero." This is why the product shot is also known as the "hero shot" — glorified with all the lighting, touch-up, and attention given to a hero. The right shoe must be confirmed (left or right), in the right size, in the right colors, with the right laces tied the right way. Various paints and sprays are on hand should the hero need a touch-up of any kind. The pampering is endless, and were it not for the money involved, quite ridiculous. There are company people, ad agency people, plus stylist, grip and lighting people, camera crew, and Director, all hovering over a dumb shoe. But everyone takes it quite seriously. It is, after all, a living.

20-00 Make-Up and Hairdressing

20-01 Key Make-Up Artist

For the talent day, make-up is needed for the basketball star and the scientist.

21-00 Electrical

21-01 Gaffer and 21-02 Best Boy

The Gaffer and Best Boy Electric come on for the two shoot days. The Best Boy is allowed 14 pay hours (12 work hours) on the second day to check inventory on the lighting package and return it to the rental company.

21-06 Equipment Rentals

The Director of Photography (for the product shot), the Director of Photography (for the video shoot of the talent), and the Producer/Director meet days before the shoot at the gymnasium to work out the lighting needs. The Producer gives the list to the lighting equipment company.

On the first day of shooting, the Best Boy checks all the equipment for inventory and breakage, and drives the lighting truck to the location. On the last day, he returns all the gear, again checking inventory and breakage to make sure the production company is not charged for anything undue.

22-00 Camera

22-01 Director/Director of Photography/Operator (Film)

For the product shot, the DP is also the Director and the camera operator. The prep day includes the site survey, a meeting with the company marketing executive about the look of the shoe, and planning for the shoot.

He is in a union, but since he works this job on a non-union basis, he agrees to a 10% invoice fee that will make up a portion of what he would have been paid for health and pension.

22-01 Director of Photography/Operator (Video)

The talent shoot is on HD video. The entire job is not shot on Super 16mm film because of expense. Also, the product shot, in addition to being used in the promotional, will be used in a commercial.

The difference between the film and video look is deliberate, and in fact will be enhanced in post when some of the video is played in black and white. It's a stylistic choice.

22-03 1st Assistant Camera

For the product shot, this person checks out the film camera package on prep day, and on shoot day, loads the magazines, labels the film cans, checks focus, and helps the DP around the camera. There is no 2nd AC on this shoot.

22-07 Camera Package Rental

For the 16mm product shot, an Arri 16SR2 camera is rented. No sound is needed. A set of prime lenses and various camera accessories are also rented.

For the talent shoot, a Panasonic HPX-170 (P2) package that includes a camera, tri-pod, sound mixer, fish pole, and shotgun mike, plus various accessories is rented.

22-12 Teleprompter

For the talent shoot, there are several pages of dialogue that both characters speak to camera. For the dialogue to each other, two monitors are placed just off the set, so each person can look over the other's shoulder and see the words. It looks as though they speak to each other, as long as they maintain eye contact with the monitors. Eventually, they learn the lines anyway, and actually look at each other when they speak. It's better that way.

22-13 Video Assist/Operator

For the product shot, a video tap is attached to the 16mm camera and run to two monitors, one for the Director/DP, and one for the company and agency people. This allows everyone to see a semblance of the shot while it's happening, and hopefully prevents misunderstandings and expensive reshoots.

23-00 Sound

23-01 Mixer

For the talent shoot, a Mixer is on hand for the production audio.

23-06 Radio Mikes

Two radio mikes are rented for the talent.

24-00 Transportation

24-03 Equipment Rental

Two trucks are needed for this shoot — a production van to carry camera equipment and sundries, and a cube truck for the Art Department to carry furniture, lumber, drapery, etc. The lighting/grip truck is included in the package (21-06).

25-00 Location Expenses

25-09 Catering Service

Approximately 25 people per day eat lunch on the set for the two days.

25-17 Location Site Rental

The Producer makes a deal with the private school to rent the gymnasium for the two days, and throw in all the electricity, for a flat fee of $1,000 per day. That includes parking, access to bathrooms, a place for the meals, an office doubling as a dressing and make-up room, and access to a telephone for local calls. The school is not in session, and is inside a gated area, so security is not needed.

27-00 Film and Lab-Production

27-01 Raw Stock (Film-production)

Here, 3,200 feet of 16mm film is brought. About 2,200 feet is shot at normal motion of 24 frames per second. That's about 24 minutes of actual shooting. The other 1,000 feet will be shot at 64 frames per second for a slow-motion effect. That's about 4 minutes worth of shooting.

27-02 Lab-Negative Prep and Processing

The 3,200 feet is cleaned and processed at .115 per foot.

27-03 Memory Cards – Production

No tape. This camera shoots to P2 cards. They rent two 32GB cards that hold 32 minutes each when recording to DVCProHD.

27-08 Telecine

The 16mm film for the product shot is transferred to DigiBeta videotape and DVCam for editing and finishing. The process takes about 4 hours at a 5 to 1 ratio, since this is the final look for the hero shoe. The DP supervises the session (as part of his deal) with the Producer and a representative from the company.

30-00 Editorial

30-08 Off-Line Editor

It is critical that the Editor be experienced in cutting comedy, since timing of the cuts is often what provokes the laugh. They find one with her own Avid Media Composer system.

30-09 Off-Line Editing System

The Avid Media Composer nonlinear system comes with the editor for the five days of editing. She uses the DVCam footage from Telecine to digitize the product shot, the P2 files for the actor footage, and her DVCam deck to digitize the stock footage.

In the Off-Line sessions, the Producer and the Editor follow the script, laying in the circled takes and building the show. The Producer records a narration scratch track that will be replaced by the real Narrator in the final Off-Line session. When it's done, it's laid off to DVD for approvals. After a few minor fixes, the Producer sends a copy of the show to the Composer for the score, and proceeds to On-Line.

30-10 On-Line System and Editor

The Producer and Editor move the edit data seamlessly into a facility with Avid Symphony for the finish. The source reels are the DigiBeta product shot reel, the HD files on hard drive, the DVCam stock footage, and the digital audio files with the narration.

For graphics, they create credits, lay in title elements from BetaSP, and create a few transition effects in On-Line.

When finished, they're ready for Audio post.

30-12 Videotape Dubs/Stock/Transfers

A DVCam dub is made from the DigiBeta product shot for Off-Line editing. The Producer logs the takes, marking the appropriate timecode. Similarly, he screens and logs the circled takes from the talent shoot.

The Producer has already selected the stock footage by screening it on DVD window dubs. The stock house transfers it to DVCam, with about 10 seconds on the head and tail of each shot for editing handles.

30-14 Video Masters

A D2 Edited Master is created in On-Line. The D2 Protection Copy of the edited master is textless, just in case someone decides to use portions of the show for something else, or in case they decide to change the text. Without the textless master, the show would have to be rebuilt in On-Line to accommodate changes.

33-00 Music

33-01 Composer

Two guys with a garage studio (albeit a good one) are hired to compose the rock and roll score. They sit with the Producer and spot for music from the off-line cut. Then they compose from the off-line cut to get started, and finally, from the on-line cut to match all the music cues frame accurately. The score is a synthesizer bed with some acoustic work and live voices laid in on top.

34-00 Post-Production Sound

34-01 Sound Editor

The sound editor digitizes the audio into ProTools. He lays out all the separate tracks, placing effects in their proper places, and prepares for the mix. He checks every single cut to make sure the sound across it is quiet.

34-05 Spotting

After the Off-Line cut is complete, the producer sits with a Sound Editor at the audio post facility to spot for sound effects. There are a dozen effects, mainly to accent the stock footage, give authoritative sound design to the hero shot, and hit the comic moments from the talent shoot.

34-05 Narration Record

A voice-over actor is hired to narrate. He's in demand, and although the Producer tries to get him for AFTRA non-broadcast scale of $311, the agent insists on double scale plus a 10% agency fee.

The narration is recorded to BetaSP at the audio post house, after the Off-Line cut is approved except for minor fixes. The narration is then digitized and laid into the Off-Line cut. For On-Line, it becomes a source reel.

34-08 Dialogue Editing

As part of the hours under "sound editing," the Sound Editor assembles, synchronizes, edit, cleans up and smoothes out all the dialogue.

34-16 Mix

Now the levels of production sound, narration, music, and effects are balanced.

34-17 Layback

The fully mixed audio is now laid back onto the D2 Edited Master. Channels 1 and 2 have a full stereo mix of music, effects, dialogue, narration, the works. Music is also recorded onto Channel 3, and effects onto Channel 4. This way, if an executive decides later on to change the narrator's copy, and he probably will, it will only cost an arm to go in and remix. Without the separate M&E (music and effects), everything is married, and the producer would have to return to the Pre-Lay stage to rebuild the tracks.

35-00 Titles and Graphics

35-01 Graphic Designer and Workstation

There are only a few graphics in the piece, mostly text points that reiterate the narrator's main points about the shoes. Even so, they must be designed with panache, and created as separate elements to be rolled into the On-Line session. In an expensive session, the graphics would be recorded to Dl, a component tape format ideal for high resolution and true colors. But cost is a factor here, so the text graphics are recorded to DigiBeta, which will do.

36-00 Stock Footage

36-01 Film/Tape Clips Licensing

The Producer selects a total of 60 seconds of footage from old silent films to use as comedic punctuation. For non-broadcast use, the license fee is negotiated at $45 per second.

37-00 Insurance

Everything is covered under the shoe company's blanket production insurance policy. One less thing to worry about.

38-00 General and Administrative Expenses

These are part of the company's standard operating expenses.

MUSIC VIDEO BUDGET

Instructions on Downloading Budgets:

- ▶ Go to *www.mwp.com*
- ▶ Click on "Virtual Film School"
- ▶ Scroll down on menu to "Resources"
- ▶ Download Excel Spreadsheets
- ▶ Save to your desktop

MUSIC VIDEO BUDGET

MUSIC VIDEO BUDGET

Fringe assumptions:		**MUSIC VIDEO**	
Payroll Tax	23%	Shoot Days:	2
WGA	13%	Location:	Local
DGA	13%	Unions:	None
SAG	14%	Production:	35mm film
AFTRA	12%	Off-Line:	Non linear
Agency Fees	20%	Finish:	Non linear

SUMMARY BUDGET

02-00 Script	0	
03-00 Producers Unit	10,455	
04-00 Direction	27,748	
05-00 Cast	3,136	
TOTAL ABOVE-THE-LINE		41,339
10-00 Production Staff	5,453	
11-00 Extra Talent	2,800	
15-00 Set Operations	9,259	
18-00 Property	1,799	
19-00 Wardrobe	3,430	
20-00 Make-Up and Hairdressing	3,106	
21-00 Electrical	6,141	
22-00 Camera	8,646	
23-00 Sound	2,076	
24-00 Transportation	2,225	
25-00 Location Expenses	10,800	
27-00 Film & Lab	12,214	
TOTAL PRODUCTION		78,184
30-00 Editorial	29,225	
TOTAL POST-PRODUCTION		29,225
37-00 Insurance	3,450	
38-00 General & Administrative	27,207	
TOTAL OTHER		30,657
Total Above-the-Line		
Total Below-the-Line		41,339
Total Above and Below-the-Line		179,404
Contingency @ 0 %		0
GRAND TOTAL		$179,404

ABOVE-THE-LINE							

	Amount	Units	x	Rate	Sub-Total	Total
02-00 Script						
02-01 Writer's Salaries					0	
			Total for 02-00			0
03-00 Producers Unit						
03-02 Producer						
Prep/Post	1	Allow	1	7,500	7,500	7,500
Shoot: 1 Day	1	Allow	1	1,000	1,000	1,000
Payroll	1	Allow	1	8,500	1,955	1,955
			Total for 03-00			10,455
04-00 Direction						
04-01 Director						
Prep/Post	1	Allow	1	15,000	15,000	15,000
Shoot: 1 Day	1	Allow	1	4,500	4,500	4,500
Payroll	1	Allow	1	19,500	4,485	4,485
DGA	1	Allow	1	2,438		2,438
04-10 Storyboards	1	Allow	1	1,125		1,125
04-11 Scout Expenses	1	Allow	1	200		200
			Total for 04-00			27,748
05-00 Cast						
05-01 Band members					0	0
05-02 Principals	2	Days	1	500	1,000	
	1	Days	1	250	250	
	1	Days	1	250	250	
	1	Day	2	250	500	2,000
Payroll	1	Allow	1	460		460
Agency fees	1	Allow	1	400		400
SAG	1	Allow	1	276		276
			Total for 05-00			3,136

BELOW-THE-LINE							

	Amount	Units	x	Rate	Sub-Total	Total
10-00 Production Staff						
10-01 Unit Production Manager						
Prep:	5	Days	1	250	1,250	
Shoot:	1	Day	1	250	250	
Wrap:	2	Day	1	250	500	
Payroll	1	Allow	1	460	460	1,710
10-02 Assistant Director						
Prep:	1	Day	1	500	500	
Shoot:	1	Day	1	500	500	
Wrap:	1	Day	1	500	500	
Payroll	1	Allow	1	345	345	
DGA	1	Allow	1	188	188	2,033
10-08 Production Assistants						

Prep: PA#1	5 Days	1	125	625		
Prep: PA#2	2 Days	1	125	250		
Shoot:	1 Day	2	125	250		
Wrap:	2 Days	2	125	500		
Payroll	1 Allow	1	374	86	1,711	
	Total for 10-00					5,453
11-00 - Extra Talent						
11-02 Extras	40 Extras	1	50	2,000	2,000	
Payroll	1 Allow	1	2,000	400	400	
Agency fee	1 Allow	1	400		400	
	Total for 11-00					2,800
13-00 - Production Design						
13-02 Art Director						
Prep	2 Days	1	300	600	600	
Shoot	2 Days	1	300	600	600	
13-03 Asst Art Director						
Prep	2 Days	1	300	600	600	
Shoot	2 Days	1	200	400	400	
13-04 Stylist Prep	3 Days	1	400	1,200	1,200	
Shoot	2 Days	1	400	800	800	
13-10 Purchases/Rentals	1 Allow	1	4,000	4,000	4,000	
13-11 Polaroid film	1 Allow	1	150	150	150	
Payroll	1 Allow	1	1,886	0	1,886	10,236
15-00 Set Operations						
15-01 First Grip						
Prep	1 Day	1	500	500	500	
Shoot	2 Days	1	500	1,000	1,000	
15-02 Best Boy Grip	2 Days	1	475	950	950	
15-20 Fire Fighter	1 Day	1	500	500	500	
15-21 Police	2 Days	1	500	1,000	1,000	
15-06 Grip Rentals	1 Day	1	1,600	1,600	1,600	
Dolly	2 Days	1	300	600	600	
Crane	1 Day	1	1,100	1,100	1,100	
Cartage				0	0	
15-07 Grip Expendables	1 Allow	1	500	500	500	
15-10 Production Supplies	1 Allow	2	150	300	300	
15-11 Craft Service	2 Days	1	150	300	300	
Payroll	1 Allow	1	3,950	909	909	
	Total for 15-00					9,259
18-00 Property						
18-01 Prop Master						
Prep/Wrap	2 Days	1	200	400	400	
Shoot	3 Days	1	300	900	900	
18-03 Purchases (+13-10)	1 Allow	1	200	200	200	
Payroll	1 Allow	1	1,300	299	299	
	Total for 18-00					1,799
19-00 Wardrobe						
19-02 Costumer						
Prep/Wrap	2 Days	1	200	400	400	
Shoot	2 Days	1	300	600	600	
19-05 Purchases/Rentals	1 Allow	1	2,000	2,000	2,000	
19-08 Fitting Fees	1 Allow	1	200	200	200	

Payroll		1	Allow	1	1,000	230	230	
				Total for 19-00				3,430

20-00 Make-Up and Hairdressing

20-01 Key Make-Up Artist		2	Days	1	550	1,100	1,100	
20-01 Key Hair Artist		2.5	Days	1	550	1,375	1,375	
20-07 Box Rentals		2	Days	2	25	100	50	
Payroll		1	Allow	1	2,525	581	581	
				Total for 20-00				3,106

21-00 Electrical
21-01 Gaffer

Prep		1	Day	1	500	500	500	
Shoot		2	Days	1	500	900	900	
21-02 Best Boy		2	Days	1	475	950	950	
21-05 Purchases (Expendables)		1	Allow	1	200	200	200	
21-06 Equipment Rentals		1	Allow	1	2,200	2,200	2,200	
21-08 Generator		1	Allow	1	650	650	650	
Driver						0	0	
Fuel		1	Allow	1	50	50	50	
21-09 Loss & Damage		1	Allow	1	150	150	150	
Payroll		1	Allow	1	2,350	541	541	
				Total for 21-00				6,141

22-00 Camera
22-01 Director of Photography

Prep		1	Day	1	1,000	1,000	1,000	
Shoot		2	Days	1	1,000	2,000	2,000	
22-03 1st Ass't Camera								
Prep		1	Day	1	500	500	500	
Shoot		2	Days	1	500	1,000	1,000	
22-04 VTR Op.		2	Days	1	350	700	700	
22-06 Expendables		1	Allow	1	250	250	250	
22-07 Camera Pckg Rental		1	Day	1	1,550	1,550	1,550	
VTR rental		1	Allow	1	300	300	300	
22-17 Maintenance/Loss & Damage		1	Allow	1	150	150	150	
Payroll		1	Allow	1	5,200	1,196	1,196	
				Total for 22-00				8,646

23-00 Sound

23-01 Playback Operator		2	Days	1	350	700	700	
23-03 Expendables (Batteries, etc)		1	Allow	1	100	100	100	
23-04 Sound Pckge (TC DAT)		2	Days	1	200	400	400	
23-05 Walkie Talkies		30	Units	2	9	540	540	
23-09 Sound Stock (+DigiBeta)		1	Allow	1	75	75	75	
23-10 Misc./Loss & Damage		1	Allow	1	100	100	100	
Payroll		1	Allow	1	700	161	161	
				Total for 23-00				2,076

24-00 Transportation
24-03 Equipment Rental

Production Van		3	Days	1	100	300	300	
Dressing rooms		2	Days	1	350	700	700	
Cube truck		3	Days	1	125	375	375	
24-04 Parking/Tolls/Gas		1	Allow	1	850	850	850	
				Total for 24-00				2,225

25-00 Location Expenses							
25-07 Permits	1	Allow	1	1,150	1,150	1,150	
25-08 Parking	1	Allow	1	100	100	100	
25-09 Catering Service							
Breakfasts	25	Meals	2	6	300	300	
Lunches	25	Meals	2	14	700	700	
2nd Meals (working)	30	Meals	1	10	300	300	
25-17 Location Site Rental	1	Allow	1	8,250	8,250	8,250	
				Total for 25-00			10,800
27-00 Film & Lab - Production							
27-01 Raw Stock (Film-Production)	10,000	Feet	1	$0.38	3,800	3,800	
Sales Tax	1	Allow	1	314	314	314	
27-02 Lab-Negative Prep & Proc.	10000	Feet	1	$0.12	1,200	1,200	
27-08 Telecine (35mm to DigiBeta)	10	Hours	1	500	5,000	5,000	
Tape to tape w/color correct	3	Hours	1	500	1,500	1,500	
Telecine stock	1	Allow	1	300	300	300	
Telecine misc	1	Allow	1	100	100	100	
				Total for 27-00			12,214
30-00 Editorial							
30-25 CGI Visual Effects	1	Allow	1	20,000	20,000	20,000	
30-08 Off-Line Editor	9	Days	1	500	4,500	4,500	
30-09 Off-Line Editing System	9	Days	1	200	1,800	1,800	
30-10 On-Line System & Editor	8	Hours	1	350	2,800	2,800	
30-12 Dubs/Stock & Transfers	1	Allow	1	100	100	100	
30-14 Safety Master	1	DigiBeta	1	25	25	25	
				Total for 30-00			29,225
37-00 Insurance							
37-01 Producers Entertainment Pkg	1	Allow	1	1,750	1,750	1,750	
Negative					0	0	
Faulty Stock					0	0	
Equipment					0	0	
Props/Sets					0	0	
Extra Expense					0	0	
3rd Party Property Damage					0	0	
Office Contents					0	0	
37-02 General Liability	1	Allow	1	1,700	1,700	1,700	
37-05 Workers Compensation (payroll svce)					0	0	
				Total for 37-00			3,450
38-00 General & Administrative Expenses							
38-05 Telephone/Fax	1	Allow	1	150	150	150	
38-06 Copying	1	Allow	1	25	25	25	
38-07 Postage & Freight	1	Allow	1	300	300	300	
38-08 Office Space Rental	1	Allow	1	0	0	0	
38-14 Messenger/Overnight	1	Allow	1	100	100	100	
38-21 Production Fee (16%)	1	Allow	1	166,451	26,632	26,632	
							27,207
Contingency @ 0%						0	0
GRAND TOTAL							$179,404

			GRAND TOTAL						$179,404

Total Above-the-Line						41,339
Total Below-the-Line						138,066
Total Above and Below-the-Line						179,404
				Check budget totals	*179,404*	*179,404*

MUSIC VIDEO BUDGET

Styles

Music videos have evolved from taking a song at its word and doing a strict performance piece to out and out surrealism. Maybe it's that "anything goes" spirit that makes many of them fun to watch. And because many are done on a budget, ingenuity is needed to get the effects. One could say that there are two key genres of videos today, "commercial" and "experimental." The "commercial" video is all about fashion and the material world, and is most popular with rap, hip-hop, and pop artists. "Experimental" videos thrive in rock, alternative and niche styles. The lines do blur, however, since some videos feature aspects of both genres.

Today's commercial video is the offspring of the performance-based videos of the '70s and '80s. They are therefore more likely to focus on performance, feature cameos of celebrities, and spend money on splashy high-end digital effects.

Experimental videos established themselves in the late '80s when labels figured out that hungry directors would pour their hearts and souls into music videos for not much money as long as they had creative freedom. Many directors launched feature careers this way and gave birth to some very creative visual effects techniques along the way. The first wave of these directors relied on practical, "in-camera" techniques to establish unique looks while the '90s generation featured directors who relied on digital visual effects. Among the latter group are directors such as David Fincher, Michel Gondry, Mark Romanek, and Francis Lawrence.

Markets

In the U.S., the king of the hill is MTV (Viacom) and its various spin offs, like VH-1, MTV2, VH-1 Pop, VH-1 Rock, etc. There are also a few specialized and independent outlets such as CMT (country music) and BET (Black Entertainment Television) broadcasting mostly country and rap/hip-hop, respectively. The newer channels are growing more successful as MTV and VH-1 continue to produce and air more original programming.

Canada has some independent music video channels, as do many European countries. For example, Canadian media conglomerate Chum Limited is successfully operating Much Music, a full-time music programming station similar to MTV.

Online music video channels are quite successful in terms of site-traffic. Yahoo (Launch), AOL, Apple (QuickTime) and other major online media companies operate "stations" with the potential of raiding televised network audiences as broadband speeds improve and access costs decline. MTV Networks may be anticipating this possibility by increasing their webcast presence.

DVDs are another market. There have been more and more of these released with music videos — compilations, for the most part, but also fillers (on concert DVDs for instance) and, more recently, very specialized releases made for collectors or fans of specific directors. (For example, see Palm Pictures' Director's Label — *www.directorslabel.com*).

Finally, just to engage in a bit of crystal ball forecasting, the impact of TIVO is worth considering. The commercial-skipping service may inspire advertising agencies to decrease broadcast advertising buys in favor of other media, including music videos — be it through co-branded online content or product placements in videos.

Average Budgets

Budgets commissioned by major labels can range anywhere from $20,000 to $1,200,000. Average budget categories usually break out as follows:

1) Indy label — $15,000 to $50,000
2) Small/alternative label — $20,000 to $100,000
3) Major label Pop/Rock — $100,000 to $250,000
4) Major label rap and hip-hop — $150,000 to $450,000
4) Major label pop visual effects videos — $250,000 to $600,000
5) Major label pop videos for movie soundtracks — $250,000 to $650,000

Attaching a star-director, soundtrack deal or significant digital visual effects work can generally increase a given music video budget by between $40,000 to $500,000. Country music videos are a budget anomaly, since they often fluctuate between low and high numbers for the same type of production.

Guerrilla production tactics are common for non-commissioned or spec projects (waiving insurance, nabbing locations without fees, permits, or clearances). Risky business. And record labels often want personal and location releases so they won't get sued.

Who Pays?

Record labels and artists share the cost of producing videos, which are primarily viewed as a commercial for the artist's single. Since the medium is intended for advertising and artists are profit-participants in album sales, the band is considered an investor rather than billed talent as in a commercial or feature.

In terms of production payments, the record label issues checks to the production company, which is essentially a directorial agency that also contracts and manages all production. Unlike commercials, the production company is responsible for all work through delivery, including post.

The Bidding Process

In commercials the producer gets a storyboard from an ad agency that represents the concept of the ad. You consult with your Director, do a budget (on the AICP form), and submit it as your bid. If you get the job, you get a fixed fee, and you are expected to come in on budget, unless they change concept on you in mid-stream.

In music videos, a record label may come to you and say, "We've got $180,000 in our marketing budget for this video, submit a treatment." You go to your Director and together work out the idea (usually one to five pages and maybe storyboards). Be careful here, since Directors in their zeal may design a concept way out of line with the budget. As the Producer, you need to bring the treatment and the budget into alignment. If you don't, you either go over budget to please the label, or you deliver a product that disappoints everyone. It's wiser to promise a smaller, more focused vision, and deliver a product that exceeds expectations. Have frank discussions with the record label, and the Director, to see eye-to-eye on concept and budget.

A *production fee* is usually entered in the budget as your company's profit. This can be as low as 10% and as high as 30% of the bottom line, but averages 15% to 20%. Since the label gives you a fixed fee, and most do not audit, you might be able to pad the budget a bit. What you don't spend is additional profit. Labels usually pay 50% up front, 25% upon completion of shooting, and 25% on delivery.

Do Record Company Execs Visit the Shoot/Editing?

Label executives, often called "video commissioners," always attend photography and keep an eye on the job through delivery. In some cases, labels have been known to hire freelance commissioners who formerly were label marketing executives. Artist management representatives frequently visit productions and are part of the approval process. The timeless entertainment industry battle between investing executives and creative directors often ensues in music videos; directors can get wrapped up in technical aspects of a shoot while label executives voice concerns about having enough "beauty," performance and artist "face time."

Negotiating with Crews

There is a shifting rate for crew in music videos, meaning the same Gaffer, for example, might get $450 for 10 hours worked in a commercial, but expect $450 for 12 hours worked in a music video. Typical are 14 to 16-hour days. Tensions between unions and the Music Video Production Association are running high at the moment because producers argue the budgets can't support them and ultimately, further increases may result in less work opportunities for crew. On the other hand, Unions claim the video industry is legitimate and far into maturity — so it's time to establish a deal. At the time of this writing, the situation is unresolved.

What Formats?

35mm film is the preferred format. HD videography is increasing in popularity, however, the cost of posting in the format is a current barrier. 16mm film may be a decent alternative for indie label productions that aren't employing a great deal of visual effects.

As with any guerilla-style production, there are stories of people using DV and even toy cameras to capture performances. However, these jobs aren't commissioned by major labels. Music is a big business; labels want the high end.

Music Playback

Most music videos do not record much, if any, dialogue or other production sound. On the contrary, they require music played back as the camera rolls, so musicians can lip-sync, and dancers can move to the right beat. Considering music videos are essentially based on the song, producing professionally prepared audio playback packages are vital to capturing good performances, yet often overlooked by new producers.

To make sure the music always plays back at the same speed, take after take, most producers use a timecode DAT player and Smartslate. The music is then synced in telecine and forever locked to picture through the edit process.

Shooting sync-sound for music videos can be a confusing process for new producers because the DAT playing back during photography typically rolls at 24 frames per second (or multiple thereof) while the audio-sync master DAT in telecine is often a 30 frame-per-second element playing back at 29.97 frames per second while the film is being recorded. This setup is used so the filmed sync performance is accurately preserved as the telecine process converts timecodes and image frames during video mastering.

Providing a solid understanding of the technical aspects behind sync sound for music videos is beyond the scope of this book. However, every music video producer on a major-label shoot should know that 1) they must at least purchase both a 24fps and 30fps DAT package for sync sound, in addition to an NTSC DigitalBetaCam recording of the track; 2) the DATs and Digital BetaCam are all recorded at the regular song playback speed from the same master; and 3) they must rent a Smartslate that converts the 24fps playback timecode for photographic display at 30fps.

Accidentally shooting with the wrong DAT doesn't create an irreversible problem but may lead to increased post costs and other frustrations. Don't hesitate to consult a local telecine engineer who's familiar with music videos before you embark on your first job.

Audio Post

The only time a producer would go to an audio post house is when there is other production sound, such as dialogue or effects, that needs extensive mixing. Most times, the music is the sole audio, and it has already been recorded to the Digital BetaCam Edited Master from the fully mixed CD provided by the record label.

Telecine

The film to tape transfer is a vital element in music videos, since it is often here that texture and color are changed, sometimes to a radical degree. A 2:1 or 3:1 ratio (3 hours of transfer time for every 1 hour of film being transferred) is considered standard. Allow more if highly opinionated record company executives are present.

Another cost increase associated with music video telecine may arise on jobs requiring digital visual effects. Many effects studios demand "simo flat passes" of the entire film transfer. The simo flat is a duplicate Digital BetaCam that is simultaneously recorded with the final color master, but has bypassed the color correction and noise reduction processes. This practically unaffected master source material is a significant aid in visual effects production since stylized color corrections can remove color information from the footage that's essential for producing good composites.

Note that in music videos, one long telecine session is booked to transfer all of the photographed footage to Digital BetaCam with both final color and sync sound. More editors are starting to use the Digital BetaCam masters for their off-line editorial process, however many make dubs on DVCam as standard procedure.

Editing

Usually, producers go right into Off-Line nonlinear editing. They present a rough cut for approval from the artist and the label. If there are important On-Line effects involved, the producer may include some of them, roughly done, in the approval cut.

Securing a talented music video editor and off-line studio (usually as a package, many editors work at home) for major label videos runs between $4,500 and $8,000 for 1.5 full weeks of work; 2 days of digitizing and logging, 4 days of editorial and 4 days of revisions. Even if the full schedule for revisions isn't used, the editorial budget is usually billed on a "flat bid." The term means no portion of the budget is refundable.

Producers warn that Post (including telecine) is every bit as important as shooting, and should be budgeted as amply as possible. If the artist and/or label demands changes that are not part of the original concept, then the producer may want to renegotiate the terms. Furthermore, the off-line edit serves as a proof for visual effects producers to judge whether or not the work-scope grew beyond the client's budget by amount of effects runtime, number of shots, type of shots, etc. In this consideration, it's the video producer's job to ensure the edit stays on track with what's budgeted for the rest of post — and thus a good idea to review the cut with post crew before sending it out for label approvals.

On-line editorial for music videos is nearly always performed on the Flame/Fire (Discrete Logic) and sometimes the Henry (Quantel) systems. Linear online systems are typically not used for music videos because they cannot accommodate the last-minute cleanup or digital fixes these jobs often require.

Talented online artists are usually visual effects compositors who typically charge between $250/hour and $400/hour for their services, although some can demand as much as $650/hour if significant digital cosmetic work is required and they have the reputation for doing it. If the project involves digital visual effects commanding more than two days of work, then producers always negotiate a flat fee for the job (based upon a detailed work spec) that includes the online edit.

Sample Budget
The sample budget is in the $200,000 range.

02-00 Script

02-01 Writer's Salary
The treatment, which is what the script is called in music video land, has either been written by the Director or a writer who always remains anonymous. Many in the biz suspect a production company's executive producer and/or director's favorite line producer often helps or even fully drafts treatments based on a director's concept and visual references.

Music video producers never budget a line-item for the writer. Production companies consider treatment development a form of marketing their ideas rather than a work-for-hire service. The payoff comes from fees and markups.

03-00 Producers Unit

03-02 Producer

Prior to the prep week, the Producer works with the Director to make sure the treatment can be shot for the money they guess the record company will pony up. He therefore starts budgeting the concept in its earliest phases. Once the treatment is approved, a budget is submitted. After the requisite amount of haggling, it is approved, and production is given a green light.

The Producer gets a flat 5% of the bottom line, which can end up as even better pay than those working in commercials. The music video producer of your average $250K video will take home $12.5K in exchange for about 3 solid weeks of actual work days. The catch is: 1) the days aren't sequential so the producer must be relatively available to work on a moment's notice while the video is in post for 2-4 weeks; 2) the producer typically works for free during the 1.5 week budgeting phase before the project is green lighted; and 3) the production company may ask you to give up a portion of your fees if the video goes seriously over budget. Although a producer may have the legal right to not concede his or her fees after going over budget, reliable music video jobs run through a tiny niche of production companies owned by a close knit group of veterans. Get it?

The Producer sees the project through from prep to post and delivery.

04-00 Direction

04-01 Director

The Director's flat fee is based on 10% of the bottom line (below-the-line costs before production fees are added), which is the standard fee, but this can vary based on a director's popularity. A high profile director will likely earn a lot more.

He is responsible for the creative vision of the video, from concept to shooting to post. In this concept, the five-member band, road weary from many miles of driving in a convertible, pull into a weather-beaten trailer park/motel for the night, only to discover that its denizens aren't exactly normal. There are plenty of animated effects to spice up the action.

05-00 Cast

05-01 Band Members

The band members are the unpaid stars of the music video. Plus there are four Principals on for one day of shooting and another Principal on for the second day of shooting. By the way, talent agency fees for commercials and music videos are in the 15–20% range, unlike TV and movie actor agents, who still get 10%.

10-00 Production Unit

10-01 Unit Production Manager

The UPM preps for five days, assisting the Producer in getting the location secured, the paperwork completed, the permit paid up on time, booking crew, organizing the casting session for the Principals and Extras, and booking equipment. During the two-day wrap, he checks all the time cards for the payroll service and completes any other paperwork. He also supervises the Production Assistants during the wrap day as they return equipment.

10-08 Production Assistants

Two ace PAs are hired for prep, shoot, and one day of wrap to help the UPM, Production Coordinator, and the Producer.

11-00 Extra Talent

11-02 Extras

The Extras are 40 actors hired on a non-union basis through an agency. They are selected for their ability to move to a beat, and their overall look. They are paid a flat $50 for a half day's work, and the UPM manages to get them out before lunch. $50 for a half day is low but legal, and it's not essential to feed them, but there needs to be enough money for them to want to show up in the first place and not flake out.

15-00 Set Operations

15-01 First (Key) Grip, 15-02 Best Boy Grip

The Key and Best Boy Grips, plus the Gaffer and Best Boy Electric, make up the four-person Grip/Electric crew. The Producer judged that this number would suffice for the two interior locations (a motel office scene and two trailer interiors), and an exterior party scene at the trailer park. There is a dolly and track to set up, plus a crane, and a decent lighting package.

Here's the breakdown for a 12-hour day:
Key Grip and Gaffer – $500
Best Boy Electric and Best Boy Grip – $475

15-06 Grip Rentals

The Fisher 10 dolly and track is picked up by a PA in the cube truck on the Friday afternoon before the first day of shooting, thus getting a two for one bonus by shooting on a weekend. The crane is delivered.

18-00 Property

18-03 Purchases

Various props are needed, including a statue of a Buddha, a small trampoline, a Ouija board, and an assortment of large paper hoops that party guests crash through in slow motion. Don't ask. The Prop Master has authority to raid the Production Design budget at 13-10.

19-00 Wardrobe

19-02 Costumer

The Costumer first works with the Director and the Art Director to select modern dress wardrobe and a color palette for the Band and Principals. Then she preps the wardrobe for the Principals and Band members, and sees to the fittings. She also works with the Extras agency to ensure that all Extras arrive with suitable modern dress wardrobe.

19-05 Purchases

There is $2,000 allowance for clothes rentals. Since the four band members are the stars and must look the best, $1,400 of that, or $350 each, goes to them, with $150 going for each of the four other principals.

20-00 Make-Up and Hairdressing

20-01 Key Make-Up Artist

Make-up and Hair are hired for the two days at $550/day for 12 hours worked. The Hair person has a half-day prep for a wig gag for one of the Band members.

21-00 Electrical

21-01 Gaffer and 21-02 Best Boy

See discussion of crew in this budget at 15-01.

21-06 Equipment Rentals

The lighting package consists of, among other things, a complement of tungsten lights, an open faced 750-watt "redhead," a 2,000-watt "blonde," several HMI 1200s, two HMI "lightning strikes" for a lightning effect, a 2K Short Throw Xenon Supertrouper follow spot, and a fog machine. It's a weekend deal, so they get two days for one.

21-08 Generator

The trailer park lacks sufficient power for all the lights, so a 350-amp generator is rented. The company tows it to the location Friday afternoon, and picks it up Monday morning.

22-00 Camera

22-01 Director of Photography

The Director of Photography preps for one day to scout the location and confer with the Director about the storyboards, film stock, camera set-ups, lenses, and overall look. He also operates the camera.

22-03 1st Assistant Camera

The 1st AC preps the camera on the Friday morning before the shoot, making sure it's working properly, and that all the lenses and accessories ordered by the Director of Photography are in the package. On the shoot, he assists the DP with the camera functions. He makes sure there is always a loaded magazine at the ready, changes the film, and labels all the reels.

22-07 Camera Package Rental

An Arriflex 435, with three 400' Mags, a prime lens and a zoom, plus sticks and standard accessories are in the package. It is on the weekend rate of two days for one.

23-00 Sound

23-01 Playback

The person who operates the timecode DAT in a music video is the playback person responsible for accurate playback of the music on every take.

23-04 Sound Package

A timecode DAT is rented on a weekend rate. See the discussion above under Music Playback about frame rates.

23-05 Walkie-Talkies

The extras get wardrobe and make-up in a trailer about 300 yards from the set, and the lighting truck has to park about 75 yards away, so the thirty walkies help the crew stay in contact during the shoot, and save a lot of wasted running back and forth.

23-09 Sound Stock

No recording is done during the shoot, but this line item reflects the purchase of both a 24fps and 30fps DAT package for sync sound, in addition to an NTSC Digital BetaCam recording of the music track. Again, see the discussion of this under Music Playback, above.

24-00 Transportation

24-03 Equipment Rental

A cube truck and production van are rented for a day of prep (picking up the camera, dolly, wardrobe, etc.), for the two shoot days, and the wrap day to return everything. A dressing trailer is rented for the cast for the shoot days.

25-00 Location Expenses

25-07 Permits

A city permit makes sure everything is legal and the Producer won't get hassled by an eager cop wondering what all the noise is about.

This brings out another point about shooting on location. The producer has already received permission from the residents of the trailer park, and even the residents of a nearby house, to make sure no one will be disturbed by the music and the activity of the shoot. Nasty neighbors can shut you down, so it's good to douse any fires before they start.

25-09 Catering Service

The producer has contracted with a catering service to prepare food and drop it off at the set, thus saving a bit of money by not having to pay servers and setup charges. The second meal is pizza and soda.

25-17 Location Site Rental

The producer negotiates with the trailer park association and settles on this fee. It's steep, but the hours will be long, there will be inconvenience to the residents, and this particular park has several elements that the Director wants to feature, like the neon drive-through portal arch that reads, "Lazy Moon Trailer Park."

27-00 Film and Lab - Production

27-01 Raw Stock

Twenty five 400-foot loads of 35mm film (10,000 feet).

27-02 Lab Negative Prep and Processing

The lab processes the negative and preps it for telecine.

27-08 Telecine

It takes about 10 hours to transfer all the film to DigiBeta in a scene to scene (color correction) session on a Spirit system. Then, after the On-Line session, there is a final Telecine session of about three hours that is tape-to-tape (DigiBeta to DigiBeta). What's this about? In On-Line, that's when the CGI effects are composited into the live action, but all those CGI effects were created by different artists with different eyes, so they all have slightly different color palettes. The final Telecine, done by a colorist with an expert eye, smoothes all that out and finishes the Edited Master. It is literally the last step in the whole process.

30-00 Editorial

30-08 Off-Line Editor

The Producer, Director, and Editor go right into Off-Line. The footage is digitized directly from the DigiBeta because they have a deck. Were that not the case, they might have made a simultaneous transfer to DVCam while they were making the DigiBeta master.

It takes one day to digitize and log, four days of cutting, and four days of revisions until approval is given by the record label and the band.

30-09 Off-Line Edit System

They edit on an Avid Media Composer, mainly because it makes a good transition to the on-line machine, Discrete Logic's Fire. If you're using another system, be sure to check for any Edit Decision List bugs between the Off and On-Line machines.

30-10 On-Line System/Editor

When the Off-Line picture is approved, the Producer, Director and Post Supervisor move to a facility with a Discrete Logic Fire nonlinear edit system capable of 8 independent layers of keying, 3D effects, 4 channel Digital Video Effects, full color correction, and other special effects software. This is where the CGI visual effects are composited into the Off-Line cut. From here it goes to one final Telecine (see 27-08 Telecine above).

30-12 Videotape Dubs/Stock/Transfers

Miscellaneous transfers that seem to pop up.

30-14 Safety Master

A DigiBeta is made of the Edited Master as a protection.

32-00 Optical Effects/Visual Effects/Digital Intermediates

32-25 CGI visual effects

$20,000 worth of CGI visual effects are composited onto the live action.

37-00 Insurance

37-01 Producer's Entertainment Package and 37-02 General Liability

The producer's insurance broker arranges for a standard entertainment policy and liability for this size production and budget. The fact that it's a local shoot with no crazy stunts keeps the cost down.

Workers' Compensation insurance is provided by the payroll service as part of its fee.

38-00 General and Administrative Expenses

A minimal amount is budgeted for general expenses like telephone and messenger. Just enough is allotted to meet these costs.

38-21 Production Fee

As its profit margin, 16% of the bottom line goes to the production company.

Note: Thanks to Ryan Thompson and Alex Garcia for their help in the writing of this chapter for the 4th edition. Heck, Ryan practically did write the whole chapter. Ryan Thompson produces visual effects for features and commercials as a co-owner of Giant Steps (*www.giantsteps. us*), based in L.A.

Alex Garcia runs *www.mvdbase.com*, with music video artist biographies to director videographies, including an index sorted by video titles, and weekly new release updates.

Many thanks also to David Robertson, who helped update the 5th edition. David is a top-level music video producer out of L.A. See his website at *www.davidrobertsonfilms.com* or contact him at drflims@me.com.

STUDENT FILM BUDGET

Instructions on Downloading Budgets:

- ▶ Go to *www.mwp.com*
- ▶ Click on "Virtual Film School"
- ▶ Scroll down on menu to "Resources"
- ▶ Download Excel Spreadsheets
- ▶ Save to your desktop

STUDENT FILM BUDGET

STUDENT FILM

Fringe assumptions:			STUDENT FILM	
Payroll Tax	0%		Shoot Days:	4
WGA	0%		Location:	Local
DGA	0%		Unions:	None
SAG	0%		Production:	Super16mm telecine to D'
AFTRA	0%		Off/On-Line:	Nonlinear
Agency Fees	0%		Finish:	DigiBeta

SUMMARY BUDGET

02-00 Script		0	
03-00 Producers Unit		0	
04-00 Direction		0	
05-00 Cast		0	
	TOTAL ABOVE-THE-LINE		0
10-00 Production Staff		0	
13-00 Production Design		25	
15-00 Set Operations		50	
17-00 Set Dressing		50	
18-00 Property		100	
19-00 Wardrobe		25	
20-00 Make-Up and Hairdressing		25	
21-00 Electrical		400	
22-00 Camera		25	
23-00 Sound		25	
24-00 Transportation		0	
25-00 Location Expenses		0	
26-00 Picture Vehicle/Animals		0	
27-00 Film & Lab		10,925	
	TOTAL PRODUCTION		11,650
30-00 Editorial		206	
33-00 Music		50	
34-00 Post-Production Sound		75	
35-00 Titles & Graphics		25	
	TOTAL POST-PRODUCTION		356
37-00 Insurance		0	
38-00 General & Administrative		0	
	TOTAL OTHER		0
Total Above-the-Line			0
Total Below-the-Line			12,006
Total Above and Below-the-Line			12,006
Contingency @ 10 %			0
	GRAND TOTAL		$12,006

```
ABOVE-THE-LINE
```

	Amount	Units	x	Rate	Sub-Total	Total
02-00 Script						
02-01 Writers' Salaries	6	Weeks	1		0	
Total for 02-00						0
03-00 Producers Unit						
03-01 Executive Producer					0	0
03-02 Producer					0	0
Prep	4	Weeks	1		0	
Shoot	4	Days	1		0	
Post	4	Weeks	1		0	
03-03 Associate Producer	9	Weeks	1		0	0
Total for 03-00						0
04-00 Direction						
04-01 Director						
Prep	2	Weeks	1		0	0
Rehearsals	2	Weeks	1		0	0
Shoot	4	Days	1		0	0
Edit	4	Weeks	1		0	0
Total for 04-00						0
05-00 Cast						
05-01 Lead Actors						
Rehearsals	2	Weeks	4		0	0
Shoot	4	Days	4		0	0
05-02 Supporting Cast						
Rehearsals	1	Week	5		0	0
Shoot	3	Days	1		0	0
05-03 Day Players (Shoot)	2	Days	10		0	0
Total for 05-00						0

STUDENT FILM BUDGET (CONTINUED)

BELOW-THE-LINE						
10-00 Production Staff						
10-01 Unit Production Manager	5	Weeks	1		0	0
10-02 Assistant Director	3	Weeks	1		0	0
10-04 Production Coordinator	5	Weeks	1		0	0
10-05 Script Supervisor	3	Weeks	1		0	0
10-08 Production Assistants	4	Days	2		0	0
				Total for 10-00		0
13-00 Production Design						
13-01 Production Designer					0	0
Prep	4	Weeks	1		0	0
Shoot	4	Days	1		0	0
Wrap	2	Days	1		0	0
13-10 Film	1	Allow	1	25	25	25
				Total for 13-00		25
15-00 Set Operations						
15-01 First Grip						
Prep	1	Day	1		0	0
Shoot	4	Days	1		0	0
Wrap	1	Day	1		0	0
15-02 Second Grip (Best Boy)					0	0
Prep	1	Day	1		0	0
Shoot	4	Days	1		0	0
Wrap	1	Day	1		0	0
15-04 Boom/Dolly Grip	4	Days	1		0	0
15-05 Craft Service					0	0
Purchases	1	Allow	1	0	0	0
15-07 Grip Expendables	1	Allow	1	50	50	50
				Total for 15-00		50
17-00 Set Dressing						
17-01 Set Decorator					0	0
Prep	4	Weeks	1		0	0
Shoot	4	Days	1		0	0
Wrap	2	Days	1		0	0
17-05 Expendables	1	Allow	1	0	0	0
17-07 Rentals	1	Allow	1	50	50	50
				Total for 17-00		50
					0	
18-00 Property					0	
18-01 Property Master					0	0
Prep	1	Week	1		0	0
Shoot	4	Days	1		0	0
Wrap	1	Day	1		0	0
18-03 Purchases	1	Allow	1	50	50	50
18-04 Rentals	1	Allow	1	50	50	50
				Total for 18-00		100

19-00 Wardrobe							
19-01 Costume Designer					0	0	
	Prep	2	Weeks	1	0	0	
	Shoot	4	Days	1	0	0	
	Wrap	2	Days	1	0	0	
19-02 Costumer					0	0	
	Prep	2	Weeks	1	0	0	
	Shoot	4	Days	1	0	0	
	Wrap	2	Days	1	0	0	
19-04 Expendables		1	Allow	1	25	25	25
19-06 Rentals		1	Allow	1	0	0	0
			Total for 19-00				25
20-00 Make-Up and Hairdressing							
20-01 Key Make-Up Artist							
		1	Day	1	0	0	
		4	Days	1	0	0	
20-02 Additional Make-Up Artist					0	0	
		1	Day	1	0	0	
		4	Days	1	0	0	
20-05 Purchases		1	Allow	1	25	25	25
20-08 Film		1	Allow	1	0	0	0
			Total for 20-00				25
21-00 Electrical							
21-01 Gaffer					0	0	
	Prep	3	Days	1	0	0	
	Shoot	4	Days	1	0	0	
	Wrap	1	Day	1	0	0	
21-02 Best Boy					0	0	
	Prep	3	Days	1	0	0	
	Shoot	4	Days	1	0	0	
	Wrap	1	Day	1	0	0	
21-03 Electrics		4	Days	2	0	0	
21-05 Purchases		1	Allow	1	0	0	0
21-06 Equipment Rentals		1	Allow	1	400	400	400
21-09 Loss & Damage		1	Allow	1	0	0	0
			Total for 21-00				400
22-00 Camera							
22-01 Director of Photography							
	Prep	2	Weeks	1	0	0	
	Shoot	4	Days	1	0	0	
	Wrap (Telecine)	3	Days	1	0	0	
22-02 Camera Operator		4	Days	1	0	0	
22-03 1st Ass't Camera							
	Prep	1	Day	1			
	Shoot	4	Days	1			
22-04 2nd Ass't Camera		4	Days	1	0	0	
22-06 Expendables		1	Allow	1	25	25	25
22-07 Camera Package Rentals		4	Days	1	0	0	
			Total for 22-00				25
23-00 Sound							
23-01 Mixer							
	Prep	1	Day	1	0	0	
	Shoot	4	Days	1	0	0	
23-02 Boom Operator		4	Days	1	0	0	

STUDENT FILM BUDGET (CONTINUED)

23-03 Expendables (Batteries, etc)	1	Allow	1	25	25	25	
23-04 Sound Pckge (702T/Mackie/mics)					0	0	
				Total for 23-00			25
24-00 Transportation							
24-03 Equipment Rental							
Production Van					0	0	
24-04 Gas & Oil					0	0	
				Total for 24-00			0
25-00 Location Expenses							
25-07 Permits (Student waiver)							
25-09 Catering Service					0	0	
Crew Meals (brown bags)					0	0	
25-17 Location Site Rental	2	Days	1		0	0	
				Total for 25-00			0
26-00 Picture Vehicles/Animals							
26-03 Picture Cars (4 student cars)	2	Days	4		0	0	
				Total for 26-00			0
27-00 Film & Lab - Production							
27-01 Raw Stock (30% off)	18,400	Feet	1	$0.24	4,416		
Sales Tax	1	Allow	1	364	364	4,780	
27-02 Lab-Negative Prep & Proc.	18,400	Feet	1	$0.08	1,472	1,472	
27-04 Prep/Clean Neg for Telecine	1	Allow	1	315	315	315	
27-08 Telecine (pix/sound to DBeta)							
Best-light	24	Hours	1	140	3,360	3,360	
Audio sync	8.2	Hours	1	90	738	738	
27-09 Telecine Tape Stock							
Dbeta	8	Hours	1	30	240	240	
Sales tax				240	20	20	
				Total for 27-00			10,925
30-00 Editorial							
30-08 Off/On-Line Editor	4	Weeks	1		0	0	
30-09 Off/On-Line Edit System	4	Weeks	1		0	0	
30-12 Videotape Dubs/Stock & Trans	1	Allow	1	50	50	50	
30-13 Screening Copies	10	DVD	1	12	120	120	
30-14 Video Master/Safety (DBeta)	3	Reels	1	12	36	36	
				Total for 30-00			206
33-00 Music							
33-01 Composer	1	Allow	1		0	0	
(All-In Package includes: Composer,					0	0	
Musicians, Instruments, Synth Studio.					0	0	
Stock	1	Allow	1	50	50	50	
				Total for 33-00			50
34-00 Post Production Sound							
34-01 Sound Editor	40	Hours	1		0	0	
34-14 Laydown	1	Hour	1		0	0	
34-16 ADR	4	Hours	1		0	0	
34-18 Foley Stage/Editor	5	Hours	1		0	0	
34-18 Foley Artists	5	Hours	1		0	0	
34-20 Mix	8	Hours	1		0	0	

34-22 Layback	1 Hour	1		0	0
34-24 Stock/Dubs/Transfers (Video)	1 Allow	1	75	75	75
			Total for 34-00		75
35-00 Titles & Graphics					
35-01 Grfx Designer/Workstation	10 Hours	1		0	0
35-02 Stocks and Dubs	1 Allow	1	25	25	25
			Total for 35-00		25
37-00 Insurance					
37-01 Producers Entertainment Package				0	0
Negative				0	0
Faulty Stock				0	0
Equipment				0	0
Props/Sets				0	0
Extra Expense				0	0
3rd Party Property Damage				0	0
Office Contents				0	0
37-02 General Liability				0	0
37-03 Hired Auto				0	0
37-04 Cast Insurance				0	0
37-05 Workers Compensation				0	0
37-06 Errors & Omissions				0	0
			Total for 37-00		0
				0	
38-00 General & Administrative Expenses				0	
38-02 Legal				0	0
38-03 Accounting fees				0	0
38-05 Telephone/Fax				0	0
38-06 Copying				0	0
38-07 Postage & Freight				0	0
38-08 Office Space Rental				0	0
38-09 Ofice Furniture				0	0
38-10 Office Equipment & Supplies				0	0
38-15 Parking				0	0
38-16 Storage (Equip./Supplies/Film/Tape)				0	0
			Total for 38-00		0
Contingency @ 10%					
GRAND TOTAL					$12,006
Total Above-the-Line					0
Total Below-the-Line					12,006
Total Above and Below-the-Line					12,006
			Check budget totals	12,006	12,006

STUDENT FILM BUDGET

Student Film

    Film and TV Departments across the country vary widely in their approaches to student projects. Some students shoot on film and finish on film. Others shoot on digital cameras, have nonlinear editing suites, and use digital post-audio work stations and mixing rooms. In some places, the school pays for 99% of expenses, the exception being food for cast and crew, and any sets, props, wardrobe or special equipment the school lacks. Other schools require students to put up money, sometimes as much as half the budget. Some produce half-hour films. Others go for five or ten minutes. Some crew up entirely from student ranks. Others get volunteer professional help.

    Sometimes it all boils down to money. If you don't have much, design a shorter film. Think in terms of simple sets, costumes, and action, and let your creativity and ingenuity carry it.

    For the students using this book, the process of creating a budget is the same as for anyone else. It's an exercise in pre-visualizing the project, and estimating the needs. The only difference is, students get to put in more zeroes in the money columns. For that reason, students can benefit from reading other sample budgets in this chapter that may resemble their projects.

    In this sample Student Film budget, we have assumed the following: this is a ten-minute dramatic story, shot on Super 16mm film, put through a Telecine to DVCam, edited on Final Cut Pro, and finished on DigiBeta. (For students wishing to read about an all-digital project shot on HD memory cards, please check out the "No Budget" Feature.) All the cast and crew are students, and at this hypothetical school, they follow the ants-on-a-cookie technique of ganging up on a project until the shooting is done. That way, many people get a taste of a variety of jobs.

02-00 Script

02-01 Writer

The 10-minute script tells a contemporary story of romantic intrigue. The time is the present, and the writer has been careful about writing scenes impossible to shoot, since she is also the Director. This means settings in a nearby house, a pet store where she knows the owner, a local lake, etc. She has deliberately made it easy to shoot.

03-00 Producer's Unit

03-01 Executive Producer

This is a faculty advisor overseeing the project.

03-02 Producer

Since there isn't any pitching to studios involved here, this job is mainly that of a Line Producer — someone who administrates the details of production, and makes sure the paperwork gets handled.

The entire project is completed inside one 16-week semester. The pre-production period is about four weeks. The shooting is in four days on two weekends. The post-production takes up another four weeks.

04-00 Direction

04-01 Director

If this is any one person's project, it's the Director's. She is creating the vision, the look, and feel of the film. She puts in as much time in pre-production as the Producer, but leaves him to final prep while she rehearses the actors for the final two weeks before shooting. On a previous project, she only rehearsed the actors for three days, and it showed. This time, she won't repeat the mistake. She took a class on working with actors, read some books, and her rehearsal schedule allows for 16 hours over two weeks.

05-00 Cast

05-01 Lead Actors

Two young men and one young woman from the Theater Department are cast in lead roles. The other young woman's role is filled from an ad placed in the local professional casting weekly. The actress agrees to perform for free, plus a DVD copy of the finished film. This time, the Director did not rush through casting. She and the Producer auditioned several actors for each role, studied the videotapes she made, and asked for call-backs before choosing. None of her friends ended up in the movie. To her surprise, it made things easier.

05-02 Supporting Cast

Two young men and two young women fill supporting roles, and to the Director's delight, a retired professional film actor agrees to play the role of an older man just for the fun of it. Their rehearsals occur during the same two-week period as the leads.

05-03 Day Players

Ten friends of the crew are recruited on the two shoot weekends to perform in bit parts and as atmosphere.

10-00 Production Staff

10-01 Unit Production Manager

For the four weeks of pre-production, and the four days of shooting, a student acts as the UPM, helping the Producer scout locations, get permissions from property owners, recruit crew members, reserve equipment, and do the budget.

10-02 Assistant Director

A student in the directing class comes on as the 1st AD, helping the Director during rehearsals to block scenes, and plan shooting schedules.

10-04 Production Coordinator

Many hands make light work, so this student comes on to help the UPM and the Producer handle pre-production.

10-05 Script Supervisor

This student sits in during rehearsals, because she's also in the directing class and wants to watch. On set, she takes script notes, marks circled takes, and watches for continuity.

10-08 Production Assistants

Two good friends of the Director agree to schlep and go-for during the shoot days.

13-00 Production Design

13-01 Production Designer

There are no sets to build, but this student wants to experiment with as many colors and textures in the existing locations as possible, to create different moods that further the story. He therefore spends about four weeks in pre-production scouting locations and rustling up set dressing and props. He consults with the Director, the DP, and the Costume Designer, so everyone is working with the same color/texture palette scene by scene — and it makes such a difference with the finished look!

15-00 Set Operations

15-01 First Grip, 15-02 Best Boy (Grip), 15-04 Dolly Grip

These three students are Cinematography majors, helping out with the grip and dolly work. Tape, black wrap, gels, and other grip/electric expendables are provided by the school.

15-05 Craft Services

Everyone chips into a kitty for on-set munchies.

17-00 Set Dressing

17-01 Set Decorator

This is a student working with the Production Designer helping out with choosing and hauling set pieces and props.

17-05 Expendables

Sundry paints, supplies, sewing machine, etc., are provided by the school.

17-07 Rentals

The school provides an allowance of $50 to help with the rental of an opulent-looking dining room set for an important formal dinner scene.

18-00 Property

18-01 Property Master

This student, also a Production Design major, helps the Production Designer and the Set Decorator organize props.

18-03 Purchases

The school allows $75 toward purchases of food used as props in the formal dining scene.

18-04 Rentals

The school allows $50 toward the rental of an expensive-looking silver-plated dinner serving and place setting set.

19-00 Wardrobe

19-01 Costume Designer and 19-02 Costumer

These two students volunteer to coordinate wardrobe among all the actors. They consult with the Director, DP, and Production Designer about the color palette for every scene. Actors mostly use their own clothes, but the color schemes and textures become part of the overall production design, and require attention.

19-04 Expendables

The school allows $50 toward sewing supplies and fabric, as several actors need to be draped for a dream scene.

19-06 Rentals

The school allows $50 to rent several police costumes.

20-00 Make-Up and Hairdressing

20-01 Key Make-Up Artist and 20-02 Assistant

These two students from the Theater Department volunteer for film make-up.

20-05 Purchases

Make-up supplies.

21-00 Electrical

21-01 Gaffer and 21-02 Best Boy

Two more from the Cinematography Department help out with lighting. They prep by scouting the locations and organizing the lighting package for each shoot day, per the Director of Photography's instructions.

21-03 Electrics

Two more Cinematography majors drop in for shooting days to help light the shots.

21-05 Purchases

The school supplies some money for new bulbs, and to repair some bad connections.

21-06 Equipment Rentals

The school supplies all lighting gear except for HMI lights, which must be rented at a discount over the two weekends.

22-00 Camera

22-01 Director of Photography

The DP is also from the Cinematography Department. He helps scout locations during prep, and drops in on rehearsals to see how the blocking will work for each scene.

22-02 Camera Operator

A student specializing in Cinematography comes on for the four shoot days.

22-03 1st Assistant Camera

Preps the camera to make sure everything is working and the package is complete, then comes for the shoot.

22-04 2nd Assistant Camera

Drops in for the shoot days only.

22-06 Expendables

The school supplies an allowance for tape and other camera supplies.

22-07 Camera Package

The entire package comes right out of the school equipment room. It's an Aaton – Super 16 A-Minima sound camera with timecode, three 200' magazines (the only way this camera comes), a zoom lens, tripod, and accessories. There's even a video tap which helps everyone visualize the shots as they're rolling.

On a traditional independent film shoot, you'd probably want to find a DP with a basic camera package that includes:

▶ Arri or Aaton camera body
▶ Set of prime lenses plus a zoom
▶ Fluid head tripod on regular sticks, plus Baby Legs and Hi-Hat

Then there are rental items
▶ Videotap plus monitor
▶ Extra Magazines, Follow Focus, filters, Mattebox, etc.
▶ Film dollies – discuss with DP

You can see cameras and camera packages on such websites as www.birnsandsawyer.com.

In terms of camera crew, even a low-budget shoot requires at least one AC. If at all possible, add a 2nd AC. The investment is worth it because it probably won't be your camera department that keeps you waiting.

23-00 Sound

23-01 Mixer

The Mixer checks out the locations on prep day, and organizes the gear.

Again, on a traditional independent film shoot, find a Mixer who has his or her own gear.

Expect to pay at least $325 – $450/day for the Mixer with equipment.

23-02 Boom Operator

The Boom Op signs on for the shoot days to handle the fish pole.

In the low-budget independent feature world, please resist the temptation to use a PA, or your mom, as a Boom Op. It's actually a very key position, and if the sound is not captured correctly here, it can get expensive in post.

23-02 Expendables

Batteries, etc. are provided by the school.

23-04 Sound Package

A Sound Devices recorder 702T two-track with timecode, Mackie mixer, shotgun mics, fishpole and accessories are provided. (For a more complete description of a movie sound package, see the Digital Feature scenario at 23-04.)

24-00 Transportation

24-03 Equipment Rental

Two station wagons and a borrowed pickup truck comprise the production fleet. On a traditional independent low-budget film shoot, try to budget for a cube truck for the gear, since film equipment generally takes up more space than video stuff does. Video shoots often get away with a windowless cargo van.

For crew, try for a 10 or 15-passenger van. It's a lot more efficient than a caravan of cars, and with one van, everybody gets lost together.

24-04 Gas & Oil

An allowance is provided by the school.

25-00 Location Expenses

25-07 Permits

Permits are routinely waived by the city for student projects. This is not so for every city, and many student projects must get permits.

25-09 Catering

A euphemism for brown bag lunches.

25-17 Location Site Rental

They luck out. One of the student's parents owns a large house and actually allows the crew in for the dining room scene. They must remove the owner's dining table, however, and replace it with the rental. All other locations are student apartments, houses, and exterior locations.

26-00 Picture Vehicles

26-03 Picture Cars

Four of the wealthier student's cars are borrowed for an exterior scene in front of the large house.

27-00 Film & Lab – Production

27-01 Raw Stock (Production)

The Producer and Director estimate that over the four days, they will shoot about two hours per day, using 23 two-hundred-foot rolls of film per day, 92 rolls total for a grand total of 18,400 feet. The school has a standing 30% discount on raw stock and processing.

If this were a more traditional feature shoot, and they were figuring their footage, they might make use of another formula that goes like this: 16mm footage runs through a camera at 36 feet per minute. If you're figuring on about a 90-minute film, and about an 8:1 shooting ratio, then 36x8x90 = 25,920 feet. It would be wise to round that up a couple of thousand feet to allow for waste. So call it 28,000 feet.

27-02 Lab – Negative Prep and Processing

The 30% discount also applies to processing.

Again, if this were a shoot outside of school, the Producer would be looking around for the best lab at the best price. Get quotes based on the footage count. If your DP has connections at a certain lab, you may be able to be there during an "unsupervised" transfer, develop a relationship with the tech, and get some extra attention.

There was no *Additional Processing* in this scenario, but this is when you ask for bleach bypass, pulling or pushing of f-stops. For budgeting, it's wise to set aside around 4-5% of this line item for these extras.

27-04 Prep/Clean Negative for Telecine

In this scenario, this function was discounted by the lab at 30%, although some labs will give it away as part of the package, especially if you are doing the transfer (telecine) at their lab.

27-08 Telecine

The 16mm film is transferred to DigiBeta in a best light pass. A best light is a cross between a one-light on the low end and a scene-to-scene on the high end. She chooses a best light for reasons of economy. From here she will take her DigiBeta into Final Cut Pro (FCP), and edit both Off and On-line, meaning she will do her final color correction on FCP as well, then output to her final master on DigiBeta.

The audio files are then synced to the DigiBeta.

FlexFiles are another optional feature offered by the lab. When doing the transfer, the lab can generate a list of takes and reels, demarcated by timecode number. The Editor can load this into the edit system and use it to batch digitize tapes. Is it worth the cost? How fast can your Editor do it? Compare the two.

30-00 Editorial

30-08 Off/On-Line Editor

A student with an emphasis in editing and post-production edits the eight hours of material into the final 10 minutes, over an accumulated term of four weeks.

30-09 Off/On-Line Edit System

The school has chosen Final Cut Pro. After the cut is locked, a copy goes to the Composer for the score.

30-12 Videotape Dubs/Stock & Transfers

The school provides an allowance for miscellaneous dubs and stock.

30-13 Screening Copies

When the show is finished, ten DVDs are made to show to faculty, and proud parents. Later, these copies will be used as calling cards to get jobs.

30-14 Video Master

The Edited Master is on DigiBeta, with a safety copy, plus a third copy for the Composer as part of his deal.

33-00 Music

33-01 Composer

A struggling composer and rock band lead guitarist, not a student, agrees to compose the score in exchange for the credit, and a copy of the show on DigiBeta and DVD.

Royalty-Free Music

There's a ton of music, some of it awful and some pretty good, that's available to producers in the form of "royalty-free" music, or "Buy-Out" music libraries. This comes in two basic forms. You can buy a package of an assortment of CDs and then have unlimited use. Some producers and editors get quite a collection going. The other way is to work with a music library and pay for each clip of music you use, or each "needledrop" as it's quaintly called. Look online under "royalty-free music" or "Buy-out music library." (Also see a short discussion of "Buy-Out Music Library" in this book in the Line Items Chapter at the end of section 33-00.)

Using Pre-Recorded Music

What's involved in using music that somebody else has written and/or performed? We can't cover the whole topic here, but the first thing to ask is, "Is this music copyrighted?" It says so on the package. If so, you'll probably need a license, and you'll need to contact the copyright owner, or whoever controls the rights. There are different types of licenses that pertain to various rights. For example, a synchronization or "sync" license lets you use a particular piece of music "in synchronization with," or in connection with, a specific motion picture, video, commercial etc. If you wanted to use "Hey Jude" in your movie, and record it yourself, you'd need a synch license from the copyright owner. And no, you're not allowed to change the lyrics without permission. But if you wanted to use "Hey Jude" by the Beatles, you'd need both a synch license and a Master Recording License from the copyright owner of the sound recording, who might be somebody else. Sometimes you have to pay musicians fees as well.

Public Domain music means the copyright has expired or was never there in the first place, but you have to be sure the music you want really is PD. "Happy Birthday to You" is actually copyrighted, and the owner gets a taste of the money cake every time it's sung in a movie.

So how do you clear music and negotiate licenses? Most producers leave it to experts, Music Supervisors. You can find them in the *L.A. 411*, and the NYPG (*New York Production Guide*), available in many bookstores or online. Or look online under "music clearance."

34-00 Post-Production Sound

34-01 Sound Editor

A Recording Arts major is the Sound Editor, Dialogue Editor and Music Editor rolled into one. First, he meets with the Producer and Director to watch the show, picking out places for sound effects. Then he does the same thing with the Composer, Director and Producer, picking out places where music is needed.

He lays out all the separate tracks, places effects in their proper places, assembles, synchronizes, edits, cleans up and smoothes out all the dialogue, and places all the music cues in the right locations. This is all in preparation for the mix.

34-14 Laydown

The production audio from the Edited Master is stripped off and laid down to a multitrack tape.

34-18 Automatic Dialogue Replacement (ADR) Stage

Now that the music is underway, it's time to consider ADR. Prior to booking the ADR Stage, in the "spotting" session, specific sections of dialogue were identified as unusable. The Sound Editor prepares the actor's lines and cue sheets for the ADR Mixer. The actors come to the ADR stage, watch the film, and they lip sync to picture as they listen to their original lines through headphones. It takes them four hours to get it right. The editing of the ADR is part of the Sound Editor's 40 hours.

34-20 Foley Stage/Foley Artists

A Foley Stage is a specially designed soundproof room in which Foley Artists watch a projection of the film, and create on-screen sounds that sync up with the picture. These student Artists are pretty good at finding ingenious ways to make sounds, and include footsteps, heavy breathing, and some body punches. They get the job done in five hours.

34-31 Mix

In the Mix, the Sound Editor, with the Director and Producer, agree on the right levels for the production dialogue, sound effects, and music.

34-39 Layback

When it's done, the show is all mixed and ready to be laid back to the DigiBeta Edited Master.

35-00 Titles and Graphics

35-01 Graphic Designer/Workstation

A student from the Graphic Design department works in Photoshop and After Effects to create the opening title sequence.

35-02 Stock and Dubs

An allowance is provided by the school.

36-00 Feature Film Clips/Archival and Stock Footage v

Feature Film Clips

Although no clips from feature films are used in this sample budget scenario, they sometimes show up in student films, having been snipped off the Internet or from a DVD from the local rental store. Luckily, nobody sees these beyond the classroom. If you want to use a clip from a commercial movie, and expect to show your film to the world, there's a certain path to follow. Please check out the Table of Contents and in the Pre-Production Chapter, find the listing for Feature Film Clips.

Archival Film Clips and Stock Footage

Generally, using stock footage and clips from archival sources, such as silent movies, training films, old news footage, old cartoons, or commercials from the 1950s, is a straightforward transaction, you just pay by the foot, or by the second. Tell them the nature of your project, and ask for a break in price. Usually they'll work with you. There are plenty of these services in the *L.A. 411*, and the NYPG (*New York Production Guide*), or through state film commissions, or look online. Please check out the Table of Contents and in the Pre-Production Chapter, find the listing for Archive Film Clips and Stock Footage.

37-00 Insurance

No insurance is provided.

38-00 General & Administrative Expenses

There are no allowances for offices, phones, legal or accounting services. It's up to the students.

On an independent shoot, insurance goes here, and you'll need to have it to rent gear, to cover the DP's and Mixer's camera and sound packages respectively, plus liability and worker's comp. The best advice is to go through a broker who specializes in entertainment or "producer's packages." Many of the associations can refer you, such as the International Documentary Association, Women In Film, American Film Institute. Look them up in the Resource section of this book, or on the Web.

APPENDIX

DESPERATE MEASURES & MONEY-SAVING IDEAS

1. Legal Services

To see what various contracts look like before you put your lawyer on the clock, check out *Contracts for the Film and Television Industry*, 2nd Edition Expanded by Mark Litwak (1999), $35.00 paper, www.silmanjamespress. com or used at on-line booksellers. (We make no guarantees.) Or go to a university law library and take notes from among the volumes of entertainment industry contracts. *Also see* Books below under Legal.

2. Obtaining Rights

Use your native eloquence and passion to convince a rights owner that your earnest efforts to get the project sold constitute sufficient consideration. Then you buy the option for a dollar (some money must change hands to make it legal). It's a perfectly valid option agreement.

3. Getting a Writer

When a writer (WGA or not) is eager to get his or her property produced, or just get some work, you can strike a "spec" deal. This means the writer:

a) becomes your partner and gets paid an agreed sum, plus a percentage of the "back end."

b) gets paid an agreed sum at an agreed time but no percentage. Or some combination of the above. What about the WGA? If a guild member chooses to work non-guild, it's not your problem. Just be up front about it.

445

4. Getting a Producer

Make the Producer your partner, and defer salary to "back end," or some future point. Or pay below rate and defer the balance. This approach can apply to anyone "above-the-line" on your project. It can work for "below-the-line" people as well, but they are not as used to the idea of not getting paid at the end of the day, so take it case by case.

5. Getting a Director

If the Director really wants to see the project made, or if it's a personal project, salary could be deferred until profits, if any, start rolling in. When you are starting out and producing low budget projects, you cannot afford to pay thousands of dollars to a Director (even if that's you!). DGA? Again, if a Director wants to work non-guild, it's his or her decision to make.

6. Getting Actors

▸ Student actors may be willing to work free.

▸ Use union or non-union actors and pay below scale (say $100/day). It's the actor's decision to work non-union.

▸ Check with SAG to see if your project qualifies for their Short Film or Ultra-Low Budget Film Agreement. See *www.sagindie.com*. You may then use any willing SAG actors and defer salaries or pay $100/day, depending on the agreement, until the film is sold.

7. Getting a Dialect Coach

If you can't afford the real thing, buy a book and CD. Samuel French Books (*www.samuelfrench.com*) has a few.

8. Getting a Choreographer

Music video producers on tight budgets often hire "choreographers" who are young people with great dance skills. Look into a local dancing school's classes. Be careful, however, since lack of experience with cameras can waste a lot of time.

9. Getting a Narrator

Narration for experimental films or "cause" projects has a cache to it. Actors often do it for love and/or recognition. Go to the biggest actor you can think of and ask if he or she will do it for minimum scale. You may be pleasantly surprised.

10. Getting a Production Assistant

When you're too broke to hire a PA, try the local college film/TV department and ask for volunteer "interns," who work for the experience, and a free lunch.

11. Getting Extras

For non-union projects you could pay below scale rates, or even just provide free coffee and doughnuts. Maybe throw in a free lunch. (Some people just want to be in — the movies!)

12. Getting a Sound Stage

Can't afford a sound stage? You can set up anywhere if all you need is a roof over your heads. Just run the sound stage checklist from Chapter 5 (12-00) on your proposed location (adding items like toilets, or honey-wagons). Spend a minute standing silently during the time of day when you'll be shooting — what you hear in the background is what you'll likely hear on your show's production soundtrack. Is there an airport nearby? A kennel? A turkey farm? Also, call your local state or city film commission and ask about converted warehouses and other less expensive structures that can be used as sound stages. But please take your audio person, as well as your DP on your scout.

13. Getting the Most from Your Department Heads

Negotiate half-day rates for travel, which is pretty standard, but also ask your Department Heads (DP, Production Designer, Costume Designer) to throw in some prep or scouting at no extra charge. It's worth a try.

14. Getting Your Crew Fed

On low-budget shows, if you don't have enough people to warrant hiring a caterer, pass around the menu from a good local restaurant and have a PA take orders. Or, if it's tighter than that, say for a student film, order pizza.

15. Getting Film Stock

Film stock companies sometimes keep "short ends," "long ends," and "re-canned" film stock. Short ends are leftover reels with less than 400 feet per reel (they can be hard to use if they're too short). Long ends have 700 feet or more. Re-canned stock means they have put the film in the magazine and changed their minds. Long ends and re-cans are used by productions big and small, but there are some possible snags. As mothers like to say, "Don't touch that, you don't know where it's been." Insist that the film be tested. The good stock houses do this anyway, processing a strip from each can at a lab to check for density levels, scratches, fogging, and edge damage. Testing is also the only way to verify what kind of film is in the can, since cans are often mislabeled or de-labeled in the field.

Also, if you are a student, some film and tape companies provide automatic discounts. If you are a member of Independent Feature Project (IFP) West or East, ask them about discounts for stock.

16. Getting Really Cheap Film Stock

Conventional wisdom says to buy decent stock no matter how broke you are. But what if even Beta oxide is too expensive? Some film and tape stock companies, or post-production houses, have recycled tape stock that has one or two passes on it. The tape should be checked for picture and audio drop outs, degaussed (demagnetized), and cleaned.

17. Getting Composers and Musicians

Hire student composers and musicians from music schools. They may well do the job for only a sample reel and a credit, if you cover the hard costs of studios, instrument rental, cartage, tape stock, etc. Yet another way is to ask the composer for any unreleased recordings you can license directly, provided the composer owns 100% of the publishing rights (sync and master rights).

18. Getting Music

If you can't afford to score with real musicians, then the composer records the score from a synthesizer. You then skip the Music Scoring Stage step, and go directly to Music Pre-Lay (*see* Chapter 5, Music 33-00 and Post-Production Sound 34-00).

19. Getting a Mix

If your "orchestra" is a combo of friends, and you can't afford a scoring stage, try packing into a friend's garage recording studio rigged for video projection. Remember, if you have not recorded a synthesizer bed already locked to picture, the recording machine needs to be electronically locked to the picture, otherwise music cues may be out of sync. Consult an audio engineer at the audio sound house where you'll do your final mix.

If you did record a synth bed, and have transferred the music to a multi-track tape with time code, you are already synced to picture, and your combo can jam along to the synth — no picture or picture lock needed.

20. Getting ADR

For bare bones ADR, you need a quiet place, a film loop of each scene to be looped, or a video playback, some headphones, decent microphones, a decent recording machine such as 1/4 inch, DAT, multi-track, or video (Beta deck or better), and the ability to lock your recording machine to your picture. If you only have some small ADR to do, you could squeeze it in during the final mix. Be sure the Mixer knows all about it beforehand, and don't be too surprised if he looks at you in horror.

21. Inexpensive Narrator Recording

Some producers record the narrator with a Nagra or comparable recorder (or onto BetaSP or DVCam videotape) in their shower stall, with blankets over the windows at four in the morning. A friend may also have a garage recording studio that will work.

22. Getting a Good Rate on Post

You can try to play one facility against another to get the bids down, but don't make up stories — all these people know each other, and word quickly spreads if you're faking low quotes. If the price is still too steep, sit down with the house of your choice and work out what services you can cut to fit your budget. Most houses are willing, and it they really can't do it, they may recommend a lower end house that can.

23. Getting Inexpensive Titles and Graphics

Can't afford time on a graphics work station or character generator? Art cards still work, and you can get quite creative, even wild, using simple press-on letters, paint, ink, and drawing tools. Talk over your ideas with your Editor. The art cards can be shot during your regular production period, while you're still renting your camera package, or you can shoot them during post-production on an overhead camera. The text images can be moved around on screen, and made bigger or smaller, in On-Line. We once saw an opening titles piece for a network sitcom done by a single artist painting one or two brush strokes at a time, and "clicking off" a few video frames. It was a great effect.

24. Getting a Graphic Designer for Less

If your graphics budget really is below standard for the kind of show you're producing, go to a Graphic Designer and say, "I have $2,000 (or whatever), do you want to get creative and take on the job?" If the Designer is busy, he or she will have to turn you down, but you may get back, "I'm swamped now, but in two weeks I'll have time. Can you wait?"

RESORCES

Film/TV/Theater Bookstores and Production Guides

A note about production guides. Several enterprising companies publish thick, expensive books that list every conceivable local product or service a film or TV maker could wish for. They are called production guides, and they are usually worth every penny. Some of the better known are: *L.A. 411 Production Guide, NY 411 Production Guide* (*www.newyork411.com*), and the NYPG (*New York Production Guide, www.nypg.com*). Other cities sometimes have their own, so check with local bookstores that carry film and TV books.

▶ **Larry Edmunds Books**
6644 Hollywood Blvd. Hollywood, CA 90028
(323) 463-3273
www.larryedmunds.com

Edmunds has a vast collection of professional books, including the above production guides. They take orders by mail.

▶ **Enterprise of Hollywood — Printers & Stationers**
1021 Lillian Way Hollywood, CA 90038
(323) 960-9191
http://quixote.com/epA.php

Enterprise stocks all kinds of production forms, contracts, budgets, script supplies, production boards etc. Ask for their catalogue to order by mail.

▶ **Samuel French Theater and Film Bookshops**
7623 Sunset Blvd. Hollywood, CA 90046
(323) 876-0570
www.samuelfrench.com

French's stocks a vast collection of film, television, and theater books, including the above-mentioned production guides.

▶ **The Writers Computer Store**
2040 Westwood Blvd. Los Angeles, CA 90025
(310) 479-7774
www.writersstore.com

Books for producers and writers, as well as all kinds of production and scripting software.

Filmmaker websites (a partial list)

www.2pop.com www

Nextwavefilms.com

www.dvinfo.net

www.digitalproductionbuzz.com

www.mydvmag.com

http://provideocoalition.com

www.bavc.org (Bay Area Video Coalition – San Francisco/Oakland)

www.filmspecific.com (Distribution Tools/Solutions for Indy Filmmakers, by subscription)

www.doculink.org (Documentary filmmaker listserv)

www.digitalcinemasociety.org

www.wmm.com (Women Make Movies)

www.woodyssoundadvice.com — great info on post audio from Woody Woodhall and friends at Allied Post Audio, Santa Monica, CA (*www.AlliedPost.com*)

DIRECTORIES

▷ **Baseline. Inc.**
520 Broadway Street, Suite 230 Santa Monica, CA 90401
(310) 393-9999
(800) 858-3669
www.pkbaseline.com

Baseline is an on-line information company that provides subscribers with up-to-date entertainment industry news, like projects in development, production and post, budgets and grosses, production company services and personnel, release dates and distributors, and more. It's usually monitored by studios and production companies with projects on the air, in movie theaters, or in serious development. If you want to be included in their data bank, give them a call.

▷ **The Industry Labor Guide**
FilmWare Products
10008 National Blvd. # 227
Los Angeles, CA 90034 (USA)
(310) 204-2421 Voice Mail & Fax (209) 433-2422
e-mail: *sales@filmwareproducts.com*
www.filmwareproducts.com

The Labor Guide contains the most requested rates, rules and practices of all the major union agreements. If you're doing union projects, it can save you hours of time and loads of frustration to have this information at your fingertips.

▷ **Hollywood Creative Directory**
Hollywood Creative Directory
5055 Wilshire Blvd.
Los Angeles, CA 90036-4396
(800) 815-0503
(323) 525-2369 (Sales)
(323) 525-2398 (Fax)
e-mail:*hcdcustomerservice@hcdonline.com*
www.hcdonline.com

Publishes the directories listed below, plus other industry survival books. Although the name says "Hollywood," the books list companies nationwide.

The Hollywood Creative Directory: Lists all major production companies and studios, their creative executives and story development people, and each company's credits, plus addresses, phones, and fax numbers.

The Hollywood Representation Directory: Lists the agency and management names, addresses and phone numbers for performing, writing, and directing talent.

The Hollywood Distributors Directory: Lists domestic and foreign distribution companies for TV and film, their sales and marketing staff, plus broadcast and cable networks.

The Hollywood Music Industry Directory: Lists composers, lyricists, music production companies, and clearance and licensing people.

HCD also publishes directories listing Writers, Directors, Actors, Composers, and Below-the-Line Talent.

TRADE PUBLICATIONS (PARTIAL LIST)

▸ *Advertising Age*
Advertising Age
711 Third Avenue
New York, NY 10017-4036
(212) 210-0100
www.AdAge.com

▸ *American Cinematographer*
The American Society of Cinematographers
1782 N. Orange Drive (the ASC store)
Hollywood, CA 90028
(800) 448-0145
e-mail: *customerservice@theasc.com*
www.theasc.com

▸ *Billboard*
Billboard Subscription
PO Box 15158
North Hollywood, CA 91615-5158
(800) 562-2706
e-mail: *billboard@espcomp.com*
www.billboard.com

▸ *Film & Video*
Film & Video Magazine
P.O. Box 3229 Northbrook, IL 60065-3229
(847) 559-7314
e-mail: *FNV@omeda.com*
www.studiodaily.com/filmandvideo/

▸ *Hollywood Reporter*
5055 Hollywood Blvd., Sixth Fl.
Los Angeles, CA 90036
(323) 525-2000 Subscriptions: (866) 525-2150 or (323) 525-2150
e-mail: *subscriptions@hollywoodreporter.com*
www.hollywoodreporter.com

▶ *Millimeter* Magazine

http://digitalcontentproducer.com/

▶ *Script*

A subscription magazine rich with resources for screenwriters and anyone interested in narrative storytelling.

www.scriptmag.com

▶ *Variety*

5700 Wilshire Blvd., Suite 120
Los Angeles, CA 90036
(323) 857-6600
www.variety.com

BOOKS

Look here first: Michael Wiese Productions. *www.mwp.com*
Shameless plug for my friend and publisher, but there are truly tons of
useful books about filmmaking here. Absolutely worth browsing.

General Information
The Filmmakers Handbook
By Steven Ascher and Edward Pincus
New York: Plume (The Penguin Group), 2008

Cinematography
Cinematography - Theory and Practice
By Blain Brown
London, UK: Focal Press, 2002

The American Society of Cinematographers Manual
A portable compendium of technical information about shooting on
film, digital intermediates, etc. It costs around $35 on-line and it's fully
loaded. Ask at any of the bookstores above.

Production Management
Film Production Management 101, 2nd edition
By Deborah S. Patz
Studio City, CA: Michael Wiese Productions, 2002

Legal
Clearance & Copyright:
Everything You Need to Know for Film and Television
3rd edition
by Michael C. Donaldson
Silman-James Press, 2008

Dealmaking in the Film & Television Industry:
From Negotiations to Final Contracts
3rd edition
By Mark Litwak
Silman-James Press, 2009

MISCELLANEOUS RESOURCES

▶ **Thomson and Thomson,**
a copyright search firm (800) 692-8833
http://compumark.thomson.com

▶ **Breakdown Services, Ltd.**
Los Angeles (310) 276-9166
New York (212) 869-2003
Vancouver (604) 943-7100
www.breakdownservices.com
If it's open casting you want — up to hundreds of actors submitting pictures
and resumes for roles in your project — call Breakdown Services. They'll
tell you what to do. For a further discussion, see Chapter 2, Pre-Production,
under Casting.

▶ **Simple/inexpensive encoding recipes for video on the web**
at *www.intelligentassistance.com*
www.proappstips.com/EncodingRecipes

▶ **Clearance Supervisors** (stock footage and clips)
Barbara Gregson
818-996-9373
barbara@usinter.net

▶ **Music Supervisors**
Dominique Preyer
512-913-8594
dominique@HearItClearIt.com
www.hearitclearit.com

Post-Production/Los Angeles area
HTV/illuminate – full service – *www.htvinc.net*

West Post Digital – finishing – *www.westpostdigital.com*

Allied Post Audio, Santa Monica, CA *www.AlliedPost.com*

Boltpix, Santa Monica, CA – production/post – *www.bolt-pix.com*

TRADE ASSOCIATIONS

▷ **Academy of Motion Picture Arts and Sciences**
8949 Wilshire Blvd.
Beverly Hills, CA 90211
(310) 247-3000

The library has *Academy Players Directories* (photos, names and agents for hundreds of leading men, women, children, character actors, ingenues, etc.). The library is also a treasure house of film research material.

▷ **Academy of Television Arts and Sciences**
5220 Lankershim Blvd.
North Hollywood, CA 91601
(818) 754-2800

ATAS is primarily a professional membership and awards organization (the Emmy), but it has a number of programs of interest to students and teachers, such as:

Student Internship Program: Students or recent grads spend a summer working as full-time, paid interns for prime time entertainment companies.

College Television Awards: Student projects in many categories compete for cash prizes.

Faculty Seminars: Annual three-day event in which film/TV teachers hobnob with heavy-hitters in prime time entertainment television.

▷ **American Federation of Musicians (AFM)**
New York Headquarters:
1501 Broadway, Suite 600
New York, NY 10036
(212) 869-1330
www.afm.org

▷ **American Federation of Television and Radio Artists (AFTRA)**
5757 Wilshire Blvd. #900 Los Angeles, CA 90036
(323) 634-8100
For a list of locals, see *www.aftra.org*

▶ **American Society of Cinematographers (ASC)**
1782 North Orange Drive
Hollywood, CA 90028
(800) 448-0145
www.theasc.com

▶ **American Society of Composers, Authors. & Publishers (ASCAP)**
7920 Sunset Blvd., 3rd Floor
Los Angeles, CA 90046
(323) 883-1000
For other offices see *www.ascap.com*

▶ **Association of Independent Commercial Editors (AICE)**
300 East 40th Street Suite 16T
New York, NY 10016
(212) 972-3556

▶ **Association of Independent Commercial Producers (AICP)**
3 W. 18th St. 5th Floor
NY, NY 10011
(212) 929-3000
www.aicp.com

▶ **Association of Independent Commercial Producers (AICP West)**
650 North Bronson Ave. #223B
Los Angeles, CA 90004
(323) 960-4763

▶ **Broadcast Music. Inc. (BMI)**
8730 Sunset Blvd., Third Floor
West Hollywood, CA 90069
(310) 659-9109
See *www.bmi.com* for other offices

▶ **Directors Guild of America. Inc.**
7920 Sunset Blvd.
Los Angeles, CA 90046
(310) 289-2000
See *www.dga.org* for information

▶ **International Alliance of Theatrical Stage Employees (IATSE)**
IATSE represents many different types of craftspeople and technicians spread across more than thirty unions. Since rates vary
by geographical location, type of project, medium (film or tape),
etc., we recommend contacting a reputable payroll service in your
area that handles union personnel. General Office contact:
IATSE General Office
1430 Broadway 20th Floor
New York, NY 10018
(212) 730-1770

▶ **International Documentary Association (IDA)**
1201 West 5th Street, Suite M270
Los Angeles, CA 90017 USA
(213) 534-3600
info@documentary.org
www.documentary.org
A membership organization with a cool magazine. The mission of the
IDA is to promote nonfiction film and video by:

- Supporting and recognizing the efforts of documentary film
  and video makers
- Increasing public appreciation and demand for the documentary
- Providing a forum for documentary makers, their supporters
  and suppliers

▶ **Screen Actors Guild (SAG)**
5757 Wilshire Blvd.
Los Angeles, CA 90036
(323) 954-1600
www.sag.org

▸ **Women In Film**
6100 Wilshire Blvd. Suite 710
Los Angeles, CA 90048
323.935.2211
www.wif.org

Women In Film's purpose is to empower, promote and mentor women in the entertainment and media industries. WIF actively supports women in the entertainment industry in four key ways:

(1) assists indie filmmakers who have demonstrated advanced and innovative skills;
(2) funds programs which provide scholarships and internships;
(3) contributes financially and creatively to the production of PSAs which spotlight issues important to women; and
(4) creates events and seminars which are educational and creatively enlightening.

▸ **Writers Guild of America-West (WGA)**
7000 West Third Street
Los Angeles, CA 90048
(323) 951-4000
www.wga.org

▸ **Writers Guild of America-East (WGA)**
555 W. 57th St., Suite 1230
NY, NY 10019
(212) 767-7800
www.wgaeast.org

CAMERA SPEED/TIME TABLES

(limited version)

The time it takes for film to pass through a camera or projector is useful to know when you are estimating how much film stock to buy and process. The figures below are for four of the most common speeds only: 16 frames per second (fps), 24 fps, 32 fps, and 64 fps. (24 fps is the speed for "normal" live action.) The range can go from 6 fps to 360 fps, but consult a book like *The American Society of Cinematographers Manual* for the complete story. It costs in the $35 dollar range, but it's loaded with information about shooting on film.

35mm film

Camera feet	16fps	24fps	32fps	64fps
50	:50	:33	:25	:13
100	1:40	1:07	:50	:27
200	3:20	2:13	1:40	:50
300	5:00	3:20	2:30	1:15
400	6:40	4:27	3:20	1:40
500	8:20	5:33	4:10	2:05
1000	16:40	11:07	8:20	4:10

16mm film

Camera feet	16fps	24fps	32fps	64fps
50	2:05	1:23	1:02	:31
100	4:10	2:47	2:05	1:02
200	8:20	5:20	4:10	1:23
300	12:30	8:20	6:15	3:07
400	16:40	11:07	8:20	4:10
500	20:50	13:53	10:25	5:13
1000	41:40	27:47	20:50	10:26
1200	50:00	33:20	25:00	12:30

BUDGETS FOR GRANTS AND DONATIONS

The Top Ten Do's and Don'ts

By Morrie Warshawski

Funders of non-commercial grant supported films and videos have a very different mind-set than investors. A savvy funder will read your budget like a book, hoping to find a romance novel and not a mystery nor a comedy. Keep in mind that most funders only rarely review film budgets. Their time is spent primarily on budgets from other types of endeavors in the arts and social services — ballet concerts, capital campaigns, programs for the elderly, etc. Begin with your generic production budget and then go through carefully to adjust for the following before submitting a grant proposal.

1. **YOUR SALARY.** Be sure to include some payment for yourself. Funders are suspicious when you either do not pay yourself, or underpay yourself. To compute your fee (and those of all other participants), use an amount that is fair and comparable for: a) the role you will play in the film; b) your level of expertise in that role; c) your region of the country.

2. **CONTINGENCY.** Most funders do not understand the concept of "contingency." Only include contingency with funders who have had extensive experience with film, or who specifically put contingency as a line item in their budget formats. Otherwise, just build in a fair contingency amount throughout your budget in all the line items.

3. **TALENT.** Do not use this word in a grant proposal. Funders equate talent with high-budget Hollywood movies. List all people under a "PERSONNEL" heading and then specifically label the roles they fulfill (e.g. "actors," "director," etc.).

4. **DISTRIBUTION.** For a non-commercial project you must include at least some start-up costs to get distribution launched. I recommend allocating funds for: package design and production, DVD screening copies, press kits, production stills, and festival entry fees.

5. **IN-KIND.** This term refers to any goods or services that are donated to your project and for which you will not have to pay cash. Reflect these items in your budget to give funders a sense of the community support you have engendered. These items can include: free lunches for your crew, a 50% discount on editing rates, donation of a box of videotape cassettes, etc. Again, use the concepts of "fair and comparable" to decide how much these items are worth.

6. **EQUIPMENT PURCHASE.** Never! It is the rare funder that will let money go towards the purchase of equipment. Always show your equipment as being leased or rented — even if it costs more in the long run than outright purchase.

7. **RED FLAG NOTES.** Because many funders are unfamiliar with films, it is doubly important that you go through your budget item-by-item and look for anything that might call undue attention to itself. Some examples could include: a higher than normal shooting ratio, extensive travel costs, transfer from tape to film if there is no theatrical distribution in your narrative, etc. Mark each and every questionable budget item with a number or asterisk, and then explain them fully in a BUDGET NOTES section at the end of the budget.

8. **STUDY GUIDES.** Any program intended for non-theatrical educational distribution should build in a fee for creating at least a modest study guide.

9. **FISCAL SPONSOR FEES.** Non-commercial projects must use the non-profit status of a fiscal sponsor in order to receive tax-deductible grants and donations (unless the filmmaker has obtained his or her own non-profit status). Be sure to include at the end of your budget the fee that your fiscal sponsor charges. Currently, anything under 10% is considered a fair fee. Anything higher than that should get an explanatory note.

10. **INCOME.** Since most funders will provide only partial funding for your project, you must demonstrate how the rest of your budget will be raised. Create an "INCOME" section divided between these two categories: "Actual To-Date" and "Projected."

Within these categories you can list the actual and potential sources for funding your project (e.g. foundations, corporations, individuals, special events, etc.), if you have given money out of your pocket to produce the film, then do not list yourself as a donor. Instead, lump your money under "Miscellaneous Individual Donations."

MORRIE WARSHAWSKI is a consultant and writer whose clients include film and video producers, arts organizations and foundations. He is the author of *Shaking the Money Tree: How to Get Grants and Donations for Film and Video*. Clients interested in working with Mr. Warshawski can contact him directly at:

E-mail: *MorrieWar@sbcglobal.net*

Website: *www.warshawski.com*

QUICK SEARCH

ABOUT THE AUTHOR

DEKE SIMON is an award-winning writer and producer of documentary, informational, and children's programming for television and video. His credits include *Help Save Planet Earth* and *Harley-Davidson: The American Motorcycle* plus specials and series for MCA/Universal, Turner, Fox, Fox Health, Paramount, Discovery Channel, ESPN, and PBS. He currently produces documentaries for social change. He has received numerous awards, including two Emmy Awards.

THE MYTH OF MWP

In a dark time, a light bringer came along, leading the curious and the frustrated to clarity and empowerment. It took the well-guarded secrets out of the hands of the few and made them available to all. It spread a spirit of openness and creative freedom, and built a storehouse of knowledge dedicated to the betterment of the arts.

The essence of the Michael Wiese Productions (MWP) is empowering people who have the burning desire to express themselves creatively. We help them realize their dreams by putting the tools in their hands. We demystify the sometimes secretive worlds of screenwriting, directing, acting, producing, film financing, and other media crafts.

By doing so, we hope to bring forth a realization of 'conscious media' which we define as being positively charged, emphasizing hope and affirming positive values like trust, cooperation, self-empowerment, freedom, and love. Grounded in the deep roots of myth, it aims to be healing both for those who make the art and those who encounter it. It hopes to be transformative for people, opening doors to new possibilities and pulling back veils to reveal hidden worlds.

MWP has built a storehouse of knowledge unequaled in the world, for no other publisher has so many titles on the media arts. Please visit www.mwp.com where you will find many free resources and a 25% discount on our books. Sign up and become part of the wider creative community!

Onward and upward,

Michael Wiese
Publisher/Filmmaker

CPSIA information can be obtained at www.ICGtesting.com
Printed in the USA
BVOW011559260712

296209BV00006B/4/P

9 781932 907735